Praise for Alan (

'His knowledge of the period is probably unparalleled and he's always unerringly accurate' - **Q**

'Having lived the life, Alan always manages to write about rock with a mixture of eloquence and irreverence' - **Jim McCarty (The Yardbirds)**

'He has some damn good jokes, and a sense of style that ties in with the era he's writing about' - *Record Collector*

'Alan is one of that rare breed of rock writers who actually knows what he's writing about' - **Ace Kefford (The Move)**

'[Clayson's biography] conveys the breathless excitement you feel when first discovering a great record, book or film – the evangelical desire to tell anyone and everyone about a new find, and seek new recruits to fight for its cause' - *Frieze*

'Alan remains the most unique musician I have ever employed – and it was entirely through him that my recording career revived in the late 1980s' - **Dave Berry**

'The perfect book to take with you next time you visit the local barber. Possibly the best account written about the petty tyrannies of tonsorial fashion' - **Simon Matthews, author of** *Before It Went Rotten*

Also by Alan Clayson

Call Up The Groups: The Golden Age of British Beat, 1962-67
(Blandford, 1985)

Back In The High Life: A Biography of Steve Winwood
(Sidgwick & Jackson, 1988)

Only the Lonely: The Life and Artistic Legacy of Roy Orbison
(Sidgwick & Jackson, 1989)

The Quiet One: A Life of George Harrison (Sidgwick & Jackson, 1990)

Ringo Starr: Straight Man or Joker? (Sanctuary, 1991)

Death Discs: An Account of Fatality in the Popular Song (Sanctuary, 1992)

Backbeat: Stuart Sutcliffe: The Lost Beatle (with Pauline Sutcliffe)
(Pan Macmillan, 1994)

Aspects of Elvis (ed. with Spencer Leigh) (Sidgwick & Jackson, 1994)

Beat Merchants (Blandford, 1995)

Hamburg: The Cradle of British Rock (Sanctuary, 1997)

Serge Gainsbourg: View From The Exterior (Sanctuary, 1998)

The Troggs File: The Official Story of Rock's Wild Things (with Jacqueline Ryan)
(Helter Skelter, 2000)

Edgard Varèse (Sanctuary, 2002)

The Yardbirds (Backbeat, 2002)

John Lennon (Sanctuary, 2003)

The Walrus Was Ringo: 101 Beatles Myths Debunked (with Spencer Leigh)
(Chrome Dreams, 2003)

Paul McCartney (Sanctuary, 2003)

Brian Jones (Sanctuary, 2003)

Charlie Watts (Sanctuary, 2004)

Woman: The Incredible Life of Yoko Ono (with Robb Johnson and Barb Jungr)
(Chrome Dreams, 2004)

Keith Richards (Sanctuary, 2004)

Mick Jagger (Sanctuary, 2005)

Keith Moon: Instant Party (Chrome Dreams, 2005)

Led Zeppelin: The Origin of the Species (Chrome Dreams, 2006)

The Rolling Stones Album File (Cassell, 2006)

Beggars Banquet (Flame Tree, 2008)

Jacques Brel: La Vie Bohème (Chrome Dreams, 2010)

Too Gone To Even Know The Words: Lyrics 1972–2022 (Aetheria, 2022)

Many books by Alan Clayson are also available in digital form, including:
Over Under Sideways Down: The Flight of The Yardbirds (via Endeavour Media)

ALAN CLAYSON

GET YER 'AIR CUT

THE ISSUE OF MALE COIFFURE, POP AND COUNTERCULTURE BEFORE, DURING AND AFTER THE SWINGING SIXTIES

Oldcastle Books

First published in 2024
by Oldcastle Books Ltd,
Harpenden, UK

oldcastlebooks.co.uk
@OldcastleBooks

A CIP catalogue record for this book is available from the British Library.

ISBN
978-0-85730-590-9 (Paperback)
978-0-85730-591-6 (Ebook)

2 4 6 8 10 9 7 5 3 1

Typeset in 11.75 on 14.4pt Goudy Old Style
by Avocet Typeset, Bideford, Devon, EX39 2BP
Printed and bound in Great Britain by
CPI Group (UK) Ltd, Croydon CR0 4YY

MIX
Paper | Supporting
responsible forestry
FSC
www.fsc.org   FSC® C171272

To everyone who fought in the same war

'It is a great disgrace and a shame for a man not to want to be what he is, what he has to be'

– Ælfric the Homilist

CONTENTS

PROLOGUE:

'Well, he had long hair, hadn't he?'

It was and is a tragedy that a pony-tailed project manager, pneumatic drill operator or computer programmer born long afterwards is likely to find incredible.

On an autumn Saturday in 1965, it was growing dark with pavements still damp following an afternoon of rain as 15-year-old Christopher Holligan strode resolutely towards the railway station that served Lancing, a West Sussex coastal village eight miles down the line from Brighton, where nothing much was meant to happen, year in, year out. Looking not unlike a cricket pavilion, the stopping place did not employ staff at a time of the week when it wasn't worth keeping anyone on to check the tickets of the few disembarking passengers who drifted like ghosts through undercarriage steam.

Chris had – sort of – resolved to kill himself by either springing in front of a non-stopping express or laying his head on the track beyond the platform and waiting with a knotted stomach. The latter would be more satisfactory in that it would flatten his disfigurement as surely as the carcasses of small animals squashed along surrounding country lanes, often narrow and twisted enough to occasion the sounding of car horns at every bend.

As extreme after its fashion as the behaviour of Frideswide, an Anglo-Saxon princess who, rather than be forced into an arranged marriage, chose years of contemplative chastity in a pigsty, Holligan's decision was traceable to the death of his mother earlier in the year – but more directly to the previous week when, without so much as a *by-your-leave*, schoolteacher John Donald – termed in the coroner's report as his 'guardian' – had switched off the television when The Rolling Stones were miming their latest single, '19th Nervous Breakdown' on *Top of the Pops*. He then forbade Chris from watching them do the same on ITV's *Eamonn Andrews Show* the following Sunday, while hissing, 'You'll be having it cut tomorrow!'

For Chris, a shearing by the barber was more traumatic than submitting to the instrument of torture that was the post-war dentist drill: sitting in the queue flicking through much-fingered back copies of *Tit-Bits* and *Reveille*; being called to the mercy-seat of cracked and tarnished vinyl; listening to the banal and mechanical chit-chat which belied the ruthlessness of an executioner in a grubby white laboratory jacket, i.e. the barber whose own hair was as short-back-and-sided, as parted and as plastered with Brylcreem as he intended to make that of the next customer. He would disregard specific instructions by any personification of adolescent narcissism whose day was made if his thatch invited sarcasm and worse from schoolteachers – or if some Oscar Wilde bellowed 'Get yer 'air cut!' from a passing car while his grinning mates twisted round in the back seat to ascertain the effect of this witticism on one who wasn't insulted, but instead proud of pulling wool over Authority's eyes long enough for it to show.

In defiance of John's dictate, Chris stayed out of the house between dismissal from school and the barber's shop closing time for nearly a week. Nevertheless, the order was enforced at last as it always had been since he'd been transfixed by the cover of The Rolling Stones' first EP in the windows of record shops, and thus became no longer 'biddable' when handed money for a scissoring and clippering that would humiliate and degrade him, as it would a village elder in Czarist Russia being punished – as was common – by the removal of a flowing patriarchal beard.

After the butchering was completed, Chris, itchy with the small strands that had gone down his collar, saw his obscene reflection somewhere in the flustered outside light. When everything turns red as hell, you don't plan precisely what you're going to do.

He shouted something with a swear-word in it. 'What did you say?!' screeched a headscarf-wearing neighbour who chanced to be passing, droplets of her spittle sparkling in neon. With head bursting, Chris turned and ran.

After the tale she told of the incident, Mr Donald, crotchety from work, had made up his mind to confiscate Chris's Dansette record player, and place him under house arrest for the rest of the weekend (except for Church) and the minute he returned from school from Monday to Friday. When *The Epilogue* on BBC television ended, however, John was about to embark on a manhunt when a police constable of blunt disposition knocked to tell him that someone who might have resembled the boy had been hit by a speeding train. His injuries were so numerous and so serious that you wouldn't have known he was a human being. He had no head.

Several months after what coroner Francis F Haddock had judged to be 'suicide while the balance of his mind was disturbed', The Beatles were to be invested as Members of the British Empire. Learning of this, the writer of a letter to the *Daily Express*, suggested that, if the group had to be so honoured, each member ought to capitulate to a 'respectable' haircut prior to being presented to the Queen.

In the wider world, the Indonesian government had already banned Beatle moptops; Singapore was to follow suit, and a leader in a British Sunday newspaper had advocated a law that made short-back-and-sides compulsory for men as a defence against what? Homosexuality? Communism? Anarchy? The abolition of National Service? Reading at the dining table? Going to the cinema on the Sabbath? Having fun? For those disenfranchised by the Swinging Sixties, did an element of suppressed envy translate into the bitterest priggishness? Perhaps it boiled down to just that. Certainly, it was understandable that many were eating their hearts out. If female, it might be because their dreary husbands were the only men they'd ever 'known' in a Biblical sense or because their own adolescences had been defined by world wars. If male, perhaps what could have been a period devoid of serious responsibility had been blighted by being compelled to fight further foreign foes or to endure peacetime national service after the dreaded official-looking envelope had fluttered onto the doormat, requiring the recipient to report for an induction medical that, unless he'd been carried in on a stretcher, was a mere formality. Next, his hair would be reduced to tiny stalks like a cornfield after a combine-harvesting, and he'd be kitted out with a dung-coloured uniform. During basic training, he'd be bawled at from dawn till dusk. When he slept, the square-bashing and the more sadistic NCOs would invade his dreams.

'There were images ingrained in us 1960s children of young men having been given very short haircuts and sent to the trenches to be "butchered",' believed post-punk Renaissance man John Arthur Hewson. 'It was partly a reaction to that – and there was the urban spread, and what's since become green politics. It wasn't really new – and, for some, long hair was just "with it". For others, however, it was a symbol. I remember cutting my hair short before going off on a camping trip in the Cotswolds with a couple of friends – and certain other long hairs I knew were really angry about it – I mean *really* angry – because I was letting the side down.'

The 'us and them' divide – and not always between youth and elders – was never more pronounced than over one of the loudest issues of, arguably, the century's most turbulent decade. As an 18-year-old with hair splayed halfway down his back, Phil May, awaiting a destiny as front man of The Pretty Things, reflected decades later, 'You can't understand what a culture shock the look was back in 1962. I was a fucking Martian to most people, decades before androgynous glam rockers or pin-pierced punks. Nothing ever had the impact of the first man to wear really long hair in the style of a female. I know. I *was* that man. Even in freethinking Soho, Chelsea and Notting Hill, I was still stopping traffic and being refused service in pubs, so what chance did I have on a council estate in Erith, grass replaced by tarmac, brick sacrificed for concrete.

'If I walked down the high street, people would jeer and try to pick a fight – and the nightly gauntlet of fire and beatings-up that I had to endure too was, in many ways, only to be expected. Nothing I can say here can explain the impact on a solid, working-class bloke of a real long-haired youth, living, working and taking up the space, on *his* home ground. I was walking that walk in Erith, and that was not to be taken lying down. Christ, I was so naïve, and, in retrospect, so lucky, to have not been maimed or even killed.'

'You'd be approached and get called "fairy" or "queer" or whatever it was,' averred Graham Nash of the more neatly coiffed Hollies. 'It was a threat to them.'

In Fleet, the Hampshire country town where I grew up – to which the nearest big town was Aldershot, 'home of the British Army' – this was exemplified by a man in the dock at one of the region's Magistrates' Courts for attacking a complete stranger, who offered the plea, 'Well, he had long hair, hadn't he?' After a Boy Scout meeting that same year, my patrol leader assured me that Mick Jagger, The Rolling Stones' vocalist, was to undergo a sex change operation. Straight up! A mate of mine told me. The origin of this myth was the 10-16 July edition of *Combo*, a short-lived pop newspaper, that had 'categorically denied' that Jagger was to fly to Sweden to have it done. Later, hearsay was to have it that Brian Jones, another Stone, was to undergo plastic surgery to look like French *chanteuse* Françoise Hardy.

While the subtext was as desperate as it could be, efforts were made sometimes to represent it as light-hearted fun. A picture of Manfred Mann showed them dragging their most hirsute *mann* towards the door of a barber's shop. As chief show-off in the Manish Boys, 17-year-old David Jones – destined for world renown as 'David Bowie' – described himself as the president of the Society For The Prevention Of Cruelty To Long-Haired Men when the fellows were interviewed by a combed-over Cliff Michelmore on BBC television's *Tonight* magazine on 11 November 1964. Among the organisation's supporters, he said, were Screaming Lord Sutch, PJ Proby, Brian Jones – and satirist William Rushton, even if the latter's hair wasn't the designated nine inches long.

In a seeming *volte-face*, Jones-Bowie's dialogue with a voice vari-speeded up to Pinky-and-Perky pitch on 1967's 'The Laughing Gnome' – the subject of an embarrassing reissue when he was famous – included the line 'Didn't they teach you to get your hair cut at school? You look like a *rolling gnome*'. This can perhaps be put into belated perspective via 'Get Your Hair Cut', a B-side three years earlier by comedy actor and novelty song specialist Bernard Cribbins, embracing a coda in which he protests, 'I'm gonna let it grow as long as I like!... There must be a place for long-haired lovely lads like me: single blokes, all with long hair all hanging down on the ground, with little trolleys behind so it doesn't get caught in the tram lines as you're walking along the street...'

There were, indeed, places for 'long-haired lovely lads' – or, at least, a sense of peer-group identity, a countercultural touchstone with political as well as sexual connotations. 'It was a kind of badge saying that we were into cool things,' averred Jim Simpson, a figure to whom a unified music scene in the West Midlands in the 1960s and beyond owes much.

'If you saw someone across the street with long hair,' confirmed Graham Nash, 'he was a person you could nod to and have an understanding. You'd know how he thought – that he hated the government and was into good music...'

Graham's Hollies smouldered into form in Manchester, the 'entertainment capital of the north' from where *Top of the Pops* was first transmitted. Nearly a decade younger than Nash and raised in a district with a glaring military presence, where the distance to any 'happening' city was measurable in years as much as miles, I was of an age to have practised being Mick Jagger before the bedroom mirror to the detriment of homework. This was on the understanding that, by the following evening, I could be before that same mirror realising that no amount of backcombing, pulling, use of a hairdryer or applications of a new thickening gel called Dippity-Do could disguise a barber's barbarity that afternoon. Thus I was obliged to make the best of a bad job, sprucing up for another small death at a dance inside some mid-Victorian hideousity with latticed windows blinded by grime, trying to pick up a girl to the amplified and gremlin-ridden sounds of the local heroes.

CHAPTER ONE

'Christ the Saviour wore long hair/And many more good men I do declare'

It's natural for guinea pigs, penguins, tigers, peacocks, gorillas, humans and more to groom and preen themselves for hygienic and aesthetic purposes. It was also a form of tribal bonding – as instanced as late as the eighteenth century by a lady at a royal banquet, remarking, 'Permittez-moi, monsieur' as a prelude to picking nits from the crowning glory of an adjacent diner who, like herself, believed that not washing hair – particularly if it had a tendency to be oily – encouraged a silky and nourished texture.

If it became too dirty even by the standards of the day, a man of means had it cropped like a convict and donned a (peri) wig – for formal occasions anyway. Made of human, goat or horse hair, wigs attracted insects, but, as a turban does in eastern cultures, also served to disguise greying, baldness and, more insidiously, the ravages of age. Men's faces were framed by a weaved artificiality, shoulder-length and longer, cascading onto the chest, frequently mountainous enough to resemble a lion's mane and sometimes powdered in violet, blue, pink, yellow or, most often, off-white – a colour that lingers in the hairpieces worn as part of the legal profession's official costumery.[1]

Such flamboyance, however, was beyond the means of the man-in-the-street, who tended to tie his hair back in what was first

---

1. More in the context of this dialogue – though beyond its chronological scope – are the wigs vital to the visual style of The B52s, a US outfit elevated from cult luminaries to mainstream eminence in the 1980s, whose chart entries included 1986's in-joking 'Wig'. As a further aside, since the sixth century, turbans 'à la turque' had been worn by gentlemen at leisure in western Europe without any religious implication or ever becoming especially widespread.

known commonly as a 'queue', but described later as a ponytail. Sometimes, it was plaited, bunched in a bag or, particularly among the navy's lower ranks, smeared with tar to reduce the risk of it getting caught in machinery. However, around the time of the Napoleonic conflicts, the regulations of most European militia made short hair obligatory.

Civilians, nevertheless, continued tying natural, tumbledown hair in a bow, and, though this was becoming *passé* when Victoria succeeded William IV, these still adorned the heads of the most conservative *paterfamilias*. It wasn't regarded as effete, and nor was the mid-century craze for elaborately tended beards and moustaches that prompted the Bank of England's executive body to forbid its clerks to join in. Indeed, the craze emphasised patriotic manliness at a time of scares that came to a head with the Crimean War.

Besides, in parish churches throughout the land, congregations were beneath the stained-glassy gape of a blond-bearded God the Father, enthroned in bedspreads and golden crown. With honey-blond tresses down to his shoulders too, God the Son would cause the hippie-ish Byrds, during their *Sweetheart Of The Rodeo* period, to be heckled by the usual 'redneck' element in the audience at Nashville's Grand Ole Opry, the shrine of country-and-western, with one ticket-holder bawling 'Get back on the cross!'

There'd also been limits to Victorian tolerance. Prior to the stroke that took him in 1902, Dundee tragedian William McGonagall, Britain's most renowned 'bad' poet, had been mocked for jet-black hair that, beneath a wide-brimmed clerical hat, was swept back into a thick immensity vaguely like the rear end of a duck. Introducing one of his readings in 1891, the compère protested on the bard's behalf 'against the persecution by boys and others who, when he's seen in the streets, advise him to get his hair cut!' Cries of 'Shame!' were capped by a cry of 'Whoever heard of a poet with his hair cut?' 'Never!' replied the crowd divided between a handful of admirers (or, perhaps, curiosity seekers) and a majority who were there to patronise McGonagall. Among these was an anonymous writer of a verse published in Dundee's *Weekly News* that closed with:

'A true rope round ye noble brow
To drive awa' dull care;
We'll decorate your learned prow
Wi' a saw to cut your hair'.

It prompted a contemptuous response from McGonagall which included this penultimate stanza:

'And, in conclusion, I'd have him to beware
And never again to interfere with a poet's hair,
Because Christ the Saviour wore long hair,
And many more good men I do declare'.

That wasn't all. The previous spring, J Graham Henderson, an affluent and admiring local tailor, had presented his idol with new tweed of loud check, and McGonagall was then addressed in an ode from some joker in Aberdeen, concluding thus:

'When ye get yer new suit, will ye swagger an' strut,
Intae some famous barber's an' get yer hair cut?'

McGonagall was as much part of the British entertainment business as the 'dames' and busty 'principal boys' in pantomime. This tradition can be traced back to the time when transvestism had been the norm on the mediaeval stage and, because women were prohibited from performing in the theatre until the Restoration, men or boys played all roles, male and female. From this root too sprang music hall drag *kings* like Vesta Tilley and – the original 'Burlington Bertie from Bow' – Ella Shields as well as post-war female impersonators such as Danny La Rue and Bobbie Kimber who made a socially acceptable living in variety. On the streets, however, such appearances attracted hostility and violence from passing strangers, as the celebrated Quentin Crisp discovered in the 1930s, when boldly he flaunted bright *maquillage*, long hair dyed crimson – varnished fingernails, and sandals displaying toenails painted likewise.

'It was simple, really,' Bunny Roger explained, 'if your ears didn't show, you were effeminate.' A rouge-cheeked and tinted-haired dandy rather than a cross-dresser, the late English couturier had been banished from the University of Oxford in 1931 because of his overt homosexuality. He was, however, also a Second World War hero whose courage under fire engendered a 'don't-ask-don't-tell' hush about his inclinations among superiors, equals and subordinates.

As it had been for veterans of Ypres, Passchendaele and the Somme during the previous global conflict, Bunny and his fellow conscripts had had their locks planed halfway up the side of the skull, a tradition of King's Regulations since the discovery that trench warfare was a breeding ground for flea and lice infestations. Many chose to keep it that way after returning to Civvy Street, either 'out of respect' or because long hair was associated with the previous century's so-called 'Gay Nineties' and the Aesthetic (or Decadent) Movement with its propagation of excess and artificiality. Among the movement's leading lights was Oscar Wilde, so disgraced by the arrest for sodomy and gross indecency that had led to his imprisonment that no child anywhere would be baptised 'Oscar' for decades afterwards.

In the Roaring Twenties there were also those who'd been called up after the Armistice was signed or missed the war altogether because of being in a 'reserved occupation'. Worse were the conscientious objectors (both those jailed and those who'd passed muster with the Military Service Tribunals), rich blokes who'd sat it out in a funk hole, and all the other Jazz Age fops who'd escaped the risk of finishing the Great War with an empty sleeve, shell-shocked or blinded, and were now going around hatless to show off hair girlishly fluffed-up or 'shingled' (whereby some brand of left-in-cream declumped curls).

Long male hair had been contentious from *auld lang syne*. Before the Battle of Thermopylae in 480 BC – as resonant a historical 'last stand' as Hastings or Waterloo – Xerxes, suzerain of the Achaemenid Empire, had expected an easy victory in the light of the opposing Spartans' habit of fussing incessantly with their luxuriant hair. It seemed to indicate men more pliant, pathetic and submissive than they should be – until Xerxes was informed that it was a soldierly ritual that primed them to fight and, if necessary, die bravely.

A millennium and a half later, the Normans also underestimated the might of Harold II Godwinson's Saxons, partly on the strength of their look – which was regarded as unmanly, particularly as their aristocracy and the king's elite housecarls were given to combing their flowing hair as carefully as the Spartans, although they were, nonetheless, confident in their heterosexuality and their standing as battle-hardened warriors. This was in the teeth of the view of St Wulfstan, prior of Worcester (and the last surviving pre-Conquest bishop) that it was a sign of degeneracy and military weakness. He went so far as to use his nail-cleaning knife to cut off a lock from a culprit and ordering him to remove the rest to correspond. This admonition appears to have been taken to heart by Harold and his retinue as the Bayeux Tapestry depicts them throughout with haircuts just above the collar.

Wulfstan's perspective was endorsed by other factions of the mediaeval Roman Catholic Church – who directed rulers within its sphere of influence to compel Muslims, Hindus and Sikhs in their domains to keep male hair short, severely parted and devoid of ornamentations such as braids in accord with law-making attempts to quell insurrection and barbarism. As late as the nineteenth century, boarding schools, riding roughshod over inbred religious observances – such as Hasidic Jewish sidelocks – forced severe haircuts on such pupils. Elsewhere, however – particularly towards the east – long hair (and a long beard) put the illiterate peasant at one with the Eastern Orthodox clergymen with their sacred wafers, blood-wine and mouthing of holy sounds at every mass and deathbed. Yet it would have been irreverent to emulate a monk's tonsure, which was supposedly pioneered by St Peter in deference to Christ's circlet of thorns. In parenthesis, no such qualms deterred some GIs stationed in Germany in the mid-1960s from forming a combo called The Monks, complete with shaved-on-top crowns. Nor did it prevent the diabolical take on it by Keith Flint, singing dancer with 1990s electronica executants The Prodigy.

What might be seen today as more outrageous than Flint, the Normans of old favoured a small, short patch of hair on top of the head to the ears with the back of the skull closely shaven. The visual division between them and their vanquished Saxons was later matched by that between the Roundheads (although they were not as pudding-basined as myth has it) and the Cavaliers with their curling-tonged ringlets. These so disgusted arch-Puritan William Prynne – who, prior to Charles I's dethroning, had suffered his ears being sawn off in the pillory and 'SL' ('seditious libeller') branded on his cheeks for his beliefs – that he condemned them with words like 'vainglorious', 'odious', 'ungodly', 'horrid', 'pernicious' and 'ridiculous'. He also regarded women who kept hair short as 'mannish, unnatural, impudent and unchristian'. So too would those Puritans who, after the Restoration, fled to North America where long-haired Caucasian men were considered akin to the painted and feathered 'savages' they were diseasing and dispossessing. To digress briefly, Charles I's grandson, the Old Pretender, exiled in Italy, tried to force a severe trim onto an unwilling Bonnie Prince Charlie to make him more presentable to certain prospective Jacobite supporters.

Nevertheless, from the ancient Greeks – who revered long-haired gods (including Zeus) and heroes – to all manner of cultures since, ornately styled hair frequently symbolised aristocratic power and wealth. Shaven heads were for slaves, the peasantry and for humiliating captured military enemies like the Gauls conquered by Julius Caesar and the Viking warlord Guthrum after his surrender to Alfred the Great – as well as disgraced political rivals and such as the target of a trumped-up charge of witchcraft in *The Devils*, a 1971 flick set in the France of Cardinal Richelieu. Moreover, members of the Roman Senate, fearful for their well-being, had kept *their* hair short to appease the Emperor Caligula whose own hair was receding. An equally sensitive later emperor, Commodus, white-haired from childhood, ensured that his curls were dyed monthly and sprinkled with flakes of gold.

Jump-cutting to Mediaeval Europe, short hair was still redolent of servitude as well as mourning – and of guilt, what with knights and those of higher rank sometimes cleaving off or yanking out their hair to show penitence for their sins. In Gaelic Ireland, you'd be liable to a heavy fine if you cut a man's hair against his wishes, and, after the Normans' annexation of huge swathes of land there, native Irish who wore their hair short were judged to be betraying their heritage. Conversely, colonists with hair over their collars were deemed to be 'going native'.

Over centuries of direct English interference in Irish affairs, descendants of such intruders preached that God was disciplining the country by delivering it into the hands of foreigners just as the Israelites had been when subjugated by others. Perhaps they overlooked Samson, eyeless in Gaza, heaving down the temple upon the hated Philistines after regaining the God-given ultra-strength lost when Delilah's betrayal caused the removal of the hair that was its source.

This was despite him telling her 'loud and clear/Keep yer cotton-pickin' fingers/Out ma curly hair' – as outlined most famously on disc in 'Hard-Headed Woman' by a certain Mr EA Presley in 1958 when his pompadour-with-sideburns had whoever copied it typecast by tidy-minded journalists as 'white trash'.

CHAPTER TWO

'Certainly the "quiff" or lock of hair which some lads
wear on their forehead, is a sure sign of silliness'

In post-war living rooms in Britain, regardless of who was present, a
parent would often switch off a radio set if it was broadcasting what
was taken to be ragtime, boogie-woogie, jazz and whatever else had
been lumped together derisively as 'swing' – because it epitomised
the cacophony heard in X-certificate films with scenes set in the
kind of juke joints, pool rooms and bordellos that prospered in
the most disreputable districts of North America. Such noise was
a distinguishing feature of the modern music that was subverting
all that was good and true. Hitler had had his faults, but pouring
contempt on that rubbish hadn't been among them.

With geometrically patterned linoleum the only hint of frivolity in
many such homes, this drab era was epitomised by a middle manager
of a father relaxing over an after-dinner crossword in slippers,
'quiet' cardigan and cavalry twill trousers with elephant folds which
obliterated any inkling of body shape round the seat. This style
was reflected in his son's school uniforms of black 'bomber' shoes,
flannels, blazer, tie and white or grey shirt. He couldn't understand
what anyone found so loathsome about a decent life in which the
only times a true gentleman's name appeared in the local newspaper
was when he got wed and when he shuffled off this mortal coil.

Whatever was wrong with aspiring to a weeded crazy paving
leading across gardens full of daffodils to front doors with silver
letter boxes, where the bell would chime and an aproned maid
might answer? Inside, the sugar was in its bowl, the milk in its jug,
the cups unchipped on their saucers on an embroidered tablecloth.
Yet the continuity of ancient conservatism could coexist with
modernism in moderation as epitomised in the world of William

Brown, Richmal Crompton's outrageous 12-year-old from a well-to-do family, whose first exploits were published in 1919. Mr Brown rarely showed any explicit emotion towards his ideally seen-but-not-heard younger son beyond an icy irritation. However, he was prepared to listen and dispense soothing, if condescending, advice to 17-year-old Robert, William's elder brother, even when the latter and his friends formed the simplistic and polite Society of Reformed Bolshevists in 'The Weak Spot' – which opened 1924's *William The Fourth* collection of short stories – despite one member being noticed leaning against the mantelpiece in Robert's bedroom and inspecting his hair in the glass, willing it to grow as long and upwardly bushy as that of, say, the young Leon Trotsky.

The upbringing of the adolescent – not 'teenage' – boy had been one in which the good opinion of their peers mattered more to his parents than their children's happiness. The bottom line was that their word was law. You were expected to do what you were told with hardly a murmur and keep your emotions in check. It all came down to a form of doublethink: training yourself not to feel bitterness or anger towards mum and dad, even when those feelings might be entirely justified – when, for instance, you could be berated in harsh and penetrating tones in the most public places, and 'answering back' (i.e. sticking up for yourself) could be met with a thrashing or being 'sent to bed with the light off'. Certainly, however much they earned private scorn rather than filial devotion, you would remain very concerned about parental disapproval even after you had ostensibly escaped from their clutches.

Shackled to homework, you'd glower and wonder if this was all there was. Perish the thought but you might be better off as the scion of some coalman or bus conductor who didn't frown should you ask to go to the cinema on the Sabbath and wouldn't threaten to disinherit you if you dared to come downstairs in an American tie.

By the time the Allies had liberated mainland Europe in 1944, the United States seemed to overseas youth the very wellspring of everything glamorous from Coca-Cola and Hollywood flicks to The Ink Spots who were to enrapture the continent's theatres during their world tour in 1947. Priscilla White, a Liverpool docker's daughter, was typical of many an English lass who 'lived in a world where the model of all that was good in life was in a Doris Day movie'.[2]

Concern was expressed in a 1957 feature in *Everybody's Weekly*, a now defunct UK journal. 'Are We Turning Our Children Into Little Americans?' it asked. For, as well as Barkis remarking that Mrs Peggotty 'sure knows her cooking' in a US cartoon-strip edition of *David Copperfield*, almost as remarkable were the Wild West films that British youth had come to consume. No one ever talked thataway. Neither would a pub landlady not bat an eyelid if some hombre was plugged full of daylight in the lounge bar. A god had descended on London once when Roy Rogers rode a Trigger from his hotel to Leicester Square Odeon. To many youngsters – including future Rolling Stones Mick Jagger and Keith Richards – Rogers, Gene Autry, Hopalong Cassidy and other singing cowboys with guitars were significant early influences.

More directly, both during and after the war, GIs on passes had burst upon the fun-palaces of places like Bedford, Kettering and Cheltenham, acknowledging bemused or envious stares with waves of fat wands of cigars. The newcomers wore garb in which only blacks, London spivs and the bolder homosexuals would be seen dead – padded shoulders on double-breasted suits, 'spearpoint' shirt collars, two-tone shoes and those contentious hand-painted ties with Red Indians or baseball players on them – and drawled in a vocabulary freighted with words like 'gotten', 'sidewalk', and 'elevator'.

'Over-paid, oversexed and over here,' they nurtured, however unknowingly, the resentment of parochial roughnecks. According to a hand-wringing media, foremost among these were Teddy Boys, the most conspicuously vainglorious of post-bellum youth sects. In existence in all but name for almost half a decade before rock 'n' roll, these had cultivated a look that, other than a touch of the Mississippi riverboat card sharp, was almost entirely British. Their Edwardian three-quarter-length drape jackets with velvet collars, bootlace ties, frilly shirts and 'drainpipe' trousers so tight that

---

2. As 'Cilla Black', she'd be the only female representative of Merseybeat to enjoy lasting fame.

it was as if their legs had been dipped in ink, provided youths, however undersized, homely and of depressed circumstances, with excuses to transform themselves into sartorial visions. With crepe-soled 'brothel creepers' (and fluorescent socks) plus glaciers of brilliantine that could render the mousiest hair heroically jet-black, they were around long before the first photograph of a saturnine Elvis Presley was published in Britain (in *Record Mirror* on 21 January 1956) depicting him as a hybrid of amusement arcade hoodlum and nancy boy. Incidentally, Presley had been blond until he chose to dye it when preparing for his first screen role, going along with an argument that it was more flattering to his face on film. He's believed to have used Clairol, a hair-colouring product aimed at women, and promoted with the slogan *Does she... or doesn't she?*

When thus greased up, a Ted might tease the mess into a lavishly whorled frontal 'quiff', a word stemmed perhaps from the French *coiffe* or, because one was worn by the titular hero of *The Adventures Of Tintin* by Brussels-born cartoonist Hergé, the Dutch *kuif* – meaning 'crest' (with *Kuifje* the diminutive given to Tintin in the Netherlands editions). On the opposite side of the Channel, a Ted might intentionally rumple or tube his hair into an 'elephant's trunk' that could flop down to mid-nose. Much rarer was what was demeaned by racists as the 'curry puff' for its semblance to a style from South East Asia involving a bob of hair waved just beyond the forehead.

Usually, however, a Ted would settle on a lavish frontal quiff and a ducktail – known colloquially as the 'duck's arse' (or, in North America, 'duck's ass') and more politely as a DA – in which the sides looked like folded wings, and the tooth edge of a preferably metal comb defined a slicing from the crown to the nape of the neck. The overall result was stiffened and held in frequently precarious 'cow-licked' place, most often by a petroleum-based gel – Vaseline or Brylcreem[3] – but also soap, lacquer[4] (a newish product from the

---

3. A surprisingly minute amount of the stuff was required to make hair shiny and fixed (and battle dandruff), hence its advertising tag line: *Brylcreem – a little dab'll do ya/Brylcreem – you'll look so debonair/Brylcreem – the gals'll all pursue ya/they'll love to run their fingers through your hair!*

4. Often purloined from sisters, mothers and girlfriends and although

USA, sprayed on from an aerosol can), a rubbed in solution of
sugar and warm water, or even lard, often daubed so thickly that
hurricane force could not dislodge a single strand.

Perfection was easier for some than others. While 'cowlicks' –
stubborn whorls at different angles to the rest of the hair – were
a constant problem for many, Ray 'Mungo Jerry' Dorset, a fellow
of mixed race, had dark brown curly hair with an inclination to
become frizzy. 'It didn't engage me with other youths thought
to be cool,' he sighed. 'It was like being red-headed.' Ray was,
therefore, able to do no more than approximate a quiff and DA
until his mother's job in a hairdressing salon led to the discovery
of a solution applied during the creation of a permanent wave
('perm'). If Ray rubbed it in, kept combing until his hair was
as straight as possible, and then used a 'fixer', he'd achieve the
desired outcome.

Many Teds couldn't pass a mirror without pulling a comb from
a breast pocket to make a quick adjustment to what amounted to
an act of passive-aggressive opposition towards strictly standardised
short-back-and-sides haircuts. These were reminders of the war,
their fathers and folk like Lord Robert Baden-Powell of Gilwell,
founder of the Boy Scouts, who in his *Scouting for Boys* manual
wrote, 'Certainly the "quiff" or lock of hair which some lads wear
on their forehead, is a sure sign of silliness.'

Worse, it got them into trouble. A newly-conscripted Teddy
Boy suffered twenty-eight days in a Hereford detention barracks
for refusal to allow the regimental barber contact with a quiff he
claimed had taken two years and God-knows-how-much to nurture
– and, as 1954's summer recess approached, a Canvey Island
headmaster announced, both during an assembly and to the *Daily
Herald* (beneath a *HAIRCUTS HORRIFY THE HEAD!* headline),
that 'these flashy American styles must stop. Have your hair cut in
the ordinary English way!'

Lone pedestrians would cross streets, particularly on desolate
housing estates and within industrial and dockside hinterlands,

---

(cont.) inflammable and toxic, it could hold unshampooed hair in place for
up to a week until washed with lotion that, from the 1950s, could contain
conditioning ingredients.

to avoid lamppost clusters of young men, some wearing sunglasses unnecessary in the twilight. They may have gathered there prior to sallying forth as swaggering phalanxes, their girlfriends trailing forlornly behind them, some attached to those who, to impress them, would pick fights with and, ideally, clobber other blokes.

Wielding bicycle chains and broken bottles – with thick brass rings (manufactured perhaps in school metalwork rooms) adorning fists like knuckledusters, and belts studded with washers stolen from work – a contingent of Cheltenham youths, desperate for things to destroy and people to beat up, took out their frustrations on the US interlopers.

One such expedition climaxed with the killing of a GI in Cheltenham's bus station toilet, and the entire town declared off-limits to North American servicemen. This was just a few years after lads blocking a pathway had refused to budge and sparked off the most heavily-publicised Teddy Boy murder trial that concluded with knife-wielding Michael Davies of a gang known as 'the Plough Boys' (after a local pub) being sentenced to death. However, he was granted a reprieve after three months in the condemned cell.

The bother had taken place on a London heath in 1954, but the previous January, would-be Teddy Boy (and former approved school inmate) Derek Bentley had been hanged after a younger brother-in-burglary gunned down a policeman.

These, plus a wealth of less reported offences enriched the demonization of Teddy Boys as post-war folk devils. Indeed, certain media found it convenient to blame it all on the 'new' cult, provoking episodes in television series to be lent Teddy Boy slants (in which violence was a predetermined element) and the commissioning of an ITV documentary (whose director encouraged some of the subjects to stage a pretend punch-up) – even though a principal thesis in Max Décharné's cohesive and worthy *Teddy Boys: Post-War Britain And The First Youth Revolution* history is 'the terms of reference are so wide as to include anyone of the right age who threw a brick through a window, regardless of what they were wearing'. Moreover, *The Teddy Boy Mystery*, a 1955 novella, contained a police sergeant who 'expresses the view that most Teds are simply in need of guidance or something to do'. He spoke the same calm sense as a non-fictional representative of the Sevenoaks force commenting on an outbreak of local hooliganism: 'if anything, they are less trouble than other youths', reasoning that Teds were too concerned about their 'elegant attire' to thus risk tearing or dirtying it. So it was that not every fine young man went to the bad via endorsement or emulation of Teddy Boys. The celebrated Viv Stanshall, for example, was one of a Southend gang of Teds prior to emergence as ace face of the Bonzo Dog Doo-Dah Band – whereas Jimmy Savile, beginning his journey to afterlife disgrace, was the manager of a Manchester palais in the mid-1950s, who discouraged the admission of Teddy Boys for all their transformation into harmless sources of gag fodder for comedians, cartoonists and the likes of Jimmy Logan, a kilted professional Scotsman, who worked a jokey soliloquy into a piece actually entitled 'Teddy Boy' on his 1958 in-concert LP, *Loganberry Pie*, which was taped at a presentation in Glasgow that marked the passing of the music hall.

Many of those ripe for more than boyish mischief had no adherence to Teddy Boys or any other movement. They weren't anything. They'd brag of getting themselves expelled from a Church youth club or somewhere else with a self-improving reek of ping-pong, slide-shows and a 'Brains Trust' on current affairs, and where sports jackets, 'sensible' shoes, cavalry twills and short-back-and-sides marked you as serviceable husband material for earnest maidens who looked as if they couldn't wait for a game of chess followed by a chat about the transmutation of souls over an orange squash.

If not reinstated after scandalised parents forced an apology for maybe blatantly brandishing a cigarette or letting slip a 'bloody', a boy might take to the streets with other such reprobates, smoking and saying 'bloody' – and even 'bugger' – unreproached whilst denouncing the youth club as 'kids' stuff'. If there was no other fun going, the boldest might return *en bloc* to wreck the place, snarling with laughter as the grown-up in charge pleaded ineffectually – though presiding clerics were sometimes able to limit the damage because of their dog-collars and the juvenile's superstitious terror of eternal punishment for sin, and, though there might be a few low mutterings, the invading entourage would shamble out meekly.

The notion of smashing up the youth club might have come from Marlon Brando in 1953's *The Wild One*, much banned because of its story of an unpunished raid on a US small town by the leather-clad 'Johnny' (Brando) and his fellow motorcycle vandals radiating an anti-everything stance. Another role model was James Dean who left this vale of misery via a spectacular car crash on 30 September 1955. In that same year's *Rebel Without A Cause*, he'd demonstrated that, unlike Brando, you didn't have to come from the wrong side of the tracks to qualify as a sullenly introspective ne'er-do-well. Even the most nicely spoken lad, even one who'd passed the British 11-plus examination and so gone to a grammar school rather than a secondary modern – where all the 'failures' went – could now saunter along to the corner shop with hunched shoulders, hands rammed in his pockets and chewing gum with a James Dean half-sneer.

He'd be obscurely thrilled when louts he'd been taught to despise barracked in cinemas; when an unruly class smashed up a teacher's cherished collection of records it deemed 'square' in 1955's *Blackboard Jungle* ('Haven't you got any bop?!'); and during the dance hall scene two years later in *Hell Drivers*. Identifying however obscurely with this boorish but not untypical instance of adult male social behaviour in the 1950s, he'd trail along when gangs barged without paying into the local palais, especially one from which 'Teddy Boys – and coloureds' – had been barred. Once inside, they'd be studied (not always surreptitiously) by 'birds' who'd make eyes at boys to whom they hoped to appear as elfin as Audrey Hepburn in 1953's *Roman Holiday*.

If pursuit of romance was either fruitless or not the principal mass objective of the expedition, the fellows would seek more brutal sensual recreation. If you so much as glanced at them, the next piece of action could be *you* via provocation as mild as turning in the direction of a sudden squawk of laughter from one of their hard-faced birds – 'Are you looking at my woman?' If there wasn't even that much righteous indignation to start something, they'd make some. So emerged hellfire sermons and scare stories, questions in Parliament and plays turned into *film noirs* like Bruce Walker's *Cosh Boy* (US title: *The Slasher*) – that suggested flogging was the only answer – while the later 1950s brought movies such as *These Dangerous Years*, in which a teenage troublemaker was reformed by a spell in the army, and *Violent Playground* (with local boy Freddie Fowell[5] as a gang boss), each set on Merseyside.

Both flicks presented rock 'n' roll as a negative influence on the young. It was, however, unmentioned in *The Teddy Boy Mystery*, published in an era when the *New Musical Express (NME)* record and sheet music sales charts was filled mostly with the North American likes of the of 'Glow Worm' from the Mills Brothers, Bing Crosby's 'The Isle of Innisfree', 1953's 'How Much Is That Doggie In The Window?' by Patti Page ('The Singing Rage'), Kay Starr's waltz-time 'Wheel of Fortune' (a favourite of Derek Bentley), Judy Garland's 'The Man that Got Away' 'Mambo Italiano' (a hit for both Rosemary Clooney and Dean Martin) and Clooney's *magnum opus*, 'Where Will the Dimple Be?'

They were directed as much at grown-ups as those condemned to put up with much the same music that their elders and younger brothers and sisters liked, even after, thanks to fuller employment and increases in wages since the war, the 'teenager' surfaced as a separate target for advertising. As far as 'pop' was concerned, the British Broadcasting Corporation (BBC) continued to give the public only that *decent* music it *ought* to like – hence *The Black and White Minstrel Show*, strict tempo supremo Victor Sylvester's *Come Dancing*, *The Perry Como Show*, *Spot The Tune* with Marion Ryan, and calypsos by Cy Grant on topical *Tonight*.

Also directed at the over-thirties were programmes monopolised by such as The Beverley Sisters and Donald Peers ('The Cavalier Of Song') and musical interludes in shows centred on the likes of ventriloquist's dummy Archie Andrews, 'Mr Pastry', and Lancastrian 'schoolboy' Jimmy Clitheroe. Otherwise, there was *Children's Favourites* – record requests aired by 'Uncle Mac'. Older siblings – and mighty square ones at that – made do with *Quite Contrary*, built round Ronnie Hilton, a former apprentice engineer from Humberside, who – for want of anyone better – was cited by

---

5. A future star of British comedy after he assumed the stage name 'Freddie Starr'.

the *NME* as 1955's most popular British vocalist, although the area had thrown up a challenger in David Whitfield, also approaching his thirties. Their rival as BBC radio's most omnipresent singer was Lee Lawrence, an ex-Entertainments National Service Association (ENSA) trouper with a similar neo-operatic tenor.

The search for anything teenage was as fruitless on Independent Television (ITV) which began in 1955 with weekly spectaculars starring Patti Page and Britain's own Dickie Valentine. While *Round About Ten* was a bit racy in its embrace of Humphrey Lyttelton's Jazz Band, the inclusion of The Teenagers, a winsome boy-girl ensemble in 'Forces Sweetheart' Vera Lynn's *Melody Cruise*, was something of a false dawn. In between 'How Much Is That Doggie in the Window' and Lee Lawrence's 'cover' of the deeply religious 'Crying in the Chapel', there was no middle ground. As in the 1940s, you jumped from nursery rhymes to Vera Lynn as if the connecting years were spent in a coma.

Young British listeners may have supposed that the sounds they picked up on the BBC Light Programme were 'square' because they were listening on one of these cheap new transistors rather than a cumbersome mahogany radiogram. Yet it was the same on all of them, what with the first ripplings of rock 'n' roll warranting no more than token spins before they were dismissed as a fad as transitory as the cha-cha-cha, Hula Hoops or Davy Crockett fake-coonskin caps. Indeed, while 'Rock Around The Clock' by Bill Haley and the Comets,[6] led by a tubby old trouper with a kiss curl swathed across his forehead, and some of its soundalike follow-ups excited all but the most serious-minded 1950s teenager, even Haley himself would tender apologies at press conferences for his Comets' knockabout stage routines – but, what with this 'rock' nonsense going so well, it'd have been bad business not to have played up to it, wouldn't it? Anyway, hadn't one of the Comets once served under Benny Goodman?

The bandleader Ted Heath, who was to 'salute' Goodman, North America's proclaimed 'King of Swing', who'd lent a sheen of

---

6. Heard over the opening credits of *Blackboard Jungle*.

respectability to mainstream jazz over an entire 33 rpm release, hadn't thought that rock 'n' roll would 'catch on in Europe at all,' explaining, 'you see it is primarily for the coloured population'.

It was also for such as *pachucos*, North American adolescents speaking a 'Spanglish' dialect of their own, and with a preference for the less slushy shades of US pop music with an erotic content no longer shrouded in stardust and roses – but usually too hard-as-nails to admit not entirely disliking 'Where Will The Dimple Be'. They originated as a clique of Hispanic descent, born in southern regions that remained as much Mexican as North American in their place names – San Diego, Pasadena, Los Angeles, Tijuana, San Bernardino, El Monte, Rio Bravo, Sacramento – where Spanish was taught as a second language in schools, Mexican decor bedecked homes, and fajitas and jalapeño peppers featured on restaurant menus.

Cruising aimlessly in shark-finned cars (with windows rolled down and radio blasting), *pachucos* collected at street corners, *puros* (cigars) clenched between teeth, and armed with flick-knives and home-made coshes.

As long ago as 1943, mutual baiting between *pachucos* and uniformed sailors in central Los Angeles had led to serious assault, temporarily precipitating a 'war' lasting the best part of a week. It prompted the prohibition by the city council of the wearing in public of *pachuco* livery hinged on oversized zoot-suits, with tent-like peg-trousers and half-belts at the back of jackets draped halfway to the knees, which, snarled mob-handed servicemen, wasted war-effort cloth.

Even before the decade turned, *pachucos* were often perceived by the US White Anglo-Saxon Protestant (WASP) media as having much in common with chapters of the Hells Angels as well as with the Teddy Boys, France's *blousons noirs*, Japan's *bōsōzoku* and the *bodgies* of Australasia. Rather than garish excess, however, some of their favoured gear, either made to last or cut-price and disposable, centred round a fundamental structure of real or imitation black leather windcheaters, jeans, motorbike boots and T-shirts.

In Britain, this was an attractive option for any who weren't in a position to afford seedy-flash finery. 'When I was at Yardley Wood

Secondary Modern – a dump, very rough,' recalled Christopher 'Ace' Kefford, preordained to be bass player with The Move, 'my school uniform was cheap black jeans sewn up as tight as I could get 'em, black shirt, red waistcoat off my granddad, greased-back hair. We had a gang at school – real dead end kids who broke into shops and pinched cigarettes.' He added, 'I think that's how a lot of pop groups formed – as an extension of that.'

Ostensibly subject to the least costly amendment were hairstyles adopted by both delinquents and the virtuous. One of the most common was the 'Tony Curtis', named after the Hollywood actor's curled-up front and DA parting at the back. This was 'the last word in cool during the middle 1950s,' recollected pop biographer Philip Norman, 'frothed out at the front in homage to James Dean – but spare a thought also for the flat-top, born of a brief Italian phase'.

The noted English novelist and pop biographer was referring to a severely upright shape, requiring fortnightly attention by a hairdresser, in which a boxy and level wedge of waxed hair from forehead to crown is the chief feature of a cutting tapered at the back with sides often shaved to the skin. Given currency in North America and Britain by returning militia during the 1940s, one of the most prominent flat-toppers was to be President John F Kennedy. With the title 'My Boy Flat Top', it was celebrated on disc to mostly chartbusting effect by US entertainers Dorothy Collins, Boyd Bennett (its co-writer) and his Rockets, the Gayles and by Liverpool's Frankie Vaughan: 'Young and strong, his top is flat/ Cool haircut, never wears a hat/I don't mean maybe, he's a real hep cat/My boy-flat top'.

Though they didn't extol in song the qualities of the style after which they named themselves, the Crewcuts, a quartet derived from a church choir in Toronto (and remembered chiefly for 1954's million-selling 'Sh-Boom') were, arguably, the first to make a connection between pop and haircuts. In their case, this was via a term coined by university boat race crews in reference to a cut designed to curb an oarsman's need to brush hair from his face. It became associated more readily, however, with the all-offs inflicted on military draftees during both World Wars with buzzing electric clippers. Crew cuts of a kind had been around since they were hidden beneath eighteenth-century wigs. They were known already in France as *coupe à la brosse* (brush cut) and in Germany – where it looked more like a hedgehog – as the *Bürstenschnitt*. More than the 'Tony Curtis', crew cuts identified bearers as, ideally, as tough as Hollywood thespian Steve McQueen, supersonic aviator John Glenn or any Major League baseball pitcher.[7]

Before import back to Europe through transatlantic seamen, popularly known as 'Cunard Yanks'[8] crew cuts had caught on in North America during the 1920s among collegians for their refreshing coolness throughout the summer, after which they might be allowed to lengthen against winter into what was known as an 'ivy league' or 'college contour'. Other variations – lent names like 'the butch', 'the front-combed boogie', 'the Hollywood' and, with two waves converging at a point high on the brow, 'the rack', depended upon customer directives. Within those parameters the barber's assessment of face and skull shape was important, as were factors peculiar to the wavy, curly or straight individual such as widow's peaks or cue ball-like bald patches that, even aided by recommended brands of wax, couldn't be readily or lastingly arched vertically into either a Californian 'breaker'[9] – top hair grown long enough to be scraped into a wavelike sleekness – or a half-inch version of what hadn't yet been termed a 'pompadour', named after Madame de Pompadour, mistress-in-chief to Louis XV of France, despite her hair having but cursory similarity to a style centred on either being swept upwards from the face high over the forehead or drooped in a 'jellyroll' (a US take on the so-called 'elephant's trunk'). This was embraced, in modified fashion anyway, by such as Frank Sinatra, the male personnel of the Ink Spots-indebted

---

7. Players of American Football, however, had had longish hair since 1889 when the Princeton team grew it as protection against head injury (and were thus caricatured in the popular press) until the introduction of helmets during the following decade.

8. Instanced by Red Bentley, a ship's engineer known to and admired by thirteen-year-old George Harrison – on whose bonce bristled a crew-cut until he adopted swiftly a more closer-to-home look.

9. Among those who favoured this style in the 1950s was the great Belgian chansonnier Jacques Brel, both a figurehead and *éminence grise* of twentieth century songwriting.

Platters and the Crosby Boys, a vocal combo consisting of the four sons of Bing Crosby.

Its official name was conferred after it had been seen in longer form on the heads of James Dean, Robert Horton (most renowned as 'Flint McCullough', the scout in television's *Wagon Train*) and other young TV and movie stars before pompadours, modified and otherwise, adorned heroes of classic rock like Chuck Berry, Little Richard, the Everly Brothers and, particularly, Elvis Presley – with 'geek chic' exhibited by the horn-rimmed likes of Buddy Holly, Roy Orbison and jazzmen like Benny Goodman – and Dave Brubeck who transported the form to the borders of blues and pop. At its most extreme was the piled up and stick-like pompadour, further enlarged with a wig and photographic enhancement, of singing pianist Esquerita – an appearance not mirrored particularly in his musical style, despite Charlie Gillett's description of it in his 1970s study of rock 'n' roll, *The Sound of the City*, as 'a chaotic symphony as a succession of chords chased each other desperately up the keyboard'.[10]

The pompadour was already prototypical of young Spanish-Americans, among them Ritchie Valens with his chartbusting 'La Bamba'/'Donna' double A-side, Chan 'Hippy Hippy Shake' Romero from the *pachuco* storm centre of East Los Angeles, as well as boys born of Italian-speaking households such as the leather-jacketed high school dropout, 'Arthur Fonzarelli', alias 'The Fonz', prominent character in the globally networked *Happy Days* US television sitcom, set in suburban Wisconsin somewhere between 1958 and 1962.

In the 2000 anthology *Prison Writing: A Collection of Fact, Fiction and Verse*, the Fonz was cited as the 'epitome of the 50s bad-boy cool', but the other *Happy Days* males, young and old, were normal and wholesome, with conservatively combed, side-parted and, as a rule, lubricated hair, referred to as 'the English cut' or 'the Prince Charles' after the then juvenile heir apparent.

---

10. Gillett is one of the few pop historians to write at length about Esquerita who, incidentally, was among black rockers like Berry and Richard who used pomade – meaning 'ointment' in French – that checked the tendency of Afro-textured locks, natural or straightened, to dry inflexibly.

That was when North American funnymen like Sid Caesar, Stan Freberg, Shelley Berman, Jack Benny, Bob Hope and Milton Berle were more likely to be esteemed than pop stars. More germane to this discussion, nonetheless, is Yul Brynner, a former singing guitarist, who shaved his head completely for the title role in the 1951 stage musical *The King and I* (later the subject of his second movie), keeping it that way for the years left to him. Enough of his male fans copied him for the style to be dubbed the 'Yul Brynner look'.

In sober Britain – where framed photographs on the walls of barber shops displayed black-and-white photographs of film actors who'd won the Second World War over and over again – efforts were also made to turn comedians such as Max Bygraves, Dave King, Dickie Henderson and Bob Monkhouse into more likely objects of adoration than singers like Messrs. Hilton, Lawrence, Valentine and Whitfield. Even Ted Lune, idiotic 'Private Bone' in *The Army Game*, an ITV sitcom, passed through cheering streets when he returned in on-screen uniform to his home town of Blackburn.

Parrot-like in profile, bug-eyed, skinny and Jodrell Bank-eared, Lune was a celebrity you didn't mind your girlfriend liking. More of a threat were the 'sensible' likes of natural history programme presenter David Attenborough; sports commentator Peter West; magician David Nixon (owner, he asserted, of 'the best-loved bald head in show business'); newsreader Huw Wheldon; disc jockey Pete Murray (who didn't disguise his detestation for Elvis Presley); Peter Elliott, (who had competed for Britain as a diver in the 1948 Olympics),[11] Eamonn Andrews, chat-show interlocutor and host of *What's My Line*, *This Is Your Life*, and the children's variety show, *Crackerjack*;[12] former heavyweight boxing champion Freddie Mills;[13] and others omnipresent on British television as a boy

11. Elliott's athletic frame and blazered air of head prefect-like rectitude as much as a wan croon provided leverage for a recording contract.
12. Eamonn's 'The Shifting Whispering Sands' monologue reached the domestic Top Twenty and Number Two in the Irish Republic in 1956. Nevertheless, he wasn't so fortunate with follow-ups, 'The Legend of Wyatt Earp' and 1957's 'The Ship That Never Sailed'.
13. In 1957, Parlophone released 'One for the Road', a one-shot 45 by Freddie

named Michael Philip Jagger graduated from Wentworth Juniors to Dartford Grammar School in 1954.

If not of gangling Ted Lune physique, Mike didn't look like he'd match up either to the clean-cut handsomeness of Eamonn Andrews *et al.* Moreover, reasoned parents like his, if you had to like pop singers, let them be heavily masculine like Uncle Sam's Tennessee Ernie Ford, Vaughn 'Ghost Riders In The Sky' Monroe, Frankie Laine and the prematurely grey Jeff Chandler, a singing actor whose screen popularity didn't translate into hit records. All these were preferable to Johnnie Ray, an exquisite from Oregon, who, with his hearing-aid discernible from the gallery, made girls want to mother him, especially when he burst into tears during some agonised *lied.* The mood changed, however, as he threw himself into an excess of pelvis-thrusting during a 1954 lewdness entitled 'Such a Night', his interpretation of the largely indecipherable lyrics implying that the conclusion of an evening out with a woman – if it was a woman – had gone further than a wistful embrace beneath the stars. The disc was also a smash hit.

While Johnnie's exhibitionism anticipated that which would pervade rock 'n' roll, it was expected that he'd 'grow old with his audience' just like everyone else. With pop regarded as a lower-class novitiate for a life as an 'all-round entertainer', as long as you didn't do anything the music establishment didn't like, after amassing a handful of hits, you'd 'mature'. A sure sign you'd 'Made It' might be a mid-evening duet on black-and-white television of some simpering evergreen with, perhaps, Bing Crosby, prefaced by a scripted chit-chat between cheeky young shaver and jovial voice-of-experience. From a subsequent comedy sketch on the same programme, there would unfold a flow chart of soft-shoe shuffling, charity sports events, 'blink-and-you'll-miss-him' roles in B-movies and life as a third-rate Sinatra in faraway supper clubs. Such was the expected fate for the luckier idol that toed a line of acceptable pseudo-rebellious behaviour. Well, we were all a bit crazy once upon a time, weren't we?

(cont.) Mills – a medley of 'Down At The Old Bull And Bush', 'I Belong To Glasgow', 'Knees Up Mother Brown' and further aged standards that poured from ale-choked mouths in pubs nationwide.

The industry would look after you, keep you in respectable work in variety, cabaret and even periodic advertising slots on TV when your time in the main spotlight was up, and the circle would remain unbroken. There was no reason why business couldn't carry on as usual with pop performers who were exactly that: purveyors of harmless ephemera to be hummed, whistled and sung imperfectly by the milkman while another ditty was prepared by reworking the same precept with either the same act or a new one developed from a similar formula.

Though the wildest act going then, Johnnie Ray's hair was no big deal in the years following the Second World War: far from excessively long at a time when nearly every boy bowed to stipulations outlined in places possessive of institutional power about it not covering eyebrows, ears, or collars. At home too, you'd go to the barber's with hardly a murmur when mum gave you the money, feeling no more trepidation than when it was your turn as class monitor to distribute the third-pint bottles of lukewarm milk provided at first playtime, courtesy of the Welfare State.

'I had no "self-image" then,' recalled photographer and author Tim Fagan of his primary school years in south-east Kent, 'and was oblivious to my appearance, doing stuff that boys did at the time: in the summer, climbing trees, making campfires... in the winter, making model aircraft and drawing...'

True enough, 'Dennis The Menace' in *The Beano* was a messily spiked *Struwwelpeter* (who, in one memorable strip, suffered explicitly when obliged by his mum to go for a trim at Slasher Brown's barber shop) and, in the more solemn pages of *Wizard*, *Eagle* and *Hotspur*, there were very occasional superheroes whose combed neatness strayed slightly over tunic necklines. The same was true in horror publications such as *Creepy Worlds* and *Tales from the Crypt*, syndicated from the United States.

Chiefly picture stories, they were frequently the principal reading matter of *pachucos*, Teddy Boys and the like in localities where the weedier A-stream pupils, being primed for higher education, earned little more than bullying contempt. Just coming into existence in the 1950s, schools like Britain's comprehensives, combining elements of both grammar and secondary modern, enabled children theoretically to follow what best suited their abilities and inclinations as they developed. However, they could be as demoralising as any other educational regime in their use of academic streaming. Moreover, a child's attendance at grammar school remained a desirable social coup for ambitious parents. When the ITV soap opera *Coronation Street* was young, Ken Barlow – then a teacher – was once depicted refusing a bribe to rig results so that a town councillor's son could attend the local grammar.

With sound reason, boys known to try hard academically were almost as afraid of their oppressors as Quentin Crisp and 'his sort' had been of 'queer bashers'. Yet, if not looking the part, there'd been nothing to stop any such not-so-Little Lord Fauntleroy making his fascinated way over to the tables in the local café where the trouble always sat. He'd feel torn between the bravado of being where he didn't think he belonged and a yearning to head for the door, never to go there again. The only alternative was to stay at home and vegetate so he strove for acceptance by avoiding highbrow topics that a Ted, *pachuco* or *bodgie* would find incomprehensible. Drawing on a cigarette (that he wasn't enjoying much), he would nod in guffawing appreciation while absorbing a dual code of morality that condoned male unfaithfulness but not that of any damsel gripping his arm proprietarily.

Sometimes he'd fight to control his features when they belched and swore, but, though it happened gradually, inhibitions flowed out of him. Determined that nothing was going to show him up for the sexually innocent boy he was (as probably most of them were too), his speech became as laced as theirs with incessant cursing. There is a similarity to a key scene in *Blackboard Jungle* where heavily accented 'Pete Morales' tells a story to a tape recorder and is obliged by censorship to change his implied and repeated use of 'fuckin'' to 'stinkin''.

At first, Fauntleroy had been an interloper, glowered at with gormless menace, but, eventually, he became a recognised satellite of the firmament, forever trying not to blow his cool with some inanity – or anything that suggested he was less than totally heterosexual.

CHAPTER THREE

'"Queer" was the insult of choice'

We're conditioned to think of events occurring during the birth-death vacuum as linear – that they have a beginning, middle and end. This history, however, is so riddled with compartments and sub-texts that I'm reminded of British historian and television presenter Lucy Worsley's pronouncement that 'History doesn't go in straight lines. It goes in curves. Sometimes things go backwards. I don't think we can take our self-defined progress for granted.'

That's why I'm jumping ahead briefly to 1964 and the baleful figures cut by The Rolling Stones on the shadowy front photograph of their eponymous debut long-player (LP). With no title or identification of the artists, every right-thinking grown-up saw five undesirables, albeit clean-shaven, in urgent need of haircuts. Indeed, many teenagers ignorant of the group's individual names seemed as aghast as their parents. Yet a significant number of boys were bewildered because what they couldn't admit was finding the Stones' androgyny guiltily transfixing – as indeed I had after I spotted the sleeve of their preceding EP (extended play) in the window of what was then Fleet's only record shop. The one I'd yet to learn was surnamed Jagger looked a little bit *femme*, as did Brian Jones who also had a face that, depending on your leanings, asked to be either punched or kissed.

Abhorrence at the physical appearance of the Stones and those who copied it spread across an adult populace that hoped long hair on males was but a passing craze. Why? 'I think that many of that wartime generation couldn't see long male hair without assuming decadence, or homosexuality or both,' confirmed Alan Franks, poet, playwright and sometime correspondent for The

Times. 'Hilarious really, were it not for the doggedness of their convictions.'

These strictures didn't apply, however, when considering British music hall jesters such as Max Wall, a married father of five whose bald crown gave way to lank locks streaming past his ears, and the irrepressible Ken Dodd, a television fixture after 1960, with, wrote an obituarist, 'sticking-up hair like an astonished ice cream cone'. It was tolerated too under the alibi of religion – like what was read of the baseball teams with tresses that matched luxuriant beards. For example, a group attached to the House of David, a commune of reassuringly depleted number by the mid-1950s, based in the Midwestern United States, claiming to be successors to self-proclaimed but long-dead English prophet of the Apocalypse Joanna Southcott.

Just about acceptable too were the more oddball university professors and rapturous-eyed orchestra conductors, preferably with twirled moustachios, from a time when 'longhair' had been a slang expression for 'classical', namely music considered 'worse' than the records hurled across the classroom in *Blackboard Jungle.* On disc, this was to be symbolised by the quote from Rachmaninoff's 'C# Prelude' that kicked off 'Like Long Hair', a 1961 instrumental single by Paul Revere and the Raiders, formed in Idaho three years earlier.[14]

By the close of the 1950s, however, it had had more to do with beatniks – whose 'cool' was defined by Amedeo Modigliani rather than Marlon Brando – and Jack Kerouac's 'Dean Moriarty' over, say, Fenimore Cooper's 'Hawkeye'. Had they got around to actually reading Kerouac, they also might have looked at Allen Ginsberg, William Burroughs and other 'Beat Generation' scribes.

Beatniks also held 'impromptu' musical entertainments involving, maybe, bongo-tapping and a saxophone honking inanely, causing the eyes of cross-legged listeners to close in ecstasy

---

14. The previous year, their future bass guitarist, Phil 'Fang' Volk, then aged fifteen, had been cajoled by girls at his Junior High School, during a lunchtime record session in the gymnasium, to sing along to Ritchie Valens's 'Donna', but their delighted response to it so irritated a cache of male students that they planned to ambush Volk after school, debag him and hew away his hair. He was, however, led to safety by Drake Levin, another Raider-in-waiting.

at the sheer joy of being revolutionary, free-loving and pacifist – or at least being seen to sound and look as if they were – though some of the fellows might exude the pensive, slump-shouldered surliness inherent in the 'kitchen sink' realism that articulated the post-war mood of the 'Angry Young Men' in whose novels, plays and visual art the common subject matter was domestic squalor and sordid scenarios from the inner city. Both genders of beatniks went in for army-surplus duffle coats draped with a long scarf, polo- or turtle-neck pullover down almost to the knees, sandals or desert boots, a CND badge and corduroy trousers that looked as if they'd hung round the legs of a particularly disgusting builder's labourer for the past five years. Had Molière been more than just a name to drop, the wearers might have quoted his words: 'Guenille si l'on veut, ma guenille m'est chère' ('Rags they may be: my rags are dear to me').

The female of the species wore either no make-up or skull-white facial cosmetics broken by maybe black eye-shadow and lipstick, conducted themselves as if in a trance and hid their figures inside tent-like jumpers. Their high priestess was svelte and spectral Juliette Gréco, the Thinking Man's French actress and singer. With her straight hair and intellectual aura, her presence was in the student bedsits where posters of works by Salvador Dali and Man Ray hung on the walls, and Genet, Nietzsche, Camus and Sartre, even if only skip-read, looked well on bookshelves.

In sock-smelling college hostel rooms and out-after-breakfast lodgings too, a fledgling beatnik boy's manner of dressing said (wrongly) that he hadn't been aware of the clothes flung on after rising that day. He contrived also to keep a day or two away from a shave or cultivated a bumfluff beard like a half-plucked Fidel Castro, the Cuban guérillero leader in battle-fatigues, admired for a perceived bewhiskered virility (oh yes, and his politics).

Needless to say, a beatnik male's hair was sufficiently longer than the norm that, on top of other de rigueur characteristics, caused a small enclave of beats in maritime Cornwall to warrant attention from both neighbours and the producers of Tonight, the BBC current affairs programme, who sent ace reporter Alan Whicker to interview all concerned. His consequent report, with its self-aware amusement, was echoed by Tony Hancock in his 1961 film, *The Rebel*, when, at a *demi-monde* get-together in Montmartre, he encountered the back of a 'weirdy with hair down to the shoulders'. '*Enchanté, mademoiselle*,' he smiled, only for the exquisite to turn round and, with a man's intonation, snap 'Do you mind?!'

During the same sequence, Hancock explained to a crowd of squatting beatniks, all dressed unvaryingly in berets and holey sweaters, that one of the reasons he'd had to quit a secure if tedious job in London was because he couldn't stand the uniformity in the accountancy office where he'd worked. As he leaves them, one beatnik commented to another, 'It must have been very soul-destroying for him. Imagine: everyone looking the same.'

The Rebel (US title: *Call Me Genius*) might have been funnier had the illustrious comedy actor been transported to a less clichéd artistic fringe. In Hamburg, for instance, where the city's university, colleges and the fee-paying *Meister Schule* were inclined to hold onto their dignity, their 'Brooding Intensity', one prominent faction – the '*exis*' – allied themselves to the Montmartre existentialists and their 'nothing matters' preoccupation with doomed romanticism and man's conquest of a disordered nature through the self-sacrificing detours of art.

Yet Hancock and his scriptwriters had already been to suburban London to crowbar public awareness of beatniks into 'The Big Night', a 1959 episode of the BBC television series, *Hancock's Half Hour*. Following the slashing of his lower face by an argumentative barber wielding an unsteady razor, Tony turns up at the cinema in East Cheam for a double-date, having opted for a false beard to hide the cuts healing beneath bloodied bits of newspaper and for beatnik casuals rather than the intended suit that fellows then wore on such occasions. The girls made their excuses and walked away and, to make matters worse, he was thought to be a hooligan and refused admission to the pictures.

Hancock's *The Rebel* character had left London for the City of Light to become a painter. 'I knew he was a nut,' exclaimed a waitress in the high street café where he'd announced his decision to go. To ordinary folk like her, 'art', if that's what you called it, wasn't a man's trade somehow. For a start, it had doubtful practical value. Put crudely, it was all right as a hobby, but could you rely on it to make a living? If you shone at art in class, it was often treated as a regrettable eccentricity. Your former teachers and classmates alike would shake their heads when they saw you entering art college portals, almost as if watching a funeral cortège.

Yet it is intriguing to tally up how many groups from every phase of mid-1960s pop had their roots in art schools. Both The Rolling Stones and The Pretty Things were hatched in Sidcup School of Art, where London invades Kent, just as the Rockin' Berries, The Beatles, the Animals, The Kinks,[15] the Yardbirds, the Creation, The Bonzo Dog Doo-Dah Band, the Move, Pentangle and Pink Floyd were in like establishments all over Britain, honing their musical skills in an atmosphere of coloured dust, palette-knives, hammer-and-chisel and lumpy impasto. As Barry Miles, co-founder in 1966 of *International Times* (*IT*), London's fortnightly 'underground' broadsheet, was to remark, 'You came out knowing a lot more about rock 'n' roll than you did about art.'

Entry standards were lax to the point of being non-existent, although Phil May of The Pretty Things, who began at Sidcup in September 1960, qualified this. 'The only way you could get into that art college without GCE 'O' levels,' he said, 'was by doing graphic design. I got in when I was fifteen after they'd seen my Bexleyheath secondary modern school portfolio. David Hockney told me that if there'd been General Certificates of Education involved, he'd never have been an artist. Once you got into art school, you didn't have to do GCEs.'

Modelling his appearance on Dave Brubeck, Shelly Manne and other jazzers, Stones drummer Charlie Watts, who studied at Harrow School of Art, was perceived as slightly peculiar for choosing tidy understatement via narrow-lapelled suits, shirts with button-down collars and a perversely short haircut (as did, briefly, Ray Davies, future head honcho of The Kinks, at Hornsey College) when 'existentialist' students were letting theirs grow long, and,

---

15. Although a mere month after enrolment in September 1962, Pete Quaife, The Kinks' bass player, was expelled from Hornsey College of Arts and Crafts for 'Teddy Boy behaviour'.

akin to the youth in *William The Fourth*'s 'The Weak Spot', studying themselves in toilet mirrors, hoping it was beginning to show.

Family approval of Charlie's choice was shown by his sister, Linda, who cut his hair as regularly as he wished, and their father who offered advice about and paid for Charlie's conservative attire. 'And I wore it as smartly as I could,' the drummer remembered. 'I didn't like jeans and sweaters in those days. I thought they looked untidy, and didn't feel somehow as good as I did in my suits with the baggy trousers.'

Elsewhere on the further education map, grey flannels, twinsets and 'chunky' sprayed hair stated either that you hadn't yet escaped the clutches of parents who expected you to be a 'credit' to them, or that you had the promise of 'jam tomorrow' if you beavered away, sidestepped the most tempting of extramural distractions, and attained your degree. Yet the other side of the coin was always represented in some way in the most unlikely faculties of academia.

If 'twinned' after a fashion with *L'Ecole Libre Des Sciences Politiques* in Paris, the London School Of Economics (LSE) was a British university by any other name. Nevertheless, while it wasn't yet the New Left furnace it would become, Trotskyites looked down on Leninists there, and words like 'materialism', 'bourgeoisie' and 'existential' filtered around the corridors. More obviously, clothes polarised each social and political group.

When he began there in 1961, Mike Jagger, who, as an act of class betrayal, was about to style himself 'Mick' as if he was the son of some London-Irish navvy, walked an uncomfortable line between the two extremes of 'straight' and 'beatnik'. If anything, in his nylon pullover and yet-unfaded jeans, he could be classed demeaningly as one of the 'Millets', called so after the Dartford branch of the 'outdoors' clothing and camping equipment store. The LSE's official broad and striped scarf was draped round his neck. Gilding an indeterminate image too was that he had started smoking – to the disappointment of his father, a fitness instructor, who'd lost most of his hair by the time he held his new-born son on a dry, sunny and very warm wartime Monday in Dartford's Livingstone Hospital.

Prised into the world in the same maternity wing were Rick Huxley, bass guitarist with The Dave Clark Five (and Mick's cousin by marriage) as well as the founder members of The Pretty Things, Dick Taylor and Phil May, who ruminated to me shortly before his death in 2020, 'Post-war Britain was a confused melting-pot of contradictions and hypocrisies. Fathers who had lost friends, brothers who had lost brothers in the war, and a ranting media all fired up the myth that long hair was a sign of depravity. When homosexuality was still a crime, if you looked different in any way at all, "queer" was the insult of choice. Wearing long hair truly made that one stick.'

'Artistic' and 'musical' were words applied to homosexuals as 'gay' is now. As Britain paid for its two world wars, parents with conformist values continued to feel that the very idea of a boy thinking of a career in any of the liberal arts was vaguely deplorable – especially as a musician in the 'popular' style – when wireless sets were still novel enough to be regarded by censorious great-aunts as meddling with dark forces, even if as indispensable a domestic fixture as the washing machine, vacuum cleaner and refrigerator. Just suppose you were 'taken' when listening to that smutty Elvis Presley on the Light Programme. You'd be cast into the everlasting pit like the Whore of Babylon. Think on that!

CHAPTER FOUR

'Man, that's what I want to do!'

It was during Phil May's two years at Sidcup that his long hair invited the first of many batterings. With malicious glee, his attackers emerged from intimidating Friday night shadows. His throat constricting, his skin crawling and his heart pounding like that of a hunted beast – which he is – Phil is seized by the shoulders, swivelled round and kneed in the balls. His eyes bulge and he collapses, gasping, trying to shield head and genitalia in a forest of kicking footwear, and thankful for duffle coat armour and sketchbook shield. He's yelling in panic, and blood is spurting from his face onto the pavement, but that isn't enough. On and on the onslaught goes until Phil is recognised by Eddie, a bloke with whom he'd once worked at a local supermarket. For a moment their eyes meet, Phil's conveying sadness as much as pain. Yet friendship defers to the joy of queer-bashing until it stops being fun, and Phil is rolled over into a pile of leaves, and the torn pages of his coursework scatter like confetti. Through a forcefield of an ever-louder ringing in one ear and various aches of needle-sharp piquancy all over him, he picks up the fading clack of running footsteps.

They'd fled with sound reason – for from nowhere had come a threnody of screeching tyres, bells and whistles. Better late than never, Kent's noble constabulary had arrived. Among their subsequent remarks were 'Christ, when will you bloody beatniks learn!', 'Take up body building not fucking painting if you want to go around dressed like that' and 'Jesus... look at the state of you, like a girl you are. Why don't you get your bleedin' hair cut?'

'I wore my scars, my clothes and my "girly" hair with pride,' exulted Phil, 'even though the ferocity of the attacks became far more intense – and they happened everywhere I went – and I ended up as a regular at the Casualty Department. They thought I was mad. So the Old Bill were probably right, it was never going to stop – but I was never going to back down!'

That first assault occurred back home in Erith, almost as far from the White Cliffs of Dover's mythical bluebirds as it was feasible to be without leaving the county. It was within one of numerous conurbations across the kingdom where encroaching urban renewal programmes had been assisted in places by the Luftwaffe. Nevertheless, sooty foxgloves sprung up beneath sepia skies on the bombsites that remained after direct hits throughout nightly aerial bombardments. 'If you were a "war baby", it was a bit gloomy and grey,' remembered Keith Richards. 'It was nothing to turn a corner and see nothing on the horizon apart from one or two miracle houses. You grew up in a wasteland.'

Across the Atlantic, Chicago, Vancouver, Los Angeles, Atlanta, Dallas, Seattle, Memphis, Philadelphia and so forth were nothing like blackened and shell-shocked Coventry, Dover, Newcastle and the like. Modern but classic, here were cityscapes of glass-walled skyscrapers, severely right-angled street grids and an undercurrent of chic confidence. Yet the splendour of the glass palaces was nowhere to be seen from tenements wrapped in laceworks of fire escapes that seemed to shiver as trains of internal railway systems rattled by – and forlorn public housing complexes where penury and unemployment clotted, built by the book for those who had no choice. There, clusters of neighbours glared as newcomers unloaded their belongings, especially if it was gleaned that they were from what was denigrated as 'the backwoods'. Hailing from one such settlement, the newly arrived 13-year-old Elvis Aaron Presley was inclined thus to be looked down upon by others at his Memphis high school. Their families had been long resident in that confluence and terminus of road, rail and river connections.

As well as 'sir' and 'ma'am' decorum, instilled into Presley and most other students from birth was that, as in Phil May's Britain, it was OK by the narrow standards of the day to be prejudiced against homosexuals, no matter how physically powerful or intellectually gifted they were. As well as being constant targets for prosecution under US law (and, as shown by the case in 1945 of Lenny Bruce – later, a well-known 'blue' comedian – dishonourable discharge from the armed forces), anyone suspected of 'faggot' tendencies could be given the works by assailants in safe assurance of leniency from police, courts and head teachers.

Hence Presley, despite being much the opposite, surfaced as such a mark when another youth surprised him combing and primping his hair – as was his constant habit – before a mirror in what he thought to be the relative privacy of the toilets.

Taunting became rough handling. 'I have never known any other human to take more time over his hair,' opined close confidant Red West. 'Elvis would spend hours on it, smoothing, mussing it up and combing it and combing it again. In a sea of pink-scalped boys at school, Elvis Presley stood out like a camel in the Arctic with his long vaselined hair in ducktail fashion. Someone was always picking on him.'[16]

For that Tibetan monk who's never heard of Elvis Presley, I ought to recount the old, old story.

If singing in public was second nature to him, Presley's had not been a particularly flaming youth, and he didn't resent having to do a run-of-the-mill job to keep alive. Nonetheless, in 1954, he joined a queue at Sun, a minuscule local studio, that offered record-your-voice facilities. Elvis, now 19, was going to sing an Ink Spots number to his own guitar accompaniment as a birthday present for his mother. His voice reached the ears of Sun's proprietor, Sam Phillips, who heard the money-making 'white man who could sing the blues' he'd despaired of ever finding.

After Presley's first release, 'That's All Right', muscled in at Number Three in *Billboard*, the US music trade journal's country-and-western (C&W) chart (although it owed as much to black rhythm-and-blues [R&B] as C&W), further such triumphs made him the talk of the Deep South. It was as a support spot to the middle-aged C&W luminary Hank Snow that Elvis was noticed by Snow's then-

---

16. In 1979's *Elvis* biopic, the brawny West character rescues Presley when locker-room terrorisers are on the point of scalping him.

manager, Colonel Tom Parker, who persuaded Phillips to auction
Presley's Sun contract to the mightier RCA in November 1955. A
few months later, the boy committed himself formally to Parker for
life – and beyond. From then on, 'Elvis occupied every minute of my
time,' acknowledged Parker, 'and I think he would have suffered had
I signed anyone else.'

There remains bitter disagreement about the Colonel. Was he
a simple funfair barker dragged into a situation he couldn't resist
or was he, in the words of movie director Sam Katzman, 'the
biggest con artist in the world'? Buttressing the latter opinion was
the ruthlessness that chilled those used to the record industry's
traditional glibness. 'Don't criticise what you can't understand,'
Elvis once said in his handler's defence. 'You've never walked in
that man's shoes.'

'Heartbreak Hotel', Presley's RCA debut, reached Number
One in Billboard's Hot 100, and global success followed after an
appearance on The Ed Sullivan Show, despite – or because of –
adult condemnation of 'this unspeakably untalented, vulgar young
entertainer', as one television guide described him. Sullivan's
programme was North America's version of ITV's long-running
variety platform, Sunday Night at the London Palladium, and it would
only risk screening Elvis from the waist up. In the UK, Methodist
preacher (and jazz buff) Dr Donald Soper wondered 'how intelligent
people can derive satisfaction from something which is emotionally
embarrassing and intellectually ridiculous'.

Of 'Heartbreak Hotel', the New Musical Express wrote, 'If you
appreciate good singing, I don't suppose you'll manage to hear
this disc all through.' Whilst engineering this conquest of an
international 'youth market', the Colonel's blunt stance on behalf of
his bestselling client compelled RCA to yield to his every demand,
such as granting him around eight per cent of monies from non-
vinyl goods officially associated with Presley, and the distribution
of one million pressings of every Elvis single. This latter judgement
proved correct because, whether the crooning of 'Love Me Tender'
or the elaborated rockabilly of 'Blue Suede Shoes', every release sold
by the ton, giving 'the King' a magnificent self-confidence about
anything he said and did.

Presley's hot-potato-in-the-mouth shout-singing and sulky balladeering on disc was as much a component of his presumed 'bad attitude' as his loud 'cat' clothes (check box-jacket, cowboy or Hawaiian shirt and tapered trousers), lop-sided smirk and truculent sensuality at concerts which often stopped just short of open riot. His choice of songs with simplistic hep-cat couplets that frequently expressed little more than a desire to get laid and sideburns to the earlobes showed he was a *man*.

As it would be with The Rolling Stones in the next decade, many of the young were as aghast as the old. Before he'd even heard 'That's All Right', Roy Orbison had borrowed his father's car and set out for Dallas Sportatorium – just over 200 miles away – to check out Presley and found he 'couldn't over-emphasise how shocking he looked and seemed to me'.

It was like nothing the bespectacled North Texas State University undergraduate had ever experienced. Elvis, sneering gently, didn't care how terribly he behaved up there – breaking guitar strings, spitting out chewing gum, doing the splits, knee-dropping and swivelling his hips in a rude way. Orbison noted too 'pandemonium in the audience because the girls took a shine to Elvis and the guys were getting a little jealous'. Yet, by the close, all potentially ugly junctures had been bypassed as everybody tuned into the epic *go-man-go* abandon.

Not finding first direct encounters with rock 'n' roll easy to forget, many municipal governing bodies began doing their bit to cast out the pestilence by endeavouring to ban all Presley-inspired rubbish, often extra-legally, as licentious and subversive. As well as the 'decadent' aspects of this new teenage sound derived from 'n***** music' – its deranged clamour, the tightness of its trousers, its dubious lyrics (that was if you could make out the words – which you couldn't) and, of course, that hair – some of its practitioners and backers compounded their infamy by either being not entirely Caucasian themselves or by promoting 'colored' artists. Didn't they realise that that was just about that in the 1950s? It was said that rock 'n' roll entertainers – and not just black ones – had been observed by backstage staff, dipping into a surreptitious pocket every now

and then for a blue or purple capsule to wire them up for the show
– just as they sampled something called 'marijuana' to unwind
tense coils within afterwards. It was, apparently, packed into a large
roll-up called a 'spliff' or 'reefer' and smoked communally.

Whatever iniquities occurred both off and on the boards,
the behaviour of thousands of teenagers, even WASPs, rippling
spontaneously stagewards at rock 'n' roll extravaganzas wasn't
exemplary either on the evidence of the liquor bottles, cigarette
packets and further litter left at arenas before outbreaks of fighting
and vandalism such as were seen outside Dallas Sportatorium.

Entranced more than he'd been initially horrified, Roy Orbison
had made his way home, turning a thoughtful steering wheel. By
journey's end, he'd decided that his semi-professional outfit, The
Wink Westerners (named after his home town) was to 'go rockabilly'
– the stuff in which Presley traded – thus outlawing itself from
the stuffy if lucrative adult dinner-and-dances and functions at
the staider youth clubs on which the group had hitherto relied for
virtually all paid work, delivering 'square' and polished staples like
'Satin Doll', 'The Anniversary Waltz', 'Tiptoe Through The Tulips',
'Moonlight Serenade', 'Ida! Sweet as Apple Cider' and '(Won't You
Come Home) Bill Bailey'. Fronting what had been rechristened
The Teen Kings, Orbison would now in extremis be witnessed in
tiger-skin garments, gyrating, snarling and rolling about as if he had
wasps in his pants.[17]

A similar scenario left its mark on Jimmy Carl Black, raised
in Anthony on the New Mexican border and with a career as a
Mother of Invention over a decade away. He was in his high school
band's brass section until, 'I realised that there was no chance in
rock 'n' roll for a trumpeter after Elvis Presley appeared at El Paso
Colosseum in 1955. When I saw the effect he had on those women,
I said, "Man, that's what I want to do!"'

Black and Orbison were but two boys in their mid-to-late teens who
became lost in dreams and half-formed ambitions to make similar

---

17. Singing guitarist Orbison was to be remembered far more for a stage act
hinged on remaining virtually stationary during 'Only The Lonely', 'Running
Scared', 'It's Over' and the rest of his run of 1960s hits.

noise and spectacles of themselves after paying attention to Presley. Then there is the even more unhinged sorcery of Jerry Lee Lewis, the keyboard-attacking fireball from Louisiana, given to sweeping an outsize onstage comb through yellow curls that kept falling over his eyes – and the outrage of Little Richard, whose father had long disowned him, with his billowing drapes, precarious pompadour and a manner best described as 'camp'. Thus was conceived, however fleetingly, the idea of bidding farewell to having hair trimmed as regularly as it had been since they were at infant school.

This applied to boys from both run-down regions and upmarket ones. Among them was 16-year-old Robert Phernetton, suspended from his Michigan high school during the Christmas term of 1956 by balding school principal, Harold F Barr, for looking too much like Elvis Presley. Robert's parents took the matter to the county court where the education committee's attorney argued that there was a 'direct connection' between student hairstyles and academic progress.

In this he was parroting a certain Eugene Gilbert, president of a 'youth research organisation', and writer of *What Young People Think*, a weekly and widely syndicated newsletter. He reckoned that three-quarters of nearly 4,000 girls and boys surveyed in 40 US cities regarded themselves as rock 'n' rollers – and that many of their guardians regarded Elvis Presley ('a symbol of destruction'), 'with abomination, not only for his performance, but also on its hypnotic after-effects'. Nevertheless, a few months later, Mr Gilbert was pleased to report, albeit erroneously, that 'Presley's phenomenal popularity among the nation's teenagers seems to have taken a nosedive' and that more boys aspired to be like President Eisenhower. He was supported by Dr Ralph D Rabinovitch, director of the University of Michigan's neuropsychiatric clinic for children, with his notion that poorly performing scholars 'wear the badge of the emptiness and lostness in their dress and coiffure'.

Apparently, Robert Phernetton had failed in every subject since he'd grown his hair, having fallen short in only one when it was short. Maybe, argued his brief, this was rooted in his disenchantment with the establishment's denial of his freedom of expression. While the judge had no quarrel with 'the right of the individual to be as ridiculous as he chooses', he ruled in the school's favour and its 'responsibility to maintain discipline'. The Phernettons refused to accept this decision, but, after their fruitless attempts to find a place more tolerant of his hair, Robert caved in and got it cut, although wailing to any member of the local press still interested, 'I'm not happy. It will take years and years to train my hair again!'

Mr and Mrs Phernetton supported their son with a zest that would be thought excessive by the vast majority of mums and dads who would, no doubt, have backed the legal outcome to the hilt. If teenagers had to have pop music, what was wrong with entertainers like Pat Boone, a clean, well-mannered compromise to that appalling Presley, and one who was – for a while anyway – as commercially successful? Through the medium of teen magazines, this palatable personification of rock 'n' roll provided copy which probed no deeper than his conception of a 'dream girl', his favourite colour, his preferred foodstuffs and the age at which he hoped to walk down the aisle. These ideals would be incorporated into 'Twixt Twelve and Twenty (the same title as one of his hits), the newly married Boone's self-written manual that preached your parents' word was law, don't talk dirty, and get your hair cut. When he, like Elvis, moved into films, he'd further parade his lack of major vices by refusing to kiss his leading ladies. Well, you never knew where these things led.

When a couple 'walked out' together, it was as if Uncle Pat was chaperoning them. Moreover, on a more fundamental level, in days before the birth-control pill went beyond clinical trials, premarital gropings were a much more serious issue. To sceptical cronies, a locker-room lothario would brag of carnal capers everyone knew were tall tales. He may have got to 'third base' after a lot of effort, but only a 'cheap' girl didn't 'save herself' for her future husband. Her whole being might be screaming for sex as much as the pimpled fumbler of her bra strap, but a true daughter of the 1950s and early 1960s would have none of it until she'd secured a husband.

This pervading moral climate, coupled with the proprieties of small town North America, thus led to 'sublimation', a word actually used in academic tomes about adolescent socio-sexual relationships rather than merely inferred in 'Twixt Twelve and Twenty. It necessitated marginalising what were considered frivolous interests such as pop music. It was gratifyingly convenient for right-thinking parents if, for example, you missed most of the nationally televised *American Bandstand* every Tuesday because of Boy Scouts or Girl Guides, that the gaiety of a 14th birthday party could be halted by mum enforcing a deflating traipse to church for choir practice, or that the only remotely romantic encounter you were likely to have was an observed kiss under the mistletoe.

During a mother's or father's obligatory and shy-making explanation of the 'Facts of Life' – which you may have learnt already in a smutty way – there'd perhaps be mention of 'camp followers'. This meant female fans who, aspiring to an orgasm at the thrust of the famous, imposed themselves on Presley and his kind. Such girls, said mum and dad, were 'not pleasant to know'.

They sounded OK to a lot of young men with raging hormones, leading them to seek openings in pop, usually as a member of a group – because it wasn't always a myth that membership of such a combo gave licence to lock eyes with the girls ringing the stage apron, tits bouncing, and ogling with unmaidenly eagerness youths who might be seen by day, bereft of the otherworldliness of the stage, as department store trainees or overalled window-cleaners.

A *droit de seigneur* prevailed for those on the bandstand at teenage dances held in halls that served more commonly as gymnasiums, canteens and for religious assemblies, where girls danced round each other's handbags, and boys shuffled about by themselves with an inbuilt sense of defeat. If you were one of the performing musicians, a tryst could be sealed during an intermission with a beatific smile, a flood of libido and an 'All right then. I'll see you later.' Sometimes, the business would be conducted immediately up against the shadowed side of the van or in the romantic seclusion of, say, a broom cupboard, and the musician concerned might then pant back to microphone or instrument, either zipping up his flies or wiping hands on circulation-impeding slacks.

During the set, he might also throw the other players into confusion by, say, messing up shifts from verse to chorus or chopping untidy endings in the air while trying to pull from the stage – and prompt irritation from male members of the audience, who'd begin a barrage of catcalls, barracking and flicking vulgar signs often inches away from his gradually more ghastly grin. If a couple of them started hurling chairs, the target of the exercise might then cease carrying himself with a ruttish swagger and quit the stage, the building and indeed the town within ten minutes. This left the rest of the group to face being watched like lynxes as the equipment was being transferred from venue to van, aware that rock 'n' roll wasn't just a red rag to some adults, but that many a local cowboy considered that Elvis Presley was a ponce with his girly haircut.

Seconds crawl by until, on the fire escape steps, the weedy-looking drummer replies 'Good evening' to a gruff "Ello'. This was the thrill divine, and there wasn't a moment to be lost. For being such a toffee-nosed so-and-so, thus would commence the same old ritual of clumsy carnage – and he'd be squirming around on the cobbles to amused jeers. With no pause for careful thought, other of the group's personnel might wade in to even the odds, perhaps landing some indiscriminate punches, and even managing to grab the belt of one of the ruffians and pull with despairing triumph before losing his grip via a sock in the mouth.

Bestial faces would get their eyefuls of the unofficial cabaret; one of them a man hugging a biscuit tin half-full of coins. Brawling outside the premises was a matter for the local constabulary, not the promoter – who hadn't let personal dislike deter him from turning a hard-nosed penny from rock 'n' roll.

CHAPTER FIVE

'Hair today, gone tomorrow'

On 20 December 1957, a month before the shooting of Elvis Presley's fourth celluloid venture, *King Creole*, was to commence, a problem arose. It could not be settled as easily as the summons to a paternity hearing that had been thrust into Presley's hand on one occasion when, as had become his in-concert habit, he feigned collapse and crawled to the stage's edge during some tortured ballad.

The US Department of War, anxious about the deadlock the Geneva Summit had reached over the reunification of Germany and an associated abandonment of east-west defences, had sent for Elvis Aaron Presley. After obtaining a 60-day deferment to complete his part in the film (which was to be judged his finest by many), with his parents and manager tagging along, on Monday 24 March 1958 he presented himself at the Memphis Draft Board offices. Assigned serial number 53 310 761, he displayed humility and good humour the following morning when, with sideburns and quiff gone already, he quipped 'hair today, gone tomorrow' as electric clippers completed the job. Next, he was kitted out with a uniform in marked contrast to his trademark 'cat' clothes.

Bravely, Elvis beamed for the cameras that greeted him outside the building, waved at distraught members of his fan club, and accepted graciously gifts of a cream pie and a Bible from its president. Then, with twenty other raw recruits, he boarded a khaki-painted bus for Fort Chaffee, Arkansas prior to transfer to a similar establishment in Texas soon afterwards.

Yet, while regulations didn't allow him to, say, re-dye his hair, Presley's experience of life in the barracks was, overall, as agreeable a stint as it could have been. Instead of taking him down a green-eyed peg or two for being the beloved of their sisters and girlfriends for the past two years, most of the other chaps in the same boat were friendly enough. Coming to be regarded by them as a 'regular guy', Elvis donated his meagre weekly pay-packet to charity, and, more pragmatically, purchased televisions for everyone when they all were shipped in September to Germany. Just before the USS *Randall* troopship pottered along New York's Hudson river to fade into a vanishing smudge on the Atlantic horizon, thirteen minutes of Private 53 310 761's quayside encounter with media, convened by Colonel Parker, was scheduled in order to be immortalised three months later on an EP, *Elvis Sails*.

In the interim between call-up and voyage, discussion about 'the King' joining the Special Services Division, founded to provide entertainment for the armed forces (but denigrated by veterans as 'the celebrity wimp-out') was quickly nipped in the bud by objections from a Republican senator which were supported by others. Elvis didn't mind. As for Colonel Tom, there was infinitely more good than harm in public awareness that his charge was to be granted no more privileges than any other fellow. However, soldiers who had close relations nearby were allowed to live with them – as Elvis's mother Gladys and father Vernon did in a luxury caravan parked discreetly in a meadow beyond the camp. Off-duty, their pride and joy could enjoy home-cooking and the hot, scented water of a non-communal bath before going to sleep, undisturbed by the snores, phlegmy coughs and wind-breaking of the inmates within an assigned hut.

Presley's periods of leave were also spent in more glamorous – and sometimes potentially dangerous – situations. When Bill Haley and the Comets passed through Germany later that first autumn, blank police bullets cracked over ear-stinging bedlam, and the employment of tear gas and rubber truncheons at a recital in Berlin caused the group to be denounced in a *Neues Deutschland* newspaper editorial for 'turning the youth in the land of Bach and Beethoven into raging beasts'. 'It was the worst thing I have ever seen,' agreed Haley. 'Worse than anything in the States.' Alsatians and water cannons brought a show in Essen to a close, but Stuttgart was peaceful, even though Elvis was known to be backstage on a fraternal visit.

More agreeable was flying to Paris on a five-day pass in February 1959 where, during one frolicsome evening amid an aroma of strong percolated coffee and mega-tar cigarettes, Presley found himself microphone in hand before a flabbergasted Left Bank club audience. This wasn't a scene from one of his films: Elvis Presley was actually there, asserting his magnetism in abundance.

At an outermost table, symbolically anyway, sat Danyel Gérard, who the previous summer had issued the first French attempt at rock 'n' roll (an adaptation of the 'Billy Boy' nursery rhyme). His forthcoming spell of compulsory National Service caused him to be overtaken by younger icons – notably Johnny Hallyday, once the resident Elvis Presley impersonator in Le Golf Drouot (and its attached 'Café D'Angleterre'), Paris's foremost blousons noirs hangout. Like their British cousins, the likes of Gérard and Hallyday accepted a second-class and, arguably, counterfeit status in good spirits, glad to breathe the air round the fascinating US aliens they'd been used to worshipping from afar.

Their chief role model appeared ecstatic at being so rapturously applauded in Paris, especially in the light of a gloomy reflection to a scribbling newshound the following month: 'I wonder if the folks at home have forgotten me. It's hard to tell from over here.' If unmindful of what was gripping backwaters like France and Britain, Elvis was conscious that his own enforced absence could be to the advantage of a crop of assurgent newcomers – Paul Anka, Frankie Avalon, Jimmy Clanton and Ricky Nelson in 1958 alone.[18]

The Colonel, however, had ensured that plenty of Presley recordings had been stockpiled to fulfil the release programme until the boy's demobilisation, following two years of conducting himself as the very epitome of the all-American soldier. Indications of another taming had been telegraphed perhaps by an element of self-mockery in 'A Big Hunk O' Love'. It was almost as if he was consoling his long-time devotees whilst smirking at those of Frank

---

18. On 3 March 1960, that's what Elvis told waiting fans in so many words after he touched down at Prestwick International Airport on the Firth of Clyde for his craft to be refuelled for a long-haul over the Atlantic. This was to be the only instance in which he ever breathed British air, and he left Europe forever before the day was out.

Sinatra's 'Rat Pack' during his homecoming television spectacular with Ol' Blue Eyes, broadcast from Miami's plush Fontainebleau Hotel. It kicked off with a uniformed Elvis crooning 44-year-old Frank's 'It's Nice to Go Travelling'. He also joined the older man in a medley of some of each other's hits, closing it with an embrace.

John Lennon, asked in 1977 to comment after his boyhood idol's passing, sniffed, 'Elvis died when he went into the army.' Yet how could this have been the case in 1960 when the chartbusting records and cinema-filling flicks continued to be released – and the King still topped three categories in the *NME* readers' poll: World's Outstanding Popular Singer, World's Outstanding Musical Personality and Favourite US Male Singer? If, as the arch-Beatle pontificated, the King had died a metaphorical death by enlisting, well, he was still ruling from the grave.

It'd been a good story, hadn't it – of the pop luminary marching off ungrudgingly to serve his country? Elvis Presley's character was never more truly tested and found sound, and he responded well to the orderliness of the military environment, rising to the rank of sergeant by the time, as 'the most publicised soldier since General MacArthur', he gave a farewell-to-Deutschland press conference in the main hall of the base when less than a week from resuming his civilian profession.[19]

It was paralleled in Britain by singing actor Anthony Newley in silver screen fiction as 'Jeep Jackson' in 1959's *Idle on Parade*, and, the previous July, in career-extinguishing fact by Terry Dene, one of several conspicuous would-be English *Elvi*. In the wake of a publicity blitz that dissolved the outlines between his public persona and the entanglements of his private life, Terry's obligatory spell as Gunner 23604106 in the King's Royal Rifle Corps reduced him to a nervous wreck after mere weeks of wheeling, turning and shouldering arms for hours on end to an NCO's roared sarcasm. 'It was grim, man, just grim,' grimaced Terry, when transferred

---

19. Two years after *King Creole*, Presley's next movie, *GI Blues* – in which he starred as a gunner stationed in West Germany – would be art loosely imitating life.

to a civilian mental hospital prior to hasty discharge (as 'unfit for duty'), and a 'comeback' tour that further transformed him into an object of scorn with a barrage of catcalls some nights after he commandeered the central microphone.

That seemed to be more or less the end, but, in 1964, Terry looked up from the bottom of his pit and saw a strip of blue sky with Jesus Christ peering over the edge. Joining the Salvation Army, he was spied as a street-corner evangelist, the ex-pop star who'd seen the error of his ways. As such, he resumed making records, albeit ones focussed on religious material – though there'd be retrospectives, notably *I Thought Terry Dene Was Dead* (also the title of a mid-1970s biography).

The next Britain at large heard of him was in 1984's *Rockers*, a light-hearted BBC South documentary, just as Terry boarded the nostalgia bandwagon where, apparently, he delivered a most compelling show.

It was, however, one of Dene's engagements in the late 1950s that marked the genesis of a 'personal hairstyle revolution' by Oliver Gray, then a day-pupil at a private seat of learning in Gloucester.

'Upon my mother's mantelpiece,' reports Oliver, 'there used to be a photo of me with a haircut which was imposed by my parents. Their idea of the only acceptable haircut for a male was very short at the back, very short at the sides and parted on the left, with the front swept to the side, rather in the manner of people attempting to conceal a bald patch. To the end of her life, my mother would point to the fading evidence and pronounce, "That's how I really liked you", and it genuinely is true to say that she never really liked me since it went away.'

It had started to do so after a story in *The Citizen*, Gloucestershire's regional weekly, about the highly strung Terry becoming embroiled in a coffee bar fracas prior to his show at the Regal, a venue on the 'scream circuit' of pop package tours. 'The locals were so outraged,' recounts Oliver, 'that I started to be interested in the image of Dene and similar British singers of the day such as Billy Fury and Marty Wilde.

'I began to gather the existence of strange and wonderful things known as Square Cuts and Bostons, both of which were ways of arranging the back of your head – which you never actually saw outside of a very uncomfortable procedure involving holding up one mirror behind you whilst squinting into another held up in front of you.'

He's discussing a kind of antithesis of the ducktail via a straight-lined cutting and razoring of US origin, particularly at the neckline. This produced a style that, if sharp, jarred with what was tolerated at the sort of schools that also frowned on ties fastened in a loose and bulbous 'Windsor Knot', regarded as sloppy and vulgar. Malcolm Noble, now host of a Sunday evening show devoted to blues and jazz on Harborough FM, recollects that, as late as 1964, 'my one ambition was to sneak into the barbers and get a Boston – which was a straight-lined fringe at the back of the neck – a couple of inches above the collar. It was banned at my school but ambiguous definition made it difficult to enforce'.

'My mother had heard of these dangerous haircut options,' elaborates Oliver Gray, 'so it was impossible to ask for them when, every few weeks, she marched me to the barber's. I would, therefore, run on ahead when she was, say, chatting to a lady in the wool shop – and so be ensconced in the seat, having already requested the crucial variation ("Boston please, Bob") before she arrived. Obsessed as they were with the parting and its position, my parents would never be aware of my Boston. Invisible to them, to me it was everything.'

Fraser Massey, later a *Radio Times* columnist, told a similar tale: 'My adolescence was spent in High Wycombe where it was rumoured that Brian, a local barber, would, for a small consideration, sprinkle loose hair from the shop floor on your scalp and shoulders so you could go home to your parents without a single one of your own hairs being cut and insist you'd had a haircut.'

You could get away with such strategies only for so long before parents saw through them and sent you back for the barber to try again – and there'd often be trouble either after he did or when you directed him to cut it in a way that would be anathema to someone like Oliver Gray's mathematics teacher. 'Mr Harley seemed to dedicate his life to preventing anyone having hair with any kind of style,' testifies Oliver, 'and would relentlessly pursue those whose neck or ears were sullied by anything more than millimetre-length bristles. He had a strong Cornish accent that was imitated in grossly exaggerated form – particularly his "*Yoo, boooy! Git yore hurrrr kott!*" catchphrase which would ring out along the echoey, disinfectant-smelling corridors during breaks and lunchtimes.

'The morning after my first successful duping of my mother into not noticing my haircut had deviated from the norm, I entered school with the completely justified fear that Jack Harley would not be similarly deceived.

"*Grayyyy, booooy,*" I heard from a number of yards behind me. "*Uzz thutt a Squayur Kott?!*"

"What do you mean, Sir?" I offered, in an attempt to appear innocent.

"*Down't playy gaymezz with mee, boooy. That izz oyther a Squayer Kutt or a Bozzton – and what'z moore, you appearrr to be growin' yore soide whusskerz.*"

'Beneath the terror, I felt a faint stirring of pride. In my just post-pubescent state, there was no conceivable chance of growing genuine *Soide Whusskerz*; however, many hours of combing small strands of hair (which actually wanted to grow behind my ears) in front of them had obviously had the desired effect, at least upon Jack Harley. He really thought I was growing my *Soide Whusskerz!* My defeat (for him) was a triumph (for me)!

'That night, the back-of-head mirror technique sprang into action and Plan B was adopted. It was important that Jack Harley should think I had been back to the hairdresser's as he had ordered me to do, so the *Squayer Kutt* had somehow to remain in a form which was acceptable to my peers as being one, but would appear to Jack to have been removed. It was hard, but possible. Similarly, the *Soide Whusskerz* had to be slicked back in such a way that Jack would think they'd been shaved off, but so that they would in fact still be available to be retrieved and reinstated on the way to the bus station and in time to impress the girls of St. Peter's on the number 56.'

Even when you hadn't yet reached an age to show an interest in girls beyond just thinking them soppy, and cared less about haircuts than model aeroplanes, you'd still invite such conflict. Simon Mayor, Britain's foremost ambassador of the mandolin, has a singular memory of 'a pitiless games master (there was one in every school!) who decided my hair was too long (it wasn't) and managed to twist a few strands round his fingers while yanking my head backwards until I fell on the floor. The words 'bald' and 'jealous' nearly crossed my lips but at the last moment I realised their utterance would only result in an even more painful experience, and promised him I'd get it cut'.

Not as compliant was the older George Harrison, whose crew cut had flowered into a gravity-defying quiff as his ignominious career as a pupil at Liverpool Institute High School for Boys reached its nadir. Yet it was odd that Alfred 'Cissy' Smith, its head of English – whose white hair, if thin, was matted and actually quite long at the back – chose to poke fun at Harrison of the Fourth for an oiled coiffure Bostoned short at the back.

Towards the city's north, Christopher Crummey had also been taunted by teachers at his grammar school for much the same reasons prior to his entering the world of work, selling prams in a furniture store, though it was understood from day one that he was just passing through. Perhaps, when he left, it was good riddance as far as his employers were concerned because, reckoned Dave Ferguson, later guitarist with Merseybeat also-rans, The Bumblies, 'he had the longest hair on any bloke in Liverpool way before Beatle mop tops became fashionable'.

This branded Chris – who went on to become Chris *Curtis* of The Searchers – as a magnet for homosexuals on his home turf. However, Ray Nichol, a Newcastle lad, was the darling of the ladies for his shockhair of the brightest red. 'Back in 1959, I had the honour of being invited to the school camp in Northumberland,' he recalled, 'at an outdoor education centre for pupils aged thirteen to fifteen. Midway through the stay, a dance was held – which I attended with a girl from Middlesbrough, turning up with this massive Brylcreemed quiff, feeling really pleased with myself.

'During the interval, my partner asked me if she could have a lock of my hair. Feeling chuffed I said yes and before I knew it there were four or five girls around me, chopping bits off. After being rescued by the teachers I was stunned to see what they had done to it. The next day I was taken to the local barber's, where I ended up with a short back and sides, utterly devastated. The only person happy about it was my dear mother, stating "It's good to see you normal again.""

Both Crummey's hair and Nichol's, before it was clipped, might not have invited much comment in Hancock's Paris or existentialist Hamburg. In Soho too, men who looked like ladies – and vice-versa – remained but minor aberrations (at least to those who lived and worked there). This village-like quarter of London's West End also embraced the 2i's, the shrine of British pop after it had won supremacy over other venues such as the Gyre-and-Gimble, the Safari, the Freight Train, the Top Ten and other shop-windows for nascent talent in the same square mile. These had all been founded during what was not so much a craze for skiffle as, in retrospect, a revolution. Although skiffle may have originated in the rent parties, speakeasies and rowdy Dust Bowl jug bands of the US Depression, in Britain it became the first self-manufactured teenage music outside North America – and, like punk later on, any amateur who'd mastered basic techniques could try it.

No one howled with derision at a tea-chest-bass, a washboard tapped with thimbles and other gear fashioned from household implements. Neither did it always matter if a group had a superfluity of blokes with digit-lacerating six-strings. Once the guitar had been associated mainly with Latinate heel-clattering but now it was the instrument played not only by Elvis Presley but by Lonnie Donegan, the movement's one-man Marat, Danton, Robespierre, Mirabeau and Bonaparte.

Not everyone was doing it as a mere hobby. The Vipers, for example, showed what was possible by appearing three times in 1957's Top Thirty, and surfacing as second only to Lonnie in the skiffle hierarchy. Furthermore, through their ranks passed Jet Harris and Hank B Marvin, prior to enlistment into what would evolve into Cliff Richard and the Shadows. The skiffle insurgency rippled over all that followed too – as instanced by the success of Led Zeppelin, whose Jimmy Page made his televisual debut on a BBC children's programme as a 14-year-old skiffler. Interviewed, he assured viewers in so many words that he didn't regard pop as a viable career.

It's likely that young Page seldom strayed from his family home in Surrey to the central London coffee bar in which the likes of Thomas Hicks, Harry Webb, Reg Smith, Brian Rankin, Roy Taylor and Terry Nelhams used to entertain and were discovered before or after changing their respective names to Tommy Steele, Cliff Richard, Marty Wilde, Hank B Marvin, Vince Eager and Adam Faith.

They'd been preceded at the 2i's by Wee Willie Harris, bruited by his agent as Greater London's very own Jerry Lee Lewis. Sporting an enormous bow-tie and hair dyed pink, Harris went along with a media-fabricated 'feud' with blue-rinsed Larry Page, 'the Teenage Rage'. Banal publicity stunts aside, the two rubbed along easily enough when off-duty: Willie presenting his congratulations at Larry's twenty-first birthday party in November 1957.

This had guests of such magnitude as Freddie Mills, chart contenders Don Lang, Laurie London, Joe 'Mr Piano' Henderson and Jack Good. The latter was producer of BBC television's *Six-Five Special*, designed to keep teenagers quiet while mum and dad put the little ones to bed, and commissioned when, despite finding rock 'n' roll noxious, the Corporation's light entertainment division was feeling more obliged to cater for its fans, not least because the continental commercial station Radio Luxembourg had commenced broadcasting pop showcases in English. Nonetheless, if Dr Soper might have watched *Six-Five Special*, as he claimed, 'as a penance', it sought to preserve a little decency by employing such upstanding compères as Mills[20] and Presley-hating Pete Murray plus pop regulars like Russ Hamilton with his gentle lisp, The Mike Sammes Singers, the middle-aged Johnston Brothers and The King Brothers who were as transparent about their dislike of rock 'n' roll as Pete Murray.

While Larry Page's and Wee Willie Harris's respective appearances on the programme prompted concerns about the BBC's role in 'promoting teenage decadence', there was worse to come in Good's epoch-making ITV pop spectacular, *Oh Boy!*,

---

20. Who, nevertheless, was to amass, however unintentionally, underworld connections through his ownership of Soho's Freddie Mills Nite Spot.

during which a principally female studio audience, urged on by Jack, screamed indiscriminately at all male vocalists. This anxiety was epitomised by Eva Jagger, mother of Mick, who 'would watch my lovely boy, sitting so neat and clean, watching that dreadful Cliff Richard, that awful hair and that sexy dancing' – even if another resident performer was Peter Elliott whose slow-moving ballads made a parade of frantic rockers by the likes of Richard, Wilde and Eager all the more piquant by his insertion of, say, a deadpanned 'When I Grow Too Old to Dream', from the 1930s.

Furthermore, Cliff Richard had been persuaded to shear off his Presley-esque sideburns by the usually liberal-minded Good – who insisted too that a barber attend post-haste to the unacceptably long hair of Vince Taylor, almost-but-not-quite the genuine North American article in that he spoke in a US twang with 'man' in every sentence despite verifiable hearsay that his name was actually Brian and he was born within the sound of traffic from outer London's Great West Road.

Good also made Taylor garb himself in a nondescript suit upon pain of his maiden appearance on 3 January 1959 being otherwise cancelled.

Cliff and Vince had to realise too, pontificated Good, that, outside scruffy jive hives like the 2i's, there were limits of behaviour and appearance in a prudish Britain that was about to hound Jerry Lee Lewis from its shores amid accusations of baby-snatching and bigamy after he took his third wife, a 13-year-old cousin, on tour. It was also to compel Billy Fury to moderate his sub-Elvis gyrations before he too could be allowed on television – and prompt astonished headlines in Wiltshire newspapers when, prior to his appearance as guitarist with The Boppers at Durrington Youth Hall in November 1959, Phil Ball had had his hair cut Mohican-style for a bet.

CHAPTER SIX

'Who are you lookin' at, pal!?'

When skiffle started losing its flavour on the bedpost overnight, the more 'sophisticated' of its practitioners who hadn't fallen by the wayside were to switch to traditional jazz ('trad'). This had come into existence in Britain through the zeal with which a post-war cell of trad jazz fanatics in Greater London furthered their cause when record sessions evolved into attempts at reproducing the stuff themselves. Among these enthusiasts was trombonist Chris Barber whose New Orleans Jazz Band had embraced the 'Washboard Wonders' – Beryl Bryden on washboard and Chris himself on double-bass accompanying guitarist and banjoist Lonnie Donegan on a brace of blues-tinged North American folk songs. For many, the Wonders slot became the highlight of the show and an arrangement of 'Rock Island Line', from the catalogue of walking musical archive Huddie 'Lead Belly' Ledbetter, was the eventual spin-off single in 1955 from Barber's Jazz Band's ten-inch LP, *New Orleans Joys*. It spent months in the domestic Top Twenty, and motivated the mesmeric Lonnie to strike out on his own – and the rest, as they often say, was history.[21]

With the passing of the King of Skiffle's period of optimum impact and the broadening of his mainstream appeal by fusing skiffle with pub singalong, showbiz evergreens and British folk

---

21. Alexis Korner, a former British Forces Network (BFN) announcer, later cited as 'the father of British blues', had been Lonnie Donegan's deputy and then his replacement with Barber in 1949 and 1960, quitting each time because he wanted to play purely blues, instead of an interval within a jazz outfit. Nevertheless, Korner's principal income was to depend chiefly on numerous unbluesy voiceovers for ITV commercials.

music, there emerged trad bands in matching Donegal tweeds, Confederate army uniforms, Roman togas, barrister wigs and similarly ridiculous variations on the bowlers and striped waistcoats worn by Acker Bilk and his Paramount Jazz Band who were forever on *Trad Tavern*, a BBC Light Programme series transmitted late on Sunday afternoons. Musically too, although, to many, every other trad outfit on the show was different, every one was the same: banjos, a confusion of front-line horns and 'dads' who imagined that a hoarse monotone was all you needed to sing like Louis Armstrong.

According to the sleeve notes to a 1958 EP *Chris Barber In Concert Volume Three*, trad was 'gay and carefree music' – on paper, the antithesis of blues. There was also something vaguely collegiate about an 'appreciation' of it. Before 'ACKER' was studded on the backs of some proletariat leather jackets where 'ELVIS' had once been – and a horde of bottle-hurling Teddy Boys disrupted 1960's Beaulieu Jazz Festival with incessant chanting of 'We want Acker!' – it was mostly the property of those who, at student union dances, would don boaters or top hats, a variety of hacked-about formal gear, drink heavily of cider, and launch into vigorous steps that blended a skip-jiving with the Charleston to 'When The Saints Go Marching In', 'Down By The Riverside', 'Swanee River' or, for gawd's sake, 'Bobby Shafto', arranged for the plinking and puffing of a trad band like The Pagan Jazzmen in Newcastle – in which an Eric Burdon slid trombone – or Ed O'Donnell's New Orleans Jazzmen, whose maiden bash at Halifax's Plebeians Jazz Club was promulgated by enthusiasts parading the streets in sandwich boards. The same equation as that linking Elvis Presley with Anthony Newley (as 'Jeep Jackson') existed between British and North American trad dads, i.e. you'd never beat the Yanks, but you could have fun and even make a little money displaying your inferiority complex.

After an absence of two years on National Service in the navy, trumpeter John Keen was astonished in 1957 to find the trad jazz scene in his native Cheltenham had exploded: 'You could go and hear it every night of the week. Rock 'n' roll wasn't considered important at all, and the only guitar group that anyone had heard of was The Shadows, who were really a show band with their funny walks and gimmicks.'

Home-reared trad performers tussled for work within easy reach in village institutes, pub function rooms, dance halls, sports pavilions and whenever swimming pools could be boarded over for such a purpose. Yet while trad was in the ascendant, many skifflers who were contemplating whether or not to donate their Lonnie Donegan 78s to jumble sales, backslid gradually, via wary amplification, to rock 'n' roll – 'a more commercial form of skiffle,' suggested Peter Gammond and Peter Clayton in their unconsciously humorous A Guide To Popular Music of 1960 – and an increasingly North American UK Top Twenty.

Yet, as the 1960s dawned, classic rock seemed to have had its day, with so many of its US cutting-edgers on a downward path. Jerry Lee Lewis was disgraced; Little Richard, with his pompadour now reduced to stubble, was in holy orders; Buddy Holly had been killed in a plane crash in 1959 (although, in the aftermath of his death, his 'I Guess It Doesn't Matter Anymore' single was winging its way to Number One in the UK); and Gene Vincent was lurching from gig to gig just to maintain a tolerable standard of living.

As for Chuck Berry, he had served in 1959 the first of two jail terms that would put temporary halts to his career. This incarceration, nevertheless, only boosted his cult celebrity in Britain now that its weekly hit parades were heaving with insipidly handsome US boys-next-door, all doe-eyes, hairspray and bashful half-smiles, moulded by their investors in the image of Pat Boone rather than the pre-army Presley. These were matched by their forenames (mainly Bobby) and their piddle-de-pat records. If they faltered after a brace of chart strikes, queuing round the block would be any number of substitute Bobbies – or Jimmies or Frankies – all raring to sing any piffle put in front of them. In addition, there were their British opposite numbers such as Craig Douglas and Mark Wynter with ballads your grandmother liked.

Crucially, Elvis caught the overall drift of the Bobby era with Italianesque ballads and lightweight tunes possessed of saccharine lyrics and jaunty rhythms. The quality of his movies also deteriorated to the extent that each succeeding effort was generally more vacuous and streamlined than the one before.[22] Others in degrees of artistic debt to the King were in the process of following the same smooth transformation from wildman to respected establishment figure via the patenting of a publicity stroke that everyone from Johnnie Ray to Johnny Rotten and beyond pulled: that the most corrupted rebel rocker could be A Nice Lad When You Get To Know Him – as instanced by Adam Faith who, after three dead-in-the-water singles (including a cover of Jerry Lee Lewis's 'High School Confidential') achieved an effortful breakthrough with 1959's gimmicky 'What Do You Want?' prior to succumbing to the following year's 'Lonely Pup In A Christmas Sh*p' [sic] Top Ten penetration, 1961's crass *What A Whopper!* movie and the title role in Bournemouth Pavilion's production of *Aladdin*. Yet his brushed-forward greaseless hairstyle was copied by no less than Brian Jones, then an office junior in the architectural department of Cheltenham District Council.

In London, Yardbird-in-waiting Jim McCarty was a trainee financial analyst in the City, another typical career option for a grammar school lad. One compensation for living in faraway Teddington was that he was able to secure a seat on the District line tube train before it became standing room only. Yet the journey's banal chit-chat and body pressure had him slouching despondently up to the offices, screwing himself up to go in. Not permitted to take off his suit jacket, even in summer, he turned pages, mulled over figures, drafted letters, liaised on the telephone and swivelled on his chair to chuckle politely when a superior bantered about what the temps were like that week. Otherwise, Jim let his body relax and mind go numb with the listlessness of the completely jaded. Taking exasperated stock, he promised himself that if ever he found the courage to jack in this soul-draining job, he'd never again set foot in the premises.

---

22. Although precisely 60 seconds into 'Song of the Shrimp' in 1962's *Girls! Girls! Girls!*, a fleeting glare mixing exasperation, aversion and resignation seemed to capture Presley's true feelings about the infantile feebleness of the lyrics (e.g. '...he showed his mama and papa, the shrimp newspaper he read...'), a sense of 'What harsh fate chose me, the rock 'n' roll messiah, to get involved with crap like this?'

Yet, however imperceptibly, Jim's and, to a greater degree, Brian's lives were to intertwine with that of Keith Richards, then a slothful and disorderly student at Sidcup School of Art where tutors could not help but imagine that he did very little interrelated reading, and that, when drawn from deep silence, he winged his way through prolonged discussion in class. His bluff was called sometimes by graphics lecturer John Sturgess whose strategies would be seen as unorthodox even now. As Phil May recollects, 'I remember one life-drawing class. I was a very naïve fifteen-year-old, standing there, looking at this naked person, and I couldn't put a mark down. John gave me ten bob (50p) and told me to go down the pub, have half a pint and come back when I was ready. He was fantastic like that.'

An educated guess is that Phil was then still a virgin, like the vast majority of his adolescent peers at a time when a 'nice' girl was 'saving herself' for her wedding night. Nevertheless, a dauntingly free-spirited nurse at Bexley Mental Hospital was reputed to have been the first to surrender herself fully to a then-unused Mick Jagger's charms when he was working there as a porter prior to starting his degree course at the London School of Economics.

Here was a wider forum for initiating carnal adventures, located as it was within walking distance of not only the bustling consumer paradises that orbit Oxford Street but also the back-alleys that spread from Soho Square, proliferating with striptease joints and – if you knew where to look, illicit gambling hells, clandestine brothels and locations where homosexuals gathered, the male ones still fearful of prosecution.

When compared to West Germany, however, professional sex in Britain was in its infancy. It tended to be furtive and grubby: shady hotels in ancient cities letting rooms by the hour with the body smells of others still lingering in the bedclothes, or common soldiers picking up whores at backstreet pubs in Aldershot, to be smuggled into the barracks for joyless assignations. A soft 'want business, man' from a doorway's dark interrupts the ambulatory brooding of an accountant on his way to the last train from Birmingham New Street.

Such chill, empty moments were rare in the brightly lit *Der Grosse Freiheit* ('The Great Freedom'), an area of Hamburg notorious since the days of three-mast clippers for its ways and means of indulging both the weirdest and the most straightforward sexual proclivities. Celebrated rather than submerged, such matters were better organised too, almost regimented in places. Though some sex workers were self-employed 'kerb-swallows' and a few of them students doing holiday work, most of their sisters-in-shame were controlled by madams and pimps who shunted them round from *strasse* to *strasse*, bordello to bordello, to ensure a continual change of faces and flesh for the regulars. 'A female friend of mine who was involved in the British "leisure industry" found the openness of what was going on in Hamburg quite interesting,' remembers Dick Taylor, 'but probably preferred the amount of independence she could have in London.'

Yet, from the client's perspective, Hamburg provided a more efficient and ample service. Though the area round Steindamm in the St Georg quarter on the other side of the Main Station wasn't far behind, St Pauli, the quarter that contained *Der Grosse Freiheit*, had the greater reputation as Europe's premier erotic fairground, the neon starting point of innumerable evenings of temptation. If you liked it plain and simple, sundry orthodox corruptions – strip clubs, peep-show arcades, pick-up joints – were to the *Der Grosse Freiheit* like steel to Sheffield.

However, a few hours in and around 'The Great Freedom' could also be an eye-opener for anyone who'd assumed that humans could only be sexually gratified without mechanical appliances and only with other humans. A veritable Pandora's Box of 'kinky' sex would reveal itself. 'Shops sold coshes like dildos, dildos like coshes,' gasped Dick Taylor, 'and the pornography you could only get from the back streets of Soho who paid the police off.'

Germans of every sex would perform any given variation of tableaux illustrated in such magazines and films, frequently inciting others to join in. Yet bare ladies wrestling in mud or fornicating with donkeys was, said Ricky Richards, one of the first exponents of English rock 'n' roll to work in Hamburg,[23] 'The sort of thing

___

23. Though it was as 'Rick Hardy' that he worked as a comedian before his death in 2006.

that you see once and don't bother seeing again – unless you're one of these blokes who can't get anything.'

The most callow youths from Britain would arrive and, like Lewis Collins of The Mojos, 'come back an old man, having experienced just about everything that's in the book'.[24] Moreover, a few UK musicians, stuck between the sensuality of their new surroundings and their own ingrained compliance to Christian values, would take sheepish communion at the Roman Catholic church next door to the celebrated Star-Club. When such a person looked about the pews, a wave of self-disgust might swamp him when he recognised a *bar-frau* whose breasts, now swaddled decently, he had squeezed the night before.

If glad of the business, the more soft-hearted tarts were saddened to see so many upstanding young Englishmen coming to St Pauli for the first time to gorge themselves on the forbidden fruit. Whatever would their mothers say? 'Everybody around the district,' George Harrison would remember fondly, 'were transvestites, pimps and hookers, and I was in the middle of that when I was seventeen.' Advisedly, lewd sniggering and shadowy thighs did not leap out of the pages of letters home – though many British ex-servicemen had wartime memories of the fleshpots of Europe, and knew that travellers' tales about them were hard fact – as their sons were thrilled to discover. As guardian of his daughter's chastity, Cilla Black's dad wouldn't hear of her going to Hamburg with the otherwise all-male group Kingsize Taylor and the Dominoes who needed a female vocalist to satisfy a contractual stipulation.

When first they came to St Pauli, Rory Storm and the Hurricanes, then rivalling Taylor's as Liverpool's boss group, had been guided round the district's diversions by The Beatles. All newcomers were introduced by groups already resident to, say, the Hippo Bar – the one with women grappling in mud – and the Telefon Club where customers could ring hostesses at the tables. *En route*, they would amble, goggle-eyed, past hucksters extolling the delights of, perhaps, 'gorgeous schoolgirls in a bath of pink champagne! Five marks!'

24. Collins became better known as an actor, chiefly as 'Bodie' in ITV crime-drama series *The Professionals*.

The jewel in the crown, however, was the Herbertstrasse, the 'Street of Windows'. 'You couldn't see into it,' said Ricky Richards, 'because of great big iron doors either end like the entrance to a concentration camp.'

The younger musicians would be ragged about notices barring minors from entering the Herbertstrasse. Unofficially, females who weren't on the game were less welcome. 'I brought over a girlfriend from England called Susan for her holidays,' chortled Ricky Richards, 'and I took her through the Herbertstrasse. As she walked through, you should have heard the catcalls and obscenities! The prostitutes hated seeing other women along there because men were the only possible customers; women could only be sightseers.'

They could be unless, of course, they were lesbians, looking the women up and down like farmers at a cattle auction. Some establishments, however, catered for other predilections. As well as homosexual dating bureaux and male whorehouses, there were places like St Georg's Pulverass (Powder-Barrel) with its Crazy Boys troupe of strippers, and, back in St Pauli, the Roxy Bar where cross-dressers congregated in their sequins and stilettos. 'The first time Skip Allen, our drummer, came to Hamburg with us, aged 16,' grinned Dick Taylor, 'we "forgot" to tell him about the sexual identity of the "girls" in the Roxy. He found them very glamorous until we told him. They in turn seemed to take to us in a big way. They particularly liked our tour manager Pete Watts' "mod" hairstyle, and I can remember him sitting there, being preened.'

There had always been a degree of cross-dressing on British stages since the nineteenth century. Thanks to the Widow Twankey-Prince Charming precedents, a Briton may not have felt as much like a fish out of water as other foreigners did in certain clubs where you'd invite stares if you *weren't* androgynous.

A hulking rock 'n' roller from the Gorbals, once over an initial revulsion, would learn that no aspersions would be cast on his manhood if he was seen in the Roxy, paying his respects to 'The Duchess', an erudite personality whose command of many languages, and encyclopaedic understanding of people and places, interactions and outcomes, provoked such lively and irresistible discussion that his-her sexual identity soon became a thing of inconsequential significance. 'None of us were gay,' Ian Amey, the 'Tich' of Dave Dee, Dozy, Beaky, Mick and Tich, assured me, 'but we used to go there because you could have such great conversations with the Duchess. She – or he – knew so many things about the world. One of his-her best friends was Johnny Kidd.'

The 'look' of Johnny and his backing Pirates, regular UK chart invaders during the early 1960s, was not as critical as their music, but, while experiences like the Roxy might not have eradicated or even tempered any of the ferociously heterosexual bluster with the lads down the pub, many of Kidd's British contemporaries in Hamburg became more receptive to a wardrobe that was not aggressively masculine. Bolero jackets, frilly shirts like whipped cream and even mascara (which Gene Vincent was man enough to apply) were not quite so out of the question when a group strode back onto the local stages from whence it had sprung. Homecoming rock 'n' rollers were now less *who-are-you-lookin'-at-pal?* defensive after experiments with dye either divided pale hair with, say, a three-inch turquoise stripe or peroxided it as two Birmingham groups, The Renegades and Denny Laine and the Diplomats, did in 1962.

They'd mooch down to the newsagent in a fluffy pullover knitted by a Roxy admirer, and not be embarrassed if caught applying lacto-calamine lotion to pimples. As the widest river can be traced to many converging trickles, so a source of the glam-rock movement of the 1970s, as well as New Romantic, Gothic and beyond, must lie as much in Hamburg as in the precedents of Vesta Tilley and Danny La Rue.

More insidiously (and enduringly) influential were the *exis*, the native Hamburg students and existentialists. After they'd dared to trespass into the red-light district to catch the imported British rock 'n' roll groups, they'd lose a little of their cultivated composure, and even start having fun – or at least, via some complex inner debate, give in to a self-conscious conviviality. So it was that fustian intellectuals would buy rounds of drinks to oil the wheels of prolonged conversation with the new messiahs of cool, willing, even glad to be accepted as unpaid and unrecompensed minions as long as they could be seen nattering familiarly with them. For some, 'ligging' during the intermissions came to be the main intention of the evening.

Many *exis*, even some of the girls, took to torturing their hair into a lubricated rocker quiff – until it drove them crazy, always tumbling forward, and causing blemishes to explode around the scalp line. However, immigrants also took trichological cues from their new admirers. By far, the most common *exi* hairstyle was *Pilzkopf* ('mushroom head') or 'Hamlet' – a heavily fringed cut, uncaked with Brylcreem. It was widespread throughout Germany – and its country of origin, France, where, rendered as *cheveux frangés*, it was seen on the heads of the seated beatniks to whom Tony Hancock was holding forth in the party during *The Rebel*. Aged 15 during the cold Easter of 1962, writer and film maker Jonathan Meades was on an exchange visit from his Somerset boarding school to Lyon where he noticed 'two fashion items I had never seen in Britain. The first was collarless corduroy jackets. The second was guys with their hair brushed forward'.

Though Adam Faith had a similar crop, it was associated more with the Kaye Sisters, a trio who were more the ilk of the BBC's cosy *Billy Cotton Band Show* than ITV's *Thank Your Lucky Stars* all-pop showcase, presented by thirty-something Brian Matthew, who, pullovered and *sans* tie, was as casually dressed as he could be without being called to task by the squarer TV programme planners. Worse, the wearing of a *Pilzkopf* would label a man as 'musical' in the streets of Wolverhampton, Cork and Liverpool where its furthest reaching manifestation came about when Stuart Sutcliffe, The Beatles' first bass guitarist, was persuaded by *exi* girlfriend Astrid Kirchherr and her fellow photographer Jürgen Volmer to let her carve one on his head from protrusions stiffened by too many layerings of daily grease. Then, after the outfit's first residency in Hamburg clubland was over and they'd gone back home in dribs and drabs, he decided he was finished with Liverpool, and, not even sticking around long enough to honour existing Beatles engagements there, had fallen into Astrid's arms again amid the gusting engine steam at Hamburg-Hauptbahnhof station.

When he rejoined the group on their return for a second season on *Der Grosse Freiheit*, John Lennon's loud scorn led Stuart to betray

Astrid by restoring his hair as best he could to the old style. Yet, before the evening was out, it was back the way she liked it. Not only that but George Harrison was to ask her to give him a *Pilzkopf* too – though, after years of quiffing, it wouldn't cascade easily into one. Although Pete Best, the group's drummer, demurred, Paul McCartney and then, unexpectedly, Lennon tried one wondering if they'd have the nerve to keep it like that, even grow it thicker and longer eventually. Just wait till the lads back on Merseyside saw it. You'll need a guide dog to stop you bumping into things, they'd say – and worse.

John and Paul were to make up their minds after a twenty-first birthday cheque from John's rich Aunt Elizabeth was blown on a fortnight in Paris from 29 September to 15 October 1961. There, they witnessed a performance by black leather-clad Vince Taylor, now focussing on France where he'd surfaced as an idol of the Gallic species of rock 'n' roll enthusiast.[25] Crucially, they linked up with Jürgen Vollmer, the visiting *exi* lensman who convinced Lennon and McCartney to restyle their hair permanently like his own and those of other friends in Hamburg – and the youths they'd observed at Taylor's show and in the *boulevards* – to wear boldly around Liverpool where, by late 1962, it was to become known as a 'Beatle cut' or 'moptop' after local lads began emulating it.

In Billy Shepherd's *The True Story of The Beatles* (Beat Publications, 1964), however, George Harrison was to state that the group's first consideration for the pudding basin look came as a result of a suggestion of two friends: 'I remember we went to the swimming baths once and my hair was down from the water and they said, "No, leave it, it's good." I didn't have my Vaseline anyway, and I was thinking, "Well, these people are cool. If they think it's good, I'll leave it like this." They gave me that confidence and when it dried off it dried naturally down, which later became "the look".'

In the same book, Lennon would recall, 'Jürgen Vollmer had bell-bottom trousers, but we thought that would be considered too queer back in Liverpool. Anyway, Jürgen had a flattened-down

---

25. Until one unhinged evening at the Paris Olympia when, so the story goes, he floated onstage in white vestments, rather than his customary biker garb, to preach a *repent-ye-your-sins* sermon to a mystified and then furious audience.

hairstyle with a fringe in the front, which we rather took to. We went over to his place and there and then he cut – hacked would be a better word – our hair into the same style.' McCartney's memory is similar: 'We said, "Would you do our hair like yours?" We're on holiday – what the hell! We're buying capes and pantaloons, throwing caution to the wind. He said, "No, boys, no. I like you as Rockers; you look great." But we begged him enough so he said "All right." We sat down in his hotel and he just got it: the "Beatle" cut! Everyone thought we had started it, so it became "the Beatle hairdo".'

Around the time Paul and John visited France, The Beatles' stage set included 'Lend Me Your Comb', a 1957 B-side by rockabilly performer Carl Perkins. This was lent contemporary resonance by the title's similarity to 'Kookie, Kookie (Lend Me Your Comb)', composed to order in 1960 as a duet for Connie Stevens and Edd Byrnes, who played 'Kookie', private eye Stu Bailey's jive-talkin' sidekick in the US drama series 77 Sunset Strip. Kookie was a kind of missing link between James Dean's Rebel Without A Cause character and the Fonz. After he surfaced as a pin-up in innumerable adolescent girls' bedrooms, Byrnes teamed up with Stevens who played 'Cricket Blake' in the companion detective programme, Hawaiian Eye, for the self-referential 'Kookie, Kookie (Lend Me Your Comb)', the lyrical thrust of which was Cricket Blake's desire for Kookie to cease his unceasing fiddling with his hair and kiss her.

It cruised into the Top Five in the States and washed up at Number 27 in the UK. Yet, though Connie had already scored a bigger hit that spring with 'Sixteen Reasons', Edd's solo singles of 1960, 'Like I Love You' and, during the December sell-in, 'Lonely Christmas', were relative failures. Nonetheless, he remained the recipient of mailbags stuffed with letters of undying love from his followers – and his brilliantine-secured hairstyle, if requiring high maintenance ('raking the ear-to-ear carpeting', he called it), was in vogue for a while.[26]

---

26. When older and sufficiently sharp-eyed, fans could have recognised a middle-aged Kookie in the 1970s films Stardust and Grease.

However, by paying a saved-up six shillings rather than the usual half-crown to a barber in-the-know, you could get a 'French cut' (a longer crew cut with a parting and puffed-up via backcombing while blow-drying into a 'bouffant'), a shorter 'College Boy' or what was popularly known as a 'Perry Como', named after the North American singer who had actually given up a successful career as a barber to take his chances as vocalist with a dance band. British actor Warren Walters retained it throughout three decades with a firm of solicitors, beginning in 1962.

Conservative though it was, the 'Perry Como' required careful razor-work and tapering – and no oily product needed to be rubbed in after this was completed. This neat and clean-looking approach was much favoured by '(Motor) Scooter Boys', who, as early as 1959, sought out those who called themselves 'hairdressers' rather than 'barbers'. For many, the most satisfactory results were achieved by going to those catering for women where it was sometimes possible to arrange an evening appointment after the usual clientele had left, with the more self-conscious fellows permitted to enter the premises by the back door.[27]

By the early 1960s, unisex salons came into being – like that of Rom Ahmed in Harringay, north London, where, as can be seen in a British Pathé cinema newsreel, there was often not much gender difference in a similarly short cut. What's more, while awaiting their turn, couples were able to dance or simply groove along to records to do with the Twist, then as much of a worldwide craze as trad was in Britain alone. Its Mecca was New York's Peppermint Lounge where, to the sound of Joey Dee and the Starliters, middle-aged trendsetters mingled with beatniks to perform what *Melody Maker* deemed 'the most vulgar dance ever invented'.

The Twist's Acker Bilk was Chubby Checker, vigorously aped on British TV by one Roly Daniels, but, from Sinatra and Elvis downwards, all manner of unlikely artists were issuing Twist 45s. Neither would it go away – probably because you were too spoilt

---

27. Some, however, were quite open about their practice afterwards of retiring to bed in hair-rollers to keep everything in place.

for choice with alternatives like the Fly, the Shimmy-Shimmy, the Locomotion, the Slop, the ungainly Turkey Trot, the Mashed Potato, the Gorilla Walk, the Mickey's Monkey, the Hully Gully, the Hitch-Hiker, the back-breaking Limbo, the Madison and, in Europe only, La Yenka and the Letkiss. Through a minor 1961 hit by The Temperance Seven, there was even a revival of the Charleston, and, a few months later, 'Can-Can 62' by Peter Jay and the Jaywalkers made the Top Forty too.

Nothing dates a 1960s movie more than the obligatory Twist sequence, and, to this day, the very elderly will slip into it unconsciously whenever the music hots up at a dinner-and-dance. By 1962, it had been turning as outdated as skiffle but 'just to make sure we stayed up to date,' twinkled Eamonn Andrews on *Crackerjack*, 'we rounded off Edition One Hundred with... The Twist!'

Ostensibly, it was all that was immediately available to those who didn't go for trad – which is why new clubs like Birmingham's Moat Twistacular and Ilford's Twist at the Top (the name echoing the 1950 'kitchen sink' film, *Room At The Top*), were very much in business. The Ilford club even had its own Joey Dee and the Starliters in Wailin' Howie Casey and the Seniors, who titled their only album after the place – and Twist exhibition teams filled the time which a skiffle group might once have done.

Dance crazes generally indicate stagnation in pop, and Britain was heaving with that. On the Light Programme if not the charts were 'Mama's Doin' the Twist' by The Viscounts, Eden Kane's 'Sounds Funny to Me', Dave Carey's homage to 'Bingo', and 'Just Couldn't Resist Her With Her Pocket Transistor' from Alma Cogan – plus unwavering 'Bobby' music. Finally, the Mudlarks, spiritual descendants of *Melody Cruise*'s Teenagers, had been voted the kingdom's Best Vocal Group two years running in the *NME* popularity poll until unseated in 1960 by the King Brothers.

Yet Joey Dee's 'Peppermint Twist' was actually quite enthralling – and Ray Charles's 'Hit the Road Jack' in 1961 traded call-and-responses with his female vocal trio, the Raelettes, like a spiritual's interplay between exhorter and congregation. Of like persuasion, Barrett Strong's 'Money' and the Marvelettes' 'Please Mr Postman' were among the first *Billboard* entries for Tamla Motown, a promising black label from Detroit – while over in Greenwich Village, New York's vibrant bohemian district, the civil rights movement was fusing with folk song to be labelled 'protest'. Among genre exponents presented in its night spots were Pete Seeger; Judy Collins; The Modern Folk Quartet; Peter, Paul and Mary; the Clancy Brothers and Tommy Makem; and, most spectacularly in retrospect, Bob Dylan, whose plaintive opening album, issued early in 1962, mingled mostly semi-traditional material and self-written items.

Mainstream pop, however, had now started addressing, initially via instrumentals, an activity that would also inspire films with titles like *Muscle Beach Party* and *How to Stuff a Wild Bikini*. Among the most notable of the vocal items was 'Surfin'', the 1961 disc debut by The Beach Boys with their chugging rock 'n' roll overlaid with infectious melodies and interweaving harmonies crowned by a cool cruising falsetto.

CHAPTER SEVEN

'In person – direct from the nuthouse!!!'

In the early 1960s, numbers involving the Twist were attempted but seldom by the few British rock 'n' rollers who didn't go Bobby-smooth, but nonetheless proved able to survive the years beyond the 1962 watershed and always have plenty of work assured with or without chart entries.

The most alarming of these was David Edward 'Screaming Lord' Sutch, who couldn't have softened up, even if he'd wanted – and this discourse would not be complete without providing some details concerning the most famous English pop star never to have a domestic hit – and about his pre-Rolling Stones long hair (briefly dyed green).

Sunday newspapers and a BBC documentary team homed in too on the leopard skin loincloth, the woad, the bull horns, the monster feet, the caveman's club, the coffin, the trademark top-hat and whatever else he'd laid his hands on in order to enhance a stage act that balanced the slickness of a Broadway musical with a sense that everything could fall to bits at any second. This was, however, but part of the package. Sutch was also to be figurehead of the short-lived pirate Radio Sutch off the Essex coast; was the chief publicist of 1972's vast Rock 'n' Roll Festival at Wembley Stadium via capering with unclothed ladies outside 10 Downing Street; and stood for Parliament in the Stratford-on-Avon by-election in 1963, setting himself on the path to becoming the longest serving party leader in British politics.

It's not possible to be completely objective about someone I knew and liked for about 15 years. However, I'd first heard of Screaming Lord Sutch at infant school when fellow pupils expressed revulsion about him sporting the longest male hair in the country. I was to see it for myself in his outrageous-for-the-time promotional film for his 1963 single 'Jack the Ripper'. This was on the short-lived 'Scorpitone' video jukebox in Macari's café in Aldershot where two bus conductors, their faces alight with vacant ecstasy, spent their lunch hour and half a satchel of silver watching David in full regalia, ghoul make-up and long-bladed dagger, stalking Victorian Tearsheets.

His career had begun one night in 1959 when he'd screwed himself up to mount the stage of a pub called the Rising Sun to entertain drinkers with a parody of a pop singer. It was located in Sudbury Hill, a suburb adjacent to his home turf of South Harrow where, as an only child, he lived at 10 Parkfield Road with Annie, his long-widowed mother. Amused cheering was enough for the 19-year-old window-cleaner to forward himself as the antithesis of the Elvis clones competing for the attention of Paul 'Dr Death' Lincoln, a former wrestler, who ran the 2i's. 'I covered my motorbike crash helmet with leopard skin, and stuck huge bull horns into it,' he'd recall in November 1998 when I conducted what I – and possibly he – didn't know would be his last major interview. 'I also borrowed my auntie's leopard skin coat. I came across as a Wild Man of Borneo, screaming out from the crowd when I was announced. I went mad, jumping onto the piano and attacking the crowd.'

So it was that the first bookings of Screaming Lord Sutch, soon backed by his Horde of Savages, formed with drummer Carlo Little, which mostly took place in that hinterland where Greater London melts into Middlesex, received instant national notoriety through an endless pressing on the nerve of how far he could take things. Though there were stories about him performing with, respectively, an alligator and a Himalayan bear, more typical routines involved a 'Grand Entrance' in a coffin carried at shoulder height, and his wrenching out of a heart and a liver (bought from the butcher's that afternoon) during the simulated murder and mutilation of a 'prostitute', played by one of his Horde of Savages in wig and padded bra.

Thus was attracted the attention of the police and Sutch spent nights in cells for sundry breaches of the peace. The Granada leisure circuit barred him after he plummeted through a house pipe organ during a rash jump from footlights to orchestra pit. More constructively, he was noticed by console boffin Joe Meek, rated by many, including myself, as Britain's, if not the world's, most adventurous record producer.

He oversaw Sutch's début 45, 1960's 'Big Black Coffin' – which had to be retitled "Til the Following Night' to humour a record company worried about what the BBC might think. This set the pattern for future singles, divided as they were between horror spoofs and rock 'n' roll ravers. In 1966, he would come as close as he would ever be to a reinvention as a 'musicianly' artiste with the single 'The Cheat' which had a fashionably mock-Oriental riff on flute and violin, although its B-side, 'All Black and Hairy', was his more traditional fare.

With commercial progress at home impeded by airplay bans, 'Jack the Ripper' – 'nauseating trash', sneered *Melody Maker* – didn't do for Sutch what the million-selling 'Monster Mash' had for Bobby 'Boris' Pickett and the Crypt Kickers less than a year earlier. However, with wall-posters proclaiming *'IN PERSON – DIRECT FROM THE NUTHOUSE – THE ONE AND ONLY SCREAMING LORD SUTCH AND HIS SAVAGES!!!'* venues filled to overflowing – and cases of fainting and hysteria were not unknown. The group criss-crossed Britain – and then mainland Europe – with line-ups that included many nascent stars, among them personnel later in The Rolling Stones, The Pretty Things, Procol Harum, Jimi Hendrix's Experience, Deep Purple, The Jeff Beck Group and Led Zeppelin, while the diverse worlds of drama and literature have been represented by keyboard players Paul Nicholas – and Alan Clayson. 'Sutch's was an outfit that every musician wanted to be in,' affirmed Tony Dangerfield, bass player, on and off, from 1964 to virtually the finish. 'Maybe the most proficient live group in the country when I joined, it was high quality, high energy too – and a great training ground.'

A horde of famous ex-Savages were the 'Heavy Friends' who turned out for their old boss after he landed a two-album deal with Atlantic Records following a visit to the USA during the fag-end of the post-Beatles 'British Invasion', putting on an upper-class accent, travelling in a Union Jack-painted Rolls-Royce and had it circulated about that he was 'the Sixth Earl of Harrow'. While 1970's *Lord Sutch and Heavy Friends* was cited in a poll amongst the UK's more unimaginative radio presenters as the worst rock album ever made, Sutch's public allure diverted attention from the essential quality of his music in which a controlled and melodic vein of heavy rock underlined compelling if gruesome lyricism.

Acts in his artistic debt spanned decades from The Crazy World of Arthur Brown to Alice Cooper to The Damned. In the 1980s, traces of Sutch were obvious in The Cramps' 'psychobilly' and the gross slapstick of King Kurt, while the Revillos had a near-hit with a revival of 'She's Fallen in Love with the Monster Man', a Sutch item from the mid-1960s.

David also became synonymous with politics, courtesy of the proposals of his Monster Raving Loony party with its retinue of deposit-losing fools like Toby Jug, Freddie Zapp and RU Serious. One symptom of this was David's ear-to-ear grin like a catatonic Benny Hill at every applicable photo opportunity; another was pot-shots at the charts with singles such as 'Rock the Election' and 1991's 'Number Ten or Bust!' Yet, might it have been not entirely laughable for a returning officer to proclaim David Edward Sutch the victor – just – of some marginal seat or other if, say, unsavoury and easily verifiable details about a front-runner's past had surfaced during the hustings, another's third lung operation in as many months made him an obvious health risk, and there was a clearer run than expected because of no other fringe miscellany?

Such a quirk of fate would be likely to hinge on an overwhelming no-vote majority. What's more, there'd probably be some immediate nonsense instanced by at least one journalist putting him on a par with 'Chance Gardiner', played by Peter Sellers in 1979's *Being There* movie, in which an idiot ended up on the brink of becoming the US President. Yet following all the knee-jerk silliness, could not common folk discover that Sutch's verbal exchanges contained a lot more sense than might have been imagined? Furthermore, many Monster Raving Loony policies proved astonishingly prophetic: votes at eighteen, the legalization of commercial radio, the abolition of the Eleven Plus, passports for pets – and pubs open all day through, so David outlined, the repeal of a stop-gap measure passed during the Great War to discourage the home front from dulling its patriotic, Hun-hating fervour with booze.

Would imagination stretch to a soberly-attired maiden speech at the House of Commons and, soon afterwards, a defection to Labour? Within months, could he have hosted a party political broadcast and been considered for a Shadow Cabinet post, having established himself as a vigorous, witty and, crucially, constructive orator? Lest we forget too, UK Prime Minister-in-waiting Tony Blair had been lead vocalist in an amateur rock group called Ugly Rumours when a long-haired hippie student with albums of 'progressive' rock persuasion on instant replay on his hostel room stereo.

With this in mind, might the fateful spring day have dawned at last when, answering the telephone, there'd be a sufficient stridency in the Leader of Her Majesty's Opposition's educated whine to compel David Sutch MP to summon an instant taxi to the party's London headquarters? During the stop-start journey through the rush hour, the twice-elected Member of Parliament ruminated that, while Labour was certain to take the country by storm in the May 1997's General Election, Tony himself wasn't too hale. Of late, the urbane mask had slipped sometimes, and the strain had shown, and he'd thought aloud to David and other intimates about packing it in.

On arrival, the normally hoity-toity receptionist conducts Sutch straightaway into the presence of Blair, who prior to getting down to business, is obliged to deal with the visibly annoying trill of his new mobile. Addressing the caller faux-jovially as 'John the Baptist', he signs off quickly with 'Let's speak later. The Chosen One's with me in the office.'

'Glad you could get here so soon, David,' Blair begins, 'I couldn't tell you this on the phone, but you know I've been suffering from intermittent chest pains over the past year? Well, the doctor reckoned initially that there was no cause for alarm, but now he's detected something sinister. Yes, really! There's no way, therefore that I can carry on – and Cherie and I have decided that I ought to withdraw from public life.'

Sutch shakes his head frenziedly as if it had become unhinged. 'Tony, the world'll look rosier after the first of May. All you have to do is convalesce and then take it a little easier. Don't chuck away what you were born to be.'

'But I'm not chucking it away. I'm giving it to you. If an actor can be President of the United States, a playwright be premier of Czechoslovakia, and a topless model an Italian government aide, why can't a rock 'n' roller be PM? You're our biggest chance. The future of the country's all yours, David.' His face fills with entreaty. 'Don't make it difficult for me.'

'OK. I'll do whatever you need me to do.' There was an inappropriately orphaned look from the older man. 'I'm going to miss you...'

Then Screaming Lord Sutch is silent for a full minute as if in a stupor. 'Yeah. Tell me again,' he says mysteriously, 'You know – about it all being mine.'

'It's all yours, David. It's all yours.'

Daydreams were all very well – and the nightmares that were to beset David Sutch lay unsuspected when 1960s teen idol Dave Berry and I were along for the laugh during an August weekend in 1987 as a certain Charlie Salt was inaugurated as Monster Raving Loony candidate for Tiverton in the midst of a concert held at an auditorium attached to the Burston Inn in Bow, a village in mid-Devon.

The main draw was Sutch, backed by a group from Redruth, 80 miles away, glad of the chance to accompany a legend. Their drummer yielded his kit to Berry prior to the latter joining in the fun on backing vocals with Charlie and then lead singing with Sutch, a session during which the strains of old-time rock 'n' roll mingled with the two celebrities' reciprocally appreciative rapping.

The following afternoon, Dave, Charlie and I were in Sutch's open-top car, waving regally too, when it shunted us round the arena of the local carnival that David had just declared open. He was in a buoyant mood at odds with those days beginning amid encircling gloom at Parkfield Road where he was still living much of the time with his mother.

He had long been a chronic insomniac, who, though near-teetotal and a non-smoker, was unable to blame this, even if everyone else did, on ingesting prescription tablets injudiciously –

and being a dedicated tea drinker, awash with up to thirty cups a day for as long as he and I began counting each other as friends – and I couldn't help but feel a frequent sense of wonderment as if he and the situations in which we became involved weren't quite real.

Where to begin? How about the midsummer day when I arrived too late to sit, feet on the warm sand of Sidmouth beach, before my copperplate place-card at the table where the cutlery and crackers were just so for a sumptuous *Christmas* banquet with Sutch and various Loony creatures plus personnel from the pick-up group (with the son of renowned comedian Russ Abbott on keyboards) used for the previous night's attendant concert.

Then there was the autumn weekend when we were both contracted to be 'personalities' at a record fayre at the University of Northumbria. That morning, April Nichol, at whose house we were staying, woke me around 7.15 am because Rosie, David's yappy little terrier, had got out during the night. Husband Ray, the redhead who'd once wowed the girls during that school trip to Northumberland, was already organising the fayre and David couldn't be raised. Could I go out to look for her? Half-an-hour later, it was my ill luck to find the animal trying to cross a busy road. She saw me, bared her teeth, ran down an alley into a garden and hid under a holly bush. Following a desperate and fruitless attempt to persuade her to emerge, I seized whatever parts of Rosie were within reach. So it was that I found myself staggering along the street with a snarling dog in my arms, blood streaming from both hands, and subject to the stares of work-bound Geordies (who reckon we southerners are soft).

After spending all morning in the Accident and Emergency Department of the city hospital – for tetanus injections, antibiotics and heavy bandaging that made the injuries look worse than they were – I arrived at the record fayre where Sutch had summoned the gentlefolk of the press to cover the incident. With *EX-SAVAGE SAVAGED* its headline, it had seeped through to the *London Evening Standard* by the following Tuesday.

To be precise, I wasn't an ex-Savage so much as an intermittent one, a position traceable to events that happened not quite a year after that function in Devon. Following a family excursion to

London's Science Museum, I suggested we round off the afternoon at a charity extravaganza in Covent Garden where luminaries like Boy George and Kate Bush were working as counter assistants in local shops. Its nexus was an open-air stage in front of the Royal Opera House. Sutch, the next act on, greeted me. One thing led to another, and within minutes, I was on the boards, pounding piano with Howlin' Wilf's Vee-Jays (then the toast of R&B London), backing Sutch and his special guest, 'Brian Tilsley' from *Coronation Street*.

After that, I was only a telephone call away if David needed a keyboard player. He thought he might if veteran musical hireling Geraint Watkins didn't make it to be part of an 11-piece band he'd assembled for a Halloween engagement in the London Dungeons that was broadcast by BBC Radio One. Frowned upon in a more innocent age, the antics of Screaming Lord Sutch could hardly have been witnessed in surroundings more bloodcurdlingly appropriate.

His line-up would also include trombonist Don Lang, once the front man of Don Lang and his Frantic Five, best remembered for the theme song to *Six-Five Special*, and for a 1958 appearance in the Top Five with 'Witch Doctor', but then dying slowly of cancer. There were also assorted former members of Deep Purple, Cliff Bennett's Rebel Rousers, Dave Edmunds' Rockpile and – by a stretch of the imagination – The Rolling Stones via Carlo Little, who had played with an early version of the group, but, during a Stones spectacular at Wembley Stadium in the later 1990s, would be operating a hot-dog trailer outside. As onions sizzled in readiness for the surge afterwards, what was he thinking as explosions of applause punctuated every segment of megawatt noise measured out by the beat of the one who'd replaced him in the Stones? 'If he hadn't scribbled down Charlie Watts's phone number for Brian Jones,' estimated Sutch, 'Carlo could have been a multi-millionaire.'

Among others on the boards too was Tony Dangerfield, who, receding and no longer peroxided hair apart, had clung onto the handsomeness and slim physique that had caused Joe Meek to single him out for solo stardom and a slot on *Thank Your Lucky Stars* in 1964. 'He said he visualised me as another Billy Fury,' Tony remarked. This, however, was not to be, and Dangerfield continued along the same journeyman path of hardship and disappointment as a guitarist that he'd been travelling since leaving school at 15. He had transferred to bass in order to join a Wolverhampton group but all routes led back to Sutch and the animal-skin stage costumes he and the others donned.

I made do with a fake leopard-skin jacket in a gig at Reading's Purple Turtle, then in its original location just before the canal bridge along King Street. It was almost like walking into someone's front room – albeit one with a bar, low stage and jukebox. It was a tiny club with maybe 20 patrons on a Wednesday evening where, on this particular occasion, as we were dismantling the gear afterwards, a barman took such exception to some bloke's remark that he floored him with a single blow, reducing him to bleeding blubber.

The night had started with the Savages alone and Tony taking lead vocals. I did not participate in this bit owing to unfamiliarity then with songs that, unlike all but two sung after David's entrance, were not straightforward 12-bar rock 'n' roll. This is clear from the set list (with keys) sellotaped above the control panel of my Roland Piano-Plus 11: *BEETHOVEN D, LITTLE RICHARD MEDLEY D, BALLS A, HOG A, MORONIE E, RIPPER Am (to C), MOLLY D, BLACK A (riff)*. I've never had the heart to remove it.

David hadn't bothered much with props during what was to him a negligible midweek gig and there was already a sense of resentment as there'd be in any too-familiar job, where you can't wait until clocking-off time, when he announced, 'Here's another good-old-good-one from the rockin' fifties' with a rancour born of dreary repetition.

Yet he made more of a show of it two months later during a packed-out concert in a Newbury pub with a huge capacity the day before votes were counted in the 1993 by-election. (Out of twenty-two nominees, Lord Sutch would come seventh, beating the SDP among several other 'serious' contenders.) Through hammering the eighty-eights so hard throughout three encores, I drew blood from a couple of fingers. Owing to volume no lower than Sutch's roar over a relentless sledgehammer beat, I also had ringing in the ears for about three days. This was despite the precaution of stuffing my ears with cotton wool as I always did when positioned next to Dangerfield's bass stack.

The Newbury show was a predictable riot, but during the 1995 May Bank Holiday, David was the surprise sensation of the Chelsea Bridge Reunion, a weekend celebration of British motorbiking in a showground near Battersea Power Station (pictured on the cover of Pink Floyd's *Animals* album), which was being turned into an art gallery. Close up, it had a ruined grandeur; an accidental work of art in itself.

Mid-afternoon sunshine and the attractions of the trade stands took the edge off our glorious leader's emergence from his coffin after the group's pulverising of Frédéric Chopin's *Funeral March*. Yet from this unpromising start, a huge crowd accumulated and tuned into the pantomime of 'Jack the Ripper' and the back-to-back rock which, by the play-out, had my right hand stuck in a triplet.

An event the media considered less important took place when David was back where it had all started, mounting the stage at Sudbury Hill's Rising Sun late in 1997 during a tribute concert for Wee Willie Harris, whose hard times had become harder since he was diagnosed with apparent prostate cancer. He was received with some affection, but, with his remaining hair no longer coloured pink, he cut a lonely figure afterwards, seated at his merchandise stall when the music was over – mostly classic rock with the subtlety of a falling ton of bricks.

More intriguing was to see what was left of other former pop luminaries who'd turned out to pay respects. A couple of those who commandeered the central microphone no longer had the figure for the cavortings of yore, but it struck me momentarily that, for simply keeping the faith for so long, the title of King of British rock 'n' roll might belong in the end not to someone like Cliff Richard, Billy Fury or even Johnny Kidd, but to hitless Screaming Lord Sutch.

That would be the last time I'd see David perform in an official function – though he was to turn the funeral of his adored mother in Pinner New Cemetery into a black carnival with a graveside press conference and posing for tabloid snapshotters. That's probably the way Annie would have wanted it, delighted as she was that 'he's made something of his life when he started out with nothing'. She'd expressed a wish – unfulfilled – that, rather than mope at her deathbed, David would stand as arranged in the forthcoming General Election against Prime Minister John Major in Huntingdon.

The interment was more or less the finish too for David, now suffering more than ever from profound clinical depression. Yet he'd explain as much to himself as me, 'I still enjoy what I'm doing, even though I've been ill, and had the stress of my mother being ill before that. It took me longer than I thought to get over her death. During that time, I felt so terrible that I was just going through the motions. I didn't want to do gigs, but now that negative side has died off. My ambition now is to lead the first rock 'n' roll band to play on the Moon.'

He'd fill hours with anecdotes about what Johnny Kidd had said to Gene Vincent in 1962. Flitting fitfully from subject to chronologically illogical subject, his mind would wander next to the pulling of minor strokes such as granting the emergent Damned the privilege of pall-bearing his coffin onstage one evening in the late 1970s. At such times I was in the company of a quiet, rather solemn chap who was endeavouring to resolve the tug-of-war between the private David Edward Sutch and 'Screaming Lord Sutch', public laughing-stock. 'My act is a kind of showbiz madness,' he confessed, 'that I've always known how to switch off when the show's over.'

Approaching pensionable age, he spoke of retirement when, late at night and wired on caffeine, he'd call me and maybe half-a-dozen others, having let an Everest grow from the molehill of, say, an insulting paragraph about him in some morning newspaper. Or, alternatively, he was wanting to talk about a mooted appearance with Los Straitjackets, the Neanderdolls and further entities of whom he'd hitherto never heard at *Hallowe'en 99: A Feast of Sixties Trash and Exotica* in Las Vegas.

With not quite a month to go, David seemed in relatively jaunty mood when we met for lunch prior to his scouring of South Harrow's second-hand emporiums with the air of a local Member of Parliament on a walkabout. He seemed in higher spirits than of late, speaking proudly, almost boastfully, about the promise of a role in an ITV breakfast cereal advert. It's difficult not to read portent into his behaviour, but as he saw me off at the tube station, David embraced me in a tight bear hug rather than shaking hands as he usually did. Also, at my house one afternoon several weeks earlier, I'd been startled when he presented me with his entire collection of memorabilia for safekeeping.

During a Rolling Stones Fan Convention at South London's Brixton Academy, he sang his swansong. Though feeling under the weather, he agreed to give 'em 'Roll Over Beethoven'. According to one eyewitness, he was drooping slightly, but pulled himself together for the big finish – a clip from which was to be broadcasted on BBC television's *Network South-East* magazine. And thus, over the play-out, the nation saw the old aristocrat of pop smile, bow at the baying blackness and, every inch a star, vanish into the wings forever.

On Wednesday 16 June 1999, a 58-year-old was found dangling from the banisters of 10 Parkfield Road, a skipping rope round his neck, paying the ultimate price for 'the nearest thing to death' that had dogged him for years with worsening episodes of lethargy, insomnia, paranoia, over-anxiety about apparent trivia and an inability to make long-term plans.

Twelve days later, David would be buried next to his mother. As fistfuls of earth fell upon the coffin lid, one of 500-odd mourners, illustrious and obscure, began dirging 'Love Me Tender' – and others took it up. A song from the repertoires of both Elvis Presley and Roland Rat, it was faintly preposterous – and somehow a fitting soundtrack to the finale of a life that was, on its own terms, as triumphant as it was tragic.

CHAPTER EIGHT

'If you look at early pictures of us, we had nothing'

In the immediate wake of Screaming Lord Sutch and his Savages had come the copycat likes of Paignton's Baron Grave and the Vampires, Mel Fear and the Fantastic Fhantoms [sic] from Torquay, Sheffield's Count Lindsay III and his Skeletons, and The Mersey Monsters. The latter delivered an appositely sinister arrangement of 'Watch Your Step' – a US R&B item that was going the rounds with myriad beat groups in the early 1960s – at a graveyard location during *Liverpool A-Go-Go*, a 1965 celluloid conveyor belt of lip-synched ephemera connected by voiceover narrative from Bob Wooler, the renowned Cavern Club's best known master-of-ceremonies.

By the time it was shown on North American television later that year, there was a sense of impending hangover in Liverpool itself. As a beehive can thrive for a while after losing its progenitive queen, so, with The Beatles gone, did combos with winsome grins, collarless suits and what would resemble spun dishmops whenever they shook their heads and went 'oooooo'. Instead of the four-eyed Hank B Marvin lookalike of yore with a Fender Stratocaster, there'd now be an unsmiling guitarist who, in imagination at least, played a Rickenbacker through a Marshall amplifier, just like George Harrison.

The Olympic torch of Merseybeat had been carried to every nook and cranny of Britain. The Grasshoppers were 'Meriden's answer to The Beatles' while Church Crookham, just outside Fleet, had 'The Termites'. Three Birmingham outfits called themselves the Brumbeats. There were also Beat Ltd, the Beatstalkers, the Counterbeats, the Beat-Chics, the Big Beats and so on. Hundreds of groups were 'pinching our arrangements too,' griped John Lennon, 'and down to the last note at that'.

However, before the two-guitars-bass-drums line-up of The Beatles, the Searchers, the Swinging Blue Jeans and other 1963 hitmakers surfaced as the beat group archetype, Merseyside ensembles of every variety and size, including sextets and octets, had been either active or in formation from Southport to Birkenhead. Some were all female, others all black. A couple were all female *and* black. For every one that admitted defeat, a dozen sprang up in its place. Most were in it for fun, but quite a few meant business.

Disregarded by the rest of the country, Liverpool and its environs – 'the pool of life' as Jung tagged it – bubbled in its isolation and built-in resilience. As unaware as his interviewers of the distant thunder too, Roy Orbison, in London during 1962, conjectured that, 'You don't seem to have the kind of rhythm groups we have in the States – and I'm sure that is what the kids want: strong, beaty rhythms that make them jump.' Nobody at Roy's press conference could predict that soon British 'rhythm groups' would be jumping up the hit parade in abundance with discs as competent and attractive as anything North American, but played with guts, like.

Yet Dick Rowe, Decca's Head of A&R, had let The Beatles slip from his then unconcerned grip early in 1962 after being persuaded to audition them by manager Brian Epstein. Rowe's verdict was that they could find their way around their instruments, but were merely competent singers with a sound that conjured up back-of-beyond youth clubs with soft drinks, ping-pong and a presiding vicar. Outfits like The Beatles could be found in virtually every town in the country.

What followed a year later provoked Rowe to saturate the company with beat groups in hopes that one of them might catch on like the 'Fab Four' who had been seized by Parlophone, a subsidiary of EMI, Decca's main commercial enemy. Others with axes to grind began alighting on the remotest indication that the peril from the north was a spent force. To Joe Meek, Merseyside had always been following rather than setting trends as shown by the Mersey Monsters copying Screaming Lord Sutch. As far as Meek could see too, 'The Beatles have nothing new about their sound. Cliff Bennett and the Rebel Rousers have been doing the same thing for a year.'

It was business as usual, therefore, for Joe with his productions of Middlesex-raised Bennett and his unit's cover of the Shirelles' 'Everybody Loves a Lover' – another beat group 'standard' – and Sutch's 'Jack the Ripper'. Even so, Meek paid heed to what he regarded as passing fads via 'You've Got To Have A Gimmick Today' by the Checkmates in March 1963, and 'I Learned To Yodel' from the Atlantics, fronted by a vocalist with the negotiable name of Jimmy Lennon.

Nevertheless, 'What's this Liverpool outfit everyone's talking about?' was a question asked with increasing frequency by various fatheads time-serving as record label directors without much of a finger on the pulse. Meanwhile office juniors were discussing whether or not The Beatles had got into a rut with their third A-side, 'From Me to You', which had the same overall melodic and rhythmic thrust as the second, 'Please Please Me'. The slowest-witted decision makers held the view that all pop groups are the same: *let's sign as many as we can, see which racket catches on, and hammer it hard. Make a fortune, eh? Pause. Where exactly is Liverpool?*

Hardly a week seemed to go by without another Merseyside act being thrust forward. Suddenly, someone who'd cadged cigarettes off you the previous month would be seen in the *NME* with his or her outfit, posing round a fire escape or on a brick-strewn wasteland. In the first month of 1963 alone, Decca – now not so cautious – made off with four, among them Lee Curtis and the All-Stars who, because of who their drummer *was* rather than what he did, had been a close second to The Beatles in 1962's popularity poll conducted by the *Mersey Beat* regional gazette. They were to lose Pete Best, however, after their first two singles missed – and it dawned on Decca that an ex-Beatle was wasted as a sideshow.

Just before their take-off, Ringo Starr had replaced Pete in The Beatles. Among purported reasons why Best became victim of intensifying character assassinations by Harrison, McCartney and

Lennon over venomous pints in a pub's murkiest corner was that
he was a quiff among the *Pilzkopfs*, chiefly because his tight curls
couldn't be fashioned into the group's now corporate style without
skilled treatment, possibly requiring application of chemicals.

In a similar quandary, Ray Dorset, then an apprentice at
a ladies' hairdresser in Egham, was able to moptop his head
following private experimentation involving a cream called *Teeda*
that in combination with *Trill* conditioner (nothing to do with the
budgerigar seed mixture of the same name) proved more effective
as a hair-straightener than the stuff he had used to tame his frizz
when he wanted to be a Teddy Boy.

Ray was to sustain financial interest in hairdressing after his
group Mungo Jerry became famous in the 1970s (after scoring a
domestic Number One with anthemic 'In The Summertime'.[28]
Also, Ringo Starr had once had an earlier aspiration to own a
string of salons, and had expressed disappointment that, as Mike
Maxfield of Billy J. Kramer's backing Dakotas had for his wife, he
hadn't acquired such premises for his own spouse Maureen, who,
on leaving school, had seen to the tortured curls of aged viragos in
Liverpool's Ashley Dupre Continental Hair and Beauty Salon.

Ringo – who was to actually spend far less time as an onstage Beatle
than Pete Best – had made his debut as an official member in front
of an audience of 500 at a Horticultural Society dance in Birkenhead
on Saturday 18 August 1962. For this purpose, he'd shaved off his
scrappy beard and, on Brian Epstein's recommendation, had had his
dated quiff reshaped at Horne Brothers – *the* place to get trimmed
in Liverpool – though it wouldn't cascade naturally into a sheepdog
fringe for another year after road manager Neil Aspinall dropped off
the immediate result at the two-up two-down terrace house where
Ringo still lived with mother Elsie. Her surprise at her son's new
look was parried with, 'It's no different change really,' registered by
Aspinall as the first Beatle 'Ringoism'.

---

28. Glance at any Mungo Jerry photographs from that period, and the face
to which you're drawn most immediately is that of singing composer Dorset
who, with mutton-chop sideburns as distinctive as the mark of Zorro was
one of the most charismatic figures to leap from the screen of *Top of the
Pops*.

Elsie might have liked his neater, shorter style but when a photo of Ringo with it was printed in *Mersey Beat* amid its venue information, news coverage and chronicling of goings-on involving key regional personalities, it took a while for readers to become accustomed to this changeling in The Beatles. His supplanting of Best had been represented in its pages as the amicable if sudden consequence of scarcely more than a mild disagreement between the parties, but the hostility when the new line-up first played the Cavern demonstrated that the truth was known on the street. Yet, while Pete would remain a Beatle morally to some who'd heard him drum with them, most fans found it in them to maintain overall loyalty to the group *en bloc*.

The country at large knew nothing of this game of musical chairs until the publication of *The True Story of The Beatles*, the first of more Beatles biographies than anyone then could ever have comprehended. You could also read the asinine poems written and sent by subscribers to glossy monthly magazines dedicated solely to both The Beatles and, for four editions, Gerry and the Pacemakers, then tussling with each other for chart supremacy. From Merseyside slang, words such as 'fab', 'gear' and even obscurities like 'duff gen' (false information) spread across *Mirabelle*, *Jackie* and further schoolgirl comics and into the mouths of young Britons. Scouse became the most romantic dialect in the country. Such was the glamour of all things Liverpudlian that a teenage girls' comic appointed as feature writer a Pete Lennon largely on the strength of his talismanic surname.

All this had happened in part because The Beatles had emerged when Fleet Street was overrun by 'serious' news of the Profumo scandal, the nuclear test ban treaty, the Great Train Robbery, racial unrest in Alabama and, to cap it all, the West Indies beating us at cricket. Between reports of England's shame and east-west-black-white tension, The Beatles were seen in their now-iconic mid-leap publicity shot, as an antidote, the epitome of the home-grown pop that was now shaking theatres across the realm with healthy, good-humoured screams.

Most knew their individual names – especially after the Moptopped Mersey Marvels had delivered their allotted four numbers when seventh on the bill on that November's *Royal Variety Show* – the very pinnacle of British show business – where Lennon's larger-than-life bluntness raised a laugh with his *'rattle yer jewellery'* directive. A lot of groups would sell their souls for a career, however it ended, that had embraced such a night, but that was only one highlight of a year that would close with seven Beatles discs in the singles chart – including three in the more expensive EP format – and the top two positions on the LP list. Other Epstein clients – Billy J Kramer, the Fourmost and Cilla Black – had been tossed hit compositions almost as licences to print money, by Lennon and McCartney, who had bolstered a precedent for self-contained beat groups to write their own material. The bigger chain stores had started stocking Beatle wallpaper, 'Fab Four' powder compacts and 22-carat 'Beetle' [sic] bracelets. The jacket of the Beatle stage suit was 'the Liverpool Look for you to knit for the man in your life' as a cardigan, its pattern obtainable via an order form in *Fabulous* magazine.[29] Learning that the manufacturers of Epstein-sanctioned Beatle boots could barely cope with demand, an enterprising Sussex company marketed 'Ringo the new Beat Boot' which also boasted elastic gusset sides and rounded toes.

As soon as another department store started stocking guitar-shaped cakes – '*The* cake for SWINGING parties' – Woolworth's came up with Beatle hairspray, Beatle combs, and, ultimately, moptop wigs.[30] This was around the time Keith Fordyce, a shirt-and-tie interlocutor, introduced the four's rendition of 'It Won't Be Long', the opening track of their latest LP, *With The Beatles*, on an edition of ITV's *Ready Steady Go!* pop series shortly after it began in August 1963.

Recognising too that the group's renown had as much to do with its principal gimmick as musical talent, the 20-salon Andre Bernard chain, fanned out from its celebrity branch in Mayfair,[31]

---

29. Which, in June 1966, would be renamed Fabulous 208 after Radio Luxembourg's wavelength number.
30. Because 'it takes too long to cultivate the hairstyle they've made popular,' stated one manufacturer in a cinema newsreel. 'You have to settle for a wig'.
31. The Liverpool shop employed Mike McCartney, Paul's younger brother, later 'Mike McGear' of musical comedy act The Scaffold.

offered not only *Pilzkopfs* gladly and unpatronisingly, but eager advice for their upkeep: 'Brush hair into nape of neck at back and from crown at front brush down into heavy fringe, and bring small section of hair at each side in front of ear.' This was not true of common-or-garden, provincial barbers who arched eyebrows at waiting adults when someone like Andy Pegg, a 13-year-old at St Albans Grammar School for Boys, ran a gauntlet of embarrassment when 'with blushing cheeks, I screwed myself up to ask for a Beatle cut'.

To younger lads like Robb Johnson, still at a suburban primary school in west London, however, 'long hair was what happened somewhere else to other people. My granny had a copy of *With The Beatles*, sitting incongruously with her dozen or so other long-playing records, because my cousin Dan used to like to dance to them, but as far as I can remember, theirs was the only long hair – and then only on the cover of a record. Otherwise, it was something you watched on TV.

'It was all curiously distant at a time when barber's shops reeked of a superficial respectability, splashed like aftershave over the cuts of an inherent seediness. The walls were uniformly off-white cream soured by nicotine, and the barbers themselves all looked like they were clinging desperately onto their late fifties. Many favoured spivvy little moustaches, like well-tended allotments, and were somewhere between thinning and balding.

'Then there were the framed black-and-white photographs on the walls. Even I recognised most of them as being from previous decades, spending as I did most Sunday afternoons watching the black-and-white 1950s films the BBC screened where decent, clean-cut British chaps won the Second World War over and over again.'

Beyond the pale of the capital, short haircuts were still forced upon other sons of provincial Britain who might aspire in vain to try to look like someone who looks like George Harrison, the most hirsute Beatle. Some, however, succeeded. 'I worked in the fruit market for about a year,' recollected Chris Kefford, then 'doing stuff the Liverpool bands were playing' with Steve Farron and the Shantelles: 'As I started at five in the morning, I'd often clock-in straight from a gig – especially if it was something like an all-nighter in Kidderminster – still wearing stage gear, and causing comment. That hardened me up, working there, especially when I started combing my hair in the Beatle style.'

If the appearance of one such as Kefford wasn't worthy of more than badinage at the Birmingham market, it would have invited dismissal at other places of work. At an engineering firm in Birkenhead one morning, manager Bill Karpinski decided he'd had enough of being powerfully affronted by 29 Beatle-headed apprentices. He, therefore, shut down the whine and throb of the machinery long enough to rant about it and instigate weekly hair inspections, sending one youth away until he'd done something about a 'ridiculous' style that was 'not reasonable, not hygienic and not smart'.

Over half a century of cranial extremities later, Swinging Sixties cultural virgins may be puzzled about why there was so much fuss. Indeed, amused by the memory of a discussion with a classmate, Malcolm Noble thought, 'The cover of *With The Beatles* seemed to us to be the best standard of hair length against which to measure our own achievement in that direction. Now, their hair seems very short in that photo.' In agreement, Ringo Starr was to point out, 'if you look at early pictures of us with long hair, we had nothing'. Indeed, it was the same general length as Harold Godwinson's in the Bayeux Tapestry, not least because, before Brian Epstein moved his organisation to London, he'd ensured that The Beatles and others of his male clients popped into Horne Brothers more often than their detractors might have imagined. As John Lennon was to remember, 'We had to take it easy. We had to shorten our hair to leave Liverpool. We had to compromise. We had to falsify a bit, even if we didn't realise it at the time.'

Though a Tory Member of Parliament bleated that 'we must offer teenagers something better' (though he did not say what), The Beatles were trotted out to discuss their hair on programmes such as a special edition of Raidió Teilifís Éireann's *The Late Late Show*. However, any serious intent was capsized by the group's interaction with fellow Liverpudlian Ken Dodd who'd been among the famous sightseers dropping by the Cavern and other teenage clubs in the city. Many a middle-aged businessman – and they were nearly all men – lured by the financial possibilities inherent in the beat boom, had also visited, feeling like he'd gone to the Moon.

In the same state of puzzlement as his late 1970s counterpart would be when looking for a New Sex Pistols, he merged into the shadows where he might be studied, as all male newcomers were, by gaggles of girls. Assessing that he was a bit *mature*, they'd resume their chatter until four louts with Beatle haircuts sauntered onto the boards. Hitting all their instruments at once with a staccato 'Right!', they'd barge into an onslaught of pulsating bass, clanging guitars, crashing drums and ranted vocals. What would strike the adult trespasser first would be the volume that precluded conversation and the ragged dissimilarity to any other pop presentation he'd ever seen. Cliff and the Shadows indulged in a little scripted playfulness, yes, but this lot were downright uncouth. They said things like '·fuck' and burped into the microphone.

After the initial shock, he'd ponder. The next day, he'd be drawn back to another sweatbath, and push through the crowd to suggest a formal meeting. Coming on as tough, untamed Scousers, the group might pretend to be nonchalantly indifferent to his overtures but would be willing to do anything to step off the treadmill of local engagements. As Brian Epstein would have advised him, his first task was to make them altogether smoother pop 'entertainers'. They had to be compelled to wear uniform suits that were not too way-out. Playing to a fixed programme, punctuality and back projection were all-important. Stage patter must not include swearing. The oldest member might have to lose up to five years from his age when annotating his life history for the press kit.[32]

Even if nowhere as heroically proletarian as they or their followers liked to suppose,[33] members of such combos were inclined to be presented as 'bits of rough' rather than *beaux ideals* in

---

32. Common to many such lists was foreign 'favourite food' when most restaurants which served a late night meal were Indian or Chinese.

33. For all John Lennon's projection of himself as a 'working-class hero', he was no more the salt of the earth than Mick Jagger, also a product of privet-hedged suburbia. The only paid work Lennon ever did, apart from as a musician, was as a labourer at local waterworks, Scaris and Brick, for a month during a summer recess when he was an art student.

Mirabelle, *Boyfriend*, *Jackie* and further literature that balanced pop
and fashion with features on pets, badminton, ballet, ponies and
making a lampshade. Typically, the front cover of one associated
annual depicted a conventionally pretty girl dancing in a mid-calf
dress with a short-haired boy in a light blue sweater, her eyes not
focussed on him.

Like Vikings of old, the contract-waving host sought plunder
elsewhere, commencing with Manchester where, again, EMI
hooked the biggest fish in the Hollies and a radical departure from
formula in Freddie and the Dreamers, fronted by a kind of Norman
Wisdom of pop. Later, the conurbation would relinquish Wayne
Fontana and the Mindbenders, Herman's Hermits and non-starters
like the Toggery Five whose recording career ended soon after it
started with a 'death disc', 'I'm Gonna Jump'. On the outermost
reaches of Greater Manchester, the Warriors in Accrington went
the same way with the Beatle-like 'You Came Along'. In Stockport,
the Stowaways were all set to be as big as the Hollies just as the issue
of 1964's *Sounds of a Swinging City*, an in-concert LP of local groups,
was cancelled because the Manchester scene had 'finished'. With
the promptness of vultures, London talent scouts began pouncing
arbitrarily on other regions.

A law of diminishing returns seemed to apply as each successive
sphere of operation yielded fewer and fewer rough diamonds to be
processed for the charts. Knocking 'em dead in Newcastle were the
Animals and the Gamblers, both of whom would make money for
somebody: the former breathing down the necks of The Beatles and
The Rolling Stones by 1965, and the latter replacing the Tornados
as Billy Fury's backing group.[34] Yet Cheshire's Lancastrians(!) fizzled
out after a fortnight in the Top Fifty with the twist-in-the-tale
number, 'We'll Sing in The Sunshine', and Bolton's boss group,
The Statesmen, were bypassed altogether.

What happened in Sheffield summarises the frenzied search for
another Liverpool. In January 1964, a concert starring the Hollies

34. A solo performer in an age of groups, Fury was still scoring Top Twenty
entries until late 1965, and was the subject of a 1964 tabloid cartoon about
the odds on his horse Anselmo winning the Epsom Derby (he came fourth).

plus a handful of city acts, who'd hoped that *claques* of supporters might suggest that, although Graham Nash *et al* had scored a hat-trick of hits by then, Sheffield groups had everything it took to do the same. Those London A&R people persuaded to attend went away disappointed: they wanted to sign the next Beatles, but also wished to keep their jobs. The only local act that did make it around that time were Dave Berry and the Cruisers who'd got their break when seen by freelance producer Mickie Most at a Doncaster Baths booking with Freddie and the Dreamers.

Then the focus would shift to the Midlands which, as the widening catchment area of *Midland Beat*[35] indicated, sprawled into East Anglia, mid-Wales and as far south as Beaconsfield. The Four Aces - nothing to do with the US ensemble of the same name - were 'Hereford's Beatles', while the likes of the Farinas and the Broodly Hoo were top attractions in Leicester. The Fourbeats were going strong in Oxford with a debut EP on Alpha Records. Winners of a 'Midland Search For Tomorrow's Stars', Ken Jackson and his Strangers hailed from olde worlde Henley-in-Arden, while 'Trentside Beat' would be represented by such as Tony D and the Shakeouts, Jet Wayne and his Cavaliers, and The Jaybirds whose high-speed guitarist Alvin Dean (later Alvin *Lee*) was 'considered by many the best in the Midlands'.

Inevitably, there came to be what might have been hyped up as a convincing sign that the 'power' might be returning more conveniently to the capital. A challenger from another EMI label - Columbia - seemed to have brought The Beatles to their knees. The Dave Clark Five had gone for the jugular in January 1964 when their sixth single, 'Glad All Over', unseated The Beatles from top spot after seven uninterrupted weeks at Number One. Another splendid racket, 'Bits and Pieces', splintered the charts a few weeks later, and even the enigmatically titled *The Dave Clark Five* EP slipped in. Yet, in Britain anyway, spring 1964 was to be the Dave Clark Five moment, never to quite return as The Beatles shut them down as surely as they had earlier pretenders like Gerry and the Pacemakers and The Searchers.

---

35. *Midland Beat* was a periodical modelled on *Mersey Beat* - as, to a lesser extent, was the Torquay-based *South-West Scene*.

That hairstyles weren't a principal part of the image for groups like the Five, the Searchers, the Fourmost, Freddie and the Dreamers, the Bachelors and the Hollies was reassuring for Dreamer Mike Quinn and Hollies' drummer Bobby Elliott, both going bald far too young.[36]

Oliver Gray regarded Bobby's guitarist colleague (and brother-in-law) Tony Hicks as 'my style guru. He adopted what to this day I consider to be the hairstyle ideal by changing to a mop top which genuinely looked like a mop, i.e. it tumbled floppily from the apex of his crown to lie in a symmetrical sugar bowl style which needed no cosmetics or attention to keep it in perfect shape. I could almost surmise that he didn't even comb it, such was its casually impeccable state at the end of energetic live performances.

'While Tony's hair (as displayed on the cover of *Stay With The Hollies*, their first LP) had been coiffed into an exquisitely Brylcreem-sculpted Eddie Cochran quiff, too, Graham Nash, who had a virtually identical style and an even more goofy grin, merely looked a twat. For me it was crucial to be a Tony Hicks and not a Graham Nash. Whatever the elusive magic was, I had to have it.

'This desirable effect can be viewed to best effect on the sleeve of the 1966 album *For Certain Because* – but why am I using the past tense? Tony still has the same sublime head of hair (plus, no doubt, an ageing portrait in the attic). When The Hollies are next billed to play near you, have a closer look at the fly posters. There, under the spotlight, stage right, clutching the cherry-red guitar, you'll see the mildly flattened hamster that is the classic "Tony Hicks".

'I worked hard on my Tony Hicks and naively believed that I

---

36. Tragic rather than merely unlucky was guitarist Mike Millward of the Fourmost, whose style (like that of Freddie and his Dreamers) was centred on comedy, but there'd be offstage tears when Mike was diagnosed with cancer, alleviated with radium treatment during which it was discovered he also had leukaemia. With the show-must-go-on stubbornness, he wouldn't let the lads down. If a scalp-revealing tuft of hair fell out the moment a compère spoke their name, he'd stick it back on with Sellotape. When unable to keep such a level-headed grip on himself, he asked bass player Billy Hatton if he ought to throw in the towel. 'It was the hardest yes I've ever had to say,' remembered Hatton. In a Cheshire hospital, nothing more could be done for Mike, and he died peacefully on 7 March 1966.

approximately attained it; photos from this Sixth Form era reveal, however, that I was far, far away. The problem was the lack of texture and substance and a horrifying propensity for "butterflies" – those irritating little wispy, curly bits – spoiling the overall picture.'

Did anyone want to look like the Rustiks? They were to south Devon what the Hollies were to Manchester. After winning a *Battle of the Bands* contest sponsored by a regional TV station, the Rustiks were taken on by none other than Brian Epstein. Nonetheless, they made perhaps too much of their defiant short-back-and-sides, their cleanliness and their implied decency – so different from certain other outfits they could mention – when interviewed for *South-West Scene* and during their only appearance on *Ready Steady Go!*, which, after the pruning of unhip distractions like Keith Fordyce and periodic send-ups of current hits by entertainers of the same age, was to be lauded as the most spirited pop programme of the 1960s just as *Oh Boy!* had been to the previous decade.[37] This was particularly so after it adopted a policy of all-live performances from April 1965 beginning with the Artwoods' 'Sweet Mary', a revival of a Leadbelly item from just after the war.

Watching non-Rustik outfits on *Ready Steady Go!*, schoolgirls would, with lacquer, Sellotape and nail-clippers, torment naturally wavy, cowlicked or curly hair into a straight, all-round Beatle-esque fringe in order to – so 'A Psychiatrist' had it – 'identify with these characters as either other girls or as sexual neuters'.[38] After 'From Me To You' became The Beatles' Top Ten debut in Australia in 1963, a prim headmistress of a girls school in Sydney barred not only the wearing of such a style but also the carrying of Beatles pictures in satchels, and membership of their fan club.[39]

37. Despite the impression newcomers were to get from Channel Four's edited reruns of *Ready Steady Go!* in the 1980s.

38. The strategies of their brothers to achieve the effect were advisedly covert. 'I had a kink in my otherwise straight hair,' records Kevin Delaney, whom I've known since primary school, 'so to get it straight, I would wet it before going to bed, and stick it to my neck with Sellotape.'

39. She was to frown too upon the mini-skirt, popularised by the late Mary Quant, *circa* 1964, initially as an outrage to public decency, prompting inspections at innumerable schools, some compelling girls to kneel down in

Throughout the Commonwealth too, all-boys schools were
becoming especially minatory about short hair as a mark of sobriety
and masculinity. As early as mid-1962, 13-year-old John Farley, later
conductor of the incomparable Portsmouth Sinfonia, 'decided to
end my visits to the gentlemen's hairdresser in Mitcham – thus
saving my parents one shilling and six pence per month. Throughout
the school holidays, my hair continued to grow and, by September,
it had reached a length never previously achieved. It looked good
and by start of the autumn term at my new school, Sutton East, a
co-ed for boys and girls, I arrived with hair reaching beyond my
collar and eyebrows. I felt relaxed and confident. The headmaster,
Mr Sykes, seemed rather old-fashioned and a little unaware that
the times were a-changing. He greeted me with a rather menacing
smile and took me aside and whispered in my ear, words which in
more grammatical parlance amounted to, "get your hair cut!" I was
gobsmacked, the older generation had not yet fully taken on board
the new order and in an instant my future hopes for a new world
were shattered.'

In a letter to *The Guardian* on 2 November 2022, a Dr Harry
Harmer of Shrewsbury mentioned that his headmaster considered
the purpose of his job – which included banning hair other than
short-back-and-sides – was to 'turn working-class boys into middle-
class men'. Moreover, at the first assembly after the half term break
in autumn 1963, the head of a Ramsgate grammar of 700 boys
announced that, from now on, no male with a fringe would be
allowed to enter the premises.

Widespread too was a correlated kind of malevolent neutrality
towards intellectually stultifying pop groups. This extended as far
as school jazz clubs that dared to devote one meeting a term to, say,
'Blues- and Jazz-Influenced Pop Singers', and Dartford Grammar
permitting sixth former *Mike* Jagger to give a talk to the historical
society during the autumn term of 1960, complete with audio-visual
aids and using Bo Diddley as a case study, about an overwhelming

---

(cont.) order for teachers to check that a given hemline touched the floor – or
at least was no higher than a negligible if regulated length above the centre of
the knees. If it was, you could be sent home to change into a longer garment.

passion that placed him in the thick of every common room controversy to do with the music of black North America. He also entered into an occasional debate on the letters page of *Record Mirror*, ready at any moment with a corrective tirade against other correspondents. Neither did he hesitate to attack the paper's very journalists. He was certainly more knowledgeable about the subject than most of them.

Even at my own Farnborough Grammar School (FGS), there was a Blues Club that folded when deputy headmaster 'Trunky' Cotgreave realised that, beyond a sociological study of aspects of black America, members actually enjoyed listening to its 'screaming idiotic words and savage music', as a US segregationalist handbill once put it.

State educated from start to finish, Yardbirds bass player Paul Samwell-Smith was to bring to mind 'a lot of opposition at Hampton Grammar. Our music master was quite good, but the head put a stop to it straightaway – because he thought that anyone in rock 'n' roll and R&B must be involved in sex and drugs'.

One of the strangest bookings of The Beatles' career took place in April 1963 at Stowe public school[40] in Buckinghamshire where 'Twist and Shout' *et al* precipitated only polite clapping from the seated pupils and their with-it headmaster. During high tea, it was pointed out to the group that school rules were so non-interventionist that you didn't risk expulsion for cultivating a fringe halfway to your eyebrows. Almost everywhere else you did, although a daily newspaper was to report that sixth-former Paul Cox who, honouring a bet, arrived at his East Sheen secondary school one May morning in 1964 with a Yul Brynner all-off, and was sent away instantly on the grounds that it was just as attention-seeking.

If condemned to endure the rigours of boarding school, as Tim Fagan was from the age of 13, even thwarted attempts at choices such as this weren't possible. Tim's account of life at his school is worth quoting at length:

'Hormones were kicking in – and The Beatles were ubiquitous. Passing senior study doors or running errands (as a 'fag'), the tracks

---

40. Whose alumni included billionaire tycoon Sir Richard Branson.

of their first LP were blaring out everywhere. All the talk outside of lessons was of The Beatles, their music and their images. Likewise, in the autumn of 1963, *With The Beatles* was on everyone's turntable and the cover of that album inspired many of us to brush our hair forward and shape an embryo fringe. We also tried – in an extremely amateurish way – to imitate a Liverpool accent when not in earshot of those in authority.

'This went unchecked for five or six weeks at a time until just before half term and the holidays when the school barber would arrive. He would set up in one of the dormitories as part of a sort of assembly line. Lessons went on as usual until someone with a shorn and sheepish look would enter the classroom and request the next five.

'Up at the appointed place, there was a line of chairs along the wall for those waiting. The atmosphere was hushed and glum. The barber was an unenlightened and muscular man who had obviously learned his trade in one of the armed forces.

'Seating you on a tall stool from the chemistry lab, he went to work. Electric clippers were the main tool used around the back and sides of the head, followed by some savage scissoring on top. The scissors were fairly blunt. There was no mirror to see the effect – nor was it any use to try to give instructions or state preferences. The procedure was over very quickly – because he had several hundred boys to do in around a day and a half. This part of the procedure was terminated with singeing at the back, using a taper. The smell was very unpleasant.

'So from the hands of the barber, it was next door to the washroom, which had possibly 20 basins, and into the hands of Matron and her assistant. A couple of basins had been set up for mass hair washing. Matron was a pleasant woman, but would brook no nonsense. She'd do the business using a thick, gloopy, piss-yellow substance that smelled of disinfectant and came in a one-gallon glass demijohn. There was no time to change the water between each boy – so Matron would push your head into some greyish cold water with a film of greasy suds floating on top; a quick dunk then application of the gunk, a massage of the scalp, another dunk and then you were passed to Miss B, Matron's assistant.

'Miss B was a young and rather plain girl with dull blonde hair – but we were all in love with her as she was the only youngish female in the whole place. To be rinsed by Miss B was wonderful, but over too quickly – just as I began to feel "stirrings" in my trousers. After this was a crestfallen return to class. No one laughed. We were truly shorn and the growing of hair would have to begin all over again.'

Some didn't bother. Before he could continue spending the Christmas of 1963 with his mother and stepfather – a Canadian army officer – at the latter's base in the Rhineland, 18-year-old Eric Clapton, who'd arrived with hair that obscured the top of his ears, was compelled to submit to an immediate crew cut from its barber so as not to cause affront when he and the family entered the mess. The sight in the mirror of the subsequent caricature of his former self brought forth tears, but Eric brazened it out on returning to England and his lead guitar duties with a group he had just joined, The Yardbirds. He found himself an up-to-the-minute fashion frontrunner of sorts for its inadvertent resemblance to the cut favoured by what were known, no longer as Scooter Boys but as 'Mods'.

In the wake of 'Glad All Over' and the wrong-headed if jubilant Fleet Street field day – with HAS THE FIVE JIVE CRUSHED THE BEATLE BEAT? a typical headline – a broadsheet cartoon had a leading politician berating a member of his staff for his 'old-fashioned' Beatle hairdo. Furthermore, even as their luck held while other stars and fashions came and usually went, John, Paul, George and Ringo still expected it to run out too. 'It's been fun but it won't last long,' avowed Lennon. 'Anyway, I'd hate to be an old Beatle.'

'A couple of Number Ones and then out eighteen months later won't make you rich,' confirmed Ringo. 'You'll be back on the buses.'

Only the most bedazzled fans thought that, contrary to definition, any pop group of choice was immortal. However, earmarked for a cameo appearance in *Coronation Street* (precluded by their tight work schedule), The Beatles were shaping up to be more than just another act as here-today-gone-tomorrow as any other. Unable to step down from a carousel that was revolving too fast, they'd been screened waving a cheery goodbye on ventriloquist dummy Lenny the Lion's show on BBC TV's *Children's Hour*. Then there was a prime time evening sketch involving the donning of boaters and a sing-along of 1912's 'On Moonlight Bay' with nutty boys Morecambe and Wise, and, like many a British showbiz evergreen, they appeared on ITV's *Blackpool Night Out*, taking part in comedy spoofs and, alongside hosts Mike and Bernie Winters, crooning 'I Do Like To Be Beside The Seaside'.

Thus the weathervane of adult toleration, if not approval, had lurched as far as ever it would in the direction of John, Paul, George and Ringo, the supposed 'Poor Honest Northern Lads' who'd 'Made It' to ITV's *Sunday Night at the London Palladium* with its otherwise endless centuries of stand-up comics, crooners, 'Beat The Clock' interludes and the Tiller Girls dance troupe. However, when parents had chuckled along with children at John's chirpy 'ad lib' to the royal balcony weeks later, 'it meant that they couldn't be any good' to teenagers like David Cook. Cook, later 1970s pop star David Essex, was then a *habitué* of the Flamingo, which, with the up-and-coming Georgie Fame and the Blue Flames one of its resident groups, had started advertising itself as 'the Swinging Club of Swinging London'.

CHAPTER NINE

'Would you let your sister go with a Rolling Stone?'

More to David Cook's taste were The Rolling Stones, the first group to be featured on the new chart-based BBC pop series, *Top of the Pops*, when it got underway in a Manchester studio at 6.35 pm on New Year's Day 1964. The Stones gave viewers 'I Wanna Be Your Man', a stabilising second single that, stopping just short of the Top Ten, cut like a double axe, having been composed by John Lennon and Paul McCartney as the *With The Beatles* vocal showcase for Ringo – now of a quartet who'd 'matured' too quickly and might be soft-shoe shuffling before you could blink.

When the Stones were still smouldering into form back in 1962, their repertoire fed not on mainstream pop but nods towards the badlands of rock 'n' roll via Fats Domino, Chuck Berry and Bo Diddley – and erudite R&B items from North America. Often desirable for their very obscurity, many had been spun time and time again on the turntable at Sidcup College of Art's Music Society gatherings – initially, no more than record playing sessions – after lectures on Fridays.

The group's overall and simple aim was, maintained Keith Richards, 'to turn people onto the blues. If we could turn them onto Muddy Waters, Jimmy Reed, Howlin' Wolf and John Lee Hooker, then our job was done'. As such, they worked in and supported metropolitan clubs as earnestly devoted to blues as other cliques were to yachting, numismatics, animal welfare and Freemasonry. Most patrons were students, weekend dropouts or middle-class bohemians who might have 'dressed down' – frayed jeans, Jesus sandals, long jumper, carefully tousled hair and CND badge – for the occasion while warming up the Dansette might be

Jimmy Reed At Carnegie Hall, Muddy Waters At Newport or Howlin'
Wolf's *Moanin' In The Moonlight*.

Yet the Stones and other young Britons, who'd once traded in
R&B and almost nothing else, were behaving dangerously like pop
performers, however much *aficionados* might refute the suggestion.
There was far less knotted-brow 'appreciation' as an old blues
trainspotter's view was now blocked by girls in paroxysms of ecstasy
over frail Keith Relf of the Yardbirds; youngest Kink Dave Davies
with his centre parting and thigh-high cavalier boots; and serpentine
Dave Berry, who, although south Yorkshire's most illustrious young
adult, was asked to leave a Chesterfield lounge bar because he and
his retinue 'looked like beatniks'.

'Brian Jones wanted to be a pop star the minute he saw The Beatles,'
sneered Keith Richards. There'd been face-to-face communication
between The Beatles and the Stones when, on 21 April 1963, the Fab
Four arrived at Richmond's Crawdaddy Club, where the Stones had
been to all intents and purposes the resident attraction since January.
Though Lennon, McCartney, Harrison and Starr drew a small cluster
of tongue-tied fans, they were not yet so well known around London's
southernmost extremities that they couldn't be steered safely through
the crowded Crawdaddy to the side of the stage.

Their more revered peers took a shine to the Stones. Lennon's
dockside mouth-organ on The Beatles' first three smashes had had
hardly a trace of Howlin' Wolf, but he loved all roots and branches
of blues, and was keen to pick up tips from Brian, who regarded
himself then as the group's leader on how to improve what he
dismissed as his 'blowing and sucking'. The cordiality between the
two outfits continued with the Stones receiving complimentary
tickets and 'access all areas' passes for *Swinging Sound '63*, an *all-
styles-served-here* extravaganza, headlined by The Beatles, at London's
Royal Albert Hall the following Thursday. In the Kensington
twilight afterwards, Jones had liked the taste of a morsel of ersatz
Beatlemania when, because of his backcombed moptop, some girls
mistook him for George Harrison and asked for his autograph.

The Stones first had reason to be grateful to The Beatles for the
endorsement that had led to a Decca recording deal as well as the

gift of 'I Wanna Be Your Man' as a follow-up to their 'Come On' disc debut (which had struggled to the edge of the Top Twenty), even if it was bestowed with the qualification from John that, 'We weren't going to give them anything great, were we?' Had they done so, Brian Epstein may have felt that they were giving too much of a leg up to potentially dangerous competitors. This was justifiable on the evidence of the *NME* readers' popularity poll for 1963, which placed the Stones behind the Springfields, the Shadows, Gerry and the Pacemakers, the Searchers and The Beatles, but ahead of Freddie and the Dreamers, the Hollies and Decca's flagship beat group, Brian Poole and the Tremeloes.

Despite finding the group and Andrew Loog Oldham, one of their two managers, personally objectionable, Dick Rowe, still the butt of *bon mots* in music business offices across London as 'The Man Who Turned Down The Beatles', had made it a point of honour to get The Rolling Stones into the Top Ten before this beat bubble burst and 'decent' music reigned once more.

Only the previous autumn, a Greater London parish institute used more frequently for amateur dramatics and table tennis had been empty for the entire four hours booked for a performance by the Stones and a stand-in drummer, who'd decided to carry on regardless. Audiences at other nascent bookings were so small that bass guitarist and founder member Dick Taylor, with a scholarship at the Central School of Art beckoning, balked when the others suggested 'going professional'.

They were then a sextet, containing pianist Ian Stewart, as ostensibly ultra-masculine as Mick Jagger and Brian Jones weren't. A sweaty aptitude for athletics had wrought in Ian a sturdy rather than slim physique. He also had a rugged, lantern-jawed face on which craggy eyebrows jutted from a forehead topped by a slicked-back smarm, all counter to the ordained outward requirements of a mid-1960s pop icon. 'He looked a bit like my dad,' smiled Taylor, 'who was a boxer. Ian was a big bloke with a big face.' To Jim McCarty, 'Ian always reminded me of "Hoss Cartwright" in *Bonanza*.'

A comparison to the obese and dim-witted character in the 1960s cowboy series is unkind, but 'my family came to recognise that how you appeared was part of a musician's job,' corroborated

Chris Kefford. So it would be that the Stones would be almost as guilty as The Beatles, as demonstrated by their dismissal of Pete Best, of pragmatic heartlessness. Both Oldham and co-manager Eric Easton – thin on top, nearing his forties and a self-confessed 'square' – had been in complete agreement, and the other Stones had acquiesced that some way would have to be found to tell Ian he couldn't be a visible member of the unit any more.

So Ian looked on as Jagger, Jones, Richards and Watts together with Bill Wyman, Dick Taylor's replacement, all squeezed into a uniform of shiny waistcoat, white shirt, dark tie and black trousers for a photo shoot with Brian Poole and the Tremeloes, to indicate, shrugged Poole, 'that they were joining the Decca "family", I suppose'. The Tremeloes and the apparently lower-ranking Stones arranged themselves standing in a half-circle behind the two Brians in pride of place on stools – with Poole seeming to impart gesticulating advice to Jones.

While he'd always feel entitled to refer to the Stones as 'us' rather than 'them', Stewart's widow was to insist that, 'Whatever Ian or anyone else said, he *did* care about being relegated. The bottom line for Andrew was that his face didn't fit. Andrew loved the pretty, thin, long-haired boys. Ian felt bitter about the savage way he was thrust aside.'

An understandable dark night of the ego passed, and, after he'd come to terms with this banishment – and his shaving mirror telling him why – Ian remained in the hierarchy, somewhere between the humblest equipment humper and the five principals, functioning as a general factotum whose duties included checking security, prising unwanted company from dressing rooms, buttonholing promoters, signing chits and bills, and, like an army batman, attending to the others' food, sleep and general health requirements. This was often before the group had played a note. When they did, the fun began. Moreover, if unseen, he remained an official Stone musically, attending when required to keyboards in the studio. 'He was the glue that held all the bits together,' was to be Keith's epitaph following Ian's death in 1985.

Another of Easton and Oldham's adjustments was the truncated surname foisted on Keith. It was to be 'Richard' now, giving him an implied affiliation with Cliff. That a Birmingham combo called the Tempests also embraced a guitarist named Keith Richards, however, had not been a consideration when the change was imposed.[41]

Disconcerting for Easton had been the muttered fulminations between the Stones and the Swinging Blue Jeans just prior to that first *Top of the Pops*, which almost culminated in fisticuffs before the combatants were left glowering at each other from opposite ends of a BBC canteen. The following month had caused ITV's *Arthur Haynes Show* to all but cancel the Stones' slot on the programme for 'unprofessional conduct' after they'd rolled up two hours late for the final run-through.

As far back as June 1963, the group had sparked off viewers' complaints for their maiden appearance on television, miming to 'Come On' towards the start of *Lucky Stars Summer Spin*, a Sunday evening supplement to *Thank Your Lucky Stars*. This was despite a concession to how a TV producer in those naïve times expected pop entertainers to look, i.e. wearing another costume (the Decca shirts, ties and trousers plus check coats with velvet collars) and directing Beatle-esque boyish grins at the cumbersome TV cameras. To Easton's further dismay, the Stones dropped 'Come On' from their stage set, even when specifically requested. Wantonly pleasing yourself by not giving the mob what could be described, with a bit of a stretch, as your 'smash hit' could kindle catcalls and more extreme reaction from riff-raff whose displeasure could be most painfully expressed by showering pre-decimalisation pennies stagewards until the lacerated visitors evacuated the boards.

Oldham, nonetheless, was OK about the disappearance of the *Lucky Stars* jackets and the waistcoats foisted on them for the photo session with Brian Poole after these acquired too many indelible stains born of sweat and spillage. Though a Wrexham headmistress was to denounce parents who permitted their sons to wear corduroy trousers 'like the ones worn by The Rolling Stones', the group's scorn of sartorial uniformity paralleled that of the fated US movie star Frances Farmer, who flew in the face of 1940s Hollywood's

41. Keith Richards himself was to ratify the official restoration of the 's' via a record company memo in the mid-1970s – though it had long been printed on composing credits and elsewhere on record packagings.

rulings about glamour by arriving garbed in slacks and sweater at premières where cameras clicked like typewriters. Just as she caused Paramount's alarmed publicity department to limit the damage by emphasising the 'eccentric habits of the star who will not "go Hollywood"', so the Stones would be classified swiftly by a bemused *New Musical Express* as 'the group who prefer casual wear to stage suits and who sometimes don't bother to change before going onstage' – while *Melody Maker* was to note, 'they hardly bother examining themselves before they wander out to the stage'.

Whatever the polarisations of visuals and sounds – and with the altercation between the Stones and the Swinging Blue Jeans thrust aside – beat groups of fluctuating equality were civil enough to each other when paths crossed in a wayside café, in a pub over the road from the venue or even in the recording studio, to the extent that a couple of Hollies helped out on the session for 'Not Fade Away', The Rolling Stones' Top Ten debut. So too did US singer Gene Pitney, in a suit and with his hair slicked back across his scalp like Eric Easton, on their first LP.

While the latter was to be one of the biggest 33 rpm sellers of 1964, such collections were mere market ballast in an era when singles mattered most, although a handful of EPs were still seeping into the *singles* Top Thirty throughout the early spring of 1963. The Stones joined this elite, and theirs was still hovering 'twixt twelve and twenty when, for a round-Britain package tour titled *All Stars '64*, the running order was subject to change after John Leyton, Mike Sarne, Billie Davis and Mike Berry – all with a backlog of pre-1963 disc triumphs – were each upstaged by the Stones and, to a smaller degree, the Swinging Blue Jeans now that the swing towards beat groups was complete.

Because of the meritocratic nature of a profession based on chart performances, the Stones' first run of post-'Come On' engagements had included support spots to such as the Hollies, then on the wings of their second hit. Yet the yo-yo progression of 'Come On' to the edge of the Top Twenty, fulfilling *Record Mirror*'s estimation that it 'should make the charts in a small way', allowed them to lord it over a diversity of other acts – though a handful gave cause for nervous backwards glances. Preceding the Stones at Morecambe's Floral Hall, Dave Berry and the Cruisers, for instance, had breached the lower reaches of the Top Fifty for the first time in the same September week with a cover of Chuck Berry's 'Memphis Tennessee'.

On a bill somewhere else, Wayne Fontana and the Mindbenders also leaned heavily on R&B, and earned the Stones' approbation. Other couplings weren't so appropriate at a time when modern pop was still seen as an offshoot of light entertainment. 'There weren't any subdivisions then,' said Dave Berry. 'There would have been nothing unusual for the Stones to have been on the same bill as a crooner, an instrumental group or a singing postman. No one thought any of the new groups would last as there was no precedent. No one could guess what was in store.'

Yet Bill Wyman, drifting into an uneasy doze with the road roaring in his ears, may have dreamt of a limousine gliding him and the fellows he wasn't yet sure he liked to a sold-out theatre where their name was in lights. He'd wake with a start as the van bumped off an early evening high street onto the gravel next to some municipal hall. From the vehicle, he and an unexpectedly large number of human shapes would emerge, numb from bearing amplifiers and drums on their laps. 'Don't go in empty-handed!' a voice shouts, causing someone to haul further gear from the overloaded van before shuffling towards the building's front steps. A janitor answers their banging, but does not help lug the equipment into a chilly and darkened venue that bears all the signs of having known better days: dust on the stage's heavy drape curtains, never unfurled these days; padded wallpaper peeling off here and there; and the front-of-house staff's depressed forbearance.

Frequently as insalubrious were the new beat clubs now springing up in every major town in Britain. Everywhere it seemed, the insides were being ripped from old factory premises, cellars cleared and bars extended to make venues for outfits with guitars and long hair, no matter how dreadful they sounded. More and more pubs began offering beat group evenings and rehearsal facilities in function rooms that assumed a separate life from the main building. Local outfits also played for church youth organisations that had sometimes embraced regular beat sessions. I went to one such function in Farnham where the music was interrupted by a 'spontaneous' on-mike dialogue between the swingin' vicar – who had little idea how teenagers really talked – and the combo's born-again drummer. They chatted about sin. His Reverence appeared to be against it.

This took place close to the heartland of a country where even an Elvis Presley quiff had yet to become a yardstick of masculinity in 1964. Thirty-five miles west of Farnham, the *Andover Advertiser* had, in September 1963, splashed its front page with '"Twist" Club Dismayed Over Fiesta Ban'. Scandalised readers learnt that the Fiesta hall's director Mr RF Knight was angry about damage to its pinewood floor by the stiletto heels of girls who'd coughed up the five shilling (25p) membership fee of the so-called Teen and Twenty Disc Club that had convened every Tuesday for several weeks. The *Advertiser* quoted Mr Knight's concern 'that the club was getting out of hand now that over 300 young people attend. The groups, some of which sing what I consider to be dubious lyrics, are often recruited from the larger towns'.

Further west, the city of Gloucester's authorities forbade the Sapphires, an Evesham-based pop group, from ever defiling its Guildhall again because lead vocalist Rodney Dawes' trousers were deemed 'crude' round the thighs and crotch. Neither Rodney nor his repressors could have prophesied that the West Midlands, the region north of Gloucester, would be where the brain-damaging practice of head banging was to be born. It would be no accident either that the annual festival at Castle Donington in Leicestershire was to be the most important date in the heavy metal year – and that *Ozzfest*, its US equivalent, was to be co-founded by Ozzy Osbourne, vocalist with Black Sabbath, who were traceable to The Rest, a soberly attired Birmingham four-piece, pictured in *Midland Beat*.

Likewise, the Black Country cradled half of Led Zeppelin, who picked up the pieces when The Yardbirds fragmented in 1968. Yet, three years before, Led Zeppelin's singer, Robert Plant, just seventeen, was still subject to his parents' incessant attempts to nip in the bud anything untoward in one whose tight-trousered blatancies and avalanche of blond tresses in an undreamt tomorrow were to make him the post-Woodstock toast of the groupies.

*

Robert had grown up in Hayley Green, a well-to-do suburb of Kidderminster, an old market town that tended to exhibit a certain insular superiority towards Birmingham, its big city neighbour. Kidderminster's principal trade was reflected in the presence of a Department of Carpet Technology at its local college of further education where Plant started a business studies course upon leaving Stourbridge's King Edward VI Grammar School for Boys.

Although he was socialising with bohemians from the town's art school, there was little as yet to indicate vocational possibilities for him other than in secure desk-bound jobs. Any attempts to discuss a different future with his mum and dad proved pointless. Variations on the same theme would just come up over and over again, and end with them not only bringing up how impractical they considered his aspirations were, but questioning whether he had any that could be taken seriously.

The similarly placed Rob Boughton, years before commencing a long career in pop, had a father who 'every day would say to me, "It's time you chose your career, son. What do you want to do in life?" Well, I knew what I wanted to do but also that it would not go down well. One day just to appease him, I answered, "I wouldn't mind selling houses." He then pulled a favour with a relative, who called me to tell me to be at an office in central London at 2 pm for an interview with a Mr Haddock, adding "Get your hair cut!" Dejectedly, I shuffled off to the local barber who took great delight in shearing off my blond locks. At the interview, Mr Haddock said I could start the following week at a £7 a week salary! Before I left he said, "Oh by the way, we're a bit square round here. Can you get your hair cut please?"[42]

---

42. Rob Boughton would have empathised with Philip Norman, who, as a cub reporter on a Cambridgeshire newspaper, recalled a generally amiable chief journalist's habit of 'pointing a finger at me and, like a joke sergeant major, barking "Haircut!", although both my forehead and collar were clearly visible. Incidentally, my mother – a beautician with the Elizabeth Arden company – went on so incessantly about my sideburns – which weren't particularly long – that I finally agreed to let her remove them with the hot wax she used on her clients' legs and upper lips. It was horribly painful and when they eventually grew back it was in weird little clumps.'

Mr and Mrs Plant and most other adult parishioners of Hayley Green would have been at one with Mr Haddock about what amounted to a symbolic castration for the sake of propriety. Furthermore, as well as the ever-increasing effort needed to force Robert to yield to each haircut, there was his rejection of dictates about what was and wasn't 'nice' music – and that subsection of R&B, later to become better known as 'soul', of which he had become fond, was definitely not 'nice'. Indeed, Robert was to reconjure how his father – also a Robert – had 'cut the plug off my record player, a little Dansette, after they heard "I Like It Like That" by The Miracles 17 times in one hour'.

Yet when Robert started performing regularly at Stourbridge's Seven Stars Blues Club whose patrons embraced both 'youths' and, half a class up, 'young people' from families like his own, Mr Plant unbent sufficiently to drive his son to the weekly session, and collect him afterwards.

In 1964 too, the UK Top Fifty would accommodate a single each by Howlin' Wolf and John Lee Hooker, justifying the latter's remark, 'the best time ever for the blues was in England in the 1960s'. In November, the risk that The Rolling Stones were to take in putting out a slow blues, Wolf's 'Little Red Rooster', as an A-side was confirmed when it was the cause of one of the most major discrepancies ever between the two principal national music journal charts. It entered at Number 15 in *Melody Maker* and went directly to the top in the *New Musical Express*. Attempting to get a handle on it, Joe Boyd, an expatriate New Yorker, contended, 'Americans, if they sang blues, were obsessed with sounding like black men, whereas Mick Jagger showed them how to sing blues and be unashamed of being white and being a kind of tarty little English schoolboy. There wasn't the same awkwardness. It was a much more relaxed position towards shopping in different cultures among the English.'

'Little Red Rooster' had ensconced itself uneasily in a Top Twenty inhabited by the likes of Gene Pitney, Val Doonican, Jim Reeves and The Helmut Zacharias Orchestra – as well as the far less anodyne Kinks, Wayne Fontana and the Mindbenders, and The Pretty Things. The latter groups were all, via exposure on Radio

Luxembourg, not to mention the newer pestilence of offshore pirate stations, making it ever harder for the BBC to give the people the music they *ought* to be enjoying.

The music I ought *not* to be enjoying had become clear during The Beatles' performance on *Sunday Night at the London Palladium* when my trance was broken by the awareness of two pairs of hostile eyes studying me. 'This isn't good music, Alan,' finger-wagged Dad from his fireside armchair. 'You mustn't get too interested in it.'

On an edition of the show just over a year later, like Winston Smith yelling abuse at Goldstein in *1984*, I joined in the sniggers when Max Bygraves, knowing the prejudices of his core audience, poked fun at The Rolling Stones with the aid of an overhead projector and a blow-up of Jagger with a superimposed Yul Brynner. Passively expressed accord in the living room for the sake of domestic harmony became private admiration in the bedroom. This wasn't the only time that I endorsed things I either cared little or nothing about or found repugnant, even supposing aloud that my father was right in remarking that the Stones were imbeciles when the family was transfixed by their miming of 'You Better Move On' on *The Arthur Haynes Show*.

Bygraves had been making hay from the Stones' standing as the anti-Beatles, an appalling antidote to an act that was now accepted as a component of the British scheme of things like Promenade Concerts, *Coronation Street* and Vera Lynn. 'The Stones' scene was strictly "teenage rebels",' noted Ringo Starr, 'but we went from four-year-old kids to ninety-year-old grandmothers.'

The Stones, however, wouldn't be above a jingle for Rice Krispies breakfast cereal: raising their thumbs in photographed endorsement of Vox amplifiers in a trade magazine, or doing their bit in a charity ten-pin bowling match. Yet it was almost foreseeable that, as had been the case with Elvis Presley following on from Johnnie Ray, there had to be an act that would go further than The Beatles in terms of outrage – and the principal focus in this case was the group's hair.

That on the heads of the Stones had been causing comment as early as the rain-swept autumn of 1963 when they had been on their first round-Britain package tour, low on the bill to the all-American

Everly Brothers, Bo Diddley and, contracted after the first posters
had been printed, Little Richard (whose pompadour was beginning
to grow back). On the tour bus too was Julie Grant, an Eric Easton
client since her childhood of talent contest victories. Although
'impressed with how polite they were', she had also confided to a
scribbling journalist that, 'I think it's longer than mine', comparing
her carefully arranged 'beehive' hairdo to the Stones' tousled manes.
Keith Richards told the *NME*, 'I've never had my hair cut by anybody.
I do it all myself.' In passing, Jagger was to add in a US publication a
year later, 'we wouldn't be so nauseatingly attractive now, would we?'

On first glance at most photographs of the early Stones, however,
the first hairstyle – as opposed to face – to which both boys and
girls were drawn would be Brian's, enviably straight and hanging
just past the eyebrow, and blond when the others were dark. 'We
don't grow our hair like this for a gimmick,' he had protested in the
NME, 'but we see no reason why we should cut it off to conform.'

Yet, just as Bill Haley had tendered apologies, both in private
and at press conferences, for his Comets' stage antics, Brian begged
pardon of girlfriends' parents about his appearance. 'I'm paid to
look like this!' he'd explained when those of Linda Lawrence, his
latest flame, had turned up during the Stones' run of consecutive
Tuesdays over the summer of 1963 at the Ricky-Tick club in
Windsor. He also described his appearance in letters to his own
mother and father to prepare them for the shock.

Outwardly, Mr and Mrs Jones were 'nice people', conscientious
rather than doting parents, and Brian would remain very
concerned about their disapproval even when he had apparently
escaped from their clutches[43] after an upbringing based on what
would today be called 'tough love'. In every family, there is always
territory forbidden and inexplicable to strangers – and we would
like the impossible: videos of scenes in the Jones family home in
Cheltenham or to see through Brian's eyes how a particular glance,
word or gesture from his mother would cow him, even as an adult.

---

43. And going so far as to put 'break with parents' as his most significant
career move when filling in the *NME*'s 'Lifelines' questionnaire.

'Brian's baby picture is quite startling,' observed mid-1960s pop star Marianne Faithfull. 'A jowly, miserable child is looking up with exactly that expression of helpless victimisation he gave off in the last year of his life.'

With his face scrubbed and hair combed until his entire scalp smarted, Brian had trudged along as the family paraded to and from divine worship at the 900-year-old St. Mary's Parish Church. Once there, his mum, dad and sister Barbara took their seats in their usual high-backed pew while Brian went round to the vestry where cassock, ruff and surplice were to cover the suit that, when he was old enough for long trousers, made him look like a miniature version of his father. As a matter of course, he had been obliged to join other boys who sang every Sunday and, when required, at weddings and in St. Cecilia's Day oratorios. As he rose through the ranks, he'd be privileged sometimes to bear the processional cross as priest and choir filed in and out. He also doused the altar candles after the General Confession during Matins.

Yet the holy sounds he sang that were slightly unintelligible (if occasionally extraordinary) at nine, were over-familiar and rote-learnt at thirteen. As it is with every intelligent teenager, he began to question the motives of adult communicants. Were the rafter-raising votes of confidence and thanks to the Lord once a week to assuage His inferiority complex, to quench His restless thirst for applause or a stockpiling of spiritual ammunition for the defence when the worshippers' cases came up on Judgement Day?

Later, Brian would profess to be an atheist, but no one was sure whether to believe him. Another legacy of his boyhood was lengthening bouts of depression and lifelong nervous disorders that either triggered or were aggravated by chronic asthma. Certainly, it drove out both a capacity for uninhibited joy and any pleasant recollections of life in an affluent but loveless home.

When still the Stones' self-appointed 'leader', Brian wrote home either on provided notepaper after he'd eased himself between the sheets in a hotel that was slightly less grim than that in which the others were staying, or on stationery of lesser quality from 102 Edith Grove, the dingy flat at the 'wrong' end of Chelsea he shared with Keith, Mick and a most singular chap named Jimmy Phelge. 'If

it's possible I would like to come to see you next Monday or Tuesday,'
Brian mentioned to his mum and dad in July 1963, 'but I warn you
– my hair is pretty long although not untidy.'

This epistle was posted during what was not so much a tour
as a string of one-nighters with the Stones transported by Ian
Stewart to mainly agricultural and factory towns in the north and
east, and to venues where the personality of the entertainers was
generally secondary to brawling and the pursuit of romance. The
Stones, however, were immediately conspicuous for their motley
appearance, notably that hair which, if only fractionally longer
than Beatle pudding-bowls then, was sufficient to brand them as
'cissies' in provincial settlements where the Second World War
was entering its twenty-fifth year. In this inland Corn Exchange
or that seaside ballroom, teenagers would be as nonplussed as
adults when confronted with Brian, Keith and Mick's greaseless
forelocks and ducktails-gone-to-seed, and Bill Wyman and Charlie
Watts not far behind. Lord Sutch's hair had been seen as part of his
endless efforts to elicit career-sustaining publicity for a 'horror-rock'
presentation as harmless and as humorous as a ride on a fairground
ghost train. This lot didn't regard the way they looked as anything
remotely funny.

From the Royal Lido Ballroom in Prestatyn to Camberley's
Agincourt to some Plaza or other in a town six counties to the north-
east, the Stones laid themselves open to incredulity and ridicule in
any given jive-hive two-thirds full of spruced-up teenagers. Although
most onlookers kept their distance, within a minute of the Stones
kicking off with, maybe, 'Route 66', some roughneck might have
to be restrained physically by Ian Stewart from slamming his fist
through a public address speaker. More insidious were the sporadic
jeers and slow handclapping which flared up, principally coming
from lads whose coiffures were governed by work conditions,
school, parental pressure and, as Brian Jones would theorise in
print, 'army discipline – you know, the barrack room thing'.

Then it was Jones who stoked up the most aggression with a
studied radiation of menace laced with effeminacy. Examples were
noted of Brian infused with an attention-grabbing desire to outdo
Mick. This was easy to do at this point as Jagger, whose movements

were often limited anyway by small stages and an undetachable skull-like chrome microphone on a heavy stand, revealed only half-hidden clues of the showman he was to become.

Jones proved capable of stealing the limelight in a more subtle fashion. While Jagger was doing his best to whip up reaction, all Jones had to do was fix his eyes on his guitar neck, as if stupefied by his own note-bending dexterity, not forgetting to look up now and then to emit a grin that would trigger ecstatic squeals from girls in repudiation of another surge of heckling further back from fellows determined to hate the Stones. It had been Brian's borderline sarcasm that had been the root cause of the affray with the Swinging Blue Jeans. That this might have been slyly calculated is supported by ticket-holder Mick Jones's report of an encounter with the Stones during their tour with Bo Diddley, Julie Grant *et al.* Arriving early for the performance at Rochester's Odeon Cinema[44] on 1 November, Mick and his then-girlfriend, Linda, crossed the road to a pub. Leaving her Babycham, Linda visited the toilet through the saloon bar. On completing her ablutions, she told Mick she'd just seen 'a bunch of beatniks'.

'My response was to tell her not to be silly. There weren't any beatniks in Rochester. Then it dawned. It was a fair bet that it was the Stones. Only recently, I'd read that the Stones respected Bo Diddley, and wouldn't be playing his material – as they usually did – and that they were avid blues fans.

'Anyway, I had no more considered it than I was in the saloon with hardly a "Won't be a minute, love". Upon opening the door, immediately before me were two tables pulled together with what must have been ten people around them. Sure enough, I recognised three of them as members of the Stones. Brian Jones, Bill Wyman and Charlie Watts were with some other guys – and some girls who I especially remember as having long straight hair – something I'd not been used to seeing around Rochester.

'I said in what must have been an aggressive tone, "Are you The Rolling Stones?", and Wyman looked up lazily and said, "You might

---

44. Where, incidentally, David Bowie was present – and 'saw the future of music'.

say that." Then I commenced to raise my objections to their claims to being blues men, feeling they weren't worthy of wiping Muddy Waters' shoes. As I was saying this, I heard my words as if they were from another's mouth, and I wondered what on earth had possessed me to put myself in this position. I mean, I was effectively slagging them off – and there were six or seven blokes looking at me. When I'd ended my tirade, I blurted out pathetically, "Hope you don't think I'm having a go."

'Brian said to me, smiling, "No, of course not" – and I have forever been indebted to him for that kindness to an undeserving stranger. He then got chatting to me quite amiably, and even asked if I was going to the show. When I replied that I was, he asked, "Why don't you shout something out to us – like 'Get yer 'air cut!'?"

"'What, and get some prearranged remark back?"

'Jones laughed, and said, "Yes, that's the idea." I thought then that it was time to beat a retreat. I've since heard that the suggested shout was used in a film of those times by either someone genuine or a plant. On it, Brian retorts, "What – and look like you?"'

Back in the safety of the Crawdaddy, Alexis Korner had seen for himself how, 'Brian went out to needle people, to really arouse them, so that they really responded. You'd see him dancing forward with a tambourine and snapping it in your face and sticking his tongue out at you not in a schoolboyish way – and then he'd move back before you actually took a punch at him. Brian had more edge to him than any of the others then. He could be really evil on stage.'

Jubilantly, Jones, then and later, would point out the pockets of violence he'd incited to the others, and, grimaced photographer Gered Mankowitz, 'always seemed ready for some sort of confrontation with the police when concerts got out of hand'.

If aching to start something after the Stones had finished, local youths would soon deduce that these weren't cissies at all. Limbering up for another long haul back to London, at least one of them might be against the shadowed side of the van, pawing some available girl. Jagger especially was discovering that a fledgling pop star's life brought more than mere money, but with the qualification, 'Ugh, we used to attract such big, ugly ones. Dreadful birds with long, black hair, plastic boots and macs.'

Mick would sense being observed with non-hostile interest by boys too. Some of them caught the Stones a second and even third time during this round of engagements, and, if most kept their distance, theirs would be the spatter of clapping that broke long seconds of thunderstruck hush when the final major sixth had resounded. Applause might crescendo as a whistling, cheering, stamping tumult with scattered screams. Under the stage lights, the ensemble certainly looked and sounded Big Time. Any would-be critic, even a backdated Ted, couldn't really fault the musicianship or the willingness of the Stones to launch into unashamed classic rock from the 1950s if they felt like it.

The Stones' ability to extract admiration from those who hadn't wanted to like them was food for thought for hipper youths. At a village institute somewhere in the eastern shires, one ogling female's nose was put out of joint when Jagger, overlooking her, introduced himself to her escort and chatted to him about the current state of pop. The bloke was Syd Barrett, set to be the greatest asset and greatest liability of the Pink Floyd, who were to begin their career in 1965 with a familiar dipping into the Muddy Waters, Bo Diddley and Chuck Berry songbooks.

Other entranced males converted to the Stones, either in person or on television, went no further than endeavouring to copy their looks. An example was Bob Geldof, then a Dublin teenager, identifying with 'the first band I considered my own. Jagger's hair was a mess, and my hair was a mess, even when it was short'.

'The Five Shaggy Dogs with a brand of "shake" all their own' – as one local rag put it – had already gone beyond the 'caveman-like quintet' description in a February issue of the NME. Now they were the Daily Mirror's 'ugliest group in Britain', establishing similar party lines among most of the other dailies in readiness for the Stones' chore on the 27th June of delivering verdicts on excerpts from latest releases as panellists on BBC television's Juke Box Jury, the Saturday before their first domestic chart-topper, 'It's All Over Now'.

While this edition of the programme ignited extreme reaction in some quarters, the Stones' languid and sometimes offhand responses to the records they heard was nowhere on the scale of, say, The Sex Pistols gaining national notoriety in the next decade by cursing on an early evening TV magazine. Nonetheless, as the *Juke Box Jury* closing credits rolled, Eric Easton drew on a cigarette and exhaled with a sigh. He'd failed miserably to turn the Stones into 'personalities' as outwardly likeable as The Beatles or Brian Poole and the Tremeloes. Take Keith Richard: a nice enough lad, he'd given his former profession as 'post office worker' in an *NME* article not quite a year earlier, but now he was telling interviewers that he'd been a 'layabout' and was listing 'policemen' among his pet hates. Moreover, if a stranger came up to him and said, 'Hello Keith. How is your brother Cliff?', Eric would rather a polite lie along the lines of 'Fine, thanks. He's keeping well' than Richards/Richard asking the enquirer why he didn't bugger off.

Finally, Easton gave up, deciding instead to place that side of things on the more with-it shoulders of Andrew Loog Oldham, who, noticed Keith, 'always made sure we were as violent and as nasty as possible'. Not so much famous as notorious now, the Stones had restaurateurs at killjoy pains to point out that any male not wearing a tie was not to be served lunch[45] and auditorium janitors promising to pull the main electricity switch the second that horrible racket overran.

As Dave Berry explained, 'hotels weren't geared up then to young pop musicians staying in them'. Looking up from the day's first edition of the *Daily Herald*, a night porter might notice one of them had a woman with him. 'Is she your missus? Another thing: I'm not leaving this desk unattended to prepare sandwiches for you lot. Something else: that sign says you're to hand them room keys in when you go out. Can't you read? No, I don't suppose you can with all that hair in the way.'

Boys would be suspended from school for grooming their locks to a style and length previously associated with queers, crazed academics and *vers libre* bards, but now linked with the Stone whose name was the first to be widely known to the general public. Indeed, sporting 'Mick Jagger' haircuts had been cited

---

45. When an officious waiter in a West Country hotel told one famous outfit that they had each to wear a tie to eat in the restaurant, the whole group plus its road crew were to parade down the central staircase and into the dining area, all wearing ties, but otherwise naked.

in the news feature beneath the *Daily Mirror's* '*BEATLE YOUR ROLLING STONE HAIR!*' headline on 27 March 1964. This appeared after 11 boys were sent away from Coventry's Woodlands Comprehensive for hair that just about touched the collar. Their return was permitted if they trimmed down to 'at least Beatle length', thundered headmaster Donald Thompson. The parents of one such offender, however, either defended their burly son to the hilt or were too frightened of him to object when he held out against Mr Thompson.

Yet Mick Jagger, whose mother was a hairdresser, would insist in interviews that he and the other Stones had their hair cut 'not short, but regularly'. A statement that some took as vague approbation came from Wallace Scowcroft, president of the National Hairdressers Federation (NHF), during its annual conference in Rothesay, Buteshire, three days after the Woodlands Comprehensive affair: 'Men's hairdressers do not object to youth wanting to wear its hair long, provided it is shaped.' Unlike that of 'bardic Beatles who believe that masses of woolly, straggly hair is a sign of intellectualism. A young man may start by wishing to look eccentric. He may finish by looking like a tramp, a social freak'.

Such was the force of Wallace's rhetoric that the NHF passed an instant resolution to charge long-haired men more for a barber's attention. Mr Moule, a member from Kidderminster, suggested it ought to be *double*, complaining 'the adolescent of today thinks nothing of coming into our salons with six to eight weeks' growth, expecting to pay only the minimum'.

Over half a century on, memorabilia curated in *Exhibitionism: The Rolling Stones*, at London's Saatchi Gallery, included the group's jestful *NME* advertisement, originated and placed by Andrew Loog Oldham, wishing 'Happy Christmas to the starving hairdressers and their families'.

Straitlaced adults were irregular readers, but nearer contemporaries of the Stones, if not *NME* consumers, were more likely to have heard not only of that 'starving hairdressers' mickey-taking but also noted tabloid incidents such as the one in which the group, conducted to their seats for a flight to dates in the Channel Islands, took such umbrage at an air hostess casting sarcastic aspersions on their personal hygiene that they gave her a (perhaps merited) hard time from take-off to landing.

Those already antagonistic towards the Stones were maddened more than ever by the now shoulder-length tresses of a group that they liked to think was 'queer', an opinion to be fuelled by such as that 'sex-change' nonsense in Combo. Here might be a suitable juncture to explain that for all the campness and androgyny, the world of 1960s pop was, arguably, more replete with heterosexual chauvinism than any other age. Most beat group musicians then would have been appalled if any man had wanted to pursue pseudo-come-hithers like that faced by drummer Mick Avory when he auditioned for The Kinks. He became immediately suspicious when their Pete Quaife made a hand-on-hip comment that he looked like 'a beautiful bitch beast', and he was addressed as 'love' in a falsetto and limp-wristed manner by both Quaife and Dave Davies.

Before the enlistment of Charlie Watts, Avory had rehearsed briefly with the Stones for whom, jotted Ray Coleman, Melody Maker's assistant editor, when backstage at Wolverhampton's Gaumont, 'face make-up is unheard of. Hair combing is rare, too. Nor do they need full-length mirrors. They hardly bother examining themselves before they wander out to the stage'.

As Coleman partook of dressing room hospitality, a cluster of blokes, paying for their drinks, might have been unwinding over a game of darts in a nearby pub. Conversation would peter out, and one of them would suggest planning a hypothetical raid on the theatre's backstage area armed with scissors to inflict depilatory barbarity on these Rolling Stones.

In August 1964, South at Six, a BBC regional news bulletin, reported a scuffle between the Stones and one such posse during an early evening walk on the beach now that it was becoming clear that darkness was the group's sole shield against the havoc that tended to accumulate round them if blithe fatalism tempted a walk abroad between sound check and show.

Hypothetical speculations in licensed premises about scalping the Stones, if ostensibly silly and tame, were symptomatic of a feeling that it was necessary to put action over the simple debate concerning

a question posed in the headline of Ray Coleman's article of 14
March 1964: *WOULD YOU LET YOUR SISTER GO WITH A
ROLLING STONE?* In so many words, it had stated the obvious
in its opening foray that, derided by grown-ups as Elvis Presley had
been, the Stones were naturally just as worshipped by the young. It
quoted Jagger's words: 'It didn't dawn on us, really, for a bit but now
we know about the parents thing. They're against us because they
think we're scruffy. We keep getting letters like the one we had the
other day, from a little girl who said that every time she put the TV
on to watch us, her mother switched it over to the other channel.'

'It was like some weird *Wizard of Oz* thing,' posited Keith
Richards in retrospect. 'Most of what made the papers by then
was on the level of "would you let your daughter marry a Rolling
Stone?" [*sic*] but all of that stuff created more interest in us. I've
never knocked it. They called us every name under the sun, barely
printable. We were vermin, basically – well that's the way we felt
anyway. The press had the white hat and the black hat, the goodie
and the baddie. So there was The Beatles... and there was us!'

To Tim Fagan, 'The Beatles were all well and good, but by 1964,
I was a confirmed member of the "Awkward Squad" at school – in
protest against the harsh and arbitrary discipline we lived under.
On a coach trip to, I think, Bristol, I first heard "Not Fade Away"
on the radio. I did everything I could to find out about The Rolling
Stones from then on. There was no television at school, but I got
hold of a music magazine that had a picture of them in it. This was
more like it! Long hair – but not neatly combed like The Beatles.
Dishevelled! Obviously with lots of scowling and "attitude". That
became my new goal.'

As the year neared its end, funnymen, whether on TV or end-of-
the-pier variety show, would only have to hold their noses and twang
'Ah *wanna be your lover baby, ah wanna be your man...*' to get a laugh –
and I, like Tim Fagan, must admit to being amused in the New Year
by Benny Hill's 'The Strolling Ones' parody on his weekly BBC
television sketch show, when he aped all the members of a Stones-
like outfit (and a screaming female), down to Jagger's stentorian
drawl and side-on microphone stance, broken by handclaps above
the head.

Yet a sea change was already occurring – as fateful in microcosm as the *Anglo-Saxon Chronicle*'s entry for 789 AD about 'three ships of the Northmen' attacking Weymouth Bay and precipitating further-reaching ravages that would trouble Britain over the next three centuries. Pop star haircuts stopped being the subject of mirthful banter. Matters were to take a serious and permanent turn, becoming a more stormy issue than any I'd ever experienced in my life.

CHAPTER TEN

'The man-in-the-street couldn't imagine any of
The Pretty Things even being married –
except to each other'

By now, newspapers no longer put snotty inverted commas round
'The Beatles' followed by 'the Liverpool "pop" group'. *The Scout*, the
official periodical of Baden-Powell's paramilitary boys organisation,
incorporated a cartoon strip about a troop's pop combo, albeit one
with short hair and fronted by a trumpeter, and *Look and Learn*,
a weekly educational magazine for children, ran a feature on
hairdressing, categorising The Rolling Stones as propagators of the
'page boy' cut. On the Light Programme, with-it vicars would slip
the latest by the Stones into *Five to Ten*, an incongruous five-minute
religious broadcast linking *Uncle Mac's Children's Favourites* and
Saturday Club, a two-hour pop showcase, hosted by Brian Matthew.

When it transpired that the Stones might not be as much of
a nine-day-wonder as many had predicted, the hunt was up for
further money-making morons who traded in noise of rougher
hew and looks more outrageous than those of passengers aboard
a Merseybeat ferry that was soon to be grounding on a mud bank.
As 1964 had left the harbour, therefore, among those on the
general public's horizon were The Kinks, Them, the Downliners
Sect and lesser lights with names like the Howlin' Wolves, the Boll
Weevil, the Primitives and the King Bees. Yet, as well as flavouring
their first two singles with Merseybeat, The Kinks had clung onto
their uniform frilly shirts and red hunting jackets for a while. The
Downliners Sect had once co-existed in war paint and feather
bonnets as Geronimo and the Apaches (with Calamity Jane), and
the Atlantix of Burton-on-Trent played a farewell engagement before
reforming the next week as Rhythm And Blues Incorporated. Other
outfits too had been straighter pop groups prior to ditching their

stage suits and 'fab-gear' winsomeness for longer hair and scruffy
taciturnity.

The Pretty Things, however, had had no such prelude when they
seemed to take the next logical step after the Stones in the same
way as the latter had followed The Beatles. According to Screaming
Lord Sutch, 'They had everything it took to overtake the Stones,
but, though they were years ahead of their time image-wise – The
Sex Pistols of their day – it was too much for the general public in
the mid-1960s. The Stones just about walked the line; The Pretty
Things went way over it. The man-in-the-street couldn't imagine
any of The Pretty Things even being married – except to each
other.'

The common denominator was Dick Taylor. 'Both the Stones
and us started in Dick's front room,' Phil May would remember,
'and Dick and I were at Sidcup Art College with Keith Richards.' It
was, indeed, from Taylor's address in Bexleyheath that, in 1962, a
tape by him, Jagger, Richards and others – in not so much a group
as a blues appreciation society – was mailed to Alexis Korner, who,
since leaving Chris Barber's employ, was leading Blues Incorporated,
the house band at a newly-opened venue which came to be known
as the Ealing Blues Club on that West London suburb's main
thoroughfare.[46] Unimpressed, Korner returned it[47], but raised
no objections when, the following Saturday, Taylor, Jagger and
Richards volunteered to play at the place.

So began Mick, Keith – and Dick's – translation to pop stardom
for, a few weeks later, the three joined forces with Brian Jones, Ian
Stewart and a succession of ship-in-the-night drummers. As there
wasn't room for three six-string guitarists, Taylor agreed to switch
to bass.

After his departure that November, mixed feelings about the
Stones' clamber into the charts the following summer had Dick

---

46. 'It was known too as "the Moist Hoist",' recalled Art Wood, one of Blues
Incorporated's vocalists (and, later, the leader of The Artwoods), 'because they
had to put a sheet of tarpaulin over the stage to stop condensation dripping
onto the amplifiers and Charlie Watts' drum kit.'
47. With an awesome contempt for historical and cultural context, Dick's
flat-mate was to erase the tape in 1965.

reflecting that the rewards of being in an R&B group might now extend beyond just beer money. He forsook higher education, and reverted to a more comfortable role of lead guitarist when he formed The Pretty Things with the younger Phil May, who'd been omnipresent at extramural jam sessions in empty classrooms at Sidcup. May was coaxed into singing and blowing harmonica until someone more suitable stepped in, but 'everyone else that came along was a better guitarist than me'.

Just as far too many would profess to have been at the Cavern for The Beatles, so there would be those who would insist they'd been present at the Central College of Art in November 1963 for the first appearance of a five-piece Pretty Things, named after a Bo Diddley shuffle, performing with *Heath Robinson* equipment and May's microphone fed through a jukebox. The group paid further dues just before Christmas with 'an eight hour stint at the Royal Academy,' shuddered Phil. 'When I came off stage, I had blood coming up from my throat.' Early fans included: David Bowie, Van Morrison, then in the midst of one-nighters in England with an Irish showband, plus Malcolm McLaren, later The Sex Pistols' man of affairs and punk Methuselah Charlie Harper, who was to front the UK Subs.

The Things' abandoned performances and their vocalist's *extra-long* long hair, although offset slightly by Taylor's cultivated beard, held instant appeal for record company moguls looking for an act to combat the Stones. With Dick's connection to those very Stones as useful in negotiation as a demo of 'Route 66', the group was signed to the Fontana label after completing only their fourth paid booking. A 45 rpm debut, 'Rosalyn', scampered to the edge of the Top Forty by June 1964.

'Success came very quickly,' considered Taylor. 'We fell on our feet. Everything was fairly innocent then, a bit of a cottage industry. There was no sense of career development. We thought we'd last maybe two or three years. We never felt that we were in the entertainment industry as such.'

In August 1964, an uproarious evening with The Pretty Things at St Andrew's Hall in Norwich would prompt the *Midland Beat* headline 'R AND B OUSTS ROCK IN EAST ANGLIA!', demonstrating that not only was the swing away from Merseybeat complete, but that the Things were likely to supersede the Stones as anti-Beatles-in-chief. The stop-start 'Don't Bring Me Down', follow-up to 'Rosalyn', riven with *dig-it-man* beatnik slang, was in the Top Ten at the same time as 'Little Red Rooster'.[48] Climbing almost as high would be a third single, the self-composed 'Honey, I Need'.

You could speculate endlessly about how it might have been. This is probably a silly hypothetical exercise, but let's transfer to a parallel dimension for a few minutes – and the following feature in the 14 July 2024 edition of the *Kentish Times*:

GATHERING NO MOSS!

As The Pretty Things cruised by limousine to Wembley during the European leg of their record-breaking world tour, their one-time rivals, The Rolling Stones, took to the stage at Eltham's Jolly Fenman (reports Jimi Henshaw). As pop historian Pete Frame mentions in his Rock Gazetteer Of Great Britain, *they have belonged to the Medway Towns for over fifty years. Appreciated as a 'group's group' for their stylistic tenacity, the Stones' rhythm-and-blues determination remains apparent but, like the Things, they have never baulked at mining less confining seams. Soul, classic rock, jazz and mainstream pop mingled with R&B set-works like 'I Ain't Got You' and a 'Roll Over Beethoven' that led one member of a near-capacity crowd to remove his shirt and cavort crazily, probably belying a daytime sobriety as a stock-controller or school janitor.*

With only vocalist Mike Jagger and guitarist Keith Richards left from the original line-up, this was the outfit's first booking after a long lay-off – one of many during decades of bad luck, administrative chicanery, excessive record company thrift and Jagger being typecast as a poor man's Phil May.

There'd been a place in the pub-rock sun for the latter-day Stones back in the mid-1970s, and they'd picked up a neo-punk audience who'd bought

48. David Bowie, who'd fronted the King Bees prior to joining the Manish Boys, was to resurrect 'Rosalyn' and 'Don't Bring Me Down' for inclusion on his 1973 album, *Pin-Ups*.

reissues of the old LPs. *Psychedelic Citadel* from 1967 even made the 'alternative' chart in SOUNDS, and a German label commissioned a new Stones album, It Should Have Been Us.

Of course, it couldn't last, and a schedule that had once signified a week's work became a month's. The only new Stones commodity during the next decade was 1986's Live At The Station Tavern – though, more recently, Mike shook his trademark maracas on an EP by Thee [sic] Headcoats, one of the mainstays of the Medway 'indie' scene.

The Stones set at the Jolly Fenman pub concluded with Sonny Boy Williamson's 'Don't Start Me Talking' during which Jagger wailed an endlessly inventive harmonica, and both Richards and pianist Ernie Grant delivered workmanlike solos while drummer Carlo Little, ministered unobtrusively to overall effect.

Brought back for an encore, the Stones affirmed their staying power once more. None of their records ever sold much outside loyal north-west Kent but, as an eminently danceable live act, they've outlasted most of the local opposition – and there's every reason to suppose that, sooner or later, they'll be providing another of those 'greatest nights anyone can ever remember' at a pub near you. Don't miss it!

Real life isn't like that – at least it wasn't for The Pretty Things – but there was certainly a period somewhere between mid-1964 and early 1965 when the Things and the Stones were on terms of fluctuating equality as belligerently unkempt degenerates, detested by adults. Even The Beatles were seen as a lesser threat to the Stones than the Things, to such an extent that Andrew Loog Oldham issued, allegedly a directive that the rival group was not to be rebooked on *Ready Steady Go!* upon pain of his lot boycotting the programme.

Head shots of both Mick Jagger and, albeit from the back, Phil May received equal space, along with those of Dave Clark and John Lennon, on the cover of the *Sunday Times* colour supplement on 12 July 1964, to flag up a main feature entitled 'THE LONG-HAIR MUSICIANS'. A chart strike with 'Cry to Me', also recorded by the Stones, began another fat year for the Things, almost but not quite as wondrous as the last, which continued with the self-written 'Midnight to Six Man'.

Projected as wilder, fouler and more peculiar than the Stones, the Things had imposed themselves upon respectable homes with a maiden TV appearance in which May's hair had flickered across a surly, blemished complexion. While even the most self-possessed parents battled for control of their features, Tim Fagan's mother 'let out a loud, high-pitched scream of horror when Phil May dashed across the stage, hair flying,' and, as for Alan Franks' mum, 'the mere name of that band very nearly killed her!' Nevertheless, embellishment aside, the effect was as keenly, if more insidiously, felt by boys like me gazing morosely through lace curtains and wondering if this was all there was.

'The last time I felt the familiar taste of blood in my mouth was the night I came back from recording "Rosalyn",' Phil May was to recall, 'and that was the last time I saw Erith for quite a while. Soon I was officially "*The Man With The Longest Hair In Britain*", 'just like a girl's', said the *Daily Mirror* – but I had earned that hair with my blood, my sweat and ten thousand stitches, and I wore it proudly. Moreover, after all the verbal abuse I was getting on the street, and the press hate mail that was aimed at all of our growing young army of nonconformist outsiders, why not wind the bastards up even more – and grow it longer? So I did.'

'There was much more hostility in the British provinces,' added Dick Taylor. 'We'd book hotels a month in advance, but by the time we turned up, they'd tell us there'd been a mistake, and there were no rooms for us. Then there was what followed one gig in Swindon. We walked out of the place, and some guy made a remark about Phil's hair, and I said something back. Then these rather heavy-looking yokels – like a lynch mob – started pursuing us, and Phil "the Greek" Andropolis, our minder-cum-driver, suddenly produced these coshes and other weapons from the car and stuck them in our hands. Next, he got this shotgun out. Instead of backing off, this guy got totally enraged and grabbed the end of it. Phil the Greek started swinging him around. Passers-by ignored it. Perhaps it was a normal Swindon Saturday night – but, fortunately, the police arrived. In the end, Phil (Andropolis) was done for not having a firearms licence. He'd have gone down for seven years today.'

Through both media reports and word-of-mouth, such outrages increased turnout at bookings. For example, Phil May remembered, 'when we arrived for one in Hull, and there were hundreds spilling out into the car park. We couldn't get near the place until it was arranged for us and our gear to be passed over the heads of the crowd and manhandled onto this tiny stage'.

'There is no such thing as bad publicity' is an adage attributed to Phineas T Barnum, co-founder of the North American travelling circus company billed as The Greatest Show On Earth. It didn't always apply to the Colchester group the Fairies, another bunch of temperamental ne'er-do-wells whose road manager Johnnie Dee wrote songs and had given them first refusal on 'Don't Bring Me Down'. In late 1964, they'd made headlines in the more trivial national newspapers when, to publicise their latest single, an arrangement of Bob Dylan's 'Don't Think Twice, It's Alright', they'd got themselves arrested for climbing a statue.

The law, however, was to come down harder on Dane Stephens, their singer and mouth organist, who was gaoled for causing death by driving dangerously in the group's unlicensed and uninsured van. Pragmatism ruled, and 'we acquired a singer who looked and sounded just like Phil May,' explained drummer John Alder, who'd adopted 'Twink' as a stage name on receiving regular gifts from a fan of a home perm lotion of that name. This was for use on an aureole of golden curls that lent him a resemblance to 'Bubbles', the child portrayed in the Pre-Raphaelite painting by John Everett Millais that was used to advertise Pears soap.

Stephens' incarceration also put the tin lid on the progress of 'Don't Think Twice, It's Alright' after the group had been signed by Decca as a riposte to The Pretty Things just as Fontana had the Things to challenge Decca's Stones. Rendering other circles, of sorts, unbroken were the Things turning down 'Get Yourself Home', also penned by Johnnie Dee, as The Fairies had 'Don't Bring Me Down'. The Things' eventual enlistment of Twink Alder and, before that, Brian Jones, someone you wouldn't trust with either your heart or your chequebook, packing his belongings and, through furtive negotiation involving Jimmy Phelge, deserting Linda Lawrence (who'd given birth while he was posing with his guitar at a Stones

photo session)[49] to ensconce himself in the basement beneath the
rented communal home of The Pretty Things in 13 Chester Street, a
freeholding of the Duke of Westminster and opposite the Belgravia
home of Reginald Maudling, the Chancellor of the Exchequer[50]
– an address that provided the title for an instrumental that used
up needle-time on the group's rush-released first LP. 'It was only a
crash-pad,' explained Phil May, 'as we'd get back from a gig at five in
the morning and leave in the afternoon for the next one.'

Brian was, in effect, 'sleeping with the enemy', to coin May's playful
expression; although, outside the context of professional rivalry, the
two outfits were actually on friendly, even intimate terms. This was
demonstrated by a particularly uproarious *esprit de corps* moment
on 7 March 1965 when, following a stopped Stones show at the
Palace Theatre in Manchester, Keith and Mick taxied across the
city to leap onstage with the Things, who chanced to be playing
the Manchester Cavern that same evening. Amongst numbers on
which Jagger duetted with May was – you guessed it – 'Cry to Me'.

Back at Number 13 however, so Phil would confide, 'Brian
used to cry on my shoulder, and say that he'd written this really
good song, but that Mick and Keith didn't want to know. You
could understand their attitude because none of Brian's songs were
suitable for the Stones. We'd tell him this, and he'd get angry and
trash our records when we went out. He'd melt them by putting
them near a lamp, and write insulting remarks about us on the
mirror. He'd boast too about getting more fan mail than Mick and
Keith. He was very uncool, very irritating, but I liked him.'[51]

During his stay at Chester Street, Brian came to understand that
there was a certain sense of *épater la bourgeoisie* about hanging about

49. Though, apparently, Jones dashed to the maternity ward as soon as the
last shutter clicked.
50. With John Paul Jones (later of Led Zeppelin), Pete Meadon, The Pretty
Things' publicist, was able to gatecrash a coming-of-age party at 11 Downing
Street for Caroline Maudling, the Chancellor's daughter.
51. Jones purloined Pretty Thing Brian Pendleton's striped matelot jersey
to wear on *Ready Steady Go!*, which caused it to became a wanted fashion
accessory.

with The Pretty Things, more so than with the Stones. 'Diana Dors[52] attended a party to celebrate our first year as a hit group,' recalled Phil May, 'and Judy Garland used to come to our flat a bit – probably because she and Viv Prince, our drummer, had a mutual interest in the bottle. Viv invited me to a double-date at the Ad Lib with him, Judy and someone for me – who turned out to be Rudolf Nureyev, the ballet star. So we danced the night away, Judy with her dress over her head and no drawers on, Rudy holding my hand. He was big news then as he'd defected only about three weeks before, and it was like having a Martian on your arm.[53] He couldn't even order a drink then. The barmen in the Ad Lib couldn't speak much Russian. The funny thing was that Rudy danced like a woodentop. All I remember of Judy is her gripping my wrist in her claw-like hand. As she spoke, I could see blood coming from under her nails as they dug into my skin, but it seemed impolite to pull my hand away.'[54]

The Ad Lib[55] was one of around ten fashionable central London nightclubs where the pop elite and their hangers-on – the 'in crowd' – could select a night out, 'night' defined as midnight to six. 'Fashionable' meant that the Ad Lib near Leicester Square would be 'in' for a while before the inscrutable pack transferred its allegiance to the Speakeasy, Blaises or Great Newport Street's Pickwick before finishing up at either the Cromwellian in SW7 for

---

52. Publicised as Britain's 'answer' to Marilyn Monroe, Dors was more like Betty Hutton, the USA's 'blonde bombshell', who rose to fame during World War II as a movie actress and recording artiste.

53. When a teenager, I'd find myself defending Phil May, admittedly without evidence, against any imputation that he was anything but the most heterosexual of men. Imagine how I felt decades later when Phil himself told me he wasn't.

54. Garland, an international entertainer, was well into her forties and near the end of a badly-frayed tether when exiled in Britain by US tax demands. She was heading, indeed, towards a fatal overdose of sleeping tablets; but a month at the prestigious Talk of the Town was a virtual sell-out. Brian Jones-plus-one would be on the guest list when Judy sang before faces and cleavages tanned on the ski slopes, bow-tied tuxedos, pearly adornments and drinks like melted crayons, all belonging to people who had paid to see a showbiz legend.

55. It was adjacent to Soho's Church of Notre Dame de France, whose live-in priests were frequent complainants about noise.

the finals of the national 'Bend' competition (a dance devised by disc jockey Mike Quinn), the Bag O' Nails off Carnaby Street, the cloistered Scotch of St James or maybe one of four other hangouts. All these places were attractive for their strict membership controls, tariffs too highly priced for the Average Joe, the non-admission of photographers and the flattering lighting that strove to make the pasty individual, accustomed to rising in the late afternoon, look more suntanned and fit.

Scrutinised through club spy-holes and not found wanting, pop *conquistadores* would hold court with only their equals to contradict them. Close at hand would be a whiskey-and-Coke and, its size depending on status, an abundance of skinny dolly-birds with double-decker eyelashes and hair cropped like that of Mary Quant. In the house discotheque's deafening dark, no one Twisted any more. The order of the day was now the Banana, the Monkey and other US dances that no Briton was supposed to have mastered yet – though the headache-inducing Shake was rife in the ballrooms.

The Pretty Things also began frequenting haunts not usually associated with their profession. 'We used to go to [The] Freddie Mills Nite Spot and these other rather strange clubs,' revealed Phil May, 'that were patronised by a mixture of leftish celebrities and gangsters – and CID flying squad, funnily enough. The Kray twins tagged onto us – because if they were Public Enemy Number One, we were Number Two. We were on the outside of society.'[56]

The group didn't find keeping criminal company entirely distasteful – nor the supposed hammer they'd taken to moral certainties being exacerbated by God-slot TV discussions concerning the depth to which pop music had sunk by the championing of such debauchees. The Pretty Things themselves were once hauled in to answer clerical criticism. 'However, our verbal retaliations were hastily

---

56. In a car parked to his Nite Spot's rear, Freddie Mills was soon to die with a rifle next to him and a bullet wound above his right eye. The coroner concluded that it had been self-inflicted in view of Freddie's demoralised state in the face of financial ruin, agonising headaches and his fast-dissolving celebrity. His widow and stepson were among the many who insisted that he'd been murdered by gangsters.

restricted,' remembered Dick Taylor, 'when we began capsizing one programme's intentions by using long words and speaking nicely.'

If they weren't exactly thickheads, then it must be made out that they revelled in higgledy-piggledy filth and slept in their vests. Thus the *News of the World* Sunday broadsheet galloped into the fray, sending a couple of its hacks to brave 13 Chester Street. If the door-stepping press on a crusade imagined aristocratic portraits gazing down reproachfully on rooms that looked as if someone had hurled a hand-grenade into them, they were soon disillusioned. 'They arrived when Viv Prince and I were having late afternoon tea,' laughed Dick Taylor. 'You could eat off the floor there.' Another depraved reprobate in an upstairs flat had just returned from an honest day's toil in a suit – and a female tenant said she'd had no qualms about inviting her parents round for a candlelit dinner.

Nevertheless, because the metropolitan police force was paying habitual visits to The Pretty Things' abode, 'local residents got up a petition demanding our removal,' groaned Phil May, 'for bringing down the tone of the neighbourhood'. One who couldn't be persuaded to sign it commented to a journalist on the scent for scandal: 'I don't approve of their hairstyles or dress, but they certainly haven't been making a lot of noise.'

CHAPTER ELEVEN

'Peter's pride'

In August 1964, the agency of the titled landlord served notice on The Pretty Things, an eviction held at arm's length briefly by the inclusion of their plight in a TV current affairs programme. To those members of the group who valued solitude, perhaps the action brought a sense of liberation, ridding them as it did of the human driftwood bobbing through 13 Chester Street.

Many people had attached themselves to the group on the slightest of pretexts and had the insolence to imagine they could foist themselves upon the official tenants whenever they wanted and for as long as they pleased. The more slyly hoodwinking of them manipulated the situation so they could stay another night – and another and another.

Often, some sort of party would be getting underway when the musicians left for a booking and it would still be in full swing when they returned to what was less a home than a depot. Feeling all the time like he was being observed, Phil May almost expected to yawn and stretch to a standing ovation, so constant was the flow of visitors.

Within nearly all outfits in the same position as The Pretty Things, all the discord and intrigues that make pop groups what they are would become all the more piquant through living on the same premises and grinding up and down the motorways and highways of Europe in the eternal van: the irresolvable feuds, conspiracies, whispered onstage spite, prima donna tantrums, backstage postmortems and interminable petulance over trivial matters. Bickering helped pass the time. So did poking ruthless fun at whoever seemed most likely to rise to it. Teasing would increase in frequency, by

GET YER 'AIR CUT

degrees less subtle and less good-natured. Intermittent retreats, as if to a prepared position, were as disconcerting as the insults. So were sudden episodes of aggressive friendliness that obliged the acceptance with a forced smile of over-hearty backslapping, nose-pulling and 'affectionate' punches.

Even those who studiously avoided confrontation would have their fill of the glory and stupidity of being in the group – because there was no reason for any let-up in the malcontented shiftlessness, the underhanded manipulations, the verbal and emotional baiting, and the general temper-charged ugliness, visible and invisible.

Complications of personal alliances included the case of two homosexuals who ended up in the same Top Ten quartet after physical attraction had been a factor in the transfer of one of them from another outfit whom they'd met when resident in the same Hamburg club. Gerry and his Pacemakers, the Bachelors,[57] The Kinks and the Spencer Davis Group all contained brothers, but sibling rivalry (and personality clashes between non-relations too) could resolve into a brusque empathy for the sake of the group. That is, until someone went too far and slanging matches and even fisticuffs would follow before an ebbing away that left the combatants muttering to respective sidekicks.

So it would be too that worms would turn, and a 'sitting duck' of a gentle drummer's barbed rejoinders to ritual antagonism could turn him into a jovial straight man to the group loudmouth's running commentary on the daily grind of stage, bar and bunkroom – that you couldn't switch off like *Dixon of Dock Green*, the BBC television police series that followed *Juke Box Jury* every Saturday.

*

---

57. A besuited trio from Dublin, they tended to be liked by those in accord with 'Are you going to let Britain's king of talent be beaten by a flash-in-the pan group like The Beatles?', an enquiry by a Cliff Richard enthusiast of *NME* readers. They specialised in good old good ones like 'I Believe', 'Charmaine' and, from the 1927 silent movie of the same name, 'Ramona'. As token pop group in 1964's Royal Command Performance, they'd been amenable to facing the Royal Box for an amended opening line – 'we wouldn't change you for the wurrrld!' – of their most recent smash on both sides of the Irish Sea.

Created by Ted Willis too, the BBC comedy-drama *Taxi!* had Sid James, its star, ferrying awful Beatles copyists with several short bookings in the course of an evening.[58] The Fourbeats turned up in an episode of the Home Service's rural soap opera *The Archers* as early as September 1963. The Swinging Blue Jeans had a cameo in an edition of mid-week *Z-Cars*, as ingrained with *oop north* 'kitchen sink' grit as censorship would allow.

Also given a beat group slant in 1964, ITV's *No Hiding Place*, centred on Scotland Yard, had Southend-on-Sea's Monotones[59] supplying the music for the all-blond 'By Boys'. A later story involved a gang of longhairs enacting an acid-throwing reprisal against a 'straight' who had offended them, and their leader enduring a short-back-and-sides by way of disguise to evade arrest (with the scriptwriter inserting a soliloquy in which the character expressed a hitherto secret relief in doing so, reverting as he was to 'when I was normal').

Beyond fiction, inmates of HMP Chelmsford were put to work assembling electric guitars as they had once sewn mailbags, and a televised debate about a political matter had a government minister reacting to a harangue by addressing a long-haired youth as 'Sir – or should it be madam?' Around the same time as this cheap laugh, Dave Davies was interviewed for the radio programme *Salut Les Copains* on the afternoon before his Kinks made their French concert *première* in February 1965, and became the first pop star to be subject to the subsequently oft-asked question, 'Are you a boy or a girl?'

This was posed in a country that was about to spawn a singer named Édouard, who grabbed attention for his perpetual Bermuda shorts and (possibly artificial) hair down to his knees. There was also 'Antoine' whose 1966 single 'Les Élucubrations D'Antoine' engendered an 'answer' disc (and domestic hit) from Johnny

---

58. This was shortly before Willis was awarded a life peerage. Like Dr Donald Soper, he was a vitriolic critic of recent pop music. A *Melody Maker* front-page feature on 'Terry', the first single by Twinkle (with a libretto about a motorcyclist who, irked by his girl's infidelity, zooms off to a lonely end of mangled chrome and blood-splattered kerbstones) quoted Lord Willis – to whom the disc was 'dangerous drivel'.

59. Who had the same name as the North American vocal group whose 1958 magnum opus, 'The Book of Love', had been subject to a UK cover by The Mudlarks.

Hallyday, still sporting a backdated quiff, in 'Cheveux Longs Et Idées Courtes' ('Long Hair And Short Ideas').

Crasser publicity stunts back in Britain had been exemplified by Jay Roberts of the otherwise unsung Primitives from Oxford, having his cascading tresses reduced to short-back-and-sides on Eamonn Andrews' TV chat show in 1965, prompting the *Daily Mirror* to publish a cartoon spoof of the episode. This, however, wasn't sufficient to lever the Primitives' new single, 'You Said', into the Top Fifty (although you could be really talking money now if you possess the Pye 45 in mint condition).[60]

Next, Brian Rossi, organist with the Wheels, pride of Belfast (and connected genealogically to Them), ceased camouflaging his retreating hairline by shaving it all off. With their beat boom Yul Brynner (and indefatigable self-publicist) in a more comfortable role as lead singer, the outfit had put themselves in the way of Decca and Dick Rowe, who, still seeking that Next Big Thing, had directed A&R outriders to fan out beyond England.

There'd been a pronounced note of urgency in Rowe's own expedition to Ireland in summer 1964 because EMI was 'interested' in the Wheels too – and had already seized the Manish Boys. Following their 'Society for the Prevention of Cruelty to Long-Haired Men' nonsense on *Tonight*, the Boys had landed a slot on *Gadzooks! It's All Happening* – a pop series on the BBC's new second TV channel – during March 1965 when their 'I Pity the Fool' debut was issued.

During rehearsals, programme director Barry Langford waylaid Leslie Conn, the group's manager, to stipulate that they all had to have a haircut before the cameras rolled. An enraged response from the Manish Boys and their small entourage of fans led Langford to relent on condition that, if there were any complaints from viewers about their appearance, their fee was to be donated to charity.

---

60. Though the televised haircut was, more or less, the end for the Primitives, they soldiered on with a new lead singer, Mal Ryder from another local unit, the Spirits – who'd functioned in a similarly mean R&B mode as the Primitives. The new amalgam made a one-shot single, 'Every Minute of Every Day' (as 'Mal and the Primitives'), and a French EP. A combo of the same name enjoyed a few chart entries in the late 1980s.

The deal with EMI was for a one-shot single with an option on further releases if this gave cause for hope. It didn't – and the group split up with David Bowie, their X-factor, after he had been given another 45 rpm chance as leader of the Lower Third, on transferring to Pye.

1964's dry summer had embraced a big moment for Pye when two of its signings, The Kinks and the Honeycombs, had tied at Number One in the UK charts. Each act represented one of the two new polarisations of the beat group. While the Honeycombs were light and instant with big smiles and a female drummer, The Kinks, born of R&B rather than straight pop, relayed that scene's angry scowls, sexual suggestiveness – and longer hair. Although newest recruit, Mick Avory, had responded to their *Melody Maker* advertisement – 'Drummer wanted for a smart, go-ahead group' by getting a neo-crew cut like that of David Bonser, an older boy at my Farnborough Grammar – and the near-epitome of the 'David Watts' character on 1967's *Something Else By The Kinks* LP, for whom high-grade exam results and school captaincy were foregone conclusions.

With a show of kindness after I'd returned depressed from the barber – as I always did now – my mother would hint strongly that David Bonser's natty coiffeur had been a major factor in his triumphs which, indeed, it might have been.[61] Certainly, Philip Allen, a fourth-year pupil I knew, suffered the indignity of being placed in the class of boys a year his junior until he had an extensive trim. Once excelling in most subjects, he was now lounging in the back row, dumbly insolent, indifferent to logarithms and the Diet of Worms – and oblivious to the jibes of both wrinkled senior teacher and trainee on teaching practice.

This punishment had been suggested to the headmaster by deputy 'Trunky' Cotgreave, who modelled himself on pre-war Prime Minister Neville Chamberlain (or perhaps Harold Macmillan, one of his Conservative successors in that post during the 1950s), but, while he'd replicated the white moustache, no one wore upturned

---

61. Purportedly, Bryan Ferry, later of Roxy Music, was approached in 1963 to be Head Boy at Washington Grammar-Technical School – but only if he had a haircut.

collars anymore. For Mr Cotgreave, hair had become as touchy a subject as it was for those he victimised.[62]

I'd never encountered Trunky before I became a name on an FGS register, but I'd known his type since primary school in days when grown-ups assumed children were always at fault, thus giving teachers licence to get away with what might land them with a disciplinary hearing, sessions on a psychiatrist's couch or even a prison sentence today. Indeed, Trunky was cut from the same cloth as Mrs Diver, a pruny and flabby-lipped 30-something who, as a person, seemed to model herself on Miss Murdstone from David Copperfield and, as a teacher, on 'Crabby', the headmistress in Cider With Rosie. She demonstrated this by relating to the class her mocking recollection of a mentally disabled former pupil smashing his head repeatedly against a brick wall. She was also quite open about whom she liked and disliked. She called an amiable nondescript named Neil by his forename while I was 'Clueless Clayson', 'Crackpot Clayson' and, most often, just plain 'Clayson'.

I digress. What happened to Steve, Phil Allen's younger brother, probably brought covert delight to Trunky, paralleling as it did that in his Daily Express in which uncontained mirth was almost audible with 'Peter's pride was his shoulder-length hair' in the opening paragraph of a write-up about the shearing of a civilian teenager by British soldiers garrisoned in Cyprus – for, in safe assurance of no more than an amused scolding with a broad wink from Cotgreave, Steve had been held fast while his nape-length locks were scissored off by some 'manly' types, i.e. the keener members of the compulsory Combined Cadet Force (CCF) that filled every Friday afternoon and seemed to thrust tentacles into too many other aspects of school life.[63]

---

62. Trunky had a soul mate in John McMillan, headmaster of St David's Roman Catholic Secondary School in Dalkeith near Edinburgh, who consigned long-haired 14-year-old Owen Holmes to an otherwise girls-only form for all subjects (except PE) because 'we don't want boys looking like girls'.
63. It was also quite in order for 'back seat hard men' on buses to and from All Hallows Catholic comprehensive on the Aldershot-Farnham border to slice off the hair of boys from Farnborough's fee-paying Salesian College, especially if they committed the cardinal sin of occupying an upstairs seat reserved traditionally for an All Hallows bully-boy further back in the terminus queue.

Another Steve – Mills – was a witness to this incident, reporting that 'it was the fact that the young sir had grown long strands of hair in front of his ears to mimic sideboards, because he didn't yet shave. They cut off one side, only assuming he'd then give up and cut the other side to match. Instead, he reappeared later with the removed locks defiantly and firmly sellotaped back in place on his cheek.

'I also recall the monthly hair and sideboard measuring on the way into or out of assembly – where a pair of prefects stood by to reinforce authority and mete out punishment while Trunky sat at a desk, waving a ruler and measuring the length of sideboards and the rest of the hair to ensure neither were below the ear or over the collar.'[64]

When yet to join the Wheels as bass guitarist, Rod Demick was 'made to stand on the stage at school morning assembly in 1963 aged 16, as an example of "today's scruffy hairstyles" and then sent home to get it cut. I was so embarrassed – but at the same time rather proud and rebellious'.

'And for me, as an Anglo-Dutch immigrant with a parent from each side of the North Sea,' relates Pete Feenstra (later, a reputable impresario, disc jockey and sleeve note essayist), 'I was thrown into a very straight school in Leicester, and the fight not to have my hair cut led to five years of purgatory. It provided an ongoing war between the formal discipline of my school and my own inclinations, fashioned by musical, cultural heroes and tightly knit friendship groups.'

Wait! There's more! 'I went to a school prize-giving after I'd moved on to art college,' relates John Arthur Hewson. 'Mine was presented by George Cansdale, a TV zoologist – a prototype David Attenborough. I was reliably informed that he said afterwards that I was "a fucking disgrace". I was wearing an old windcheater jacket

---

(cont.) Once on board, within minutes, such a thug might have the fellow's head under one burly arm with the fist on the other going back and forth on his face like a piston.

64. Imagine Trunky's reaction to one of my classmates who'd instructed a barber to 'lighten' his hair. 'Be a man!' raged Cotgreave on passing sentence of a week's detention.

with the collar up, like John Lennon on the front of the *Rubber Soul* album, and I had paint on my jeans.'

Speaking to a local reporter on 13 May 1964, Harry Davies, director of the Institute of Education at the University of Nottingham, deplored what seemed plain fact that 'teachers are too obsessed with haircuts'. Nonetheless, when studying at Merseyside's Merchant Taylors' Boys' School, John Townsend noted 'a master drawing on a pupil's face with a felt tip pen to indicate where sideboards were allowed to extend to – which was nowhere. Bizarrely, the view on sideboards was that they were both effeminate and made you look like a gigolo. Go figure.

'A boy with longish hair was told to go home and not come back until he'd had it cut. He returned with a short crop with razor parting. He was suspended until his hair had grown. Another with long straight hair used to wet it down and stick it down inside the back of his collar. Strangely, he got away with it, although it can't have been very comfortable.'

Now dig this from Tim Fagan: 'There was a steady stream of "Get your hair cut!" or "What do you think you look like?!" from masters and prefects alike. During one maths lesson, a Mr Baldwin reacted to some smart alec remark of mine with, "Look at you, Fagan, with your stupid grin and your girly fringe. You'll never amount to anything." I wasn't in the mood for this, and I found myself in front of the class, holding Mr Baldwin by his jacket lapels and saying "Don't you ever speak to me like that again!" He sent me to the headmaster, who duly caned me – but agreed that I should not bother my head with maths again.

'At that point, people like myself who had the qualifications but not the appearance or attitude to be accepted into the Sixth Form were housed in a remote classroom away from the main school building. The deal was that we could attend classes if we wished, and come and go as we pleased, but would not be welcome to attend school functions where parents might be present such as speech day or sports events. There were five or six of us in 'Five Remove A'.

Let's hear too from Charlie Salt: 'When I was in my public school's CCF, I was an obvious target because my hair was then in a

Beatle cut, and my father was a colonel in the Royal Military Police. At some parade or other, we were drawn to attention for inspection by an RSM who had served with my dad. He went along the ranks, got to me and bawled, "If your father saw you with hair looking like that, he would be beside himself! It would look better on a girl!" Then he pulled my hair at the back, and yelled in my face "Get that 'air cut, you 'orrible little man!'"

Such singling out extended to places of work, as outlined in Ray Nichol's narrative of a pertinent episode in which he played a central role: 'Being a male teenager and having red hair in the early 1960s had drawbacks. The girls would like it – but the fellows would sometimes give you hell. At seventeen, I'd been working in an engineering factory for two years. Because I was wearing my hair fairly long by the standards of the time, I took a bit of stick from some of the thickies there. They called me "darling" and stuff like that. Then The Beatles came along, and my hair became a lot more respectable in certain circles, but when the Stones appeared on the scene I became the long-haired monster again.

'One of the workmen used to cut the other men's hair for a couple of cigarettes or a shilling or whatever. This usually happened during the lunch break. One day, I was beckoned to the haircutting area, whereupon I was restrained and they proceeded to cut mine. After the incident, I went to report it to the foreman, but before I could say anything, he came out with, "Now that looks better!" What, therefore, was the point in complaining? When I went home that evening, my mother said she would come to my workplace and make a complaint, but my father asked her not to as it may have made things difficult for me.'

In every factory like Ray's, there always seemed to be a Dutch uncle dispensing grave and level-voiced guidance when, say, shaking his member in an adjacent urinal in the gents: 'I'm gonna give you some advice, son. Take it or leave it. When you get home tonight, have a good look at yourself in the mirror. You *must* have a haircut and smarten yourself up – because if you don't, you'll never get on in the world, marry a decent girl – or win my respect or that of any of the other blokes who work here or anywhere else. Just a friendly warning. Think on, son.'

Not every adult was so militantly against the new aesthetic. 'I didn't wear my hair particularly long,' protested Jonathan Meades, 'but it was still too long for a neighbour of my parents who used to phone my mother to complain of my appearance. Cuban heeled boots also irked this busybody. My mother eventually got shirty with her.'

After her 15-year-old brother had a chunk of hair that 'had started to struggle over his collar' slashed off by a master at his provincial grammar school, a teenage Penny Baldwin's parents – who 'weren't necessarily progressive but were always there to stand up for us, threatened to have the teacher charged with assault. Said teacher came to our house that evening and apologised profusely for his actions.'

Protests from parents were loud and clear too at Harraby Secondary Modern in Carlisle when, in June 1964, 20 boys were marched from classrooms by the deputy head, William Boak, to an eager 17-year-old army barber on the grounds that 'long hair is anti-social because it is a sign of boys' association with groups that are anti-social'. After the threat of solicitors' letters and the action of one mother in wrapping a scarf round her son's head to hide his shearing, Boak's high-handedness was defended by Alderman Gerald Coogan, the education committee vice chairman: 'Sometimes teachers are forced to take over parents' responsibilities.'

Not in agreement with Coogan, Boak or even her own husband over the matter was the mother of journalist and radio presenter Eddy Bonte. As a 15-year-old in 'this conservative, Flemish *townette* called Veurne', he had 'found sense in pop music and youth culture, bicycling 40 miles to Ostend to buy the latest issue of *Rave*.[65] Thanks to my understanding mum, I had somehow "secured" a Beatles jacket – the brushed and dusted foursome being considered acceptable for most mothers. A Stones fan at heart, I now entered the next phase on the road to revolution: a rougher look and long hair. There wasn't enough money for any sort of dress code; hence hair became the main issue.

---

65. Founded in 1964, *Rave* was a UK pop magazine (distributed to France, Luxembourg, Belgium, Spain and Italy) of more literary and visual depth than most such publications.

'In hindsight, my hair then looked ridiculously short, but at the
time it was quite a feat of provocation and pure rebellion. It's easy
to be so unique in London, Paris, Amsterdam or even Antwerp
but, in 1964, it took courage and perseverance in Saxmundham,
Truro – or Veurne.

'I found myself in a particular situation what with my father
being a former *gendarme*. His son a "Beatle"? Over his dead body! At
heart, my dad was a good person, but somewhat easy to influence
when he'd had a few pints. He worried about what other people
thought about a policeman's son. If he and his family didn't set
the standards, how could you expect others to be law-abiding
citizens? To top it all, he had trained as a hairdresser during the
war before joining the army to avoid deportation to Germany. Oh,
it can even get worse: we rented a house from the neighbourhood's
hairdresser. Whatever I may have preferred, my dad gave the
landlord-hairdresser strict instructions. I was unable to beat that
pair, particularly because my dad threatened to get out his 1940s
scissors himself – with my mother imagining subsequent horror
scenes!'

'Oh, they're so far away,' was my mother's argument when I pointed
out the pictures of long-haired pop stars from the pages of *Rave*
and *Jackie* on the walls of my sisters' bedroom, although she knew
as well as I did that most of them had surfaced from communities
like ours. If, as Eddy Bonte implied, the pastime of 'shocking the
establishment' took on at times an almost good-humoured aspect
in London, Paris and other European big cities with accepted
traditions of counter-culture, it was opposed with uncompromising
gravity in regions where the function of pop-crazy boys like me was
just to absorb the signals as they came.

Ready Steady Go! (or what I was able to catch of it before setting
off for another long, boisterous evening of Scouts), *Top of the Pops*
(which I always missed because of choir practice) and so forth were,
indeed, 'so far away' – and the excesses of the 'permissive society'
were merely a distant rustling, belonging to speculation while
sharing a communal cheap cigarette behind school bicycle sheds,
and through soothing reading in the scum press on Sundays.

Local newspapers reported on whist drives; the Opera Society's production of HMS *Pinafore* Geoffrey Adams ('PC Lauderdale' in *Dixon Of Dock Green*) opening a new High Street department store; commotion about the gypsies camped on the disused aerodrome; and the Borstal runaway hiding somewhere in the everglades. Gossip sufficed for harder news that came via *Melody Maker*, the *NME*, *Disc*, *Record Mirror* and *Music Echo*[66] for youths who, on a flaming August afternoon, would be shuttered up inside the coffee bar, making a cup of frothy coffee last for hours, while once upon a greensward a few hundred yards away, archers had rehearsed for Agincourt.

Since the discharge of the last National Serviceman in 1963, there seemed to be nothing as horribly exciting as the prospect of slaughtering foreigners, no apparent avenue of rescue from the near-stagnant river of the rest of your life. This crawled towards a gold watch on retirement to tick away the seconds before ideally, a comfortable and respected old age of liver spots and the bowling green, and then the silence of eternity.

So far, so unworthy of comment. Yet domestic powder kegs were exploding with increasing frequency, and there'd be frightful exchanges that neighbours may have found immensely entertaining. Previously, these had manifested themselves in the time-honoured turmoil over a pubescent boy's choice of friends, late hours, speech, manners, slouch and, more recently, the 'crude' drainpipe jeans he wore to go with the purple shirt, winkle-pickers and denim jacket, and the ridiculous Teddy Boy side-whiskers he was trying to grow. He had an 'attitude' as bad as the constant pimples on his face.

In such traumatised households, grandmothers found themselves pleading for calm amid blazing rows between parents and once tractable sons over post-Merseybeat hair, a matter that was to ride roughshod over all the other problems. A sea-change – a sin against God – was occurring, and bringing with it a running battle amid years of incomprehension, lamentation, deprivation, uproar, assault, interminable domestic 'atmospheres' and derision (especially derision).

---

66. Which was to merge with *Disc* in 1966.

CHAPTER TWELVE

'The Chicago stockyards smell good and clean by comparison'

In Rancho Cucamonga, a community in southern California's San Bernardino County, pinch-faced matrons of the type who delight in delivering nagging lectures to strangers about breaches of social etiquette, had taken to emitting an exaggerated *tcch!* whenever their paths crossed those of 21-year-old Frank Zappa and his friend Jim 'Motorhead' Sherwood.

Frank's hair had been causing comment almost from the moment he arrived among the several thousand-odd souls who lived in a town where the 1940s hadn't ended yet. While it was only just beyond the limit that marked sobriety – and his ears were still visible – he'd stopped plastering it with mannish brilliantine, and started brushing it forwards. 'It was aiming downwards too,' Frank would remember, 'and was about three inches long. In that day and age for that part of the country, I was a mutant in striped shirts unheard of to a population that thrives on the white, short-sleeved sports shirt plus bow tie – because that's what you wore to work.'

Zappa ran Studio Z, a three-room recording complex with blacked-out windows that stood on North Archibald Avenue, bounded by a malt shop, a school, a Holy Roller church and, precisely opposite the studio, San Bernardino County Courthouse. It was but one of many such shoestring enterprises dotted beyond the outer rim of Los Angeles where music was manoeuvred through reverberation units, echo chambers and further contrivances amid tape spools and a spaghetti of jack-to-jack leads through which only the sound engineer could navigate.

Lately, Studio Z had been redecorated. The overall colour scheme was olive-green and turquoise, broken by framed items including letters beginning 'I regret to inform you... ' and a threat from the Department of Motor Vehicles to revoke Frank's licence. He also painted large signs saying RECORD YOUR BAND and $13.50 AN HOUR for display at the entrance.

For a while, Zappa and Kay, his soon-to-be ex-wife, had paid the price of sharing the same address by driving one another mad. In the first days of their marriage, however, Frank had appeared to pursue a path of conventional maturity, amenable to functioning by day variously – and sometimes concurrently – as a window dresser, a door-to-door encyclopaedia salesman, behind the counter in a jeweller's and, lasting the longest, as a greetings card designer. He was also a newspaper advertisement copywriter for businesses that included the bank where Kay, her hair glaciated with spray, was a clerk.

With jobs presented to him on a plate, a sagacious and good-looking spouse and their parents' financial safety valve, the story might have ended there, but, to cut to the chase, Frank upped and quit, decamping to rough it in Studio Z with 'Motorhead' Sherwood – whose student grant helped with the rent and who also filched food from the refectory at his college, adding to a larder consisting mainly of peanut butter, instant mashed potato, white bread, coffee, honey, processed cheese and a cheap brand of gravy powder of institutionalised lumpiness. Because they also had to have their cigarettes, empty bottles were accumulated and returned to grocery stores for the two-cent deposits by Zappa, Sherwood – and Lorraine Belcher, a strapping titian-haired beauty in her late teens, whom Frank had chatted up in a Los Angeles snack bar, implying that he was a film director who could make her famous.

A Studio Z endeavour to branch out into movies had got underway with the purchase of a job lot of scenery in an auction at a Hollywood studio in receivership. The consequent focus was on Captain Beefheart Vs. The Grunt People, a screenplay of an outer space persuasion, set on Mars with a role earmarked for Don Vliet, a youth who'd been in Zappa's year at high school, and was the possessor of a bestial Howlin' Wolf-ish bass-baritone.

For the local Ontario Daily Report, the projected flick was enough for a scoop about a local man bringing a touch of Tinseltown glamour to the district, even if *Captain Beefheart Vs. The Grunt People*, should it ever be finished, was unlikely to match *Ben-Hur* in terms of cinematic and dramatic quality. The centrefold article mentioned, too, that its director was on the look-out for folk to be extras, even to take bit parts.

Reading of this, a Jim Willis became interested in auditioning to be 'Senator Gurney', one of the 'bad guys'. Jim was a police sergeant assigned to the vice squad. Among duties to which he applied himself most exultantly was patrolling public toilets, usually in plain clothes, to either traduce homosexuals or catch them in the act.

Pop music wasn't Sergeant Jim's domain at all. He didn't know, therefore, what to make of an episode of CBS television's comedy series, *The Lucy Show,* in which stooge 'Mr Mooney' had wanted to book, for a hundred dollars, 'that English combo everyone's talking about' for the bank's dinner-and-dance. Jim's teenage relations had been like an alarm clock that couldn't shut off since The Beatles' vividly documented and messianic descent on New York's John F. Kennedy International Airport on 7 February 1964. They were there for *The Ed Sullivan Show* two nights after a press conference on touchdown in which questions like 'Do you guys think there'll be another war soon?' ('Yeah, Friday') and 'Will you be getting your haircut soon?' ('I just had one yesterday') were fired at them.

So began British beat's subjugation of the commercial territory that mattered most via a large scale rerun of the hysteria known at home. Even a few weeks earlier, no one would have assumed that The Beatles would be anything more than a strictly European phenomenon. Why should the USA want them anyway?

Why should British beat groups want the USA? A lot of them disliked the glimpses they'd had of the place. 'When the Dave Clark Five started,' reflected their drummer-leader, 'we used to play US air bases in England. It was hell because the American servicemen kept getting drunk. It was the only side of America I'd seen, and I didn't care for it.'

Yet Dave would be made to care after his Five embarked on an exploratory tour prior to taking Uncle Sam for every cent they could get. The 'Great Adventure' had begun a few weeks after that of The

A man of means like **Charles II** had cropped hair covered by a (peri)wig for formal occasions.

Dundee tragedian **William McGonagall** – Britain's most renowned 'bad' poet – was mocked for jet-black hair swept back into a thick immensity (vaguely like the rear end of a duck).

November 1958: Durrington Youth Hall. Wiltshire, thrills to the sound of **The Boppers** featuring Dave Dee (central microphone) – and Phil Ball (far left) who had had his hair cut Mohican-style for a bet.

The King in his mid-1950s pomp

Teddy Boys remained active long after their post-war emergence – as seen in an image captured during a musical evening in 1977 at the Queen's Hotel in Southend.

The Rolling Stones (left to right seated: Bill Wyman, Brian Jones, Keith Richards, Mick Jagger and, obscured, Charlie Watts) during a press conference at Amsterdam airport on 26 March 1966 prior to commencing a European tour in Belgium that very evening.

As a Canadian schoolboy, pop music jack-of-all-trades **Gary Pig Gold** (right) modelled himself on David McCallum (left), who starred as secret agent 'Illya Kuryakin' in the internationally-syndicated spy drama series *The Man from U.N.C.L.E.* (and was the subject of a correlated tribute disc, 'Love Ya, Illya' by a pseudononymous Alma Cogan).

What a difference a decade made: **the author** in 1967 and 1977.

From a comparatively safe billet in Germany, some US soldiers formed **The Monks**. The title track of 1966's *Black Monk Time* LP outlined how much the group, with their gimmick tonsures, loathed the army.

Singing pianist **Esquerita** was among black rock 'n' rollers who used pomade that checked the tendency of Afro-textured locks to dry inflexibly.

Frank Zappa in session during spring 1965 after his barrister suggested a haircut to help his presentation in the best possible light for a forthcoming trial for 'conspiracy to commit pornography'.

A 1964 Dutch release by **PJ Proby**, visually conspicuous for a pre-Victorian ponytail, first known commonly as a 'queue'.

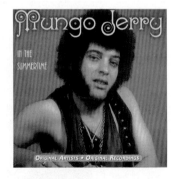

Ray Dorset of Mungo Jerry was one of the most charismatic figures to leap from the screen of BBC1's Top of the Pops during the 1970s.

The Beatles are accosted by a fan in the era before darkness became their only shield against the havoc that would surround their every public appearance.

Led by Frank Zappa (centre top), **The Mothers Of Invention**'s first toured Europe almost as a freak show, thanks not least to a media primed to accentuate a notoriety amassed within their native USA.

The Who's Keith Moon (right) with fellow Middlesex-raised outrager **David, 'Screaming Lord', Sutch** (left), the finest Prime Minister this kingdom never had.

From 1967's shock of corkscrews, **Jimi Hendrix** was to adopt more of an African 'natural' look before his death two years later.

Robert Plant during Led Zeppelin's 'imperial' period in the 1970s. Years before, however, Plant was noticeable as 'a local Mod with very short hair' by guitarist Dave Hill, then yet to form Slade, formerly Ambrose Slade, who, in 1969, adopted a corporate 'skinhead' look.

The greaseless hairstyle of **Adam Faith** was among factors that assisted his UK chart breakthrough with 1959's 'What Do You Want?'.

Schoolgirl comics and their associated annuals tended to reflect their editors' idealisation of teenage life – hence this girl in a mid-calf dress dancing with a short-haired boy, her eyes not focussed on him. In parenthesis, he looks about twelve – while she could be as old as twenty-eight.

David Bowie in concert at London's Hammersmith Odeon on 3 July 1973, which culminated with him announcing the 'retirement' of his 'Ziggy Stardust' persona.

The Small Faces (left to right: Steve Marriott, Ronnie Lane, Ian McLagan and Kenney Jones) in transition from Mod to hippy.

The Pretty Things (left to right) John Stax, Dick Taylor (beard),
Viv Prince (hat), Phil May (lower front) and Brian Pendleton in 1965.

Phil May exudes septuagenarian joviality on 13 December 2018 during The Pretty Things'
televised farewell performance.

Beatles. Some would argue that they shut down the latter fleetingly as Uncle Sam's top British act. They endured disembarkation at JFK; long corridors of light and shadow; and stick-mikes thrust towards their mouths in the hopes that, like John, Paul, George and Ringo, the Five would crack back in their alien dialect at banal, ill-informed enquiries, as repetitious as a stuck record, from circling media hounds.

'I don't think anyone expected musicians playing rock 'n' roll to have any wit or repartee at all,' reckoned the Five's Mike Smith. As pedestrian as their interrogators at times, it was the Britons' overall combination of zaniness, bluff unsentimentality, unblinking self-assurance and the poker-faced, *what-are-you-laughing-at* way they said 'em that capsized what might have been expected from incumbent pop stars who were relatively devoid of independent opinion when providing copy for *16*, *Datebook*, *Hit Parader* and similar US teen periodicals, often with text by men with female pseudonyms, and bought primarily for their pictures, and full of probing items about the gorgeous smile of some cosseted and distanced idol. 'Our appeal,' summarised Ringo Starr at a press conference in Milwaukee, 'is that we're ordinary lads.' As it had in Blighty, this proved effective in soothing the woes of a country depressed by recent traumas: vehement opposition to the Civil Rights amendment, the first boy-soldiers blown to bits in Indo-China and John F Kennedy's assassination by Lee Harvey Oswald in Dallas (and Vice President Lyndon B. Johnson assuming supreme office on the same November day in 1963 that The Beatles' forthcoming US trip was announced). John Lennon's more forthright theory was 'that kids everywhere all go for the same stuff and, seeing we'd done it in England, there's no reason why we couldn't do it in America too'.

What's more, the US Top Twenty was sodden with Bobby-ballads, forgettable instrumentals and anthems like The Beach Boys' 'Be True To Your School'. To the chagrin of The Beach Boys, the Four Seasons and others on the same record label, Capitol, the intruding Beatles were launched with one of the most far-reaching publicity blitzes hitherto known. As a result, their 'I Want To Hold Your Hand' would be stuck at a timely Number One on 2 February while clambering up the chart would be all those Beatles discs that, in 1963, had been aired to negligible listener response on those few US radio stations that could be bothered to spin them.

Beatle chewing gum alone netted millions of dollars within months – because, as is their wont, the North Americans, once convinced of something incredible, exhibited a fanaticism that left British Beatle-maniacs swallowing dust. Our transatlantic cousins were devouring the grass on which the group had trodden, and swooning on fingering a guitar autographed by all four and owned by someone who'd declared himself 'The Beatles' Oldest Fan'. Whingeing from their children would cause well-off US parents, just coming to terms with them squandering their allowances on, say, a six dollar can of 'Beatle Breath', to interrupt European holidays in order to fly, garlanded with cameras, to Liverpool, where back copies of *Mersey Beat* would fetch inflated prices, and the seat on which Ringo had, allegedly, always perched when in the Cavern bandroom was kissed like the Blarney Stone. Next, a US record label – the first of many – got hold of poor old Pete Best, who, with his group, was hauled over the ocean to milk his connection via a sell-out North American tour at odds with ebbing interest in him at home, even on Merseyside.

Pete benefited too from the unearthing of items he, John, Paul and George had recorded in Germany as backing group to Tony Sheridan, a guitarist-singer who'd created a ripple on *Oh Boy!* in 1959. While it had been his old Hamburg club underlings who had brought Tony to a wider public than he may have warranted in the normal course of events after a repromoted one of these, 'My Bonnie', sold a supposed million in 1964, he was uneasy about pieces by The Beatles and him that were planned to be doctored for rush-release. However, it was to his advantage to stay malleable for the time being by, say, re-recording his vocal to their arrangement of the 'Sweet Georgia Brown' pre-war jazz standard, inserting money-spinning references, e.g. 'In Liverpool she'd even dare/to criticise The Beatles' hair'.

'Just about everyone is tired of The Beatles,' cried *Billboard*, 'except the record-buying public.'

'Britain hasn't been so influential in American affairs since 1775', read the same editorial as the summer approached and the

Animals became the second UK beat group to top the US chart. Fascination with all things from the land of Good Queen Bess – Robin Hood, fish 'n' chips, Oxford and Cambridge, Beefeaters, monocled cads and kilted Scotsmen *et al* – was to peak in that autumn week when two-thirds of the *Hot 100* was British in origin, and The Beatles occupied *nine* positions in the Canadian Top Ten. Until then, this sceptre'd isle had been the provider of short-lived chart contenders – with the Tornados' 'Telstar', the quintessential 1960s instrumental, playing Erik the Red to the Columbus of the seven weeks 'I Want To Hold Your Hand' spent at pole position in *Billboard*.

Yet what has passed into myth as the 'British Invasion' had less to do with the entertainers themselves than with the way the imagination of the North American public was captured – and, more pragmatically, that of the many US music industry bigwigs and individuals – songwriters, recording artists, producers and just plain scene-makers – who, correctly anticipating further demand for UK talent, were debating whether or not to cross the Atlantic to stake claims in the cultural diggings.

Although one executive was overheard cawing, 'I tell ya, Elmer, you heard one Limey outfit, ya heard 'em all,' most of Britain's major pop acts[67] made progress to varying extents in the previously unchartered United States and Canada. Some minor ones did too. Thanks to the printing of a photo of them in *16*, Middlesex's West Five acquired a New York fan club. Grander still, the Hullabaloos, able to amble unrecognised down the sleepy streets of their native Kingston upon Hull, risked being set upon by libidinous fans not much younger than themselves after scoring twice in the *Hot 100* and being inevitably omnipresent on *Hullabaloo*, which rivalled *Shindig!* as the most popular nationally broadcast US pop show.

A crucial element in the Hullaballoos' good fortune was their shoulder-length peroxided locks[68] – and The Beatles' gimmick

---

67. Perhaps the most unexpected such entertainer to strike lucky was Adam Faith, whose domestic B-side, 'It's Alright', reached *Billboard*'s Top Forty.

68. The similarly bleached-blond Blackwells were losers in a 'Battle of the Bands' contest that provided much of the plot in the Gerry and Pacemakers' film, *Ferry Cross the Mersey*.

moptops had also been a principal focus of US fuss before they'd crossed the Atlantic. Capitol required its merchandising staff to wear Beatle wigs during business hours, and tried to foist them on radio presenters and other potentially useful human publicity outlets. Paul McCartney was to suggest, 'the money was mainly spent in Los Angeles, getting people like Janet Leigh to wear the wigs and be photographed in them. Once a film star like her did that, it could get syndicated across America: "Look at this funny picture; Janet Leigh in this wacko wig" – and it *did* get us noticed!'

While the group was yet to jet back to England, record company executives were being accosted by songwriters who, the morning after that pivotal *Ed Sullivan Show* with 74 million tuning in, had been adding the finishing touches over breakfast to cash-in; numbers like Donna Lynn's 'My Boyfriend Got a Beatle Haircut' and 'The Boy with the Beatle Hair' by the Swans. There were also plenty of hastily assembled soundalike and 'tribute' discs by such as the American Beetles, the Bug Men, John and Paul, the Merseyboys and others *ad nauseam*, mostly groups consisting of session musicians who probably bitched about The Beatles during coffee breaks.

'Ringo, I Love You' and 'Santa, Bring Me Ringo' were among anthems of adoration issued before the year was out, but there were others such as the more generalised 'Are You a Boy or Are You a Girl?' from the Barbarians, a Hot 100 entry which contained the line, 'You're either a girl, or you come from Liverpool'. Further examples were 'The Beatles Barber' by Scott Douglas and 'To Kill a Beetle' [*sic*], a 45 of unconscious presentiment, by somebody called Johnny Guarnier. Its lyric was from the perspective of a US teenager, insanely jealous because every other girl at high school had lost her marbles over the new sensations from England.

There was no mention in Johnny's lyrics of local outfits who'd found it paid to break up and reform as soon as they'd either grown their hair or acquired wigs. They even rehearsed tortuous Liverpudlian accents and slang – 'wack', 'gear', 'fab' and so on – for onstage continuity during a set consisting wholly of *yeah-yeah-yeah* Beatles/Merseybeat imitations. Some tried passing themselves off as genuine Britons while those in 'redneck' climes – such as San

Antonio's Sir Douglas Quintet – were apprehensive about sporting a *Pilzkopf* offstage for fear of disapproval expressed in terms stronger than simply hollering 'Get your dad-blasted hair cut!' from across the street.[69]

Frank Zappa's parents in Lancaster, an hour's non-stop drive away from Cucamonga, had come close to washing their hands of him, despite his sister pinning pictures of The Beatles on the walls of her bedroom, and despite their reading that what had originally been deemed a 'British phenomenon' now had a Chicago barber reporting that 80 per cent of his young customers wanted moptops. Perhaps even more revealing, not one of a competition-level rowing crew at Pennsylvania's Eastern University, affiliated with the American Baptist Churches, had a crew cut anymore.

For many of Cucamonga's citizenry, colour was as sensitive a subject as Zappa and Sherwood's hair, particularly to the local Holy Rollers, vexed as they were by a white woman with a black baby – overnight guests of Lorraine Belcher – playing together on the pavement in front of Studio Z. Also, the studio's proprietor was, so they'd gathered, the guitarist in the provocatively named Muthers, a guitar-bass-drums combo who'd gained a regular gig at the Saints and Sinners, a tavern catering largely to Mexican agricultural labourers.

Hence, when word of this, plus disputed complaints about noise escaping from Studio Z's double glazing and infiltrating the surrounding non-residential buildings, reached the Cucamonga

---

69. Conversely, longhairs on road trips below the Mason-Dixon line would indulge in a cowardly game of slowing down and yelling 'motherfuckers!' at kerbside groups of rednecks, and then pressing down the accelerator. Sometimes the car would stall, and they'd have to face the consequences. For those who don't know, 'rednecks' was the name given to whites from North America's Deep South. It was first used in reference to field workers whose backs of shaven necks were exposed and scorched red by the sun. Later, it became a derogatory term for all those parodied as unsophisticated, clannish, bigoted and anti-intellectual, given to right-wing sloganeering, inciting suspicion of labour unions and minority groups. This was laced with alternate matey camaraderie and pious fear towards not so much 'God' as 'The Lord', 'The Man In the Sky', 'The Boss Of The Riders' or, if you'd swallowed a dictionary, 'The Big Architect', a homespun prairie Plato with a crewcut and a Charles Atlas-like physique.

police station, it provided additional excuses to put the bite on the parish oddball.[70] The operation got underway during a beer break at the Saints and Sinners when a plain clothes officer sidled up to the Muthers' guitarist to enquire about the price of him making training films for the force's vice department. Unbeknownst to Frank, the same vice squad were to begin a stake-out of Studio Z, going so far as to bore a spyhole through the wall from the shop next door. As, after a few weeks, there was nothing illegal worth pursuing, Jim Willis, posing as a car salesman, called one Thursday in March 1965 to ask Zappa about the production of a stag movie for his firm's party the following Wednesday. It wasn't feasible at such short notice, calculated Frank, who, nonetheless, offered to put together an audio alternative, and directed Willis to return the following day. Via a mini-microphone attached to the sergeant's wristwatch, the entire exchange was heard in a truck parked opposite.

Overnight, Zappa and Belcher simulated 20 minutes of orgasmic moans and heavy breathing on faked bedsprings from which their laughter was erased and backing music added. 'We didn't even take our clothes off,' affirmed Lorraine. With no prior knowledge – and minus the contrived creaking – you might have mistaken it for the sound of two people who had been sprinting. Yet it was enough for the siege of Studio Z to enter its next stage with tip-offs to the printed media about what was to happen bright and early next morning when *agent provocateur* Jim bowled into Studio Z with only half the agreed fee. When an irate Frank refused to surrender the tape, Willis pulled out his badge – and then came the shouting at the door, the uniforms in the execution of their duty, the ransacking, the seizure of all recorded material, the monotonal caution, and the click of cameras as, so the *Ontario Daily Report* put it on its front page, 'vice squad investigators stilled the tape-recorders of a free swinging A-Go-Go film and arrested a self-styled movie producer and his buxom red-haired companion'.

---

70. There were, too, embryonic plans afoot by the Chamber of Commerce for the studio to be demolished to widen North Archibald Avenue.

Every pore of his ashen complexion was bestowed with a pinprick of sweat as Frank was charged with 'conspiracy to commit pornography' for which, so the gleeful desk sergeant informed him, he could receive decades in jail. Zappa's livid father grubbed around for the bail, and he and Frank bounced thoughts off the assigned barrister, who suggested Frank had a haircut to help his presentation in the best possible light during the trial in the courthouse facing the studio where the defendant's counsel argued that there was no case to answer for what amounted to entrapment. Through the oratorical skills of an unctuous 26-year-old prosecutor, however, the bench overruled this plea, feeling perhaps that, among the other concerns, a thirst for vengeance for the indignation that Zappa's 'long hair' had inflamed, needed to be quenched.

A 'guilty' verdict was announced, and an intrinsically law-abiding young man was steered out of the dock, having received three years probation. In addition, Frank was to serve an evil and slow ten days of a suspended six-month sentence in San Bernardino County Jail.

After the convict transporter bus jolted into the prison, the occupants' hair was cruelly mowed. Then they were issued with regulation ill-fitting garb with the texture of a horse blanket, and escorted to Tank C where strip lights glimmered day and night, and a solitary shower unit was so filthy that Zappa chose not to wash or shave for his entire confinement. The only advantage derivable from the episode was that, even when Zappa's 'criminal record' was expunged from files after a year, his ten days inside remained enough to exempt him from the draft just as the actuality of the Vietnam War began gripping harder. Otherwise, the shock of Tank C and the debasing haircut provoked ever more palpable stirrings of resentment of authority beyond the family circle and school, turning him into a distrustful cynic.

His years were divided now into before and after the vice squad's forced access to the studio. Justice had been seen to be adjustable and subjective. Yet Frank's bitterness was pointless if it couldn't be directed at getting even, not on Willis and his pals, shaking each other's hands in congratulations in the courtroom, but on whatever higher power had allowed them to do so.

He was almost as emaciated as a Nazi death camp internee, but otherwise seemed undamaged physically, although 'after my release, it took me two years to learn to drive without looking over my shoulder,' Frank glowered. 'I was convinced I was under constant surveillance'. The psychological conflicts born of his incarceration were, therefore, a long time resolving themselves as a shaken Zappa acquired skills in the evasions needed to make life halfway bearable in a society sustained largely by pretence. For a while, he went to any lengths, however hard he had to rein in his rage, to avoid public conflicts in case they backfired and involved the police again.

Yet, with nowhere else to go, he'd screwed himself up to return to Cucamonga where he tried to disregard the smirks of passers-by at the spectacle he presented of transgression rebuked, namely the severely 'decent' haircut from which nothing could deflect attention, even when, after much mental debate before the shaving-mirror, he began cultivating what was to become his trademark moustache and dagger beard (that one day, would actually be known as 'the Zappa').

After he was effectively railroaded out of Cucamonga, the prison trim was still so apparent that he 'was kind of freaky-looking' to Jimmy Carl Black, drummer with the Soul Giants, a 'covers band' with sporadic one-nighters in and around Los Angeles' dance hall circuit. Even Black and bass player Roy Estrada who resided in Orange County, a region more conservatively 'redneck' than Cucamonga, didn't quite like to laugh at a guy with the shortest hair in the city.

Owing to the on-going obsession with all things British, becoming the Giants' guitarist might not have been a sound notion during what Frank would recall as 'a strange time. We didn't have long hair, so didn't work very much'. The competition was there for all to see. There were the Standells,[71] operational around Hollywood since 1962, but whose second B-side was entitled 'Peppermint Beatle'; the Factory, who'd obtain a cameo in a TV sitcom as 'The Bedbugs'; and the Turtles, once surf instrumentalists the Crossfires at Westchester

---

71. Another group who wore Beatle wigs until their own hair had grown the required length.

High School where chalk-and-talk was interrupted by the whooshings of passenger jets from Los Angeles International Airport.

Some such outfits were driven by market expediency. A common complaint was that of Zappa: 'If you didn't sound like The Beatles or the Stones, you didn't get hired.' However, the reasoning behind the formation in 1964 of Captain Beefheart and his Magic Band, fronted by Don Vliet, was mostly their enthusiastic absorption, irrespective of financial gain, of The Rolling Stones' style and onstage mannerisms. They did this to such an extent that some imagined the group weren't counterfeit Limeys like everyone else, but had been imported from R&B London.

Back then, they could have been categorised as a 'garage band', which by original definition is 'punk', a word first applied to outfits like the Shadows of Knight, the Sonics, the Seeds, the Standells, the Thirteenth Floor Elevators, ? (Question Mark) and the Mysterians, and those that contained Lou Reed, Iggy Pop and future members of the Alice Cooper group. Furthermore, Jim Morrison, the son of a rear admiral (one of a long line of military careerists), had been avidly digesting answers to enquiries on how to get started in pop, even before the Invasion, keeping an ear to the ground for a combo that could use him after he commenced a degree course in theatre and film.

Especially after '(I Can't Get No) Satisfaction' topped the US chart in summer 1965, most garage bands tended to owe less to The Beatles and more to the Stones – the Barbarians whose 'Are You A Boy Or A Girl' referenced the Stones ('You can dance like a female monkey, but sink like a stone... yeah a Rolling Stone')[72] and Toronto's Ugly Ducklings, who, while actually supporting the Stones at the city's Maple Leaf Gardens, sounded more uncannily like the English ensemble on the radio than too many similar offerings by other lookalikes.

Though the Ducklings were fronted by a vocalist with a passing resemblance to Brian Jones, more desirable was a Jagger-like singer who, when he wasn't also blowing mouth organ or wielding maracas,

---

72. The Barbarians are remembered as fondly for the hook-shaped artificial left hand of drummer Victor Moulton.

would be like the one in Benny Hill's spoof Strolling Ones, right down to kicking one leg backwards as if dancing a half-hearted Charleston. To his right, the blond – possibly bleached – fellow transfixing the girls with his 'Brooding Intensity' would be playing what could either be mistaken, for or actually was, a Vox Teardrop Mk. VI. With its sensuous if lozenge-shaped table, this was to be as synonymous with Brian Jones as the Stratocaster was with Hank B Marvin.

Many weeks before The Rolling Stones had threaded through customs at JFK in June 1964 for their first tour of the States, almost as a freak show, the US media had been primed to accentuate their notoriety ('dirtier, streakier and more dishevelled than The Beatles', London Associated Press had raged) which reached such a pitch that adolescent North America and its exploiters had anticipated a resounding outcry that here were not four but *five* Horsemen of the Apocalypse, spreading plague and destruction wherever they passed. Gene Pitney had seen this coming when he'd landed in New York in 1963, with the screams from an edition of *Thank Your Lucky Stars* with The Rolling Stones still in his ears. In the *Daily Mirror*, he had joked, 'When I first saw them, I didn't know whether to say hello or bark.'[73]

Though the *Los Angeles Times* considered the group worthy of a major write-up, its emphasis was almost solely on that hair: 'One of them looks like a chimpanzee. One resembles the encyclopaedia drawings of Pithecanthropus erectus. Two look like very ugly Radcliffe girls.[74] The fifth is a double for Ray Bolger in the role of *Charley's Aunt*.'[75]

In August 1964, another article in that same newspaper cautioned that the Stones' 'loose-lipped, loose-hipped, long-haired

---

73. Yet Pitney tinkled piano on the Stones' first LP, and would penetrate 1964's British Top Ten and the US Hot 100 with 'That Girl Belongs to Yesterday', a ballad penned by Mick Jagger and Keith Richards.
74. Radcliffe College in Cambridge, Massachusetts was a sister institution to the all-male Harvard.
75. The 1892 play *Charley's Aunt* by Brandon Thomas was the basis of a Broadway and West End musical and, later, a movie also starring Bolger and requiring him to dress as a lady.

(at least three inches longer than George Harrison's) eccentricity frightens parents, thrills teenagers and makes The Beatles look as crony as a crew cut'.

'The kids were fascinated by us,' confirmed Keith Richards. 'They'd all had a taste of The Beatles so it was like, "Oh look, there's more!" – but the older generation, the real entrenched conservative American types, they didn't take to us at all. It was the same thing as the English press but with the American spin on it. If anything they were even more horrified than the English.'

Particularly put out were those with an inbred hatred of 'commies', blacks – and 'queers' like this new breed of 'musical' Limey longhairs headed by the Stones who, during a second jaunt to the USA in 1964, snatched a few hours of serenity round a Savannah swimming pool only to be interrupted when, recounted Richards, 'we were arrested for topless bathing. Some people were driving by, and swore that there was a load of chicks leaping in and out of the pool with just a pair of drawers on. So the cops came zooming in to bust these "chicks" – and, of course, the closer they got, the more stupid they must have felt – especially when they heard these London accents'.

Yet, in comparison to that of The Beatles in February – when they'd been greeted by the unison banshee scream they'd mistaken for engine noise on touchdown – the Stones' initial welcome to the USA had been muted, mainly because, unlike the Fab Four, the way hadn't been paved by a *Billboard* Number One. 1964 was half over, and the Stones' progress in that same tabulation had been negligible. 'Come On' had not been considered worthy of a US release, and 'I Wanna Be Your Man' had B-sided 'Not Fade Away', which, beginning a creep around the *Hot 100*'s lower reaches at Number 98, became the chief selling point of 33 rpm *Britain's Newest Hitmakers* a volley fired at the LP list.

A few hundred fans converged, nonetheless, on the airport's upper terraces as the newcomers were subjected to the *woomph* of flashbulbs and a rush of microphone-held questioning. Coming across as more rivals to the Dave Clark Five than The Beatles, nothing particularly funny or even significant emerged from the Stones' lips, either then or during their first jetlagged radio interview

– at cock-crow on New York's WINS radio interview station, an episode of wry shallowness conducted by a yapping presenter with the *nom de turntable* 'Murray the K'. The brashest of them all, he'd had the unmitigated audacity to proclaim himself 'the Fifth Beatle' and now 'the Sixth Rolling Stone'.

From Manhattan's Astor Hotel, Brian Jones hazarded a stroll around Times Square on the afternoon prior to an internal flight to Los Angeles for a mismatching on a television variety show hosted by Dean Martin, one of Sinatra's 'Rat Pack', who dished out derogatory quips at the Stones' expense ('You're under the impression they have long hair. Not true at all... it's an optical illusion... they just have low foreheads and high eyebrows'). In passing, sixteen-year-old Stephen King, watching at the time, was to recall, 'I thought, "Fuck you, you old lounge lizard. You're the past, I've just seen the future."'[76]

They made their US concert debut before a crowd of not quite 5,000 at San Bernardino's Swing Auditorium on a bill with three Bobbies (Vee, Comstock and Goldsboro). Generally, the remaining shows were either like that or poorly attended headlining affairs like the one in Minneapolis's half-empty Excelsior State Ballroom. Yet, as it had been when punishing seasons in Hamburg had toughened up The Beatles in readiness for what lay ahead, weeks of exploratory hard graft in the States were the Stones' 'Hamburg'. They were often arduous but contained hidden blessings. With nothing yet describable as a 'hit', the group was obliged to melt the *sangfroid* of the most unresponsive audiences. Although they were judged and found wanting on a couple of occasions, some of the crowd felt a compulsion to dance only a few bars into the first number, and Mick Jagger was twisting 'em round his little finger by the finish on the evidence of the bedlam you could hear back in the dressing rooms.

During two performances, compèred by the Sixth Rolling Stone, at Carnegie Hall – New York's premier auditorium – 23 June, capacity crowds went crazy enough to provoke a ban on pop extravaganzas there for the foreseeable future. On this final day of their most testing public journey thus far, the group had been determined not

---

76. As a novelist in later life, King would be dubbed 'The King of Horror'.

to quit the stage until the entire place was jumping, while making a run of the most frantic ravers all the more piquant by hanging fire midway and inserting the doe-eyed 'Tell Me'. This was a Jagger-Richards original on their first British LP, which, as a US-only single, was inching at last into the national Top Thirty (guaranteeing a fair hearing for a rapid follow-up, 'It's All Over Now') and *England's Newest Hitmakers* commenced its pedantic climb to Number 11.

Amassing further widespread support between their first and second visits, the Stones' breakthrough was, nevertheless, as low-fat margarine to full-cream dairy butter when compared to that of The Beatles. The New World would be almost as commercially hospitable towards Peter and Gordon, an upper-class duo who released five US albums to every one they did in Britain, and to the Zombies from Hertfordshire, who seemed the epitome of well-mannered, educated choristers, straight out of *Tom Brown's Schooldays*. With Frankie Avalon playing it posh too as 'The Potato Bug', an English pop-singing 'refugee from a haircut' in *Bikini Beach* (one of those sun-kissed movies made over and over again then), differing from The Dave Clark Five's 'common' *norf* London accents (and those personnel in the Stones with *sarf* London ones), a male in a post-Beatles US group in the British image had to make up his mind whether to come on as a proper Lord Snooty or a Cockney barrow boy using often-redundant east London colloquialisms such as 'blimey, guv'nor' and 'blighter', and addressing other men as 'mate'.

What were they to do, therefore, after hearing talk by Manchester's Freddie and the Dreamers and Herman's Hermits, led by Peter Noone – a former cast member of the *Coronation Street* soap opera based, apparently, in one of its outlying towns – who had a boyish aspect like a young JFK or an older John F. Kennedy, Jr., then less than ten years of age but beginning to look less like a schoolboy with a head of well-groomed short hair than a Beatle?

Emerging from a long-haul internal flight, groups like Peter's and Freddie's might be greeted, even in the graveyard hours, by hundreds of hot-eyed teenagers, many chaperoned by parents who hadn't chastised them for shirking household chores to ogle a TV 'documentary' of Freddie and his Dreamers' first US press conference – with surreptitious hand-held studies of Freddie's ear lasting minutes on end – for, if nothing else, they, Herman's Hermits and, before them, The Dave Clark Five with their sporty image and matching threads, were palatable compromises to 'hairy monsters' like the Stones, The Kinks, Them – and The Pretty Things, whose line 'I laid her on the ground' from 'Don't Bring Me Down' required censoring by US radio (and the issue of a cleaned-up rendition by something called 'On Her Majesty's Service').

For the Stones, the danger of being superseded by an outfit that would make them look tame – which had led to that blockage by Andrew Oldham of any re-engagement of The Pretty Things on *Ready Steady Go!* – was as worrying a psychological undertow in the States too. On the strength of sound alone, let alone its makers' appearance, 'Don't Bring Me Down' wiped the floor with the twee 'Tell Me', didn't it? In theory, the ubiquitous Pretty Things were likely so delightfully horrify the Land of the Free that the Stones might be lost in their shadow.

The group's office rang with proposed tour schedules from US entrepreneurs yelling 'Klondike!' at the notion of a grotesque carnival of even greater magnitude than those dreadful Rolling Stones. The Things' domestic reputation – with Phil May's cascading tresses publicised now as the longest of any male not only in Britain but everywhere else – was highlighted via trade advertisements ('Proof positive that long hair *can* be popular!'), filmed TV snippets and mention in that *Los Angeles Times* feature about the Stones.[77]

Dollars danced before the Things' eyes as their management dithered: big place, America, isn't it? In any case, in 1965, US immigration authorities were temporarily to refuse visas for more Limey longhairs wishing to propagate their filth in Uncle Sam's fair land, supported by those like an Illinois newspaper's critic: 'You walk out of the amphitheatre after watching The Rolling Stones perform and suddenly the Chicago stockyards smell good and clean by comparison.'[78]

---

77. 'A member of a group called The Pretty Things wears his longer still, and has it cut and set in a style that calls to mind Clairol ads.'
78. Charlie Watts was to design a comic strip for a concert programme for a Stones US tour the following year, which included a Jagger figure singing on

Such denigration was balanced by the hippest of the hip digging the Stones – who had already visited Studio 54 in midtown Manhattan at the insistence of Andy Warhol – whose mannered revelling in kitsch and trashy commodity, which included listening avidly to Top Forty radio, was part and parcel of Pop Art, a movement descended from Dada with its broad and provocative premise that anyone could create art, no matter how absurd, trivial or pretentious the end result – and there needn't necessarily be one.

Warhol also asked to be sneaked into the backstage area of a New York theatre because, as he put it, 'I wanted to be in the presence of the Yardbirds.' Furthermore, Bob Dylan[79] had asked to meet The Pretty Things on his first UK tour, and the Animals' take on 'The House of the Rising Sun' hardened his resolve to 'go electric'. For The Byrds – whose Hollywood version of Dylan's 'Mr Tambourine Man' ('folk-rock' rather than 'folk') was sent on its chart-topping way in June 1965, it had been the Searchers' fusion of Merseybeat and contemporary folk. Furthermore, Them's 'Gloria' B-side was to be subject to a US Top Ten reawakening in 1966 by Chicago's Shadows of Knight, by which time it was a fixture in the repertoires of three-chord 'garage bands' across North America that the invaders had outfitted with vestiges of musical personality.

Among the inestimable number of 'Anglophile' outfits that were crawling from the sub-cultural woodwork in every state of the Union, Vince and the Spiders,[80] although besuited and mop-topped, counted the Yardbirds as a principal inspiration. They would have been bemused by Paul Samwell-Smith's recollection of 'an interview with a disc jockey in the middle of Disneyland – which was going out on the radio. The guard at the door said, "You can't come in. Your hair is too long." "But we're the Yardbirds." "Don't care. Those are the rules." Five years later, I went there independently, and the bloody guards had longer hair than I did'.

Some US groups, nonetheless, chose to remain defiantly un-

(cont.) a stage that grows higher with each frame, the first and final ones captioned 'He's very good... if only he'd have his hair cut.'

79. Who was to confess, 'I was trying to look like Little Richard, my version of Little Richard. I wanted wild hair, I wanted to be recognised.'

80. A group that had transformed itself into Alice Cooper by 1968.

reconstructed. Chicago's American Breed showed this in their very name; Cannibal and the Headhunters from East Los Angeles retained their towering quiffs even when opening for The Beatles at the Hollywood Bowl – and Paul Revere and the Raiders in the Revolutionary War costumes they'd worn since 'Like, Long Hair', managed a spectacular chart comeback in 1965.

Becoming slightly long-tufted themselves was Paul and his Raiders' only concession to the British Invasion, but others from similarly wild and remote North American zones weren't prepared to go even that far. Like certain blood-brothers in Britain – and Australasia – they expelled much hot air planning to accost certain British groups and their imitators to hack off their hair, knowing that such an assault would be applauded by right-thinkin' folk like those in Massachusetts Bay Colony where a 1634 law forbidding long hair on males had yet to be revoked.

Taking more sober stock, parents and teachers kicked up as much dust as those in Britain. While none of their children was to go to the extreme lengths that Christopher Holligan would on that Sussex railway track, Kathi Fowler, a former student at Pattonville Senior High School in Missouri, 'had a friend in school who was pressured to shear his locks. He suffered pneumonia when he ran away from home!' Moreover, according to a diary a Bob Greene kept in 1964 when an adolescent in Bexley (a white 'mom-and-apple-pie' suburb of Columbus, Ohio), his father, while captivated by The Beatles' televised personalities, wouldn't allow Bob to have a moptop, and supported the school principal in the now constant confrontations with other boys who, returning from the summer recess, tried to grow one too. However, that same autumn, Edward T Kores of Connecticut's Westbrook High School preferred suspension to combing his Beatle fringe off a forehead at the front of a scalp otherwise covered with hair shortened at the sides and back. In Vancouver, three senior students of both genders decided that, after shampooing the evening before mass photography for 1964's yearbook, they would apply no expected fixative. However, almost as soon as they presented themselves, they were sent away with fleas in their ears, and told not to return unless they'd 'done' their hair.

Yet to come was the expulsion of 15-year-old Francis Pelletreau from his school in Trenton, New Jersey, for his 'Beatle-length' haircut, an action upheld by acting State Commissioner of Education John Clayton ('it is inconceivable that a pupil must be allowed to dress or appear in some such bizarre, grotesque or outlandish fashion') until the New Jersey chapter of the American Civil Liberties Union (ACLU) rebuked what it construed as a violation of a Supreme Court ruling in 1925 that forbade the use of state power to 'standardise its children'. After an absence of six months, Francis, still pudding-bowled, was back in class.

In autumn 1966, three members of a teenage pop combo named Sounds Unlimited were to go so far as to sue their W.W. Samuel High School in Dallas for its dictates about hair. Protesting that a clause in a recording contract forbade them from having short hair, the group took the case as far as the federal Circuit Courts of Appeals (who declared against them).

Sounds Unlimited was but one of over a hundred masculine, long-hair cases before US federal appellate courts and beyond, and there were instances matching that of Penny Baldwin's brother, of teachers being indicted for cutting pupils' hair. These usually ended either in an out-of-court settlement with reprimand or in cases being dismissed because they fell under a given school's corporal punishment provisions.[81]

It was also OK for two high-flying senior students at a school in New York's Forest Hills to be obliged to wait in the dean's office day after day until they got 'suitable' haircuts, and for Assistant Principal Ray Martin at Fordson High School in Dearborn, Michigan, to shift the goalposts about rules to do with 'excessively long hair on boys'. When some of the better-off fellows offered the

---

81. One court adjudicator cited the USA's Founding Fathers who not only had long hair, but covered it with wigs of greater length 'to enhance their appearance of dignity'. 'We can't mould people who are going to run the world in the 1980s into the shapes of the 1920s. We just can't expect to make the future look like the past. It's bad education even to suggest it', would be the supportive response of Chicago's District Court Judge James B Parsons when he ordered Barrington Consolidated High School to readmit two students who'd been suspended for wearing their hair too long.

compromise of purchasing 30-dollar wigs for classroom use, they were still threatened with punishment until Mr Martin made a scowling show of acceptance with the remark that, 'you care more about how you look than about your education'.

Then there was Norman Limoges, a school administrator in Concord, New Hampshire, who put 18 students on a bus chartered specifically to transport them to a barber, and an education committee in New Jersey which decided that 'ears are usually considered to mark the borderline of propriety', and claimed that a majority of students had voted for this too.

In the wake of the Robert Phernetton affair, a cell of Philadelphia fraternity brothers had plotted to kidnap Elvis Presley and shave him bald, but, by 1964, if a boy had an 'Elvis haircut', it was no longer of much concern to parents. Yet, for moptops, Ringo Starr reckoned, 'everyone, especially in America where it was Crewcut City, they all said "these long-haired creeps"'. Even at a flag-waving British Embassy reception in Washington, patronising Foreign Office males in dull suits and short-back-and-sides, jostled, politely insulted and hailed members of the group like taxis. Despite a woman snipping off a souvenir lock of his hair, Starr seethed only inwardly when asked to present the raffle prizes to these nicely spoken if 'silly people because they hate to admit they like you too. They think it's wrong'.[82]

Among the natives, Roy Orbison, on returning to his Tennessee home from a British tour with The Beatles in 1963, voiced a not entirely universal feeling that, 'As a male, I personally don't like feminine hair on men, and I imagine women don't like it either, but if the fellows are wearing their hair, not just to be different, but because they like it, then I say that's great. The important thing is to be yourself.'

Not everyone was as tolerant below the Mason-Dixon Line, where, as bullet holes in the undercarriage of one Beatle chartered flight testified, some were maddened enough to lie in wait at the end of a runway, shotguns at the ready. Mirroring one of the Big O's

82. Yet when touring Australasia later in 1964, three Beatles consented to the cutting of miniscule sections of their hair by two females who then tried to sell strands of it to fans queuing outside Melbourne's Festival Hall.

observations, Chris Britton of The Troggs[83] was to ascribe such hostility to jealousy, 'probably because their girlfriends liked the new "English" pop songs instead of traditional USA country music'.

As a less acute protest against boys who looked like girls, Jerry Lee Lewis, while not understating his onstage edginess, sheared back the long, crinkly wavy mane that had been his since he first hit the big time. In the 'Bible Belt' too, hellfire sermons were being preached of the divine wrath to fall on communicants who did not subscribe to the casting out of this latest pop pestilence and its flaunting of I Corinthians XI.14: 'Doth not nature itself teach you that if a man have long hair, it is a shame unto him?'

From the likes of the Savannah police, The Rolling Stones had been able to slip smoothly away into the skies and back to England, but, for Sir Douglas Quintet and other incumbent Anglophiles attempting to shape up to breadwinning UK specifications, there remained much suffering, not only in the Deep South, at the hands of cops, rednecks – and even their own parents. According to the *Daily Express*'s 'This Is America' column, a lead guitarist was hauled off stage at one New Jersey venue by his mom for not being home at a specified time.

The group's name wasn't mentioned, thus preventing its capitalising on the affair – unlike Providence's Georgie Porgie and his Fabulous Cry Babies who, like the Ugly Ducklings in Toronto, reached the apogee of their career as the warm-up act for the Stones at the Rhode Island capital's Lowe's Theatre. Already they'd copied the British visitors' repertoire, offhand stagecraft and appearance to the degree that Porgie was cast out of high school for hair length that exceeded the establishment's dress code and, reckoned Principal Joseph E Joyce, Jnr, could 'disrupt and impede' what he called 'school decorum'.

The resulting fuss after his parents pursued the matter, taking it all the way to the US Supreme Court, helped procure Georgie and his Cry Babies a recording contract, although 'it wasn't long at all,' he would protest. 'It would be considered less than average today. By the time the case was heard, everybody had long hair. There was no longer any point in proceeding with it.'

---

83. Who didn't actually perform in North America until the spring of 1968.

CHAPTER THIRTEEN

'In his day, we would all have ended up in the death camps'

In 1949, it had been at a radio station in the Bible Belt city of Houston where the career of the incredible PJ Proby was rooted, but it started to flower 15 years later after he was spotted by Jack Good – then jetting between London and Los Angeles – and soon to be making his mark as a Hollywood movie stereotype of a bowler-hatted, pinstriped Queen's Englishman, complete with furled umbrella, when appearing on and superintending the TV programme *Shindig!* which held its own in a ratings war against *The Beverley Hillbillies*, *Flipper*, *The Munsters* and a cartoon about a pop group called 'The Beadles' on rival channels.

After an introduction effected by songwriter Sharon Sheeley late in 1963, Jack's interest began when he yanked PJ's pre-Invasion long hair and exclaimed, 'By God, it's real, dear boy!' Brought to Britain in April 1964, Proby made hit parade hay over here, following a memorable appearance on *Around The Beatles*, a one-off 1964 special for ITV, overseen by Good along the approximate lines of *Oh Boy!*. For this, Proby donned buckled shoes and a bat-winged blouson shirt but was most visually conspicuous for a ponytail like a pre-Victorian.[84]

On the wings of his first (and biggest) British hit, 'Hold Me', PJ rented a Knightsbridge mews abode with Jimmy Phelge – and Kim Fowley, a Hollywood jack-of-all-trades, who, if a long-jawed beanpole of a fellow, boasted of 'a non-stop river of naked women flowing through the place. We had a cat there too – and Brian Jones stole

---

84. Which must have heartened defiant boys at Bude-and-Stratton Secondary School, Cornwall who, also in 1964, had been commanded by headmaster Mr P R James to 'have a trim or wear ribbons'.

it. Proby and I chased him down the street, and retrieved our cat –
which he'd put up his shirt'.

PJ's outrageous public demeanour as well as a magnificent if
often mannered vocal style sustained him until a fall from grace
in 1965 when his too-tight velvet trousers split, allegedly, from
knee to crotch during the second house at the Croydon ABC and
he was ordered off the stage. It happened on two more occasions
during that same package tour – and there grew suspicions that
the offending garment had been rigged via weakened stitching to
tear at a climactic moment. If this was a repeated publicity stunt,
it backfired. Proby was removed from the remaining concerts and
put other engagements on his calendar (including TV slots) in
jeopardy.

He was replaced on the tour by the ascendant Tom Jones,
who, with his stalwart build, lustrous sideburns and *mucho macho*
aura, was a more orthodox tracer of the Proby scent than Beau
Brummell, Esquire – alias Mike Bush from South Africa – who
attired himself just like his Georgian dandy namesake to cut a dash
on *Ready Steady Go!* where he bowed from the waist over resident
compère Cathy McGowan's hand during the introit to his maiden
45, 'I Know, Know, Know'. The record's failure spurred his return
to the Transvaal after the ungallant tactic of selling the story of his
backstage love-life to the *News of the World*.

Travelling with Brummell-Bush in a converted London
ambulance, equipped with a cocktail cabinet, were his accompanists,
the Detours, a combo from Bognor Regis he'd renamed the Noble
Men. As the Detours, they'd been seen on *Thank Your Lucky Stars*
by a London group of the same name who, to avoid confusion,
became the Who – soon to be among a batch of chart newcomers
in early 1965.

These included The Byrds (whose *Top of the Pops* mimings left their
mark on such as Pete Feenstra who was 'drawn in by the cool
shades and hair' of Roger McGuinn), and the Walker Brothers,
an unrelated amalgam of singers John Maus and Scott Engel,
respectively the guitarist and the bass player in the Dalton Brothers
(a Los Angeles outfit who'd released a Proby number, 'I Only Came

To Dance With You', as a 1963 single) and Gary Leeds, once of the Standells, and also the drummer behind PJ on early UK stage bookings. On returning to California, Gary had suggested to John and Scott that there might be Proby-sized rewards for them in Britain too.

On arrival in London with hair yet to reach Rolling Stone length, their first single, 'Pretty Girls Everywhere' (with Maus on lead vocal), was a flop but, aided by a spot on *Thank Your Lucky Stars*, 'Love Her' peaked at Number Twenty in June 1965. It also set a precedent for all the trio's A-sides until disbandment two years later. Engel would emote in a golden-brown baritone one funereal-paced smash after another, veiled in heavy orchestration, while Maus waded in with supporting harmonies. Omnipresent in Britain, the Brothers emerged as top pin-ups in girls' magazines and once had an entire edition of *Ready Steady Go!* devoted to them. On a more basic level, on the evening after the Brothers' 'Make It Easy On Yourself' had prised '(I Can't Get No) Satisfaction' from Number One in Britain, The Rolling Stones' circle flicked lighted cigarettes towards Scott's table in the Scotch of St James.

On the road, the Brothers were augmented initially by Birmingham keyboard player Jimmy O' Neill but, as manhandling by hysterical females became more frequent, Engel and Maus shelved their instruments to concentrate on singing, accompanied by Leeds and by Coventry's Johnny B Great and the Quotations. This was all prior to a disturbing hat-trick of comparative flops, and disagreements between John and Scott that caused the three to go their separate ways in 1967 when our throne of kings was just about clinging on to its standing as the planet's prime purveyor of pop.

The rest of the world had been a walkover after Uncle Sam capitulated. Even Soviet Russia threw down a gauntlet with Соколы (The Falcons) and what was decipherable as 'The Candid Lads' – as did the USSR's satellite state, Czechoslovakia, via such as the Glow Worms and the Matadors while Los Shakers were Latin America's 'answer to The Beatles'. The pronunciation of their all-English lyrics by Los Shakers (Caio, Hugo, Osvaldo and Pelin) was so anonymously precise that they wouldn't have been out of place in Hamburg's Star-Club, circa 1963.

Unhindered by the clipped solemnity of mouthing lyrics in a foreign language, like outfits in Australia were surfacing in both city centres and out-of-the-way villages. All across, say, New South Wales or Victoria, you'd come across a combo formed or reinvented as an ersatz British beat group. Sydney's Bee Gees, for instance, mutated from an updated Mills Brothers to quasi-Beatles. Over in Melbourne, a bunch of skifflers had found a Mick Jagger-type in future accountant Rod Turnbull, and bowdlerised The Rolling Stones' very name. What's more, the Spinning Wheels hired Roger Savage, lately emigrated engineer of the Stones' first Decca session, and worked up a repertoire filled with what were often the same Diddley, Berry, Wolf, Muddy and Jimmy Reed favourites. Perhaps in some other cosmos, the Wheels are slaying 'em at the Hollywood Bowl, while it's Jagger who's ended up amongst the ledgers when his time as north-west Kent's 'answer' to Rod Turnbull was up.

In New Zealand, Chants R&B[85] in Christchurch had formed in The Pretty Things-Yardbirds-Them image, spooning out genre elixir from Howlin' Wolf to Motown among the likes of 'Don't Bring Me Down', 'Gloria' and tracks from 1964's *Five Live Yardbirds* LP. As far as they were able, personnel from Chants R&B had followed The Pretty Things' trek round the country's two main land masses in 1965 with Eden Kane and a laryngitic Sandie Shaw, famous for performing in bare feet.

THESE, BELIEVE IT OR NOT, ARE MEN!, bannered the national *Daily News*, although the furore centred not on Phil May, but on drummer Viv Prince setting a standard for 'TV-sets-out-the-window' behaviour that would mean certain groups would be banned by hotel conglomerates across the globe. 'It would reach the point,' fretted Ray Dorset, 'where proprietors assumed that if you had long hair, you were an unruly person who'd wreck the premises.'

Sometimes this supposition was justified, and other guests would be either incensed or derived vicarious enjoyment from the

---

85. Nothing to do with a Merseyside vocal ensemble of similar name.

larks of someone like Prince, a man for whom the highlight of the day wasn't always the show, but the building up and the winding down with associated deeds of destruction.

Arguably, rock 'n' roll excess would be taken to its limit most conspicuously by Keith Moon of Who. Already a known exhibitionist and prankster by 1964, he'd become legendary for creating mayhem from nothing. The most frequently documented example was his purported disruption of a party in Chertsey by steering a Rolls-Royce Silver Cloud into the host's swimming pool.

He'd learned much from studying Viv Prince. 'I always remember Keith standing in front of the drums,' expounded Dick Taylor. 'Later, he would admit he idolised Viv. Before that, playing drums was quite sedentary, even boring – and through Viv, you'd suddenly realise you could be a drummer and also an extrovert. You could be a star, and play your drums too. I think Keith realised he could let out all his lunacy through the drum kit – because Viv was amazing. He'd hit anything: mic stands, fire buckets, the floor, the guitar you had in your hand... '

Usually when in a condition of alcoholic or narcotic disrepair, Prince's antics offstage (so the sometimes ill-founded tales were and are told) included chopping at a hotel's dining tables and water pipes with a fire axe. Another tip of a vast iceberg of hell-raising was his refusal to tread the boards one evening because the pub opposite the venue wouldn't serve him. 'What he forgot,' grimaced Phil May, 'was that the night before, he'd gone there with a bunch of musicians and smashed the place up.'

The trip to New Zealand concluded when TV cameras were on hand to immortalise an inebriated drummer being escorted from a (grounded) Kiwi Airlines aeroplane after an altercation with an air hostess and pilot. Stories abound still too about Prince, say, spraying Sandie Shaw's feet with his urine; bringing the same very dead crayfish to every press conference; and crawling beneath a proscenium, slurping whiskey from a shoe and attempting to set fire to the stage. Most of these had such substance that Down Under was sealed off altogether for The Pretty Things as if they were deadly microbes threatening a swift epidemic. Certainly, the tour is on a par, in retrospect, to the chaotic fortnight in the USA that was to finish The Sex Pistols in the next decade.

Overridden with resounding hue-and-cry too, The Rolling Stones' visit to Australia in January 1965 had sparked off headlines like SHOCKERS! UGLY LOOKS! UGLY SPEECH! UGLY MANNERS! Yet Richard Neville, founder of Sydney's Oz magazine, wasn't so alarmist, writing that, 'Seeing Mick Jagger felt like seeing part of myself – as if the Stones and I, and all our mates, belonged to a secret tribe. The mode of the music was alchemical, Mick's strut signalling a burning impatience with the *ancien regime*, and a sharing of common aspirations, inspirations, strategy, style, mood and vocabulary. Long hair was our declaration of independence, and pop music our Esperanto.'

Tarred with the same brush, other long-haired musicians would shuffle through customs areas, strangulated by every fibre of red tape bureaucracy could gather. Even the Fab Four suffered. After frenzied protest demonstrations about those Beatle *ketōs* polluting the Budokan Hall, Tokyo's temple of martial arts, for three nights in summer 1966, worse was to come in the Philippines. Faced with less of an invitation, more of a command for John, Paul, George and Ringo to be guests of honour at a palace party to be thrown by Imelda, wife of President Ferdinand Marcos, Brian Epstein let the weary Beatles sleep through the comings and goings of lackeys instructed to bring them to the waiting Imelda and the families of the totalitarian government and military junta. George Harrison would recall his bafflement when, over a late breakfast, 'someone turned on the television and there it was, this big palace with lines of people, and this guy saying, "Well, they're not here yet", and we watched ourselves not arrive at the party'.

The following day, the expected crowd of teenage well-wishers at Manila International Airport were puzzled that no security measures had been laid on. Close enough to be touched, their agitated idols lugged their own baggage up static escalators a few steps ahead of a jeering mob of adults, apparently guaranteed clemency and even commendation no matter how they behaved in cooperating with official harassment. This had started the previous night when incessant interference contrived by studio engineers had wiped out every word of Brian Epstein's televised apology for his boys' unwitting insult to the hallowed person of Imelda Marcos. The First Family's honour was further assuaged by vast tax deductions from box-office receipts still in the grasp of accountants employed by the stadium where The Beatles had played the previous day.

Water off a duck's back to The Beatles and their high-ranking sort by then were insulting placards and the rarer peltings with decayed fruit and more revolting projectiles, thrown mostly by males. So too were intransigent hoteliers at pains to stress that no minor was to be served alcohol, their faces falling when the youngest member of a group produced his passport.

An unlikely scheme for a Rolling Stones recital in Moscow would cause the Soviet Ministry of Culture to send an emissary to the group's only concerts in the Eastern bloc in the 1960s – two shows at Warsaw's Palace of Culture on 13 April 1967. He returned so deeply horrified that the ministry made a firm decision not to let any Western pop into Russia, and to turn the heat on those groups that existed anywhere within the USSR's sphere of direct influence.

One case study is that of the Primitives Group, based in Czechoslovakia – under Communist rule since 1948. They were to flourish belatedly during the fleeting 'Prague Spring' of 1968 which ended when Alexander Dubček's liberal regime was eradicated by the military dictatorship of Leonid Brezhnev gaining supreme control of every aspect of national life, including culture. Thus the Primitives Group achieved easy renown in the hardest possible way, provoking the authorities with an approximation of beat group garb, coiffure and attitude, and an assimilation of the more left-field pop from the free West.

Even there, so Dick Taylor was to recollect, 'I was standing next to some local long-haired guys on a street in Hamburg one afternoon, and we were being harangued by a shouting old man. When I asked what he was saying, I was told he was ranting about how in his day we would all have ended up in the death camps. I must say that this was the only incident of this kind that I ever experienced abroad.'

On mainland Europe, the effect of a record like the 'Don't Bring Me Down' was such that it was possible for listeners in Oslo or Madrid not to understand a word, but still be swept away by the spell that was being cast. Usually, it didn't work both ways – because the biggest stumbling block for even the more mainstream pop artists outside North America, Australasia and Britain was that their chosen genre had developed into a music built on English lyrics, and was likely to remain so for all time. This has meant that, while there have been isolated exceptions across the decades, whether 'Dominique' by Belgium's Singing Nun or Los Del Rio's bilingual 'Macarena', the only way to break free of domestic orbits has been either to trade in instrumentals, as easy-listening German bandleader James Last did, or to sing and compose in a tongue not your own. Such was the way of Spain's Los Bravos whose 'Black Is Black' was kept from a UK Number One in 1966 only by the Troggs' 'With a Girl Like You' – or Charles Aznavour who was to last a month at pole position with his 'ow-you-say 'She' in summer 1974, the same season that, via the Eurovision Song Contest, 'Waterloo' opened the floodgate that established ABBA as the most enduring Scandinavian act to penetrate charts in every territory on the planet.

Though no Stockholm Sound or Fjordbeat was to do the same during the beat boom, ABBA's native Sweden might serve here as a case study. According to Lennart Wrigholm, an authority on its pop history, it's 'the European country that was sometimes seen as an extra US state'. This was down to its thorough, even scholarly, absorption of post-war culture from North America – and, by implication, the UK. 'All the great stuff came from England,' agreed Hans Alehag, in later life a respected blues guitarist and record producer. 'The luxury cars, the music, the agents and those red double-decker buses. We lived in black-white-grey times covered with snow half the year. Spring and summer seemed to flash by with a bit of colour – so anything English was inspiring. America at the time might as well have been in a different galaxy.'

Many groups from the UK, unlucky at home, were to thus prosper in Sweden. After their solitary week in the UK Top Fifty in 1961, with 'Night of the Vampire', had been and gone, north London's Moontrekkers had been on the point of disbanding when a 1963 single, 'Moondust', swept into the Swedish Top Twenty.

Earlier, an ever increasing workload there made the Deejays (with singer Clive Sands, brother of Eden Kane) worthy of a Musicians Union-legislated exchange with the Spotnicks, the country's Shadows. Also from Cambridge, Ken Levy and his Phantoms found it convenient to emigrate after supporting The Beatles for dates in Sweden during October 1963.

'Sweden was an excellent country for The Beatles' first real tour outside of Britain,' comments Lennart Wrigholm, 'but, after the final stage show, they took part in the TV programme *Drop In*, transmitted from Stockholm, where, as the main attraction, they ended the programme in front of a cheering audience. It was not broadcast until one month later, and it seemed like every Swedish teenager watched it. Everyone agreed that The Beatles was a musical explosion – but it was their hair and clothing style everybody was talking about more. Of course, the older generation believed it was the worst thing they had seen and heard. My music teacher at school said that no one would like to see or hear this kind of noise after a few years. He'd said the same thing about Elvis Presley a bit earlier.

'Yet who cared? Now there was only one thing to do: let the hair grow and keep up with the trend. The biggest critic of my new style was, of course, my mother. The culmination of this family drama came when we were to receive a visit from mother's aunt Ellen and her husband who lived in Gothenburg, our second largest city, and who, reckoned my mother, were a few steps higher on the social ladder than us.

'"Go get a haircut, you can't look like a sheep when Aunt Ellen comes to visit" was a censure I heard on a number of times each day before they came. Of course I ignored this call and, when the day finally arrived, my mother had an expression on her face like a thunderstorm when I entered the room to greet the visitors.

'Aunt Ellen lit up when she saw me and said: "Lennart, you also have that modern hairstyle that all the guys in Gothenburg have these days! So nice!"

'The silence in the room became monumental before my younger sister started giggling. After that, the mood became quite cheerful and my mother's nagging about my hairstyle stopped. Hadn't Aunt Ellen said this was the modern style? Then it must be so!'

The effect was felt by younger children too. Hans Alehag was six when he first heard The Beatles, even recollecting the precise day. 'On 20 March 1963, 'Please Please Me' hit like a bolt of lightning! I didn't know who or what it was, but that was it! Fantastic! In school the next day "The *Bee-tells*" was all we talked about. We hadn't started to learn English yet so we sang along phonetically to "Please Please Me" and the later records that year: "*she laffs yoo yea yea yea*". I got to see them on *Drop In*, playing electric guitars and drums "live", smiling, having a good time in their nice suits and "long hair", which caused my dad to turn off the TV and break my heart.'

More qualified than that of The Beatles was the impact of the Downliners Sect who, if their thwarted 'try-try-again' ambition at home still provokes sympathy, all but topped Sweden's chart early in 1965 with 'Little Egypt'. An imposter calling himself 'Keith Grant', after their bass player, was to base himself in Gothenburg where he demanded and received huge fees as leader of a Sect-like outfit, Train.

For a while, the Sect were on a par with not so much The Beatles as The Who. As well as overcoming pre-emption by local hopefuls like the Hi-Balls (who copied their 'I'm A Boy' note for note) and, also in 1966, the Lunatics who played 'Pictures Off Lily' [sic] with a lead vocalist sounding even less like he understood the words,[86] The Who undertook quasi-royal treks round Sweden, attracting a record-breaking audience of 11,000 to an outdoor stadium in Stockholm. Historically, this was Keith Moon's first performance with a double-bass drum kit (with images of 'Pictures *Of* Lily' postcard Victoriana painted round its shell), but otherwise it was a delivery of their now-expected feedback-ridden, loudspeaker-stabbing, microphone-hit-on-cymbal goods. The indigenous Hep Stars compounded their own infamy with cavortings exemplified by a guitarist swinging the neck of his instrument round on each off-beat to trigger lead vocalist Svenne Hedlund's rhythmic ducking to avoid it clouting him on the head. If nothing else, such antics gained attention.

---

86. In similar vein – but a hit in northern Europe – was the near-meaningless 'Chris Craft Number Nine' with a melody close to that of Herman's Hermits' 'A Must to Avoid', by another Swedish outfit, The Shanes.

'The groups all had long hair or much longer hair than what we children were allowed to even think about,' observed Hans Alehag. 'Every now and then, always on a Saturday, my dad took me down to the basement for a cut – with the allowed fringe a maximum of one centimetre above the eyebrows and absolutely no hair over the ears or the shirt collar. I could have joined the army based on my haircut.

'Fifty years later – actually when the anniversary of The Beatles' appearance on *Drop In* was in the papers – I asked my dad why. He shook his head and looked somewhat embarrassed and said "That's what the times were like back then. I'm so sorry."'

CHAPTER FOURTEEN

'Long hair isn't "with-it" anymore'

Herr Alehag's fierce mowing of his son's scalp seemed to align exactly with a pontification by the *Daily Telegraph* in the summer of 1965 which was seized upon by exultant parents across the UK. 'The metaphorical gloves were off,' affirmed Tim Fagan, 'and any ploy was considered fair to gain our ends, both by my mother and myself. On passing through the kitchen on my way to school, one morning, she glanced up from reading the *Telegraph* to announce that "It says here that long hair isn't 'with-it' anymore." I replied with a contemptuous snort.'

Yet many teenagers found such news, however questionable, reassuring, even perhaps as much of a comfort as their elders did, stuck as they were between the 'so far away' and their own compliance to stolid adult values. Retired after decades in the offices and factories of Britain, how many are the 70-somethings who took the then wise course of leaving 1960s pop groups that later made it? Exemplified by his pumping Buddy Holly's 'Peggy Sue' with one hand in his pocket, bass player Paul Arnold's condescension towards the Zombies had become intolerable by 1963. He was to become Dr P Arnold, M.D. Maybe comfortably-off retired solicitor Jim Spencer too had been well-advised to cease blowing sax for the Dave Clark Five in 1961, but perhaps kicking himself now is Victor Farrell who resigned from the Hollies in May 1963, and was dwelling in a house called 'The Hollies' 30 years later.

It had still been possible, nevertheless, to be a bank clerk or mail room boy and be recognised as being 'with it' by other initiates via signs as conspiratorial as a Freemason's handshake, such as simply leaving all suit jacket buttons undone except the top one. Without inviting the sack, you'd make out you were a Mod, a soft option because employers were less likely to grouse about your turnout – and, on the strength of appearance alone, so-called Mods wouldn't get turned away from the parish dance. You'd even earn praise from the vicar for looking so smart. Mods were no longer exclusive now.

Late in 1963, a 'beat-ballet' entitled *Mods and Rockers*, soundtracked by Beatles music, had opened in the West End. Since then Mod for the masses had spawned two types: 'peacock' (or 'smooth') and 'hard'. Gathered mostly round London and the bigger cities, the former were more concerned with clothes and trancing out in front of mirrors. Everything had to be just so: double-breasted bumfreezers with back vents precisely seven inches one week, exactly five the next. How wide are lapels now? This shirt's got a pointed tab collar which means I can never wear it again. At the Flamingo, Glasgow's Picasso or the Twisted Wheel in Manchester the previous Saturday, you had to look Parisian. Go back the following Thursday and it'd be electric-blue Italian.

In regions beyond, however, 'Mod' clothes weren't much more than gang uniforms in which no pretence was made of dandification or of keeping up with the on-the-spot front-runners. You could be ostensibly 'Mod' as long as you had Chelsea boots, hipster flares in Billy Bunter check and a corduroy jacket with faint faecal odour – which were worn to every local hop until you outgrew them. In any case, by the time any gear hit a local high street, it was probably 'out' anyway.

Both within and without such events, 'hard' Mods were as inclined to look actively for trouble as their Teddy Boy forebears had been. Spiritually ugly people with desires to make everything else ugly too, they might encircle a victim and discuss loudly how they were going to slash off all his hair. Street life in night-time Uttoxeter or Reigate could be as much a jungle as the Belgian Congo, but the only alternative was to stay at home, maybe on the sofa before the farewell edition of *Blackpool Night Out*, with parents who might even help pay for a motor-scooter[87] as long as you didn't

---

87. Mods tended not to ride with headgear for fear of it ruining their hair style more than wind or the breeze of motion. In 1973, a compulsory helmet law was introduced.

get into fights with rough boys in leather windcheaters or *smoke* those 'Purple Hearts' you read about.[88]

Open hostility between Mods and Rockers was never as virulent as the newspapers or *Quadrophenia*, the Mod retrospective movie from 1979, made out. Respective tribes would merely congregate at opposite ends of somewhere like the Rendezvous, Fleet's high street coffee bar-cum-transport café which had a jukebox and pinball machines. There, wayward girls and boys could loiter for hours without buying so much as a single cup of frothy liquid. There was a flurry of activity at lunchtime, but otherwise there were hardly any customers who paid for much more than coin-operated pop and to flipper silver balls. Nearly everyone had known each other since infant school, and there were enough small ghosts accumulated since then to fill a Gothic mansion.

My most piquant memory of the nearest the town had to a house of ill repute is a mingled essence of leather, motorbike oil and cheap perfume – because parked outside were fewer lawnmower-sounding Lambrettas than the chrome steeds of the Rocker majority. There was hardly any enmity, however, between either of the principal youth cultures of the mid-1960s. In any case, a lot of the Rendezvous' youthful patrons were neither Mods nor Rockers. They weren't anything.

Whether Mod, Rocker or neither, using dress as provocation was a bloke's way, I suppose, of drawing attention away from hair that nothing could make long, although 'a parting down the middle was a trendy, rebellious substitute,' recollected Malcolm Noble. That had been among my own strategies when making the best of a bad job, sprucing it up with not only a centre-parting to the crown, but also a *bouffant* the rest of the way towards the back with the sides

---

88. I know it's distasteful to mention such things, but, alas, it's true: certain Mods and members of 1960s pop groups took outlawed drugs. However, although all too aware of 'Purple Hearts', 'Black Bombers', 'Yellow Submarines', 'French Blues' and an appetite suppressant containing amphetamines known as 'speed', marijuana was still a bit too cloak-and-dagger for many. However, after no less than The Beatles giggled through the shooting of their *Help!* movie vehicle in a marijuana haze, many of those who read about it, sampled its short-lived magic.

brushed to partly cover the ears (until I was no longer able to get away with it) in the style of Steve Marriott from The Small Faces, more the ultimate Mod group than The Who were (and I still comb it that way today).

Already free of the strictures of school, Oliver Gray and a fellow university undergraduate John Yorke also emulated the Marriott style. 'Other favourites were the Action and, distressingly, in retrospect, Tich (of Dave Dee, Dozy etc), because they not only had no "butterflies" but also sported a little backcombed bit at the crown of the head, like a kind of fluffy skullcap. John was adept at creating one of these, but the shape of my head meant that it just refused to work on me.

'He never actually attended any lectures or seminars or wrote any essays, thus allowing himself to party all night and spend all day sleeping – and "smoothing", a word he'd invented about a complicated but vital procedure whereby all butterflies must be killed. First wash your hair carefully, rinsing several times. Dry very lightly, using a towel. During this process, take strands of hair between folds of the towel and pull down slowly but firmly from the top of the head to the end of the hair. Then switch on the hair dryer. Using a specially purchased round hairbrush, insert it underneath the hair above the ears and very slowly draw the hair down to the ends with the brush, applying the dryer (set on medium heat) all the while. Just as you reach the bottom, gently twist the brush one more time towards the head, thus ensuring that the ends curl inwards, if at all. On no account may they curl outwards; the optimal result, of course, is complete straightness. Repeat the entire procedure all round for at least 45 minutes or until hair is completely dry. Do not on any account go out in the rain or the wind, or all your work will be wasted.

'John Yorke taught me how to do this and in our rooms we would spend Saturday afternoons preparing for an evening where we'd do the little Mod dance which involved shuffling of feet, clicking of fingers but very little shaking of heads. We thought the girls in the hall would be irresistibly attracted by our butterfly-free styles. Sometimes they were, but I didn't go as far as John, who refused to let girls run their hands through his hair for fear of disturbing it.'

*

My own grooming turned from routine to fetish too, even if my
interest in variations, old and new, pictured with instructions on
Rave's new 'Fashion And Beauty For Boys' section, was cursory.
Neither did I go for the severe Beatle-ish cut of David McCallum,
who'd graduated from arch-juvenile delinquent 'Johnnie' in the 1958
film *Violent Playground* to co-starring as a secret agent of Russian
extraction, 'Illya Kuryakin', in the internationally syndicated spy
drama series *The Man from U.N.C.L.E.* Emerging as its chief source
of appeal to girl viewers, he was the subject of a tribute single, 'Love
Ya, Illya' by Angela and the Fans.[89]

During an initially desultory period as a professional entertainer,
Rod Stewart was known to those who'd so much as heard of him as
'Rod the Mod' – and for hair backcombed to rise halfway towards
the back to a height of just under an alchemically-stiffened six
inches. He'd been one of Long John Baldry's Hoochie Coochie
Men when they performed in February 1964 at a Birmingham
Town Hall concert in which Mississippi bluesman Sonny Boy
Williamson, bowler-hatted and vulture-like in posture, headed a
bill of British attractions.

When Sonny Boy's bass harmonica was stolen afterwards, a prime
suspect was Robert Plant, who was to abandon a career as a chartered
accountant after about a fortnight to pursue an extramural objective
with which none of the other trainees could have identified.

He was travelling 'a rocky journey with my parents. They just
didn't understand it at all, any of it. In the beginning, they thought
it would pass'. Yet, for a while, their reproaches and comparisons to
boys who were a credit to their families had had the desired effect.
Robert dressed with reticence and adopted a style almost redolent
of nineteenth century Prussian militarism. Indeed, he was 'a local
Mod with very short hair' to guitarist Dave Hill, who, with three
other veterans of several Midlands beat groups, was to form Slade.

Had he still been at King Edward VI Grammar, Robert might
have been castigated for wearing his hair too *short*, like Steve Mills

---

89. A pseudonymous Alma Cogan. McCallum himself was the conductor
and principal tunesmith of 1966's *Music... A Part of Me* LP. Its spin-off 45,
'Communication', harried the lower reaches of the UK Top Fifty.

was at Farnborough, 'after leaving an early growth of sideboards,'
recalled Steve, 'a lower sixth form master accosted me, moaned that
I'd had too much off and then sneeringly pointed at my sideboards
and said "and the barber missed a bit".'

Such customising was available from the likes of Ivor, the lesser
of two scissor-wielding evils in Fleet. He asked me to model for him
in an amateur fashion show in which he was involved, to be held at
the local Secondary Modern's assembly hall. It wasn't exactly show
business, but, chiefly because I liked Ivor, I meandered, ill at ease,
along the catwalk in my old hipsters and corduroy coat to subdued
laughter from other lads there. A commentary included the telling
sentences, 'Alan's hairstyle is the result of the compromise we have
had to make between his parents' wish for him to have his hair cut
and his determination not to. The finished dressing is a "Mod"
type, now short enough to please his parents, but well-suited to
today's clothes, and also satisfies our model himself.'

Like hell, it did. All that Mod pseudo-suaveness, whim-conscious
dress sense and, especially, the short hair was at odds with how I
really wanted to be. For a start, I couldn't care less how old-fashioned
the *Daily Telegraph* reckoned long hair had become.

CHAPTER FIFTEEN

'Because you have reached exalted heights in your profession, it does not mean that you can behave in this manner'

'John Yorke was a Mod,' recollected Oliver Gray, 'and I would initially have been interested in going in that direction, but I was relieved that we were on the cusp of the transfer into general long-hairedness as a fashion.'

An earlier harbinger of this was Don 'Captain Beefheart' Vliet, the only child within a household of such relaxed informality that he was given free rein to do things on his terms, in his own way, and whenever he was in the mood. When visiting the place to listen to music after school, Frank Zappa observed that Don said 'motherfucker' within earshot of his parents, something he'd never dream of doing himself. To Mr and Mrs Vliet, however, it was all quite marvellous.

So was their son's long dark hair which had been almost to his waist by 1964 – a likely story – when he and his Magic Band made their stage debut at a teenage dance in Lancaster, when old school friend Frank, yet to take over the lease of what would be Studio Z, was still neatly trimmed and clean-shaven.

Yet this manifestation of an apparent willingness to pursue a path of conventional maturity would take its toll, commensurate as it was with emotional pressure to 'be good', to 'be worthy' of all your parents had given you. You were born, you tried hard at school, you worked diligently at a decent job, you got married, you had children – and that was it. There was no time in between for much fun. After you were over that developmental stage known as 'rebellious adolescence', expressed most conspicuously in loutish affectations and inverted snobbery, you were supposed to change into a serious, thoughtful young adult.

Yet, more than ever now, you were brooding about whether there might be differences between yourself and Normal Sensible People. Your hair told the world that, unlike other humans, you were strangely fascinating – that your life had gothic aspects. Furthermore, deep absorption of 45 rpm pop was making the words on certain discs more than just syllables strung together to carry a tune.

'I'm Not Like Everybody Else' by The Kinks and, also buried on a flip-side, The Pretty Things' 'I Can Never Say' became particularly articulate speeches of the heart for me as I traced a guitar in the vapour of the kitchen window and wondered why Mum didn't understand as she pointed out that the posh Fulford brothers,[90] who lived next door, got their hair cut without fuss, even volunteering to go beneath the clippers before their parents asked.

Circa 1965, my Dad was wondering aloud why the hell I wanted to look like 'a ruddy poet', and Mum would make it clear that she too didn't like long hair on males. She even hated it. Her attempts to transform me into a 'young adult' rather than a common 'youth' included, therefore, an inflexible imposition of a short-back-and-sides every few weeks – to which I'd become resigned then with much the same attitude as that of a Great War trench private to the *bullet-with-his-name-on-it* at 'Wipers' (Ypres).

Men don't have periods and can't get pregnant, but pillars of women's liberation might note how difficult the issue of hair could be for teenage boys by this point in the 1960s. You had to fight every inch of the way – and nowhere was the battle more fierce than in the provinces after matters were turning much more serious than they'd been when the fan hysteria surrounding The Beatles was still good-humoured. Police patrolling the round-the-block queues kept eyes peeled for the odd runaway, but no bother was expected from the sleeping bags lining the pavements with comics and transistor radios. Once they might have wrung their hands, but then mums and dads would bring provisions to their waiting children.

---

90. One of the three was to be England's first openly homosexual high court judge.

Well, it was only The Beatles – who could not be imagined urinating, passing wind, committing a felony or being truly obnoxious any more than sexless cartoon figures when their unchallenged procurement of sexual gratification was not yet brought to public notice by a press who judged any besmirching of their cheeky but innocent images as untimely: save the scandal for The Rolling Stones.

Yet, though 1960s pop musicians were frequently most admirable young men, they had their share of young men's vices. Although dressing room scenes were sometimes how susceptible fans might have imagined them: a card or board game on the middle table, the TV on, someone tuning a guitar, another shaving at the wash basin, time which hung heavy between one concert and the next wasn't only killed with snakes-and-ladders and *Dixon of Dock Green*. Like *omertà* in the Mafia, a vow of silence concerning illicit sex has always persisted among bands of roving minstrels. Feted wherever you went, a Roman emperor might never have had it so good, and you'd get quite accustomed to requests to meet a certain type of female in, say, the romantic seclusion of a backstage broom cupboard. Indeed, there was a young North American lady known as 'The Torpedo', one of many female music-lovers notorious for evading the most stringent security barricades to impose themselves on chartbusting beat groups. Conversely, the story goes that a midnight raid on a girls' Borstal was foiled when a warden woke up to find one of the Animals prowling about her bedroom.

It was hard fact, however, that, as Phil May reminisced, 'In Stockport one night late in 1965, Viv Prince stopped drumming to rip the blouse and bra off some screaming bird, and sock her in the mouth. All the bouncers jumped on us, and we got beaten to fuck, and our equipment was smashed. Viv retreated over the road to the pub leaving all this chaos, and I followed him in, sacked him and put him on a train back to London.'

'When we appeared on *Sunday Night at the London Palladium*,' added Denis D'Ell of the Honeycombs, 'we'd borrowed Viv from The Pretty Things so Honey Lantree, our usual drummer, could go centre stage to sing a duet – 'That's The Way' – with me. Viv had quite a reputation as a raver so, after the rehearsal that afternoon, he was locked in the dressing room until it was time to go on – in case he went on a binge and either didn't show up or else was so far gone that he might do something untoward in front of an audience of millions. The next day, one of the tabloids ran a feature headlined *WHO WAS THE OTHER HONEYCOMBS GIRL?* because of Viv's hair.'

'That's The Way' turned out to be the Honeycombs' last UK chart hit, but continued success overseas held the group's demise at arm's length for a while longer. Four consecutive Number Ones in Sweden entitled them to headline over the Hep Stars – and an exhausting but exhilarating international itinerary included a month in a capacious night spot in Rome where, noted Denis, 'we got into diabolical trouble. When it got hot, I undid my shirt. This sparked off some screaming. The second night, the police were there, holding sheets in front of me so the audience couldn't see – so I clambered up on top of the amplifiers'.

With The Beatles' performances came instances of fainting – and heightened blood pressure brought on nose bleeds. The odd tip-up chair would snap off its spindle too – but afterwards the screeching would cease for the National Anthem, to resume half-heartedly before everyone filed quietly out.

However, fire hoses and arbitrary manhandling of fans by shirt-sleeved security manning the low barricades before the stage – ensuring all could register their visible importance in the proceedings – were needed, apparently, to quell riots at shows by those sinister Rolling Stones. A judgement on them was that, after one such fiasco, Keith Richards lay among the 22 people unconscious, hit by a flying bottle. On the sodden carpeting, auditorium cleaners had come across soiled knickers among smashed rows of seating.

That same tour embraced a private prosecution by the manager of a Romford petrol station (and local youth club organiser), intent on striking a blow for decent entertainment for decent folk. This was to conclude with Mick Jagger, Brian Jones and Bill Wyman being fined for relieving themselves against the garage wall. 'Because you have reached exalted heights in your profession, it does not mean that you can behave in this manner,' barked the magistrate.

Dave Berry had been in the convoy of cars from which the three desperate men had spilled: 'The pissing in the forecourt was blown out of all proportion to what it was. A *Daily Mail* journalist was travelling with us, and it was his job to find stories – like us, say, getting refused entry to a night club in Scarborough, things like that. He'd be straight on the telephone as soon as the doorman said, "I'm sorry. You can't come in."'

By inviting bother about hair, a boy in the provinces would feel as if he was sharing something with the Stones, especially if he'd embroiled himself in garage rehearsals with a group while daring to dream of global renown – or at least, however deludedly, imagining that such sessions might be a means of breaking loose from social immobility. Often, pushy parents, mindful of their own foiled ambitions, teased glamorous ambitions from reticent offspring. Yet even they would intimate that considering this shabbiest and most corrupt branch of pop for so much as a moment as a full-time living was neither honourable nor permissible. It was roughly the equivalent of wanting to shake your body in a burlesque troupe.

'Pop music was completely banned in our house,' grimaced composer and painter John Whittaker, a former pupil at Merseyside's Waterloo Grammar School. 'I had to sneak downstairs early in the morning to listen to the latest hits on the radio or go round to a friend's to hear their 45s played on a Dansette Viva record player whilst studying who was in the charts and how their position had changed with time via the appropriate page in a magazine or newspaper. I suppose it made it all a bit more exciting!

'I was not allowed to grow my hair long either – and always had to have a short-back-and-sides when I visited the barber. It made my life as a teenager rather difficult at times, although I don't ever remember being particularly teased about it. I just felt a little bit "out of it" when you just wanted to be part of the crowd growing up.'

John was far from alone. In too many family circles, there had evolved a nakedly open anti-pop domestic policy. No longer were children to receive records for birthday or Christmas presents – at least not from mum and dad. If some other relation gave a teenager a record token, he or she would be warned not to waste it on doubtful

pleasures. 'What should I buy then? Shakespeare's speeches,' they'd
say, or, more vaguely, 'classical music'. If money was spent on a pop
LP, this was to be confiscated as soon as a reason was presented to
do so by the sort of parents who'd sniggered at the 'Peter's pride'
article in the *Daily Express* – which, like BBC television's *Six O'Clock
News* also made much of the scream-rent heroes' welcome laid on by
womenfolk of both officers and lower ranks when the Greenjackets
infantry regiment touched down in Gatwick in December 1964
after their peace-keeping chore in Borneo was over.

In my neck of the woods, 'squaddies' – low-ranking soldiers –
were the common foe of Mods, Rockers and those who'd pledged
allegiance to neither. In south-east Kent, it was the lower ranks
of Royal Marines garrisoned in Deal where 'long hair could be
inconvenient,' warned Tim Fagan. 'You could pretty much expect
some sort of unpleasantness, verbal or physical, if you were caught
alone at night and alcohol had been consumed.

'That was around the autumn of 1964 when I'd just been
expelled from boarding school and was now at somewhere local as a
day pupil. The hair was coming on fairly well by then – but endless
jibes from my parents and the three-weekly visits to the house of a
local barber, one Ernie, meant I had to argue hard and even throw
temper tantrums to keep my hair at collar length.

'Others had it worse than me. Any objection, even rolling the
eyes, by one fellow student from a large Roman Catholic family
would be met with violence from his irascible father, a former Army
boxing champion, who'd send him regularly for a brutal cut from a
barber known as "Holy Joe". He had religious icons in his salon and
would quote scripture while going about his business.'

I suppose I was luckier with Ivor. At least he listened to polite
protests even if he countered them with, say, 'I need to take a
little more off to balance the other side.' This was after I'd been
dispatched to him when restyling my Steve Marriott to a combed-
back flatness at home couldn't hold it off any longer. Nor was I
articulate enough then even to try to reason my way out of it. With
hardly a murmur, the likes of me was still expected to do what he
was told by a 'responsible' grown-up, particularly if such a person
was as contemptuous as your parents were on hearing of some

young twit kicking up a fuss because his poor old mother told him to get off to the hairdresser's for an all-off!

What sort of lunatic world was it, thought the middle-aged Average Joe or Joanna, when you switched on the telly and there was that Mike Jaggers or whatever his name was, hair all over his surly, lippy mug, prancing about in his tat, and caterwauling that he was a king bee buzzing around some tart's hive or something? 'What with all these long haircuts and *beards*,' put in a letter to BBC television's *Points of View*, 'you can't tell the difference between the girls and the boys!'

The more populist newspapers weighed in obliquely with such as a letter-writer in the *News of the World*, sounding smug about her deck-chaired holiday-making where 'in our cardigans and bonnets, we think we look rather nice – and so do our husbands in their braces, rolled-up shirt-sleeves and with bald heads either in knotted handkerchiefs or glistening in the sun!' Then there was the tale of a young ledger clerk who dwelt in a West Country village socially divided between 'tea-shoppe' gentility and what our colonial cousins would call 'trailer trash'. His evenings were squandered by frequenting an espresso bar patronised by bikers. In order to fit in, he'd bought a ladies' wig to cover the severe haircut required by both his parents and in the office.

As late as 1968 Terry M, another alumnus of Tim Fagan's day school, would be in similar circumstances. He became 'the epitome of white soul cool in Margate nightlife, sharply dressed and sporting mirror shades and a black Afro hairdo the size of a medicine ball, but come the 7.30 am commuter train to London, he would set off for the office in a grey suit and tie with a short-back-and-sides. Presumably the Afro wig lived at home in his bedroom. It just showed the lengths to which people had to go!'

CHAPTER SIXTEEN

'He looks more like a bleedin' lavatory brush'

When The Rolling Stones were miming to 'The Last Time', their first self-penned Number One, on *Top of the Pops* during the early spring of 1965, 18-year-old George Best was among the dancers over whom the cameras hovered. If the footballer's two goals capped Manchester United's victory in the European Cup quarter-finals later that year, it was his dark moptop that caused an enthralled Portuguese newshound to hail him as 'O Quinto Beatle' – 'The Fifth Beatle'. It was a nickname that was to endure long enough for painter Stewart Beckett to superimpose a likeness of Best at that very match on a reproduction of the group's famous march across the Abbey Road zebra crossing.

Yet, because the world of soccer was associated by tradition with the grizzled manliness epitomised by combed-over Bobby Charlton, prominent in 1966's World Cup final, *United!*, a contemporaneous and short-lived BBC1 drama series about a fictional second division team, had manager 'Gerry Barford' ordering a player to have a haircut ('You're a footballer, not a pop star!'). Champion wrestler Mick McManus – notorious for bending the rules as far as he could without being disqualified – was, nevertheless, genuinely charmed to be photographed with The Rolling Stones. In 1964, he was *Ready Steady Go!*'s Man of the Year (its Sound of the Year was Tamla Motown), an award he received during the New Year's Eve edition in which he, character actor Harry Fowler and British music business jack-of-all-trades Kenny Lynch mimed to the Newbeats' 'Bread and Butter' in Victorian bathing costumes.

McManus might have kept his hair short, but Jackie 'Mr TV' Pallo, with whom he maintained a decade-long professional rivalry, would tread the canvas in a bleached and ribboned pigtail. Like Pallo and McManus, Billy Two Rivers, raised on an Indian reservation in Canada, was forever on the regular 40-minute slot devoted to the sport before ITV's broadcast of the football results on Saturday afternoons. He would war-dance into the ring in a feathered head-dress which he'd remove to reveal a Mohawked scalp, i.e. shaven to the skin on both sides with a rigorously upright strip in the centre.

Jimmy Savile had been a wrestler while simultaneously achieving regional renown by spinning the discs in northern ballrooms from the late 1950s. However, it was a well-received stint at a palais in Essex that brought about his presentation of Radio Luxembourg's Decca-sponsored *Teen & Twenty Disc Club* and it made sense for the company to allow Savile a couple of singles of his own. After these had ended up on the deletion rack, he rose to greater fame as Britain's most eye-stretching TV disc jockey of the 1960s, dolling himself up in clothes that were very much more than just a little bit daft, and even when his regular appearances on *Top of the Pops* were broadcast in black and white, dyeing his lengthening hair a different colour for every edition – even trying stripes and tartan before settling permanently on peroxide white.

He reached the big screen, too, as the anchor of B-featured *Pop Gear* (*Go Go Mania* in the USA), a 70-minute conveyor belt of 'blink-and-you'll-miss-'em' clips of lip-synched pop. It was bookended by the in-concert Beatles, six months before they were driven in a black Rolls-Royce through cheering masses to receive those MBEs from the Queen at Buckingham Palace on 26 October 1965.

This honour had its origins when, in the run-up to the post-Profumo general election, BBC television's satirical and much-watched *That Was The Week That Was* series was cancelled at short notice while a *Daily Express* cartoon had the two main political leaders, Alec Douglas-Home and Harold Wilson, soliciting the four for their support, thus lending credence to the words, 'I care not who makes a nation's laws as long as I can compose its songs.'

Camouflaging vote catching as acknowledgement of John, Paul, George and Ringo's contributions to the export drive, and that British pop generated vast financial power, Wilson's new

Labour Government had, seemingly, also taken to heart a March headline in *Melody Maker* that ran, 'Honour The Beatles!' No such decoration, before or since, has ever been as divisive. 'I didn't think you got that sort of thing,' exclaimed George Harrison, 'just for playing rock 'n' roll music.' Neither did the disgusted civil servants and retired admirals who returned their medals to Her Majesty.

There had been milder rumblings from such quarters two months earlier when Donovan, a Hertfordshire lad who'd come across as a beatific and initially non-doctrinal Bob Dylan, had showed he had teeth with *The Universal Soldier*, a bestselling EP that was accompanied by a promotional film shot on location in old cordite-ridden trenches, provoking letters of disgust to *The Times* from military folk about this 'long-haired pacifist'.

He was also the subject of *A Boy Called Donovan*, an ITV documentary, transmitted in January 1966 and advertised on the front cover of that week's *TV Times*. Because he and the film crew were screened smoking a reefer, two cars containing nine of Scotland Yard's narcotics squad pulled up outside Donovan's London apartment in the graveyard hours with reason to believe that the premises were being used for the consumption of controlled drugs, contrary to the provision of the 1965 Dangerous Drugs Act, Section 42. When they displayed a search warrant and 'effected entry', Donovan, hair tousled with the disorder of disturbed sleep, leapt unclothed onto one constable's back. After that, arrest was a mere formality.

The programme also captured the attention of BBC television's *Not So Much a Programme, More a Way of Life*, a sub-*That Was the Week That Was* satire series, also hosted by David Frost, which was to embrace a sketch centred on 'Hooligan', a Donovan-like character whose 'poetic' commentary lapsed into bleeped-out abuse when confronted by a housewife shrieking with laughter at his hair. In passing, another episode had a dad in an armchair, gazing with disgust at his teenage son and exclaiming to all and sundry 'Oh, look at his 'air!'

As well as on the output of Donovan, Bob Dylan had left his mark on the varied likes of 'Eve Of Destruction' by Barry McGuire from 1965 when 'protest' was all the rage; Jonathan King's 'It's Good News Week' for Hedgehoppers Anonymous; the Downliners Sect's 'Bad Storm Coming', a euphemism for impending nuclear holocaust; and Sonny and Cher's 'I Got You Babe'[91] with its telling couplet 'So let them say your hair's too long/'Cause I don't care, with you I can't go wrong' – directed at those who found Bob too harsh and impenetrable, especially now he'd stopped going on about war being wrong and fairer shares for all, and was singing through his nose about myriad less wistful topics that, couched in surrealism, looked beyond fifth-form sermonising.

Furthermore, Dylan, whose short trim of 1963 was to transform into an explosion of trichological barbed wire on the front of 1966's *Blonde On Blonde* double-LP, was no longer considered to be 'ethnic' by outraged folk purists. The opening 'Subterranean Homesick Blues' on the transitional *Bringing It All Back Home* LP lifted salient points from Chuck Berry's 'Too Much Monkey Business', and he took the stage at that summer's Newport Folk Festival bearing a solid-body electric guitar with the Paul Butterfield Blues Band, followed by a 1965 tour of Britain with the Hawks (later, the Band) who used to back the Canadian rock 'n' roller, Ronnie Hawkins.

Alexis Korner's tight curls would be bursting out of his head like Dylan's when he blazoned the strangest symptom of R&B's new acceptability by leading the house band on *Five O'Clock Club*, an ITV children's programme. Continuity was provided by Wally Whyton, who seven years earlier had invited Alexis to join his chart-riding skiffle group, the Vipers. The memory of Whyton's glove puppet co-compère, Pussy Cat Willum, introducing Korner's gritty rendering of Ma Rainey's 'See See Rider' isn't easy to forget.

Was the tempest dropping further? Mick Jagger was now 'the most fashionably modish young man in London,' according to a condescending *Evening Standard*. 'We are told he is the voice of today, a today person, symptomatic of our society. Cecil Beaton paints him, saying he is reminded of Nijinsky and Renaissance angels; magazines report that he is a friend of Princess Margaret; gossip columns tell us what parties he failed to turn up at.'

Most of it was true, even if the Queen's prettier younger sister was a fan of other pop stars too, remarking to the nominal leader

---

91. One of myriad records I love to hate.

of the Spencer Davis Group that 'your music has given me a great deal of pleasure'.

Mick was also soon to be a neighbour of Commander David Birkin, a hero of Dunkirk, his wife, comedy actress Judy Campbell and their daughter, Jane, listed as 'Blonde' in the closing credits of *Blow Up*, a portrayal of Swinging London that had already become a little antiquated by the time it was on general release late in 1966.

Now the British public seemed to have got over the initial shock, even accepting the Stones as not a pop combo as ephemeral as all the rest, but a mostly objectionable part of the national picture – but part of it all the same – on a par with *Till Death Us Do Part*, the BBC1 series that seized upon racism, religion, sex before marriage, the Royal Family and other issues plus language hitherto deemed too uncomfortable for mid-evening viewing. Stoking up most controversy in the programme were the loudmouthed opinions of East End patriarch 'Alf Garnett', played by Warren Mitchell, so reactionary and freighted with reluctance to adapt to changing times that they would have earned him the unquestioned approbation of rednecks[92] and those who brought about Frank Zappa's arrest, especially when bald Alf was sparring with his not-immoderately long-haired Liverpudlian layabout of a son-in-law, 'Mike Rawlins' (Anthony Booth), an adherent of opposing values, ideological, cultural – and aesthetic.

'When I had hair, I kept it cut and looking a bit tidy,' he wailed at Rawlins, adding, 'Look at all your top brains – all your scientists, all your leaders of industry, all your top politicians – they're all a bit thin on top. All your better class people, I mean, they don't go in for hair.' Yet, while ostensibly unbothered by his exposed cranium, Garnett still went along with suggestions in the same episode (titled *Hair-Raising*) to apply friction and various home-made potions to stimulate a resumption of growth. 'Leave off your hat,' advised his barber. 'Let it breathe.'

'He looks more like a bleedin' lavatory brush. Fancy going around with a barnet like that!' were among Alf's remarks about Mike's

---

92. Especially after *Till Death Us Do Part* was remade as *All in the Family* for North American television.

appearance, referring to him as 'Shirley Temple' – or 'randy Scouse git'. This was a phrase that caught the ear of Micky Dolenz of The Monkees while they were on tour in the UK, inspiring him to use it as the title of the group's next single. Their record label renamed 'Alternate Title' in the UK market to avoid any of the rumpus *Till Death Us Do Part* had aroused rubbing off on The Monkees – not a group but a 'project' whereby a quartet of amenable young men had been put together by a cabal of investors to play an Anglo-American pop group in a transglobal TV sitcom with musical interludes. The result was then sent on its way with one of the most ruthless merchandising strategies imaginable.

As well as coping admirably with simple, self-contained weekly scripts, The Monkees also sang on records for which the services of top songwriters, session players and producers had been negotiated. The overall blueprint was the *Hard Day's Night*-period Beatles and, to a lesser extent, Herman's Hermits. Indeed, it was noticed that, like Herman, Davy Jones, The Monkees' dreamboat-in-chief, was a Mancunian and had been in *Coronation Street*.

With almost mathematical precision, success was immediate, dealing as it did the hardest blow to the waning British Invasion. Even prior to the opening show in 1966, their debut 45, 'Last Train To Clarksville', had been high in the US *Hot 100*, a month after The Monkees' principal role-models, The Beatles, stopped touring following a performance in San Francisco, a city soon to be as vital a pop Jerusalem as Liverpool had been. Indeed, Frank Zappa was to remember an approach late in 1966 'by a group of lawyers and businessmen who wanted the Mothers of Invention to move to San Francisco, which they were trying to turn into a centre of music for commercial purposes'.

Sprouted from the Soul Giants, the Zappa-helmed Mothers Of Invention issued 'It Can't Happen Here' as the spin-off 45 from *Freak Out!*, their first album, issued in June when the USA seemed to be riding high on the post-war economic boom and an unprecedented rise in consumerism. This, nonetheless, marginalised the down-trodden and a spreading subculture in which there'd be a disparity between confrontational 'freaks' and pacifist 'hippies'.

In Britain, 'It Can't Happen Here' was voted a unanimous

'miss' one Saturday in November on *Juke Box Jury* by a panel that included Ted Rogers, resident stand-up comedian on the *Billy Cotton Band Show*, who always raised a polite laugh with his Mick Jagger impersonation. My 15-year-old self hadn't watched this particular edition, but, on the following Monday, after eavesdropping on a serious-minded classmate's uncharacteristically vigorous dismissal of it as the worst record he'd ever heard, I became intrigued as I always was by the unusual in music.

When Zappa's Tank C all-off was still growing out, he'd kept the Mothers under wraps, earning what they could at venues mostly local to Los Angeles, while they worked on 'image'. Among insurmountable problems were vocalist Ray Collins with his receding hairline, and Jimmy Carl Black who wore a visible wedding ring, thus transgressing the rule that applied to all pop idols – which was to play down long-term attachments. Then again, on paper, Freddie and the Dreamers had been theoretically unmarketable too with their podgy bass player and a prematurely balding guitarist. Finally, there was Freddie Garrity, four-eyed and spindly, the weed who got sand kicked in his face in Charles Atlas advertisements, and whose onstage antics had an element of that lip-trembling pathos that some find endearing. Nevertheless, because it was visually obvious that some Mothers were already subject to the ravages of early middle age, they looked older than not only Freddie and his boys but also, say, the Byrds with their high-status residency at Ciro's, the former hangout of Frank Sinatra's Rat Pack along Sunset Strip.

That most of the Mothers tended to be defiantly bearded didn't help either, but they went along with Zappa's intimations about stage wardrobe: 'I never actually told the guys what to wear, but thought it silly to be playing the kind of music we were in suits and processed pompadours.'

Thus, after a period in a vague uniform of black homburgs and purple satin shirts like tailboard-riding Prohibition hitmen,[93] the Mothers went visually as far beyond The Pretty Things as the latter had beyond The Rolling Stones, causing the very teen columnist

---

93. Pre-empting the gangster look that was to intimidate hippiedom as flowers wilted during 1967's unsettled autumn.

of the *Detroit Free Press* to write, 'Mothers and fathers, you thought The Beatles were bad. You got up in arms about The Rolling Stones. Sonny and Cher made you cringe. Well, as the man said, you ain't seen nothing yet.

'The Mothers of Invention are here with an album called *Freak Out* (someone suggested it should have been called *Flake Out*). They come from Hollywood. Their clothes are dreadful – and I dig mod clothes. Their hair and beards are filthy. They smell bad. You just can't believe it!

'Tuesday afternoon, the Mothers appeared on Robin Seymour's TV show *Swingin' Time*. As Art Cervi, its talent coordinator, said, "We've never had anyone that brought anything near the controversy they caused. The switchboard was flooded with viewers either saying the Mothers were great or awful."'

Yet, however much their more intense aficionados might refute the suggestion, the Mothers were as much of a pop group as The Monkees. They even had a fan club in all but name called United Mutations – with a membership certificate signed in ink by 'issuing officer' Zappa who, if not offering himself as a prize in 'meet-and-greet' contests, wasn't above wanting teenage endorsement for the Mothers. He submitted gladly to interviews in periodicals such as *Hit Parader* and *16* which was to step way out of character with its editor's obituary for Lenny Bruce.[94] Playing it safer were *Mod* (*16*'s sister journal), *Datebook*, *Tiger Beat* – and *Teen Set* ('the nifty music magazine with the misleading name') which, nonetheless, was about to radicalise itself by inserting a Mothers-flavoured teabag into its customary cupful of pop and fashion.

On *Sunday Night at the London Palladium* half a world away, singing comedienne Margo Henderson was belting out the traditional gospel song, 'Down by the Riverside', updated to include a reference to 'the

94. The suspected homosexual ejected from the US militia in 1945, Bruce is now remembered vaguely as some dirty wisecracker by those outside the USA who have heard of him. Bruce styled himself as an 'oral jazzman' for his satirical monologues in hip-restricted code about politics, religion and sex – with titles like 'White Collar Drunks', 'Don's Big Dago', 'How To Relax Your Colored Friends At Parties' and 'Psychopathia Sexualis', heard perhaps as nascent rap.

good old Rolling Stones'. At wedding receptions, a drunken uncle might don a woman's wig and do a flawless imitation of Mick Jagger as '(I Can't Get No) Satisfaction' shook the Dansette. The Stones were even worthy of a modicum of unwilling respect as stubborn eccentrics who would not 'go showbiz' by fork-brandishing fathers who, if disparaging them in breakfast rooms, could differentiate between individuals other than Jagger.

The purchase of a fourteenth-century manor deep in the South Downs by Charlie Watts sent an electric thrill throughout the entire postal district. A few fans would sink into a languid daze induced by the fixity of gazing up the drive. Commuting schoolchildren learned that you could see more from the top deck of buses to and from Brighton, where Charlie and wife Shirley ate at a favoured Chinese restaurant, certainly more favoured than one in Lewes after some unpleasantness when another diner's open insults – which embraced the phrase 'long-haired pansy' – culminated in a scuffle.

Jonathan Meades' father nicknamed Charlie's fellow Stone Brian Jones 'Mrs Wormold' after a *gorblimey* character played by Patricia Hayes in the BBC sitcom *Hugh and I*, starring Terry Scott and Hugh Lloyd. Brian's provocatively shuddersome face on the front sleeve of the group's *Between the Buttons* LP indicated a heroically foolish defiance which was rooted in a feeling that he had gone past the reaches of convention and authority. The Ancient Greeks had a word for it: *hubris*, which defies succinct translation. Now, in an adolescence extended by adulation, Brian's *hubris* was learnt not through asceticism and self-denial but via the dynamics of careless sex, the sub-criminality of his past – and making it up as he went along. Jones had also gone beyond using chemicals to stay awake, fall asleep, calm nerves or lift a blue mood (and imagining he could give them up any time he liked).

By way of simple experiment, regardless of the repercussions, lysergic acid diethylamide – LSD – had been part of the 'anything goes' spirit of Swinging London for about a year before it was outlawed for recreational purposes in 1966. The Moody Blues and Small Faces were outfits who'd come to know LSD well. So had The Pretty Things if one was to assume the worst of titles like 'LSD' and 'Trippin''. Certainly, it had already launched Brian (and Keith

Richards) on a voyage that was to carry them further from old-time beat music than any consumer of 'Come On' could have foreseen.

To Marianne Faithfull, 'acid only worsened Brian's condition and compounded his paranoia into a full-blown persecution mania'. Now an unhappy supporting player in the Stones, Jones with *inamorata* Anita Pallenberg had turned their studio flat in South Kensington, according to Marianne, into 'a veritable witches' coven of decadent illuminati, rock princelings and hip nobility'. Less qualified 'insiders' spoke of sado-masochism, coprophagy and the dark arts, all taking place in a dimly lit aura of either cartoon scariness or fascinating depravity, depending on a given visitor's credulity.

The garments observed scattered on the bedroom floor were symptomatic of Jones channelling much of his creative energy into being the best-looking member of the group – of *any* group. The duty of attending to his now highlighted hair fell to friends made aware that any mistake would be comparable to a medical emergency. As the ordained slow-motion operation neared completion, Brian would be dumbstruck in an unremitting contemplation of his own beauty in a three-way mirror. With the Stones, he once elected to wash his hair in a handbasin ten minutes before showtime, causing a half-hour delay. Well, there was no point, was there, in mounting the boards unless you looked like a million dollars? The fans expected it.

He'd also taken to topping his head with floppy, wide-brimmed hats. Elegance in those days, see, no longer meant invisibility. Turning his back on Carnaby Street, by 1966 no longer an epicentre of menswear, Brian – like PJ Proby and Beau Brummell, Esquire before him and countless others later – scoured Portobello Road, Chelsea Antique Market and boutiques like I Was Lord Kitchener's Valet (which thrived on a craze for Victorian military uniforms), Hung On You, Granny Takes a Trip and similar establishments that sprang up in London and the bigger cities, peddling variants on vintage garb, and imported Oriental exotica.

Hence Brian made himself resplendent in lace ruffles, frock coats, costume jewellery, pendants, necklaces, bandana-like cravats, and trousers that, prior to dyeing, may have once adorned the legs of an Edwardian navy deckhand. Later, near-transvestism was offset by experiments with dundreary whiskers and, briefly, a beard. 'He was an effeminate kind of guy,' confirmed Jim McCarty, 'but totally heterosexual. We used to share a girlfriend, Winona. Brian's driver used to pick her up from my flat in Fulham.'

What cannot be denied, however, is that Jones was as self-adoring as any Regency dandy or Teddy Boy, treating his appearance as a work of theatrical art, made afresh before he faced each day. To what extent may be discerned in remarks by Bobbie Korner, wife of Alexis, after she saw Jones 'in that period of dressing up in eighteenth-century clothes. We went to a concert and Brian came into a box above us, and I looked up at him and thought, "My God, he's gone. That isn't somebody dressing up. It's somebody who has disappeared."'

The old inferno of antagonism towards the Stones was rekindled when Brian made his most jaw-dropping fashion statement via the black jackbooted uniform of a Second World War stormtrooper in which, grinning evilly and stamping on a doll, he appeared on the front cover of *Stern*, a glossy magazine published in West Germany, a territory in which Jones was, arguably, more revered than Jagger. This was particularly inflammable in the light of a recent election triumph by neo-Nazis in Bavaria, not to mention a US Beatles album, hastily withdrawn, with a front illustration showing the group as white-smocked butchers among bloody wares that also contained the limbs and heads of dolls. There was also an incident in which Keith Moon, Vivian Stanshall and Screaming Lord Sutch paraded round London clubs in Nazi attire, although, after morning came, Sutch cried off when Moon sought further fun in one of the city's most Jewish quarters.

An *NME* interviewer noted a swastika flag draped over one of Jones's armchairs, but believed his avowals that the *Stern* picture was 'a put-down. Really, I mean with all that long hair in a Nazi uniform, couldn't people see it was a satirical thing?' It was also a 'satirical thing' when all five Stones garbed themselves as middle-aged ladies for the US picture sleeve of the 'Have You Seen Your Mother, Baby, Standing in the Shadow?' single. A few months later, they delivered four numbers under apparent sufferance when, on 22 January 1967, they topped the bill of *Sunday Night at the London Palladium*, a performance given in the light of narrowing opportunities for what Jagger reasoned was 'a good national plug', now that opportunities for television exposure for the more *outré* pop musicians seemed to have narrowed after *Ready Steady Go!* had been taken off the air just before Christmas.

'Personally I didn't want to do it,' griped Charlie Watts. 'I suppose it was a challenge.' As had happened long ago with *The Arthur Haynes Show*, the Stones arrived late and, carped sixty-year-old producer Albert Locke, 'I was confronted with ill-mannered, studied rudeness.' Next, their 13-minute slot was completed with Jagger singing over pre-recorded backing to which the others mimed because, claimed Keith Richards in *Disc* the following Thursday, 'The show's so bad we couldn't rely on them to get the sound we wanted. It's not as if we can't play live.'

Additionally, despite roundabout persuasion giving way to naked pleas by Locke – and Andrew Loog Oldham – the Stones refused to join the rest of the cast, which included a comedian, acrobats, a formation dancing team, a lady balladeer and compère Dave Allen, at the end of the show when they lined up to wave goodbye on the Palladium's revolving stage while the pit orchestra sight-read the 'Startime' theme tune. Whenever members of a pop group came into view, this play-out would be swamped by screams that would ebb abruptly as they were carried off to the back, and replaced by an almost palpable wave of goodwill washing over, say, some national treasure of a comedian like Max Bygraves or Frankie Howerd.

The affront was resonating still during the next edition's rotating curtain call when, interpreted by some as a show of solidarity, satirical comedy duo Peter Cook and Dudley Moore stood next to commissioned cardboard effigies of the group. The fall-out trundled on into February, beginning with predictable affronted scorn from the 'straight' press and its letters pages. A typical epistle came from an Oxford lady who wrote that the group 'should take a lesson from the real stars like Gracie Fields, Margot Fonteyn, Frankie Vaughan, etc., none of whom would dream of being so rude to either their fellow artists or the public'.

CHAPTER SEVENTEEN

'It was the end of the innocence, the end of the fun'

By making their stand at the Palladium, the Stones were not only gilding their notoriety, but identifying with a spreading subculture disturbing enough to warrant a celebrity-laden campaign to curtail it. At a public meeting, Frankie Vaughan – who, back in 1958, had ousted Dickie Valentine as Britain's most popular male singer in the *NME* readers' poll – declared, 'Hippies are leeches on society,' and spurned a flower proffered by one such leech in the audience.

Frankie's counter-revolution was to gather pace in 1967 with his new single, 'There Must Be a Way' and other 45s by the likes of Tom Jones, Engelbert Humperdinck and Des O'Connor which sat awkwardly in the autumn Top Twenty amongst entries from such as the Small Faces, the Jimi Hendrix Experience, Traffic, and the Move. If nothing else, this showed that the opposite of a prevailing trend is always represented to some extent – but what *was* the prevailing trend? Paradoxically, the watershed year of 1967 was as much a *bel époque* for schmaltz as for psychedelia, what with Humperdinck's mind-expanding 'Release Me' being spun as frequently as 'I Can Hear the Grass Grow' by the Move on the Rendezvous jukebox.

Failing pointedly to reach Number One in September, The Rolling Stones' 'We Love You', bracketed by topical prison door sound effects, was a mock-placatory riposte to an ugly episode during which the 'establishment' had all but won a decisive victory, and the conclusion to what would remain the best-known drugs trial in pop, 'which gave us this image of being like a real bunch of dope fiends,' sniggered Mick Jagger.

The preponderance of 'decent music' in the charts apart, the us-and-them situation had intensified, initially with laughable minor attritions such as the arrest of a youth for blowing bubbles – a 'breach of the peace' – in Trafalgar Square. Well, he had long hair, hadn't he? Just as Antisocial Behaviour Orders (ASBOs) would be regarded as badges of honour by post-millennium teenage delinquents, it was perversely glorifying if you looked hippie-ish enough to be stopped and searched for drugs. 'As boys' hair grew longer and longer, we often were stopped by police and searched,' recounted Penny Baldwin, 'or had our names run through the system to make sure we weren't up to no good.'

Vans transporting groups and equipment were pulled over by squad cars, who'd prise off speaker cabinet covers when looking for 'sub-stances' too. Sometimes it was motivated by ennui, but there were instances of just sheer malice. 'I met a fellow who'd been at school with Mick and I,' glared Dick Taylor. 'He'd become a cop in Chelsea, and he said, "I saw Jagger the other day, and I was thinking of busting him just for the hell of it."'

Why were the screws tightening all of a sudden? 'The hippie revolution was beginning to make an impact,' answered Caroline Coon, a London student whose boyfriend was serving time then for possession of marijuana, 'and causing the establishment to recoil in horror. Young people were disappearing off the streets. Nobody knew where they'd gone. Doors were being kicked down at two o'clock in the morning and the police would barge in.'

It wasn't, therefore, just the ineffectual Alf Garnetts who took as gospel what certain Sunday newspapers – for example, the *News of the World* in its three-edition exposé, *DRUGS & POP STARS – FACTS THAT WILL SHOCK YOU* – saw as the encroaching godlessness of the age.

Marijuana – now popularly known as 'pot' or 'grass' – was more and more a herbal handmaiden to creativity as certain pop practitioners started thinking of themselves as not merely entertainers, but pseudo-mystics whose songs required repeated listening in order to comprehend what might be veiled but oracular messages. Even the Troggs from Andover, the market town in north-west Hampshire, would be singing about 'the bamboo butterflies of *yer* mind', and were to suffer airplay restrictions for 1967's 'Night of the Long *Grass*' on the premise that it referred to drugs.

'1967 was the explosion of the drug culture, if there is such a thing,' elucidated Keith Richards. 'It came out into the open, and everybody started talking about it.' That it was going beyond mere reefers and pep pills was implied in the self-consciously 'weird' debut singles by chart newcomers like the Move and Pink Floyd as well as in the transition of The Pretty Things, Small Faces and other established groups from 'boy-meets-girl' compositions to musical insights that were not so instantly comprehensible. Not yet versed in hip jargon, the universal aunt that was the BBC allowed airplay for the Small Faces' 'Here Comes the Nice' single, which dealt with the rush of 'speed', and Bob Dylan's 'Rainy Day Women Nos. 12 & 35' with its 'everybody must get stoned!' refrain. However 'The Addicted Man' by the Game, a group from Surrey, and just plain 'Heroin' by the Velvet Underground (an arty New York combo led by Lou Reed that had come to fruition as part of the Exploding Plastic Inevitable, a series of multi-media events under the aegis of Andy Warhol), hadn't a hope of a solitary spin on the Light Programme (soon to be Radio One). Although Peter Cook and Dudley Moore's spoof 'LS Bumble Bee', a 45 that was indicative of general knowledge, if not use, of lysergic acid diethylamide, passed muster, the Corporation had frowned on the Byrds' 'Eight Miles High', and 'Tomorrow Never Knows', the eerie omega of The Beatles' latest LP.[95] 'Dropping acid', indeed, had become so widespread that Dave Dee would insist to *Melody Maker* that, as far as the clean-minded lads in his group were concerned, LSD still stood for pounds, shillings and pence. Moreover, the Troggs were confined to provincial bookings in the UK to minimise the chances of drug publicity sticking to them.

Matters would climax halfway through 1967 with three Rolling Stones on the very top of the midsummer bonfire. Yet Mick Jagger, as befitted the son of a physical fitness expert, had had little to do with narcotics of any description (though 'Connection' on *Between The Buttons* seemed to contain references to the non-prescription drugs that helped the time pass quicker in this bandroom or on

---

95. Designed by Klaus Voorman, the monochrome front cover of *Revolver*, the album in question, had hair tangling round bits of photographs.

that long-haul flight). He'd hesitated before sampling marijuana for the first time (reportedly, in a cigarette rolled by Paul McCartney at the Beatle's house in St. John's Wood). Nevertheless, once Jagger got round to LSD too, he was loud in its defence: 'You see everything aglow. You see yourself beautiful and ugly, and other people as if for the first time. You should take it in the country, surrounded by all those flowers. You'd have no bad effects. It's only people who hate themselves that suffer.'

The music and underground press in 1967 would be sodden with quotes along similar lines – such as this one from the lips of *International Times* columnist and Radio One disc jockey-in-waiting John Peel: 'There are sparrows and fountains and roses in my head. Sometimes I don't have enough time to think of loving you. That is very wrong.' To *Melody Maker*, Traffic's Jim Capaldi spoke of trying to 'get as much colour into our lives as possible. We see movements and roam through the temples of our minds'.

During 1967's so-called 'Summer of Love', inanities like these were thought worth publishing now that the peace-and-love 'flower-power' ideology had gusted over from San Francisco. Cluttering the pavements in and around Haight-Ashbury, that city's flower-power suburb, were many who seemed to be still living out part of LSD guru (and defrocked Harvard University professor) Timothy Leary's 'turn on, tune in, drop out' slogan by begging from the very 'straights' they mocked. 'Bands' – not 'groups' any more – were still played on and on and on at the 'be-ins', 'freak-outs', 'mantra-rock dances' and 'love-ins' that were held on the greensward of the city's parks, in its transformed ballrooms, and nearby at the Monterey International Pop Music Festival.

Back in London, 'happenings' such as *The 14 Hour Technicolor Dream* at north London's Alexandra Palace embraced the emulation of the paranormal effects of LSD via the contrast of glimmering strobes and ectoplasmic projections on the cavernous walls. One after another, 'bands' appeared on platforms erected at either end of the exhibition centre – Pink Floyd, the Move, Tomorrow, John's Children (with a guitarist called Marc Bolan), the Flies and many others. During a rare intermission, the promenading audience was treated to a turn by a Japanese-American 'concept' artist named

Yoko Ono who many saw as walking evidence of her own conjecture: 'You don't need talent to be an artist.'

In attendance was Ono's future husband, John Lennon. Lately, the music press had been full of how 'mellow' he was now he was in his late twenties. He had the still-noticeable haircut – swept-back fringe, short sides and shaved-off sideburns – from the previous September when it had been required for his role as 'Private Gripweed' in *How I Won The War*, a movie on general release in the period between Brian Epstein's untimely death in August 1967 and that December's interesting-but-boring TV spectacular, the self-produced *Magical Mystery Tour*. 'It's a groove, growing older,' John confided in *Disc*. It was also a groove to attend hippie 'happenings' without an outbreak of Beatlemania obliging a hasty departure. Shouting 'It's John Lennon!' if he edged past you wasn't 'cool' in the capital nowadays.

All this even reached the Netherlands, where Eddy Bonte 'got myself a *chemise à fleurs*, a flower shirt as worn on TV by Antoine, who'd now become France's very own Dylan-styled and long-haired protest singer', and in Tuscany where Andrea Bocelli spent his childhood. The blind classical tenor had a father who 'did not like my long hair, which, at the time, was all the rage. "Cut that hair!" he used to say and I'd reply, "Father, I think I look good like this" and he'd say, "Yes, but you can't see yourself!" I found this unfair, but it was the same for my sighted brother.'

'Flower power' may not have gripped the imagination of the young in agrarian Italy as hard as it had their cousins in Amsterdam or London, but its adherents were becoming commonplace enough for the droll 'Give Him a Flower' to grace the B-side of the debut 45 by the Crazy World of Arthur Brown, whose focal point danced in an idiosyncratic sideways-jumping flicker and emitted a penetrating glare. Robed exotically, he sported a helmet spouting flames (originally a candlestick attached to a sieve). Now and then, however, things went dangerously awry and Arthur's drapery was set ablaze to ovations from those who thought it was as premeditated a stunt as the crane that had lowered him from a great height onto the podium at some outdoor 'happening' during that hot summer.

*

The weather, nonetheless, had become changeable in early August when one of the national tabloids and a couple of regional newspapers reported that a handful of teenagers in kaftans, beads and similar flower-power tat had gathered outside a West Midlands magistrates' court where one of their number was to face a charge connected with marijuana. Placards reading HAPPINESS IS POT-SHAPED, NO CONDEMNATION WITHOUT INVESTIGATION and the like were hoisted high enough to be inches above the head of the tallest protester.

This was Robert Plant, cited by local media as 'leader of Midland Flower Children', who had a beard that hadn't really taken and hair, that if longer than his Mod trim of yore, confirmed Jonathan Meades' observation that, 'Shoulder length hair was still the exception in the late 1960s. Essentially the longest haircuts then were grown-out Mod.'

'I never knew anyone personally with such long hair as Anthony Booth's in *Till Death Do Us Part*,' confirmed Robb Johnson, now a 13-year-old, 'Some found this an issue, but they weren't given to such voluble expressions of fury as Alf Garnett. It was all amusingly academic. When watching BBC repeats of David Frost's black-and-white programmes, I noticed Frost's hair had grown a bit longer over the decade, but mine hadn't or my Dad's nor that of any of my school chums or teachers.'

These observations – and those of Jonathan Meades – were counter to that of Leicester's Mick Pini who 'must have been the first in the area to have really long hair. It went down to my waist for a long time, and I got banned from a café where I used to hang out. Also, I couldn't get a job because of it. Totally ridiculous! Yet being a musician I really didn't care what *they* thought'.

Mick spent much of his day idling in a public park, having 'started a hippie movement, calling ourselves *Shower* People rather than *Flower* People. Passers-by would just stare at us'. Among his companions was Pete Feenstra who'd likewise 'decided to be a hippie with flowers in my hair and a totally free lifestyle. Well, that was the ambition but there's a limit to what a 16-year-old in Leicester can actually be free about. Yet I seriously intended to try. To avoid actually working forty hours a week, I went to Charles Keene College of Further Education for the next two years. Studying didn't take up much of my time, and I concentrated on the more important occupation of living an alternative lifestyle and being a part of the grooviest bunch of people that ever walked the face of the Earth.

'The grooviest of all was Mick Pini, blues guitarist, first class inspirational clown and one of the most beautiful people in existence. In the year above me, he was spectacular looking with long, flowing hair and really expressive Italian features and hand movements. He was the business. I made it my duty to get to know him. We soon realised we had a lot in common. Both of us wanted to make the most of every minute, trying all sorts of things – art, poetry, singing – and, in my case, playing the clarinet and, later, harmonica and guitar. We were the college's artistic vanguard, its avant garde!

'The Art Centre on Cank Street became a hub for the hippies, but maybe the best times were when we just wandered round town, acting the fool, being holy idiots and singing.' Leicester may have been a pocket of cool, but Fleet wasn't.

Nevertheless, *International Times* was purchasable in a back-street newsagent close by the bus station in nearby Aldershot, along with *Oz* – now uprooted from Australia and regarded spuriously as *IT*'s colour supplement – plus San Francisco's groovily subversive *Rolling Stone* and *The Process*, mouthpiece of the Church of the Final Judgement.

An edition of *IT* in 1967's early autumn had a centre spread of Frank Zappa stark naked on the toilet, but with his modesty strategically hidden. That same week, he told *Melody Maker* that his Mothers of Invention 'seem to thrive in areas where there is unrest between the generations', and pinpointed those who constituted what he'd divined as the group's core audience: 'In every small town, there's one person who's crazy – but in a strange way, that village idiot is respected by the rest of the community. In the back of their minds they're thinking, "Is it possible that this nut knows something I don't know?" – and there are times when this strange person will come across new, unexplored avenues of free expression.'

I'd been the first in Fleet to buy *Freak Out!* after the Mothers reeled me in without effort – and were to be the stars of the first formal pop concert I ever attended which would fly by as quickly as reading the most page-turning thriller. Try to imagine the effect that that pop-Dada junk-sculpture of a show had on a despondent if excitable schoolboy from the wilds of Hampshire where I was a misfit, a 'freak' if you like. Moreover, for the rest of my adolescence, Frank Zappa became a barometer against which matters could be evaluated and tested. If watching a television programme, listening to a record or being asked to consider some new idea, the immediate thought might be... yes, but would Frank like it? More often than not, the answer would be 'No, he bloody well wouldn't!'

There were plenty of others like me from north of the Baltic to the coast of Africa because, through mysterious means, copies of *Freak Out!* and the next Mothers LP, *Absolutely Free*, which living up to its 'underground oratorio' subtitle, even leaked beyond the Iron Curtain. Thus, in Czechoslovakia, Mothers numbers infiltrated the repertoire of the Plastic People of the Universe (formerly the Primitives Group), whose lamentable name was derived from *Absolutely Free*'s opening track, and whose output was actually referred to as 'Zappa music'.

Through the same channels, issues of *International Times*, *Oz* and *Rolling Stone* would also wend their way to Eastern Europe. As well as reading them as far as they were able from cover to cover, dissidents would take heart, too, from what they translated as further incitements to revolution, particularly from the Mothers and the Velvet Underground, to supplement those they imagined were in the grooves of the records.

Ivan Martin Jirous, the Plastic People's manager and creative pivot, encouraged the incorporation of English lyrics into their *modus operandi*, going so far as to enlist a Canadian as lead singer for two years – until it became clear that compositions sung in their own language were having more of the desired, challenging effect.

Needling the authorities with their approximation of hippie coiffeur[96] and garb, the Plastic People of the Universe were lucky not to be sent to the salt mines, although certain members endured

---

96. Though the outfit's 16-year-old original drummer wore an onstage wig to cover a mane he was obliged by his day job to keep short.

months, even years in jail for 'organised disturbance of the peace' and other dubious offences.[97] Next, the government revoked the musicians' performing licences, and suppressed the distribution of record releases that, to those in the West who heard them through exported albums, reaching playlists on foreign radio programmes broadcasting non-mainstream pop, conveyed a sense of tuning in to coded musical messages from youth oppressed by tyranny.

What amounted to a reign of terror paralleled the Nazi oppression of the *Swingjugend* ('Swing Youth'), who jitterbugged to banned 'N*****-Jew Jazz' in bars, cafés and behind closed doors. This *Entartete Kunst* ('degenerate art') led to many of its performers and supporters being dispatched like political prisoners to extermination camps. Post-Dubček Czechoslovakians involved in 'underground' music suffered too from a policy of 'normalisation', i.e. attempts at forcing conformity to the regime's own idea about what 'rock' should sound (and look) like – namely, bland, ideologically acceptable pop. After the Plastic People failed to turn up for a compulsory audition before a Ministry of Culture panel, a process began in which they lost their professional status as well as state-supplied instruments and access to rehearsal space on top of cancellation or curtailment of such concerts as there were. These deprivations forced the outfit eventually into acceding to a performance (with hair tucked inside collars) before a specially convened committee that granted them a licence, revoked a fortnight later on the grounds of 'morbid' music that would have a 'negative social impact' on those who might be subject to shadowing to and from school by secret police with powers to detain the most intransigent of them on the flimsiest of charges.

---

97. Jirous was to accumulate eight years under lock and key; his final stretch completed weeks before 1989's 'Velvet Revolution', and the election as first President of the Czech Republic of his friend Václav Havel (who, in the month of his inauguration, was to host a quasi-royal visit to Prague by Frank Zappa). Though a qualified art historian, Jirous had been prevented from obtaining academic posts through his outspoken belief that the force of 'alternative' artistic expression – what he called the 'Second Culture' – might undermine repression. Moreover, he was often central to spectacular brawls over ethical matters in Prague taverns, earning the nickname (and eventual stage alias) 'Magor' ('the crazy one').

*

This was the 'real thing' as opposed to a boy in Limoges, Loughborough or Laramie trying to disregard his parents' belly-aching about his so-called long hair. It even went beyond Ronald Reagan, the freshly elected Governor of California, proclaiming open war on any liberals seeking to extinguish his Republican fire. This included the voicing of any blatant opposition beyond simple conscientious objection to American intervention in Vietnam.

From a comparatively safe billet in Germany, some US soldiers with ragged nerves had formed the Monks. They might have wound up in the glasshouse had they not been demobbed weeks before the release of a 1966 LP, *Black Monk Time*. As well as highlights like 'I Hate You' and 'Shut Up', the title track outlined how much the group, with their gimmick tonsures, loathed the army and the possibility of being sent off to the slaughter in Vietnam. Theirs was an outlook in defiance of age-old right-wing bigotries that were to manifest themselves in the twice-over firebombing of a Houston radio station by some good ol' boys who begged to differ with its anti-war bias.

That Christmas was brightened with Roy Orbison's 'There Won't Be Many Coming Home', which, however briefly, earned him the approbation of the blossoming drop-out sub-culture as a rebuttal of RCA's fastest-selling disc of the year, 'The Ballad Of The Green Berets' by fellow Texan, Staff Sergeant Barry Sadler. It extolled dying 'for those oppressed' (by, presumably, the Vietcong), and citing one lofty wearer who, before being killed in action, requested his young wife to ensure their son follows in his footsteps as 'one of America's best', i.e. 'have him win the Green *Bereeeeeet!*'. Patriotic hearts swelled too when, standing smartly to attention in full uniform, Sadler piped it out in a strong baritone on *American Bandstand*: the ultimate camp or what?

Opposition to US military involvement in south-east Asia was shared by 13-year-old Mary Beth Tinker, a Greta Thunberg of her day, who, with some friends and her brother, had worn black armbands to their Iowa high school a week before the Christmas holidays of 1965 – an action that precipitated not only her immediate suspension, but, as she was to report, 'a man who had a radio talk show threatening my father on the air. Red paint was thrown on our house. A woman called on the phone, asked for me by name, and then said, "I'm going to kill you!"'

The children returned to class in January without the armbands, but chose to dress in black for the rest of the academic year – and Mary Beth got her parents to file a lawsuit. Though backed by the ACLU, there were to be four years of legal to-ing and fro-ing prior to an ambiguous ruling that affirmed the students' rights to free expression as long as it didn't infringe school regulations about clothing, hairstyles and deportment.

While what posterity would call the 'Tinker case' had been trundling on, Mr Reagan became particularly keen to patch up what he called 'the morality gap' in higher education. This was epitomised by long-haired happenings like the Mothers of Invention headlining a 'rock & roll dance benefit' in a gymnasium at the University of California's Berkeley campus. There, lighting like that at *The 14 Hour Technicolor Dream* on wall-bars, ceiling and audience simulated an experience lately given the adjective 'psychedelic'.

It was all in aid of the Vietnam Day Committee which had forged links with those of similar left-wing mind in that same San Francisco Bay area where a leading local newspaper laid into this and like affairs, calling them 'a deluge of filth' for all the usual, exaggerated sex-and-drug related reasons. All that stuff in *Mister Democrat* Lyndon B Johnson's State of the Union address about having to 'honor and support the achievements of thought and the creations of art' had, it seemed, got out of hand. It was time to reinforce clean-mindedness, the Motion Picture Production Code, short-back-and-sides, mid-calf skirts, and the repudiation of the monstrosity that rock 'n' roll had become since the coming of that version of it from across the Atlantic.

If as a gnat round a tent in comparison, how eminently satisfactory what happened to Mick Jagger must have been to Reagan when – as it would be for Johnny Rotten of The Sex Pistols ten years on – the Rolling Stone had been foremost among 'their' most wanted outlaws?

'It was the end of the innocence, the end of the fun', a middle-aged Mick would sigh about a year when he'd started as a mere bystander when the curtains had risen on the most arrant act in a drama, hitherto exceptional only for a divertissement in which *News of the World* witch hunters, banging out those *DRUGS & POP STARS – FACTS THAT WILL SHOCK YOU* pieces, assured readers several months after the fact, that, in Blaises one evening, 'Jagger' – actually Brian Jones – had, quite openly, swallowed some amphetamine tablets and invited the eavesdropping reporters back to his flat to smoke some marijuana – or was it LSD? When a fuming Jagger served a libel suit, the editor carpeted the journalists responsible and plotted a damage limitation scheme whereby the truth – or *a* truth – could be retimed.

By prodding investigative nerves, he discovered that Jagger (and Marianne Faithfull) were to spend a weekend during 1967's mild February at 'Redlands', Keith Richards' moated grange in the peninsula banked by Hayling Island and Chichester. It was a matter of a couple of telephone calls to West Sussex Regional Police Headquarters to arrange for the place to be invaded on the Sunday evening.

Sure enough, the officers found enough 'substances' on the premises to justify the arrest of Richards and, to the *News of the World*'s relief, a now subdued Jagger. However, in his case, charges had to be trumped up to make something of the four pills that, so it was pointed out in court four months later, were available over the counter across the Channel, and that his doctor had permitted him to retain in order to combat pressure of work. The bench overruled this defence – and, less than ten minutes later, the jury, which, according to folklore, included the comedian Terry Scott, returned a 'guilty' verdict. Two days later, a 23-year-old who'd only wanted to get to the dock quietly was ushered from his cell in unnecessary handcuffs and, amid extravagant rejoicing and lamentation, sentenced to three months in jail.

He managed not to faint, but the trademark mouth was almost comical in its gaping shock, and tears weren't far away as he was hustled out of the Chichester courtroom and off to Brixton Prison, more convenient than it might otherwise have been for visits from his parents, still in suburban Dartford, and, as he'd admit long after this particular storm had passed, 'unhappy with what I do'.

Taking the witness stand after his colleague had already been sent down, Keith Richards gave a remarkably unruffled and articulate declaration of himself, though he may have overplayed his hand as the anti-establishment young rock 'n' roller up against the nasty, short-haired old squares. It was almost an open-and-shut case anyway that the Crown would enjoy a complete triumph. The television evening news was full of 'Mick Jagger and his guitarist Keith Richard' being jailed – with Keith receiving his sentence of a year 'without expression'. By the time the bulletin was over, he'd be picking without relish at a meal that included toffee-coloured chips and congealing custard in Wormwood Scrubs as Prisoner No 7855.

In search of a new angle after years in which the lead singer had been seen as the personification of the Stones, many journalists wondered whether to focus more on Keith, with his forbidding aspect and crow's nest thatch, now slightly spiked like that of one of Procol Harum, men of the moment with their 'A Whiter Shade Of Pale' vying with The Beatles' 'flower-power' anthem 'All You Need Is Love', as the most plugged single on Radio London's playlist before the Marine Offences Act became law in August 1967. Thus was effected the demise of those floating pirate stations moored just outside the realm's territorial waters. While this paled beside the troubles of teenage Czechoslovakia, Radio London's final hour would be in its way as poignant for the millions who cared as the Johns Kennedy and Lennon's respective slayings – in that you'd always remember exactly where you were, and what you were doing.

During the period before Jagger and Richards were each granted bail, after not quite two days behind bars – thus cheating warders who'd anticipated dining out on their escorting a Rolling Stone to the prison barber – the BBC had wrung its hands over whether or not to pan away from Mick when that Thursday's *Top of the Pops* broadcast the pre-recording of 'All You Need Is Love' – in which the miscreant had been among the turn-out of The Beatles' eminent friends assisting on the *omnes fortissimo* chorus. That same week, The Who's manager, Kit Lambert, placed an advertisement in a national daily objecting to the two Stones being 'treated as scapegoats for the drug problem'. This was just as The Who themselves were knocking out revivals of 'The Last Time' and 'Under My Thumb', Stones album tracks, for a single whose royalties from what turned out to be its three weeks in the lower reaches of the Top Fifty, were to be donated to Richards' and Jagger's legal costs.

As well as a poster with Mick's image and the paraphrased caption, *LET HE WHO IS WITHOUT SIN JAIL THE FIRST STONE*, on sale in what were to be known as 'head shops' in flower-power London, a protest march along Fleet Street was broken up with the aid of police Alsatians. A last-minute insert in the latest edition of *Oz* disclosed the home address of the *News of the World*'s editor, together with a cunning caution that, 'It would be inadvisable for our readers to mail him cannabis resin and then tip off the police in an effort to have him busted.'

Other periodicals turned on the *News of the World* too. The party line of both *The Sun* and the *Daily Sketch* suggested that Jagger's incarceration was too likely to make a martyr of him, while the *Sunday Express* weighed in with its opinion that it was 'monstrously out of proportion to the offence'.

On the evening after an appeal in which his sentence was commuted to a conditional discharge (and that of Richards dismissed), and the judge reminded Jagger of his 'grave responsibilities', the nation's eyes were glued to ITV when he was trotted out to debate the repercussions of his conduct since he'd first touched the brittle fabric of fame, with two high-ranking priests, a former Home Secretary and the author of an angrily sympathetic editorial in *The Times*. Belying the assumptions of many viewers – as they'd had about The Pretty Things before that God-slot TV discussion – that he was some anomalous nitwit, the former LSE undergraduate who was now the kingdom's most worshipped as well as reviled celebrity, gave an intelligent and gently spoken explanation. If not exactly repudiating the recreational use of narcotics, he argued calmly that he wasn't the one who'd made a bother about it in the first place. As a mere pop singer, he'd been unqualified to do so in any case, unconsciously agreeing with the *Daily Express*'s James MacMillan, then sharpening his quill to express indignant wonder that such a discussion had ever wasted television time.

The same journal published a cartoon in which a John Bull-like figure is incredulous that 'Mick Jagger, Rolling Stone' had become 'Mick Jagger, Saint!' – and heavy-handed endeavours to punish Mick Jagger for being Mick Jagger backfired further when his case, following so soon after that of her boyfriend, escalated Caroline Coon's foundation of Release. 'The first youth organisation that was really an alternative social service run by young people for young people,' she affirmed with quiet pride. 'I felt people needed to know what to do when they were arrested – that you didn't have to be pressured into a confession. You didn't have to make a statement before you've seen a solicitor. What the police claim to be illegal drugs must be confirmed by analysis. You are legally entitled to a telephone call etc. One of the first practical things we did at Release was put out a "know-your-rights" Bust Card. We had thousands printed to distribute free.'

These were yet to be designed when, on the very afternoon Richards and Jagger's case had come up, Brian Jones's apartment in South Kensington was ransacked by the drug squad, who found grains of cannabis and miniscule quantities of harder stuff. It had been, philosophised a fatalistic Brian, as inevitable as, say, an oft-seen episode in the BBC's recent reruns of Hancock's Half Hour. It was almost as if he'd willed it to happen. A psychologist might have theorised that by placing himself in the same agonised boat as Mick and Keith, Brian, consciously or unconsciously, believed he'd be a big wheel in the gang again. Alternatively, perhaps it was to beef up his bad boy image. Whatever those two could do, he could do it worse.

Raw fact is that Brian had answered and ignored telephoned tip-offs of the impending intrusion, possibly from sympathetic journalists who'd been told themselves by contacts inside the force. At any rate, a photograph of Brian on the balcony of the flat during the actual raid was published in one rag, and a phalanx of further press was already crowding the pavement outside Chelsea Police Station when he was escorted inside for the formal charge.

After the trial date was fixed for 30 October, Brian considered that the amount of drugs in question wasn't sufficient to warrant making much of a fuss. All right, so he'd be fined a couple of hundred quid, taking into account inflation. Maybe a conditional discharge as well? That had to be the limit.

His solicitor shook a doubtful head. Judging by the atmosphere at the West Sussex Quarter Sessions where Jagger and Richards were under scrutiny, Jones ought to expect the stiffest possible penalty and be pleasantly surprised if it was less. Hope rose slightly after Mick and Keith's favourable appeal, but Brian's puffed, slitted eyes in the promotional short for 'We Love You' told their own tale. Those two were off the hook. He wasn't.

It might improve matters, thought his lawyers, if it could be argued that Brian needed psychiatric treatment rather than jail. As well as being frail and haggard from the arrest, who could regard him as 'normal' after so many years of being under pressures that John Citizen couldn't begin to understand? Taking this to heart, Jones got himself admitted to a residential clinic in rural London. After an unpromising beginning, the new patient reacted well to its order and discipline, and was able to re-encounter the outside world with his ways changed – or so both Jones and his counsel assured the bench. Neither this nor the defendant's neat pinstriped suit softened court chairman Robert Seaton's heart. Loudly, as if addressing a crowd beyond the wrought-iron gates of the Inner London Sessions Crown Court, he spoke of pop musicians setting an example to their admirers, and said he would be failing in his duty if he didn't send Brian down for nine months.

Although it was not on the scale of the demonstrations that followed the internments of Jagger and Richards, a rally of about 30 people in the pouring rain around Sloane Square was unruly enough to necessitate 12 arrests. This exercise in futility made no difference, however, as the hours dragged by for Jones in Wormwood Scrubs where he'd been clothed in regulation garb, allocated a cell and told that a pair of scissors was hanging over him like a sword of Damocles. Then came the hour when his belongings were returned to him and a thumb jerked at the cell's open door. Twenty minutes later – with all his hair still on his head – Brian Jones was free.

An expert appointed by a High Court judge had examined him and had been convinced that Brian's mental state was precarious, even suicidal, and this had tipped the balance in favour of a hearing at the Court of Criminal Appeal on 12 December 1967. On that day, the bench agreed that Brian had learnt his lesson, and that he had every intention of staying out of trouble for the foreseeable future. He was, therefore, to pay a hefty fine and be put on probation for three years. His behaviour was to be monitored, too, via regular consultations with a psychiatrist.

Five months later, Brian's supposed resumption of his drug habits was in less secretive focus via another run-in with the law. This time, rather than respond to the relentless bell-push, he dialled the Stones' office before the police gained forced access. When a car driven by one of the Stones' aides pulled up outside, Brian's persecutors were belabouring him about some cannabis uncovered in a ball of wool from the drawer of a desk.

'I don't knit. I don't darn socks. I don't have a girlfriend who darns socks,' he'd plead when, after two nail-biting adjournments, the case came up early the following autumn. All that was true enough, but the jury still thought him guilty as hell. Under the circumstances, Brian had no right to expect mercy, but those psychological problems of his proved helpful again, and he got away with a fine as small as the amount of dope with which he'd been caught – or had had planted on him.

CHAPTER EIGHTEEN

'Cop kill a creep! Pow! Pow! Pow!'

Ten days after the arraignment of Brian Jones at the Appeal Court, I, well, experienced the Jimi Hendrix Experience at *Christmas on Earth Continued*, an all-night spectacular on 22 December 1967 at Kensington Olympia's vast Exhibition Hall. Just as it was reported of the Alexandra Palace's *14 Hour Technicolor Dream*, the walls squirmed with light shows like those you might see if you were on LSD – about which I knew nothing apart from what I'd read in the papers. Sets by the Move, Tomorrow, the Soft Machine, Syd Barrett's Pink Floyd, Traffic and more from the very top drawer of British psychedelic rock begged the question of a last hurrah to flower-power, so *passé* then that it was the subject of 1968's belated 'Flower Power Fred' (coupled with 'Harry Krishna') by Harry H Corbett in his 'Young Steptoe' guise, and fuelled jokes for stand-up comedians at Batley Variety Club, 'the Las Vegas of the North' and, in its own way, the other side of the same coin – particularly as the Summer of Love had been no more the dawning of the Age of Aquarius than the Twist had been.

I paid heed to this at *Christmas On Earth Continued* with an Al Capone slouch-hat and, in my mind anyway, a shoulder-padded zoot-suit (with a belt at the back) instead of an eyesore of pink-striped plastic topcoat and floral trousers from a bargain rail in Laslett's, Fleet's High Street clothes shop – through which I'd been risking a beating-up in the town's streets.

Ringo Starr ascribed the supplanting of flower-power in Britain by slouch-hatted Prohibition gangster chic to 'those lightweight clothes. You'd freeze to death. So flower people are putting on their overcoats again'. The week before *Christmas On Earth Continued*,

Georgie Fame had been at Number One with 'The Ballad of Bonnie and Clyde', which, complete with machine-gun sound effects, was to create the misconception that it was actually part of the score for the then current Oscar-nominated biopic *Bonnie and Clyde*.[98] While this revitalised Georgie's flagging chart career, another London-based act, the Artwoods, missed the boat. Even more than Fame, 'we badly needed a gimmick', surmised Art Wood. Sensing what was coming, they'd rechristened themselves St Valentine's Day Massacre and rush-released a revival of the Depression-era anthem, 'Brother Can You Spare A Dime'. This was gilded with a suitable wardrobe and stage presentation and a publicity stunt involving Faye Dunaway (who'd been 'Bonnie' in the film). Unvarnished opportunism pervaded too on the self-composed, 'Al's Party' B-side – named after Capone, the brains behind the historic massacre in Chicago on 14 February 1929.

Because the once invincible Al and his cohorts had kept theirs short, maybe the *Daily Telegraph*'s assertion that long hair wasn't 'with-it' anymore might have carried more weight than it had back in 1965.[99] Certainly, it was no longer 'with-it' for rhythm guitarist Brian Pendleton, who'd anchored Dick Taylor's attractively rough-hewn solos and riffs in The Pretty Things – in which he'd also been required to pluck bass whenever the usual player, John Stax, doubled on harmonica.

After a second LP, *Get the Picture*, failed to chart, and the Things bid a final farewell to the UK singles Top Fifty with a cover of a Kinks album track, 'House in the Country', Pendleton had been the first to quit. According to Phil May, 'We were on a train to Leeds – and when we got there, Brian was gone. He'd got off somewhere, so we struggled through the five or six dates we had in the north

---

98. Also relevant in this context are 'Al Capone' – a 'sleeper' hit by Prince Buster as early as February 1967 – and the following January's semi-spoken 'Bonnie And Clyde' by Serge Gainsbourg and Brigitte Bardot.

99. Though fighting a largely unnoticed rearguard action was 'Long Hair', released in December 1967 as the B-side of the only release by the Infinite Staircase from San Antonio, Texas. It had lyrics that named US mass murderers of the decade such as 'Texas Tower Sniper' Charles Whitman, along with Lee Harvey Oswald (who 'all had short hair and not a flower').

as a four-piece. When we got back to London, Dick went round to Brian's flat, and the door was swinging open like the Marie-Celeste. He'd taken his wife and baby and just vanished. We never saw him again until we had a wind-up meeting about four years later.'

Viv Prince, however, had not become a relative nobody after his time in The Pretty Things limelight was up. Within weeks of being fired in November 1965, he'd emerged as the host of Knuckles, a new metropolitan in-place where, on one occasion, he'd been beastly drunk at the bar when, so *Melody Maker* testified, 'The Spencer Davis Group arrived to be greeted by the Animals and PJ Proby.'

'Don't Bring Me Down' – not The Pretty Things' song – had been the Animals' final hit prior to a relaunch as Eric Burdon *and* the Animals. During the old group's farewell tour of the States in 1966, bass player Chas Chandler had decided to diversify into behind-the-scenes branches of show business for fun and profit, and had 'discovered' Jimi Hendrix through the latter's casually cataclysmic performance in a half-empty Greenwich Village club. When spending much of the previous four years as a hireling musician on the R&B/soul package tour circuit, Afro-American Hendrix had been photographed 'in a tuxedo and a bow tie playing in Wilson Pickett's backing group with my hair slicked back and *my mind* combed out'. Nevertheless, during a stint in Little Richard's backing Upsetters, 'he began to dress like me,' noticed Richard, whose hair was now more untamed than it had been before his bout of born-again Christianity. 'He even grew a little moustache like mine. He watched me work and just loved the way I wore these headbands around my hair and how wild I dressed.' Once, fans, spotting Jimi and mistaking him for Richard, cornered him for autographs (as happened to Brian Jones when mistaken for a Beatle after the *Swinging '63* show). Years later, a cover drawing on a posthumous Hendrix album of dubious legality represented him, at first glance, as just like his erstwhile boss.

On persuading Hendrix to come to London, Chas Chandler held daytime auditions in Knuckles for personnel who would make up the rest of a trio and would be fluid complements to Jimi's playing – and his image.

From an array of bass players, Chas and Jimi chose Noel Redding, a lead guitarist who was willing to transfer. As well as owlish John Lennon spectacles plus a fretboard dexterity above the ordinary, Noel was also conspicuous for a hairstyle vaguely like that of shock-headed Jimi – unlike that of chosen drummer Mitch Mitchell at first. 'When the Troggs used to frequent the greasy spoon up Denmark Street[100] in 1966,' recounts Chris Britton, 'we knew Mitch as a short-haired Mod. At the end of the year we were on the edition of *Ready Steady Go!* on which the Experience made their TV debut – and I hardly recognised Mitch with this alarming Afro like Jimi's. A few months later you'd see that hairstyle everywhere, even back in Andover.'

Over in Dover – where my family lived before Fleet – an elderly relation of mine came to refer to Hendrix as 'that cannibal' for his brown skin and the nimbus of corkscrews round his head. A contemporaneous edition of *Good Evening*, an ITV chat show presided over by Jonathan King, would feature Mitch and his parents conversing about how much Mr and Mrs Mitchell had become reconciled to the way their now similarly haloed son earned a living in the employ of wildman Hendrix. The foreseeable conclusion was that he was the axiomatic 'Nice Lad When You Got to Know Him'. As for Hendrix himself, a brash outer shell was found to contain surprising gentleness, sensitivity and generosity. An *NME* article referred to Jimi's 'sad Dylanish air' while agency assistant Melissa Chassay's observations of his carnal antics backstage were belied when calling on 'the most charming, polite person in the entire world. If you went to his house, he took off your coat, that kind of thing'. Moreover, a touching image in *Disc* was of Jimi dressed up as Father Christmas at a children's party within the Roundhouse, the converted railway engine shed in Chalk Farm that had hosted the launch of *International Times*.

He also gave hope for such as Ray Dorset who, 'when Jimi Hendrix came along, my mindset was still wanting to have straight hair'. Mike Cooper, soon to be a cult celebrity during a second wave

---

100. Then London's Tin Pan Alley for its confluence of music publishing firms and equipment shops.

of British blues in the later 1960s, would recall, 'after seeing Jimi Hendrix, I had my hair permed and dyed black for fun by a friend who was a hairdresser'. As for styling the result, both Ray and Mike might have had to do as little as Jimi himself. 'A girl asked me if she could comb my hair,' he once laughed. 'Nobody can comb my hair. I can't even comb my hair.'[101]

Three months before *Christmas on Earth Continued*, I'd spotted Hendrix at play rather than work after Stefan Mlynek, a childhood friend who'd just become a police cadet at a college in north-west London, very kindly bought me a ticket for the Mothers of Invention's first recital outside the Americas on 23 September at the Royal Albert Hall. This proved a 'happening' which, for ages afterwards, I was to recount in detail at the drop of a hat to anyone who would listen.

I'd had to work delicately on Mum and Dad for their 'I suppose so' permission to go before I boarded the train for London half a day before the show and met up with Stefan.

As evening fell, we passed 30 TV sets in a domestic appliances shop transmitting silent TV stills of Zappa on a *London Weekend News* bulletin. What were they saying about him? I was to be told that the thrust of this break from heavier reportage was that, though the *raison d'être* of the Mothers seemed to be comedy, they weren't like Freddie and the Dreamers.

Stefan and I then entered a snack bar where two older boys, apparitions in chiffon, paisley, crushed-velvet and, crucially, impressively shoulder-length locks, were tunnelling into sausage-and-chips. One – addressed as 'Nige' – was looking at us as if he'd like to talk. Through forkfuls of food and puffs at a cigarette, we gathered he and his pal were off to see the Mothers too. It wouldn't surprise him, he reckoned, if all they did was sit immovably on onstage chairs, remarking about 'plastic people like you!' Nige snarled abruptly. He'd assessed that I was a yokel, a little disorientated in the metropolis, too aware of a recent haircut and who'd bought *Freak Out!* simply because I liked it.

---

101. Later, however, Hendrix was to adopt what was called an African 'natural' rather than either continuing as a fashion leader for whites or going in for a chemically straightened 'conk' worn by many young blacks.

Nige was probably an undergraduate who'd end up as a primary school teacher with a clipped beard and brown leather elbows. For now, however, he was probably one of the hipper-than-thou *illuminati* – subjects of Zappa's private contempt – for whom the main purpose of a concert was to see and be seen during the intermission, and who were preoccupied with what to say afterwards. Having absorbed the show in a knowing, nodding kind of way, everyone would be babbling about how 'interesting' it all was. Dropping the appropriate names and catchphrases, they'd assume a pitying superiority towards those who either hadn't 'appreciated' it for the 'right' reasons or were among those Zappa recognised as 'on the fringe of everything, the ones who don't care if they're in or out, don't care if they're hip, hep, swingin' or *zorch*, even if you have short hair and watch TV 18 hours a day'.

We noticed Nige again – with his toffee nose still asking to be punched – in the same upper circle block as ourselves, which afforded a back view of the Albert Hall stage. After I'd shuffled towards seat 113, row 15, there was a burst of applause somewhere in the stalls as Arthur Brown, an aura of rock eminence spreading from him like cigar smoke, took his seat. From a distance too, I was also to spy Hendrix, who grinned and waved at my uninhibited shout. 'Shut up, Alan! Shut up!' whispered Stefan.

As I might have done, strangers had pressed their noses against windows of espresso bars to watch Frank Zappa *eat* – and, on one occasion, answer a waitress's question about whether his inky mane was genuine – after he'd breathed foreign air for the first time when he and manager Herb Cohen had checked in at the Royal Garden Hotel – from where you could see both Hyde Park and the Albert Hall – a month before the big night. As well as a photo call where Big Ben rises from the Houses of Parliament – with Zappa in a bowler hat – MEET A MOTHER! blazed above a picture on the front page of *Melody Maker* of Frank in full mini-skirted drag – false breasts, floral dress, fishnet stockings, Phil May hair in ribboned bunches (inducing a deluge of letters from sickened readers). The feature inside, however, revealed that Zappa was a pop musician who provided good copy: plain-speaking, with a quirky wit and, unlike John Peel with his 'sparrows and fountains and roses' or Jim Capaldi roaming through the temples of *yer* mind, faultless logic.

Of the fading Summer of Love, Frank asked 'How can you love complete strangers when a lot of them are unpleasant people? I want nothing to do with flower-power,' pointing out that its inherent elitism was as prone to the same narrow-mindedness that defined the most right-wing square. Indeed, while *We're Only In It For The Money*, his Mothers of Invention's yet-to-be-issued third LP[102] was to be one of the funniest records ever released – funny ha-ha or funny peculiar – there are no laughs at all in its 'Mom And Dad' selection, even if it took a gentler tone than might have been expected with the 'plastic' adults indifferent to police turning guns on some hippies lazing in a public park – until the revelation that their daughter was among them. Presumably, this scenario was in municipalities that had adopted laws to keep the long-haired weirdo in check or, preferably, beyond their outskirts. To this end, Carmel, California made tree-climbing and sleeping on the grass illegal. Swedesboro, New Jersey classified those kissing, hugging, and indulging in further 'improper or indecent action' as being criminal.

'Cop kill a creep! Pow! Pow! Pow!' was a key line when *We're Only In It For The Money* also dwelt on the rumoured internment of dissenters in 'Concentration Moon' – and, Zappa told *Melody Maker*, 'The system is crumbling. The old don't see the mess they have caused and are wallowing about in. Their egos won't allow it – but the kids say, "Well, society is a joke. Let's go to San Francisco and drop out, join a tribe and live back on the land." So what happens to society? It *does* crumble and there's a chance to change

---

102. Melody Maker's MEET A MOTHER! photograph was from the session for the *We're Only In It For The Money* sleeve. While it spoofed that of The Rolling Stones' 'Have You Seen Your Mother, Baby, Standing in the Shadow' 45, it was contrived as far as possible on what Zappa called 'a direct negative of that for *Sgt. Pepper's Lonely Hearts Club Band*' – with the Mothers' name spelt in semi-rotted vegetables rather than flowers, a thunderstorm instead of a blue sky, and background figures that included a policeman, JFK's assassin, groupies, characters from horror flicks, Lyndon B Johnson (twice), a Pope, Elvis Presley, the Statue of Liberty and Theda Bara (the silent movie star on the *International Times* masthead).

it, but all you've got is a lot of tribes not equipped to take over on the technical and political side.'

Interviews that filled other of Zappa's waking hours were all grist to the publicity mill for 23 September but, behind the closed door of the Royal Garden's most nicotine-clouded suite, Zappa and Cohen were shouldering difficulties such as the unavailability of *Absolutely Free* in European shops until October. In the States, however, it had been released on the same day, 26 May 1967, as the now-moustachioed Beatles' *Sgt. Pepper's Lonely Hearts Club Band*, which had been assured a gold disc before its conception, let alone completion. With every vinyl crevice filled likewise, *Absolutely Free* was to grapple its way to the brink of *Billboard*'s Top Forty but no further.

Yet both were among the albums that laid the ground rules for pop's fleeting 'classical period' when it surfaced as a feasible means of artistic expression. As trade figures were to signify, record companies were now underwriting further syncretic 'concepts' (*Their Satanic Majesties Request* by The Rolling Stones, John Mayall's *Bare Wires*, and the Moody Blues' *Days of Future Passed*), 'rock operas' (The Pretty Things' *SF Sorrow*, *Arthur* from The Kinks, The Who's *Tommy* and, in 1971, Frank Zappa's *200 Motels*) and *nouvelle vague* 'works' by artistes entering realms even further removed from their humble beat group origins. With Twink from the disbanded Fairies now in the ranks of The Pretty Things, *SF Sorrow*, for example, was, elucidated Phil May, 'an album that was one piece. That's why it had a story – the only way we could give it continuity'.

Dick Taylor continued: 'EMI – probably because they didn't know what was going on – actually seemed quite willing to accept it – though they still took a single off it.'

With the long-player no longer a testament to market pragmatism rather than quality – too frequently a throwaway patchwork of tracks, a hit 45 and its B-side – it was becoming feasible for acts that carried any artistic weight to operate ambiguously with 'musicianly' fancies on 'rock' (not 'pop') albums that only the most sophisticated could appreciate, whilst keeping a weather eye on the singles Top Fifty (often with the LP's most trite excerpt) on the understanding that po-faced *Top of the Pops* excursions were marginal to a main body of work on these here 'albums' (not 'LPs').

Into the bargain, 'serious' composers like Terry Riley and French electronics boffin Pierre Henri (who was to record an album with picked-to-click Spooky Tooth) were to be promoted like rock stars. The most sensational discovery of this resolve was by CBS's record division of Louis Thomas Hardin, alias 'Moondog', who, with his 'image' enhanced by blindness, had been a familiar sight at his pitch on New York's Times Square, busking with home-made instruments, attired in army blankets and a sort of helmet that made him look like a hybrid of Druid and Norse jarl.

Other labels saw similar potential in England's tall, long-haired John Tavener and 'Samurai of Sound', Stomu Yamash'ta, a hirsute and exotically garbed young man from Japan. He was a percussion virtuoso awarded a Classical Grammy for an album of pieces by Henze and Maxwell Davies who, with Stravinsky, Schoenberg, Holst, Penderecki, Stockhausen, Ives, Berio and Varèse were as likely as anything from the charts to pulsate from the car stereos of self-improving pop musicians such as Pink Floyd, three of whom had met during a degree course at Regent Street Polytechnic.

They had surfaced as darlings of London psychedelic clubs like the Spontaneous Underground and The Night Tripper (later UFO) where an act's appeal to a tranced hippie clientele, either cross-legged or 'idiot dancing' with catherine-wheel eyes, depended less on looks and hip-hugging trousers than the dazzling atmosphere that thickened during incessant extrapolation of tracks from both its album debut and the unfamiliar successor that was being created during a studio block-booking of weeks and, if affordable, months.

Such behaviour was infused with an accelerating absorption of 'underground' culture and the associated rebellion, though 'underground' was becoming a misnomer as, by the mid-1960s, it was being pushed into every one of your provincial senses. Joss-sticks were burnt in sixth-form common rooms and, as early as 1966, Stephen MacDonald, a Farnborough Grammar schoolboy in the year above me, possessed a US import of the Velvet Underground's first LP – which he lent to me in exchange for a few days with *Freak Out!*.

*

Yet pop music was still a vocational blind alley where Stephen and I lived during an era long before parents bought synthesisers as 16th birthday presents for children who could even con grants out of the government to form a group. No one lasted long – so you might as well get accustomed to the prospect of holding down mortgage-paying but humdrum jobs and marrying each other's siblings. As for those of higher academic caste, you could daydream forever, but, whether you shook off local fetters or not, the reality seemed to be a dismal and inflexible eternity of exams and, when you were through with being further educated, the continuing mundanity.

After reaching the Upper Sixth Form at the grammar school in St Albans, Andy Pegg was among the few deemed by headmaster Ronald Bradshaw to be 'too irresponsible to be prefects, because our hair was too long. On more than one occasion Mr Bradshaw pursued me around the school quadrangle trying to catch me to demand I cut my hair. By the time it came to leaving school, he gave me an ultimatum: "cut your hair so that it rests above your collar, trim your sideboards wear a school tie and have a school badge on your blazer and report to my office tomorrow morning or else I will not write a reference for you." I wanted to go to college, so reluctantly, I duly complied'.

Ending up at the same teacher training establishment as Andy, Brian Harrington had also been 'a long-haired hippie from around 1967 onwards. When in the Canadian army, my father had been billeted on the Isle of Wight where he met my mother, who he married and took back to Canada until we returned to the island. Like many parents they wanted me to do better than them in terms of job prospects. They wanted me to be a banker (or other respectable profession), but I was very much into music (and art) and worked briefly as a disc jockey at an island disco.

'As the vast majority of my family were still in Canada, I went there for holidays and worked on an Ontario radio station where the boss liked my English accent. He then left to work on Radio England[103]

---

103. Swinging Radio England broadcast from a ship in the North Sea, and was categorised as a pirate station.

and, when I came back to Britain, he offered me a job. My father, as a shipyard welder, was on £11 a week and I was offered £90 per week for a fortnight on board and one week off. It might have been worse if I had told my parents I wanted to be a ballet dancer, but DJ was a close runner-up. It didn't help that on an early trip back home I went out with them, saw a jacket I liked and paid £70 cash for it!

'I fully embraced the hippie image, with shoulder-length hair, velvet trousers, silk scarves and more. The Marine Offences Act brought it all to a screeching stop, of course, and so I returned to the Isle of Wight and applied to teacher training college. Suddenly I was respectable again (apart from the long hair and fashion choices). Although I never taught post-qualification, I did end up (after more training) as a Probation Officer. I was still "the one with the long hair" according to the judges and magistrates.'

On the strength of appearance, it may have been assumed by uninformed court officials that Brian was the lawbreaker rather than perhaps the appointed supervisor in a place like New Jersey which, on top of the 'improper or indecent action' in Swedesboro, had earned such a reputation for harassing long-haired males without sound cause that a British travel guide cautioned them to steer clear of a state where prosecutors had been obliged to order highway patrollers to be more circumspect about pulling over folk of that description. Of a random sample of thirty-seven, a mere seven had been arrested – one for possessing a bottle of aspirins.

On the other side of the far-famed New Jersey Turnpike tollbooth, a letter to the *New York Times* complained on behalf of a man who was 'an honest citizen of the United States' and a disabled Vietnam veteran to boot. He had been stopped and body-searched not once, but twice at the city's LaGuardia Airport – one of but three passengers so confronted. That each was distinguished by having long hair drew no response from the Customs Bureau in Washington, but 'a spokesman' pleaded, 'We are engaged in a nationwide crackdown on narcotics, and unfortunately many innocent travellers face some inconveniences. However, the idea that people with long hair are being picked upon for special treatment is nonsense.' In a quieter passion would be

Good Housekeeping magazine whose poll on a connected matter had 76 per cent of those balloted siding with schools that regulated student hair length.

This was countered by a statement from Ernest Besig, executive director of the ACLU office in San Francisco, that the laws directed at the unkempt and unshod were 'unreasonable and arbitrary. We're talking about minority rights. There's just no rational reason to discriminate against people who have long hair'. That was all very well, argued Norman Bramall, who, in June 1968, was to resign after forty-one years as a tennis instructor at Pennsylvania's Haverford College because of an executive decision to rescind a ruling that 'an athlete must be shorn and shaved to suit the needs of the coach', following a student petition demanding that 'neat beards, or neat but long hair, could not automatically be used to exclude men from teams'.

Although he became an unwilling subject of national editorials, typified by one defending his refusal 'to be stampeded into submission by this weird new breed of hippies which infest many of our campuses today', Norman was willing to yell from the rooftops a belief shared unknowingly with 'Gerry Barford' of BBC television's *United!* series, that sportsmen would not command respect if they took the field with long-haired, bearded players.

On reading headlines like *HIPPIES 'KO' TENNIS COACH* and *COACH RAISES RACKET, HIPPIES NET VICTORY* – and noting that undergraduates at a sister establishment were picketing outside an employment office because it would not hire a student mail carrier on the grounds that he had long hair – Frank Navarro, in charge of football at New York's Columbia University, remarked 'We don't have time to grow hair, to be sidetracked. We're playing football. We're concentrating. Long hair and beards lead to other things like lying under trees and singing songs.'

CHAPTER NINETEEN

'Will any girl spare you a second glance when you're twenty-five, unemployed – and bald?'

On 6 October 1967, Haight-Ashbury was the stage for a mock-funeral, 'Death of Hippie', involving a public bonfire of associated clothing and literature, to signify the corruption of the Summer of Love utopia with its drug peddlers and teenage runaways plus the sightseers and weekend ravers who kept the newly sprung record stores, boutiques and restaurants in profit.

A glance at the charts also told you that the music industry had been at the forefront of this inevitable commercialisation of flower-power. Cashing in quick had been Scott McKenzie with 'San Francisco (Be Sure To Wear Flowers in Your Hair)' and Eric Burdon with 'San Franciscan Nights' – while specific to Britain, the Flower Pot Men also got lucky with 'Let's Go to San Francisco' and, garbed in chiffony robes, tossed dead chrysanthemums into the audience when appearing at London's Finsbury Park Astoria.

In the air, too, as 1967 ran its course was *Hair: The American Tribal Love-Rock Musical*, an off-Broadway enterprise that, in a profit position within weeks, premièred on the Great White Way the following spring. Next, understudies were brought in so that the troupe could hit the road, coast to coast. Other than the odd outburst of heckling, it was hailed across the nation. The rest of the world – well, most of it – followed gushing suit. Imported to the West End, *Hair* was destined to run at the Shaftesbury Theatre for 11 years after opening on the very day after the abolition, via the 1968 Theatres Act, of stage censorship, thus permitting the murkily lit nakedness which closed the first half[104] as well as the

---

104. This would also allow a presentation by a combo from Leicester, Black

extremity of improvisation – and audience participation, extending beyond the show *per se* when those allowed to stay up past their bedtimes pitched in, too, as 33-year-old Alex Harvey led the 11-piece house band through current favourites by the likes of Bob Dylan and The Beatles.

While the fundamental plot of *Hair* centred on a youth eligible for induction into the US army and sent to do his bit in Vietnam,[105] it also delved into aspects of pacifism, environmentalism, spirituality and astrology, although the tabloids made more of the nudity and profanity than the memorable songs with their echoes of jazz and Las Vegas cabaret. There was an immediate rash of cover versions such as 'Aquarius' by both Paul Jones and, in German, Spencer Davis. The title song became a smash hit in Australasia, South Africa and North America for the Cowsills, a fresh-faced family from Rhode Island, who wore jokey wigs to promote a number from which they'd removed all references to religion in rather contrived lyrics exemplified by a verse glorifying hair that's too short if you can see the eyes of a wearer letting it grow 'down to where it stops by itself'.

Members of the London cast were all to crack the domestic charts, one way or another, among them Marsha Hunt whose face, framed by wide and fuzzy black hair, was worthy of a full-colour double-page head-and-shoulders portrait one week in *Disc and Music Echo*. She also fitted Mick Jagger's apparent penchant for 'girls with long dark hair, who are small and gay'. Perhaps calculated to needle Marianne Faithfull, still clinging on as his official 'constant companion',[106] that's what he told *Boyfriend* – because the Stones weren't so dismissive of the adoration of schoolgirls that they didn't have recent photographs available on request for *Boyfriend*, *Rave!*, *Fabulous 208*, *et al*, even though the

---

(cont.) Widow, that featured a bare lady prostrate beneath singer Kip Trevor's sacrificial sword amid chilling screams and abundant spilling of fake blood.

105. Post-millennium reheatings of *Hair* in the context of later wars, beginning in 2001 with productions at theatres in Los Angeles and New York, were still active over 20 years later.

106. A reference to 'Mick and Lady Faithfull' began a verse of 'Melting Pot' by Blue Mink, a UK Top Ten entry early in 1970.

latter magazine seemed to be reflecting, erroneously as it turned out, overweening teenage interest in rugged cowboy types like Doug McClure who played 'Trampas' in *The Virginian* on BBC 1 as much as, say, pretty Peter Frampton of the Herd, the soon-to-cease *Rave's* 'Face of '68'.

As demonstrated by period pin-ups of Keith Potger of the Seekers and Engelbert Humperdinck, McClure's looks were in line with a mid-to-late 1960s concept of male beauty that hinged chiefly on an intensity of the jaw line and lips. Him (or his management) giving printed thanks for a *Fabulous 208* award for which he wasn't actually nominated also corresponded with a seeming repudiation of all that marijuana-smoking hippie nonsense and, indirectly, an indication of the cautious post-pirates programming of pop by the BBC – which had hastened the shallower and less subversive content of *Top of the Pops*. This reached its nadir one 1968 week of wall-to-wall balladeers apart from, over the closing credits, the Tremeloes, now *sans* Brian Poole, who were, with Marmalade and Love Affair, a prong of a grinning triumvirate that were hopeless pretenders to The Beatles' throne during this silver age of British beat.

It also coincided with a long period when The Rolling Stones had downed tools as a touring entity for over two years, from a date in Athens on 17 April 1967 to 7 November 1969 in Colorado. In between, the only stage appearances would be ten minutes at an *NME* Poll-winners Concert on 12 May 1968 and the fabled memorial to Brian Jones – who drowned a month after leaving the group – at Hyde Park on 5 July 1969.

During this phase too, Mick Jagger alone, rather than the Stones *en bloc*, was also being courted by theatre and movie moguls – either on the lookout for new big-screen talent or driven by cynical expediency, because the words 'Mick Jagger' in the credits would guarantee attention. In autumn 1968, he not so much dipped a toe as plunged head first into a film, *Performance*, with a screenplay by Donald Cammell, a leading light of the bohemian post-war 'Chelsea Set' of jazzers, painters, debutantes, ex-public schoolboys, the more glamorous criminals – and, by the mid-1960s, pop musicians. Cammell was also a godson of Satanist wizard Aleister Crowley (who was also included on the front cover of *Sgt. Pepper*).

Warner Brothers, its investors, had been led to believe it was a
breezy crime caper fixed in what was left of Swinging London of
Blow-Up, but *Performance*'s cinema release had to be postponed until
it had been subjected to the cutting room's scrutiny. The violence
was considered too sickening and the sex too weird and graphic.
Cammell's script delved into existentialism and identity crises,
notably when the outlines dissolved between Jagger as 'Turner', a
pop recluse, and 'Chas', played by James Fox – in a departure from
his usual upper-class parts – a bisexual hitman, fleeing from both
rough justice and the police to Turner's 'right piss-hole' of 'longhairs, beatniks, druggers, free love... You couldn't find a better little
hidey-hole'.

In view of the hippie subculture's supposed trafficking in
promiscuity and drugs, you could understand unhip Chas's scorn
towards Turner. He probably felt the same about the 'controlled
weirdness' of 'Apple Corps', an umbrella term for myriad maverick
ventures under the aegis of The Beatles' self-managed business
enterprise, founded the previous January. After moustaches, LSD
and, more recently, meditation, John, Paul, George and Ringo
hadn't suddenly latched onto bourgeois greed. No more qualified
to run Apple Corps than Brian Epstein had been to play guitar,
'we had this mad idea of having Apple there,' said George, 'so
that people could come and do artistic stuff and not have a hard
time'.

Advertisements appeared, therefore, in both national and
underground outlets soliciting the public to bring 'artistic stuff'
to the Apple Foundation for the Arts in London. Not a postal
delivery would go by without a deluge of manuscripts and demo
tapes thumping onto its doormat, begging for cases to be heard.

Setting off on the journey to his pathetic and gore-splattered
end in 1980, John Lennon, his *How I Won The War* serviceman's
cut now pushing Phil May length and centre-parted, ordered
the issue on Zapple, Apple Records' short-lived 'experimental'
subsidiary label, of his *Unfinished Music No. 2: Life With The Lions*,
the second of a trilogy of albums with Yoko Ono, who'd become
to Art as Screaming Lord Sutch was to politics – while Lennon
had overtaken Jagger as the chief representative of all that the likes

of Frankie Vaughan despised. Now a generalised disenchantment with the hippie counter-culture was to be epitomised in the USA by the Sharon Tate bloodbath in summer 1969. Had it been only the previous October that *International Times* had declared, 'Charlie Manson is just a harmless freak'?

Through Yoko Ono's catalytic influence, the world was confronted with a Lennon they'd never known. Annihilating completely any cosy illusions that Fab Four traditionalists had left were his and Ono's headline-hogging 'Bed-Ins' for world peace,[107] 'Bagism' and other 'Art statements' too indecent for a family newspaper – as well as going beyond the bounds of acceptable ickiness with autumn 1969's *Wedding Album* on which half the needle-time was consumed by Yoko and a now bearded Lennon's repeated utterances of each other's name over their own pounding heartbeats. As an aside – and writing subjectively – I sensed, perhaps speciously, that John felt obliged to lend pragmatic support to matters about which, deep down, he cared little or found embarrassing, even repugnant and, as a result, mutated from a hero into some sort of cosmic *wally*. There! I've said it!

'The change in him was like Jekyll and Hyde,' agreed Cynthia, his first wife, who, like other of his intimates had not associated penis display with him. Here was a man who, only three years earlier, had hissed 'You don't do that in front of the birds!' when he, Cynthia plus George and Pattie Harrison had been confronted

107. Taped at a 'Bed-In' in a Toronto hotel, Lennon's 'Give Peace a Chance' anthem, attributed to the ad hoc 'Plastic Ono Band', was his first smash without Paul, George and Ringo. During the event too, Lennon and Ono debated with the fashionable Canadian communication theorist Marshall McLuhan, who'd been nominal host of a 1967 festival in San Francisco where hippie listeners to his tutorials took up his slogan 'the medium is the message' and his talk of a 'global village'. To him, the wearing of long hair was akin to 'a frame' – and his chat with the Lennons included the following exchange: McLuhan: 'The minute you've got long hair and the minute you're popular with the kids, the whole adult on the other side of the gap says, you know, you're a bunch of left wing communists and that.' Lennon: '...and it's the same as if you'd only get your hair cut and wear a straight suit, you'd be more effective. One, I wouldn't be myself. Two, I don't believe people believe politicians, especially the youth.

by a drunken Allen Ginsberg wearing only underpants – on his head – at a London *soirée* held on the beatnik bard's birthday. What then had they made of Lennon and Ono's *Unfinished Music No. 1: Two Virgins* with its sleeve photographs of the pair naked, back and front?

In London's tube stations, a poster promoting the newly released *Till Death Us Do Part* movie tie-in gave prominence to an unclothed Warren Mitchell as Alf Garnett, albeit covering up his genitalia with hands and tobacco-pipe, and a caption thanking John Lennon for 'pioneering this form of publicity'.

The ordinary fan's reaction to *Two Virgins* was articulated in the topical disc, 'John You Went Too Far This Time' by Rainbo, alias Sissy Spacek, a future star but then less even than a starlet. Her love, she sang, would 'never be the same'.

Me? Well, it's difficult to articulate how extremely shocking a first sight of Lennon's flaccid Beatle willy was to a 17-year-old product of a straitlaced, churchgoing upbringing – not unlike John's own ('Sunday School and all that,' so he informed Ray Coleman). How could he have been so rude? Whatever would adorn the cover of the follow-up? A pile of his turds?

Nevertheless, *Two Virgins* aligned after a fashion with what had been building up within me since gazing with yearning at the cover of 1963's *With The Beatles*: if only Mum would let me have my hair like George's then I wouldn't go on about it anymore. Into the equation too had come Jane, a girlfriend vigorously encouraging me to grow my hair because it made me look more like Led Zeppelin's chiselled Robert Plant with his classic Viking facial bone structure.

Having spat out the Hayley Green plum in favour of a Ray Charles-with-a-hernia tenor, Robert had been drifting from pillar to post, from group to unsatisfactory group whose names were surfacing as regularly as rocks in the stream in *Midland Beat*. As 1966 had drawn to a close, however, a Plant solo 45, 'Our Song' – a translation of an Italian ballad – had been issued by CBS and its follow-up, 'Long Time Coming', had elicited a favourable review in the *NME*. Nevertheless, Robert had been obliged to take up employment as a labourer, laying asphalt on roads in West Bromwich.

Then 1968 brought a godsend. Led Zeppelin rose from the ashes of the Yardbirds with Robert at the central microphone after Jimmy Page had rung to summon him to his riverside abode in Pangbourne, Berkshire a few days after rubbing his chin over Plant's performance with something called Hobbstweedle at a college in Walsall.

As Plant commenced rehearsals with what was yet to be named Led Zeppelin at a studio in central London during that rainy summer, there came the day when my mother handed me money for a haircut and I refused point-blank to go. The drama that followed led me to try unsuccessfully to placate her by slicking down my mop with brilliantine. The upshot was her turning off a furious main water tap after I'd started to shampoo it out, me beginning to pack my belongings, and her conceding an inch or two.

Elsewhere a strong-willed boy in a similar dilemma also found it necessary to desensitise himself to parents and other older relations vibrating with animosity if he so much as entered a room after a war of attrition began with the old invocation, 'long hair's old-fashioned', often contradicted with 'why do you have to follow fashion?' Next, they'd move on swiftly to plaintive supplications to what they called his 'better self' with 'how can anyone with hair like yours be taken seriously?', 'you're otherwise such a good-looking lad. It's tragic!' and 'you're in the public eye' among laments recurring like a broken record.

Then came perhaps, 'You are breaking our hearts. What have we ever done to you that you should bring such shame on us by looking the way you do?' It wasn't to rile anyone, he'd explain. He just liked it like that. Rallying, they'd try scare tactics with, say, a statement that male hair fell out if it was too long, and assuring him that his was already: 'Will any girl spare you a second glance when you're 25, jobless – and bald? When that day comes, I shall *dance!*' A riposte that he'd take the risk would prompt greater fury – as would the argument that if he *had* gone bald, would he want to be employed by someone small-minded enough to care about such a thing?

Appeals to honour, common sense and filial duty didn't wash either, so mothers in particular would bring in the emotional artillery: sending him to Coventry for weeks on end; pretending to have hysterics at the mere sight of him; promising no sympathy should he suffer grievous bodily harm in the street for his 'effeminate appearance'; 'funny' letters left in bedrooms; and, on observing him preening himself in the mirror, asking if he was homosexual. Strategies as subtle as a flying mallet were exemplified by shampoo for *damaged* hair as birthday and Christmas presents, and perhaps an artlessly strewn magazine on the kitchen table, open on a page with an advertisement for one of these new Ronco hand-held comb hair trimmers (with a small-print warning that, if manipulated too close to the scalp, left 'mis-cuts', i.e. bald patches). Bribery in the form of, say, a 20 pound cheque when 20 quid was worth something didn't work either. Neither would a childish ploy of shielding eyes from him as if he were a leper, and inciting other family members to do the same.

Though Mick Jagger, Phil May and even Frank Zappa replicas weren't entirely uncommon by then in English country towns like ours, my own hair was a source of remark – albeit emotionally uncharged – at Fleet's new Waitrose supermarket where I'd gained a Saturday job. I was a popular enough employee, regarded as very much part of the weekend furniture despite being missed on the occasions in summer 1969 when I absented myself to attend the respective Hyde Park concerts by Blind Faith and The Rolling Stones.

Mr Wray, the youngish manager, didn't probe the lying excuses about where I'd been. A visit from a head office inspector, nonetheless, obliged him to direct me to make up my mind between a haircut or the sack, even though I was hidden from customer view as operator of the cardboard baler round the back. I hesitated. It wasn't the principle, it was the money. Then someone piping out a comment about me not having the courage to make a stand stung me into the least sensible decision, even if, unlike Mick Jagger, Frank Zappa *et al*, I couldn't afford to do so.

I told my parents I'd been laid off, but they commenced investigations, culminating in a telephone call to Mr Wray when my job was among vacancies on Waitrose's notice-board the following Friday. Thus a third-degree awaited when I came in that evening – with my three siblings gathered round to watch the fun. Mum and Dad had me bang to rights, and I saw ahead of me an intensification of the former's now customary nagging, cliff-hanging silences, scoring of catty points against me and moody discontent which went from a tinge of vapour to a heaven-darkening Wagnerian thunderstorm of home truths.

In how many other families as well was the issue too far gone for any kind of rapprochement? 'My mother was as fanatical as yours in her own way,' considered Alan Franks, 'just as unhinged and void of rational discussion when my – and my older brother's – hair had the nerve to creep down over the collar.' For either side to have given way, however slightly, would have been conceding some kind of defeat. 'Early Rolling Stones shoulder-length would have suited,' mused Tim Fagan, 'but I was driven to an extreme because I didn't want to back down.'

Yet, as the decade began to turn, you'd hear of parents, especially in the USA, supporting their boys' modish caprices with all the vivacity of the parents of would-be Elvis lookalike Robert Phernetton back in 1956 (though black families tended to do so over issues other than hair length as instanced by the suspension from his Pennsylvania high school of 18-year-old Darius Lovelace for growing a moustache).

When, on returning from the summer recess, 20 others complied with the order by the physical education teacher and the principal of their El Paso high school to have haircuts, 16-year-old Chesley Karr held out against modifying what he referred to as his 'freak flag'.[108] This was a pudding basin about as long as that of Peter Noone in Herman's Hermits. With his mom and dad right behind him, he took the matter to the school board. After it failed to rule in his favour, he approached the ACLU, who advised taking it to federal trial.

---

108. This was an expression Karr heard in 'If 6 Was 9' – which closed the first side of 1967's *Axis: Bold as Love*, the second LP by the Jimi Hendrix Experience. This 'acid-fuelled blues' (as one reviewer described it) contains a line expressing the narrator's apparent indifference 'if all the hippies cut off all their hair'. 'Freak flag' was to surface too in 'Almost Cut My Hair' by Crosby, Stills and Nash in 1970, and sung by the thinning David Crosby, 'the Byrd nobody fancied' according to the late Tom Hibbert, UK music journalist.

In the witness stand, Mr Karr, an insurance agent, testified that 'nobody told me how to cut my hair when I was in school,' and that, while he didn't like his lad 'breaking rules for the fun of it,' Chesley had the rights of any individual to choose the way he looked. Isn't that the American Way?

No, it isn't, believed a local mayor who thought all long-haired boys were troublemakers. A head teacher in a Wisconsin village elaborated, 'whenever I see a long-hair youngster, he is usually leading a riot; he has gotten through committing a crime; he is a dope addict, or some such thing. His hair reflects a symbol that we feel is trying to disrupt everything we are trying to build up and by "we" I mean God-fearing Americans!'

Despite it thus coming to wide attention that began with over 50 letters to *El Paso Times* and *El Paso Herald-Post*, evenly balanced between the freedom of the individual and the opening of chaotically permissive floodgates, the Supreme Court declined to hear the case. It was the same with that of a firefighter in Sacramento, California who was suspended from his job for 30 days because, so the chief of the brigade argued, his long hair, even if stuffed beneath a helmet, posed as serious a question of personal safety as that of, say, a mechanic entangling his too-long hair in moving parts. He had a point. Ricky West of the Tremeloes recalled 'Our old bass player was taking his turn at the wheel of the van, and had the window open for a while before closing it while still driving. The draught pulled his long hair through the window and trapped it. He lost quite a bit of hair trying to free himself.'

CHAPTER TWENTY

'The same bastards are in control. The same people are running everything'

Most of the cultural and social commotions that occurred during the high 1960s appeared to be transient within old-fashioned communities in which, it sometimes seemed, Queen Victoria's death was still a tragedy too grievous to be borne. A sense of an ending less absolute pervaded too after things didn't so much go back to normal as remain as rigid as ever. Indeed, soon after 1970 came into view, John Lennon was grimacing in *Rolling Stone* that, 'The people who are in control and in power and the class system and the whole bourgeois scene is exactly the same, except that there are a lot of middle-class kids with long hair walking around London in trendy clothes. The same bastards are in control, the same people are running everything.'

In agreement, Pete Feenstra would reckon, 'It could be justifiably argued that in terms of the establishment very little had changed. At school, there was still an inspection each Monday morning from top to toe of both your hair and school uniform – and, though I mercifully never used Brylcreem or the like, I used to dampen my hair with water and comb it back flat behind the ears. This frequently led to adverse and somewhat hurtful comments, which only diminished once my cricketing skills came to the fore and, as a result, they seemed to subside, though again there were fraught moments at the wicket when my hair would sprout out all over the place as I pivoted when attempting a hook shot.'

In *Good and Bad at Games*, a UK television drama first shown in 1983 but focused chiefly in flashback to the late 1960s, an outsider has only become part of a clique of prefects because, like Pete Feenstra, he is 'good at games'. He ingratiates himself further by being on the periphery when the fellows single out a pupil with a certain 'otherness' for constant and pitiless bullying. One of this unfortunate's lesser humiliations is being compelled to have a clipping by a persecutor who actually has longer hair than himself, and who has been observed by the sickened victim, lost in a common room dream, playing air-guitar to 'Badge', Cream's valedictory hit single before disbandment.

'Power trios' like guitar-bass-drums Cream were the thing then with any muted subtleties or restraint that might have been displayed in the studio being lost on the boards to high decibels and 'heads-down-no-nonsense' rock with some numbers cut, dried and dissected for nigh on half an hour, each to Emperor's-new-clothes applause. Some featured a singing non-instrumentalist as did Free who accrued support in European colleges for their first blues-derived albums which were musically unambitious but punchy and proved worthwhile exercises financially. One music journal was prompted to cite Free as 'the New Stones'.

Though they never became such, Free were esteemed by the discerning likes of Oliver Gray, although, 'tonsorially speaking, it was hard to justify this, because the band was a hairstyle disaster area, with only one member out of four being really well-smoothed. Andy Fraser, the bassist, had an awful poodle-cut; singer Paul Rodgers' locks were long and flowing, but coarse and unacceptably wavy; while Paul Kossoff... well, no wonder he got himself a drug habit. Drummer Simon Kirke, however, was the Man. His hair was blond, straight as a dye and fell forward to completely obscure his facial features as he walloped his drums.

'One fantastic Tuesday evening, Free played live at the Spektrum club in Kiel after any meaningful relationship with my parents became a total impossibility. The shame of being associated with a long-hair was too much for them to bear, so they requested that I should come home as little as possible. It was fortunate that I was due for my "year abroad" – which to the university authorities meant improving my standard of German but to me meant a glorious nine months of total turpitude.

'The weekend after Free were at the Spektrum, I hitched to Copenhagen with some friends, and ended up in the Tivoli

Pleasure Gardens. Eager for further pleasure, we tried to impress some young ladies by taking them repeatedly on the Big Dipper, but eventually impressed them much more by pretending to be members of Free on a night off from their European tour. Dark-haired Jochen Schmidt, slightly dishevelled, was Paul Rodgers and I, of course, was Simon Kirke. Just for one night, we got a mild feel for what it must have been like to be in a pop group, because, yes, the girls believed it and yes, they were impressed. Once again, "smoothing" had proved its worth.'

Pete Feenstra preferred Hawkwind, who'd taken shape when breathing the same air as Tyrannosaurus Rex, Mick Farren and his Social Deviants (led by the mainstay of the UK wing of Detroit-based political activists the White Panthers), the Edgar Broughton Band, the Pink Fairies,[109] Eire Apparent, the Third Ear Band and like denizens of the hippie community centred round west London's Ladbroke Grove. Deep in the east Midlands, Pete's function then was simply to absorb the signals as they came, sometimes in a negative fashion, 'being witness to pointless raids on "head" shops, whose only crime was to stock informative books, anarchist pamphlets and joss sticks. The drug squad always seemed to be on a job creation scheme when it came to what were selectively termed "freaks". Everyone with long hair has a story, but perhaps my most memorable one concerned a trip from a friend's house near Mansfield to Derby for a Hawkwind gig.

'We were all suitably stoned, laughing at the most trivial of things, when out of nowhere one of our number, a guy with really unkempt hair, suddenly shouted: "Stop the van. This is a raid and you are all being arrested!" We naturally laughed it off, and only realised after he'd whipped off his wig in what seemed to be slow motion that he was serious.

'Two things sprung to my mind. Firstly, we hadn't actually smoked anything in the van *en route* to the show, while my second thought obviously resonated with most of the others, a thought given purchase by the driver who shouted out; "Er, arrested by you

109. Consisting of musicians who'd assisted John 'Twink' Alder on a solo album recorded in 1969 after he'd left The Pretty Things.

and whose army?" In a flash the van stopped, the back door was opened, he was ushered out and we went on our way.

'Travels and social life aside, there was also the question of looking after your hair. What at first seemed a tiresome enterprise eventually led me to a couple of helpful women who advised on split ends and sheen. Coconut oil and henna and the like quickly became part of my regime, though too often my best intentions were thwarted by inadvertently setting fire to it. By the time I could boast truly long hair, help was at hand with the fact that it was "cool" to either wear a headband or more usefully wear your hair in a ponytail. When I went to California not long afterwards, virtually everyone had chosen this option and I couldn't help but feel we'd all been lulled into a new sense of uniformity.'

That might have been the case in Los Angeles and San Francisco, but in San Diego, 23-year-old James Wallace, a Marine Corps reservist, was court-martialled along with fourteen others for non-compliance with regulations stating that hair should be no longer than three inches. Most of the guys submitted calmly to weeks of hard labour, but Wallace managed to get the decision reversed by a civilian court on the grounds that he was also a student at a local college and therefore exempted from military punishment.

The same would apply to New Yorker Harold Raderman, an army reservist, who pleaded that he was obliged to keep his hair shoulder length to maintain credibility as 'a rock and roll talent scout'. Nevertheless, during autumn 1970 in Buffalo where the state borders with Canada, Judge Ann T Mikoll, cut from the same cloth as Trunky Cotgreave, dismissed assault charges against three construction workers who'd dragged adolescent John Pierce into an alley, worked him over and cut his long hair.

In Michigan's Oakland County two summers earlier, arresting officers had an alibi of officialdom when, with a delighted 'We'll soon have you looking like a human being again!', they scalped to fist-shaking abuse the luxuriant hair of John Sinclair, a propagator of revolutionary rhetoric in his capacity as co-founder of the White Panthers and manager of the MC5, who were to the political collective as the Velvet Underground were to the Exploding Plastic Inevitable. Over a raw musical attack, the group barked rude words and slogan-ridden orations about matters that included the decriminalisation of marijuana.

It was through a 'honey trap' (offering two spliffs to an undercover female cop) that Sinclair had been caught. His prison term began with another shearing that was 'what the pigs are all about. They want everyone to look and be just like them... and they'll pay for this one way or another!'

More high profile was a show in Florida on 1 March 1969 by the Doors, a Los Angeles foursome that had most successfully brought 'underground' sounds to a mass teenage market with their 'Light My Fire' (which was to become as much of a showbiz 'standard' as 'Yesterday', 'Up Up And Away' or 'You Are The Sunshine of My Life'). At Miami's packed-out Dinner Key auditorium, nonetheless, their booze-addled vocalist, Jim Morrison, that son of a rear-admiral, was alleged to have sworn and, worse, exposed himself during what the group's organist, Ray Manzarek, was to describe as his colleague sending up his sex symbol status with a routine involving a towel. Backstage opinion intimated that the resulting accusations were cooked up by authorities, as keen as the *News of the World* had been over Mick Jagger, to pull down a tight-trousered longhair who had been corrupting their children. Especially one who, testing the tolerance of officialdom, had been turned into a cross between a modern Dionysus and a singing Marlon Brando.

Morrison's attempt to avoid prosecution by flying back to California was thwarted when he was detained by the FBI as soon as his craft touched down in Los Angeles. While he awaited trial, all Doors bookings over the next five months were cancelled, and later ones threatened with instant closure at the remotest hint of a cuss-word or unzipped fly. During this period of enforced inactivity, Morrison sought the company of those prone to similar traumas and immoderate tendencies, among them Brian Jones whose death would inspire Jim's 'Ode to LA While Thinking of Brian Jones, Deceased', published in *Disc and Music Echo*, the week after the funeral.

His hearing was scheduled for September 1970 when the prosecution called upon 17 onlookers at Miami to verify that the offences had taken place. Thus the defendant was found guilty, and condemned to eight months hard labour. However, directly after sentence was pronounced, his brief requested and was granted leave to appeal. Neither did the judge oppose Morrison's application for bail.

Now bearded to the cheekbones, Jim had put on weight alarmingly. His face was rounder, his complexion pasty, and his eyes emanated a burned-out look when he exiled himself to Paris. Weeks became months, and an incommunicado enigma deepened. Few of Jim's intimates were entirely unprepared for his body's final rebellion after a lifetime of violation. He was found dead in a hotel bathtub on Saturday 3 June 1971, and buried in Père Lachaise cemetery in Montparnasse, traditionally the Ville-Lumière's artists' quarter.

Several weeks later, the coroner concluded that a heart attack had killed Morrison, whose distraught father, George, had answered a letter from the Florida Department of Correction concerning Jim's character. Here are three crucial paragraphs:

'In 1965, I began a two-year assignment in England. Although I invited him to join us in London after graduating, he declined in order to start his own career. Since that time he has been completely independent of me financially and in every other way. We have had little contact with him since that time due partly to the physical separation and partly because of some criticism from me.

'While in London, I was called by an old friend in California who had been approached by Jim for a loan to finance his first record. Concerned by his appearance, particularly his long hair, the friend called me. I, in turn, wrote Jim a letter severely criticising his behaviour and strongly advised him to give up any idea of singing or any connection with a music group because of what I considered to be a complete lack of talent in this direction. His reluctance to communicate with me again is to me quite understandable.

'I have followed his career with a mixture of amazement and in the case of Miami, great concern and sorrow. While I obviously am not a judge of modern music, I view his success with pride. Based on my knowledge of Jim, I firmly believe that his performance in Miami was a grave mistake and not in character, and I stand by my conviction that Jim is fundamentally a respectable citizen.'

*

As autumn leaves had started falling on the Doors too, Morrison had become friendly with Screaming Lord Sutch who was completing a season at Los Angeles' Thee Experience. Though a near-teetotaller, his Lordship had gone clubbing with Jim, 'but I couldn't keep up with him. He was so totally gross'. Nevertheless, they accompanied each other to the open-air Toronto Rock 'n' Roll Revival Show in September 1969 where the Doors were on a bill that, as well as the likes of Alice Cooper and John Lennon's Plastic Ono Band, embraced more fervently Jerry Lee Lewis, Chuck Berry, Gene Vincent and further giants of classic rock.

The very name of the event was reflective of an aspect of late 1960s pop that had caused Bill Haley and Buddy Holly reissues to hover round the middle of the UK charts during 1968's cold April; an overhaul of 'Good Old Rock 'n' roll ', a North American smash by Cat Mother and the All Night News Boys, to return the Dave Clark Five, their overseas exploits over, to the domestic Top Ten; and olde-tyme rock 'n' roll medleys to close shows of 'nice little bands' with names like Tea-and-Symphony, Warm Dust and Puce Exploding Butterfly.

Entertaining a truer underground than these denizens of Students Union stages were provincial outfits led by extant Teddy Boys like Crazy Cavan, Shakin' Stevens and others such as Sha Na Na and Flash Cadillac and the Continental Kids on the opposite side of the Atlantic, who carried a torch for the 1950s. Though not so obviously 'regressive', 'Fire Brigade', the latest smash from the Move, had been freighted with an antique Duane Eddy twang while The Beatles' 'Lady Madonna' was reminiscent of Fats Domino.

Off the blocks in time – just – for 1968's Yuletide 'silly season' had been *Cruising with Ruben & the Jets*, i.e. the Mothers of Invention under a pseudonym, which peppered its 13 tracks heavily with lyrical and musical clichés from the annals of combos like the Five Keys, the Penguins, the Sharp Tones, the Larks, the Flairs and the Pelicans that had evolved largely from fellows singing together for their own enjoyment across the USA. Partly because that type of pop had never really caught on in Europe might have been among the reasons why we were short-changed with regard to

Cruising with Ruben & the Jets via a cheap sleeve marred by typing errors. In the States, it had been packaged in a gatefold jacket which also contained a sticker, a full libretto and sheets detailing dance instructions and how to comb and set a jellyroll (i.e. an elephant's trunk), as modelled in cartoon form by Frank Zappa. Frank's youthful portrait (shirt, tie and white sport coat plus a neat trim with just a hint of sideburns) from the year he gained a high school diploma for which he'd barely qualified, dominated the back cover.

Sniffing the prevailing wind, the BBC scheduled a season of Tuesday evening rock 'n' roll movies and, during the week of *Jailhouse Rock*, a fellow student named Malcolm minced into Farnborough Technical College's[110] canteen one morning with a brilliantined quiff fashioned overnight from a thick, collar-length moptop. Correspondingly, he was all for me and him starting a group that conducted itself as if Merseybeat, psychedelia and so forth had never happened.

Malcolm understood too that long hair wasn't always a requirement for acceptance by those of general 'alternative' demeanour. Though most outside France, Belgium and their colonies hearkened to the *chansons* of Jacques Brel – still combed in 'breaker' style with as much attempt to distinguish between each as a shopper does between wedges of supermarket *muzak*, he was otherwise very much the property of undergraduates flirting with bohemia before becoming teachers – and on their record-players were *The Transfiguration Of Blind Joe Death* LP by thin-on-top US 'roots' guitarist John Fahey and, also first released in 1965, *The Paul Simon Songbook* by one whose 'The Sound Of Silence' with Art Garfunkel[111] had been suddenly at Number One in the States, almost doing the same for the likewise clip-maned Bachelors in the UK chart, better placed as they were to plug their version on the domestic media.

Without hippie-esque long locks either were Serge Gainsbourg and the maker of *Songs Of Leonard Cohen* – and further vinyl exercises by one stereotyped for decades as a merchant of melancholy, despite trading in what amounted to stand-up comedy before he reached

---

110. Where I went after an ignominious six years at the Grammar were over.
111. With whom he'd penetrated the 1959 *Billboard Hot 100* with a ditty in quasi-Everly Brothers vein.

out to self-doubting adolescent diarists. Usually keeping his hair short and tidy too was Lou Reed, who one day, with thumbs hooked in his belt, was to sneer, 'I don't shake hands with longhairs' to a hippie journalist with his palm held out.[112]

Yet Malcolm's single-mindedness in the smaller world of Farnborough Tech, if bold, was also a sort of voluntary surrender in the light of him, me and boon companions who, prior to becoming brave enough for rebellion, still had regular cuttings imposed by parents quite aware of how unhappy they made us. Peter Scott was one subject to 'that familiar command to the nearly adult son who'd overtaken him height-wise, from a father who had words that were not merely on the tip of the tongue, i.e. "you're not going out like that! I thought I had two sons and a daughter, not your brother and two sisters! We didn't bring you up to embarrass us!"

'An appointment was made by him on my behalf for a Saturday morning at the barber, and paid for in advance (probably with a tip). I parked my motorbike outside and went in. "Ladies' is next door. This is for men and boys only." Eh? "Sorry, sir! I didn't realise... "

'I gave precise instructions how I wanted it to look - a Boston with the top layered and left over the ears. Feeling like a prisoner in the electric chair, I watched helplessly until, happy the job was completed, he showed me the result in the hand mirror. The lower Boston line was not straight, but curved from one ear to the other; the layering had reduced the length to match and my ears were exposed to the world (and larger than I had remembered).

'I put on my crash helmet and got the hell out of there. After I arrived home and removed it, my distress was obvious to the whole family, particularly as I realised that there was only a day and a half

---

112. Though not possibly or remotely ironic was an incident that was to occur after former *Midland Beat* picture editor Jim Simpson's Big Bear organisation began bringing American Blues Legends revues to Europe from the early 1970s, when he drove to Heathrow airport to collect Cousin Joe Pleasants, a sexagenarian from New Orleans. 'A more dapper and well-dressed piano player you couldn't imagine, and when I introduced myself after he strutted into Arrivals, he looked me up and down with horror, particularly at my hair and said "I get here after three thousand five hundred miles on the red-eye, and my tour manager's a goddamn, fucking hippie!" It was a long time before he got over that moment.'

before I had to face my college mates – unless I could go sick, but that wasn't really me.'

As much as rock 'n' roll revival and the continuation of parental harassment over hair were in the air, *circa* 1968, so too was 'revolution', derided as 'this year's flower-power' by Frank Zappa – who was invited to give a talk one Tuesday at the London School of Economics where catcalls would greet his submission that, rather than protest marches and so forth, the students ought to infiltrate the 'system' by becoming lawyers and politicians. To this end, he stressed too the importance of self-motivated study – but maybe that was too much like hard work? A war of words was charged with, for example, some hothead denouncing 'yet another bourgeois liberal with inert reactionary tendencies' after Zappa wanted to know whether the LSE activists had planned who was to take post-revolution charge of the sewage system.[113]

Mick Jagger too was criticised by agit-prop extremists for not inciting the multitudes at the Stones' free concert in Hyde Park to take over the capital, even if the thrust of the group's much-banned 'Street Fighting Man' was that there was no place for such a person in 'sleepy London town'. Besides, argued Jagger, 'it's stupid to think that you can start a revolution with a record'.

Yet John Lennon was putting his mind to an eponymous number about revolution (which would surface as flip-side to The Beatles' 'Hey Jude')[114] that, however irresolute, would be his most far-reaching assessment in song of the political undercurrents pertinent to the culmination of the Swinging Sixties. Likewise, The Pretty Things were to come up with 'October 26 (Revolution)', which took its title from the USSR public holiday in commemoration of 1917's *coup d'état*.

The Stones' old friends and rivals' living still depended on earnings from the road, but they were amenable to playing for

---

113. Melody Maker scribe Chris Welch was to travel with The Mothers Of Invention during a British tour that began not quite a month later. At a motorway service station, a check-out girl asked Welch if his hirsute companions were 'a group – or just Americans?'
114. 'Revolution' was an A-side by Tomorrow, released a year before The Beatles' item of the same title.

just expenses on a stage erected within the barricades of a sit-in at London's Goldsmith College at the request of Germaine Greer, then a professor of English there. With New Left radicalism the common denominators, there was so much to spark off such tub-thumping takeovers: the assassinations of Martin Luther King and Robert Kennedy; the growth of feminism; the ongoing slaughter and starvation of Mao Zedong's cultural purge; Ireland, bloody Ireland; the increasing encroachment of Russian troops on Eastern Europe; and, of course, Vietnam where Lieutenant William L Calley Jnr. had just overseen the slaughter of the women and children of an entire village. He had then been immortalised in 'Battle Hymn of Lieutenant Calley' by one Terry Nelson, which was to go on sale ten days prior to a long-awaited court-martial verdict on Calley. Nelson and his record company's prayers that the officer *wouldn't* be acquitted were answered. To the tune of 'John Brown's Body', the song strove to vindicate Calley on the grounds that he and his death squad were merely obeying orders, 'even though they made me out to be a villain, my truth was marching on'. At least a million US music lovers – largely 'rednecks' – agreed.

This market triumph was a trace of sulphurous mist when kaftans were mothballed as their former wearers trailed along with the crowd to genuinely violent anti-war demonstrations, riots, disruptions of beauty pageants and pop festivals plus further student sit-ins. Girls lost their marbles over Daniel Cohn-Bendit, known as *'Dany le Rouge'* ('Danny the Red'), organiser of the 'situationist' *évènements* in France – but not as much as they did over the late Che Guevara, Fidel Castro's seemingly more ascetic second-in-command, whose familiar high-contrast poster had had the length and tousle of his hair exaggerated via dark room techniques as Esquerita's had been in the 1950s.

Two years before massacre had come to horrify viewers of the *Six O'Clock News* no more than a shootout in a spaghetti western, the touring Beatles' final press conferences had swung in seconds from chit-chat about moptops and mini-skirts to two-line symposiums on far more combustible subjects while Brian Epstein cringed. 'He always tried to waffle on at us about saying nothing about Vietnam,' the four's most instant pundit, John Lennon, would claim later, 'so there came a time when George and I said, "Listen, when they ask next time, we're going to say we don't like the war and we think they should get out.'" As fingers scribbled and Harrison sniggered beside him, he defended the group's infamous 'butcher sleeve' with the unfunny quip, 'Anyway, it's as valid as Vietnam.'

Even The Monkees' 'Last Train to Clarksville' was thought by some to concern a drafted lover off to south-east Asia ('and I don't know when I'm ever coming home'), bidding farewell to his lass. There was, however, no ambiguity about the Saigon Saucers' 'Howdy Doody Doctor Death' which, in a swirl of buzzsaw-toned guitars, greets and blames President Johnson whose ordinances, it claims, were at the root of whatever 'blowed my mind out in the ditch' in Saigon where there's 'no Beatles... no Dylan... no nobody'.

Among more coherent (and lucrative) examples had been 'I-Feel-Like-I'm-Fixin'-To-Die Rag' from Country Joe and the Fish, Eric Burdon's 'Sky Pilot' (slang for a regimental chaplain), Freda Payne's 'Bring The Boys Home', 'Talking Vietnam Pot Luck Blues' by Tom Paxton or, when sung *en masse* outside the White House during the Vietnam moratorium, The Kinks' ballad, 'Every Mother's Son'.

When pressed about the distant hostilities and similarly combustible topics, Keith Richards was active after a detached, arm-sweepingly pop-starrish fashion in verbally endorsing both pacifism and Cohn-Bendit's *soixante-huitards*, while also enquiring, 'How many times can they use those words – justice, freedom? It's like margarine. You can package and sell that too.' He might have spoken vaguely too about, perhaps, 'unemployment' without going into economic ramifications, but more pointed anger was directed at Decca who, so Keith comprehended, were ploughing back monies amassed through record sales into its radar division – which made parts for air force bombers in Vietnam.

Interviewed by Richard Branson, then editor of the leftish *Student* magazine, Mick Jagger too seemed to be all for dissident popular opinion, though he was inclined to follow reason as much as his heart, and felt compromised if waylaid by factions who wanted him to join with them. Yet, if he made no doctrinal statement, Jagger had been visible on a traffic island on the periphery of militants outside the US Embassy in London – and had, apparently, rescued one of the tens of thousands there from the hooves of a mounted policeman's horse.

At either school or home, I'd been told off for wearing a US GET OUT OF VIETNAM lapel badge, but that was less for its political statement than its implication that I was a would-be long-haired menace. Exacerbating this after I started at Farnborough Tech was my involvement in two of the Arts Laboratories that had been closing as fast as they opened since 1967, while encouraging all to make use of their workshop ambiences. The one in Aldershot was to find an eventual home in a parish hall, although, despite the haranguings from an old woman next door ('Go away from my house, you... you... beatniks! Get out of my street!'), I preferred the previous address within pre-war terraces and old-fashioned street lighting like Jack the Ripper's Whitechapel. One of the attractions was that there was no electricity in there – because the evening somebody brought along a record player to the new place, Aldershot Arts Lab became as unexciting as a church youth club.

Never mind, it was fun for a time while having the impact of a feather on concrete on 'the System', 'society' and all that – with being 'subversive' going little further than some roaming the town centre with a loud hailer proclaiming a fund-raising dance that evening in a space above the library. 'As we walked down Victoria Road,' recalls Mark Stokes, one such Lab assistant, 'I was making an announcement about it, and some squaddie with a northern accent came up and told me that they didn't need my kind of people in the town. Being brought up in an army settlement still wasn't really great when your hair was long.'

It wasn't all that brilliant in places with no military clout either. 'The late 1960s were a bad time to walk around much beyond "trendy London" with past-shoulder-length hair,' surmised Peter Miles, now proprietor of a Devon garage, 'but once ordinary people had seen groups, bands, singers – whatever you want to call it/ them – be hugely successful, then attitudes *did* change.' – but not fast enough for John Townsend: 'Once I was in a pub toilet in Crosby when a guy came in and told me aggressively that my hair looked like rat tails. He wanted me to say it didn't so he could start something. I declined – and then a friend of his entered and told him to leave me alone. I left them to fight it out.

'I also remember being in a rural pub in Ireland where the barmaid came over to tell me where the toilets were (although I hadn't asked) to enable her to inform me aggressively that the ladies was up the stairs.'

Sometimes the insult was unconscious as illustrated by Ricky West's memory of when, 'I would walk into shops and the assistant would say, "May I help you madam... er, sorry, sir?" Once when I was choosing shoes, I had a long conversation with a salesperson who didn't catch on I was a geezer at all, partly because I've always had a high, girly voice – so with that and hair touching my shoulders, he was convinced I was female.[115]

'I was also on an aeroplane going somewhere with Alan Blakley, our keyboard player and rhythm guitarist, and a lady – probably only about fifty, but seeming old to us in our twenties – asked Alan "Is that your girlfriend or your wife?"'

Echoing Frank Zappa's preparation in 1965 to face that 'conspiracy to commit pornography' hearing, West also remembered, 'when the whole band had to go to court on an instrument smuggling charge, we were told that we should all have our hair cut short to make a better impression on the judge, but we were making a film at the time and it would've messed up the continuity, so we went to court as long-haired gits. By the way, it was not us doing the smuggling, but, as the Tremeloes owned the equipment, we were the ones fined.'

Travel overseas also brought trouble to Dave Brubeck who'd now given his hitherto defiantly short, white hair its head. It obliged him to cancel part of a tour across Singapore. Joe Cocker and Cliff Richard were also barred from playing in the city-state for the same reasons, and so too the Bee Gees and Led Zeppelin.

In Thailand, schools were commanded to maintain (by scissor-wielding force if need be) earlobe-length bobs for girls and crew cuts for boys. Powers of similar direct action were granted to South

---

115. Ricky's easy falsetto had been to the fore on the group's 'Silence Is Golden', a UK chart-topper over summer 1967.

Korean police under a Minor Offences Act that as well as limiting the length of hair for males, mandated a minimum length of skirt for females. Furthermore, no foreign man could enter Albania or Turkey while wearing a banned hairstyle – as shown by the arrival of Vodak Pryliński, yet another Farnborough Grammar old boy, at Istanbul Airport where he was detained for looking like Pink Floyd's Roger Waters.

As shaggy-headed too was Pete Feenstra when he and some friends decided to travel by bus, boat and train from England to Morocco: 'Macho Spain provided its challenges. It was not uncommon to have your sexuality called into question there – but Morocco had more of a *laissez-faire* approach towards "heads" with mutual lifestyle ambitions, unencumbered by drug squads, parents, work or the reactionary UK media.'

Similarly relevant issues of the later 1960s and early 1970s were articulated too in further songs by artists present, among them Ray Dorset who, in 1969, composed the hard-luck story that was 'You Don't Have To Be In The Army (To Fight in The War)' with an opening verse bemoaning the consequence of meeting a girlfriend's 'folks' who 'grab you by the collar and throw you through the door' because 'they say that your hair's too long'.[116]

That's also why, in 1969's *Easy Rider* film drama, Dennis Hopper, Peter Fonda and Jack Nicholson as freewheeling 'Billy', 'Wyatt' and 'George' weren't served in a café and suffered disobliging remarks about their appearances from coffee-sipping policemen and other locals, some of them cudgelling George to death that evening during a storming of the three's kerbside camp.

---

116. As a Mungo Jerry single, this composition was to reach Number 11 in the UK over autumn 1971.

CHAPTER TWENTY-ONE

'The town skinheads knew us and tried to hunt us down'

Though *Easy Rider* might have been its film, *the* hit song of 1969 was 'Sugar Sugar' by the Archies. The next logical step after The Monkees, these were a happy-go-lucky cartoon pop quintet containing three short-haired boys. It idealised high school coming-of-age in a Midwestern United States town a bit behind the times, although the promotional film for the single centred on a local carnival that included a stall with a girl offering her 'candy kisses' at a dollar a go. Almost as insubstantial were Ohio Express, Crazy Elephant, 1910 Fruitgum Company and other acts manufactured as chart fodder within the walls of Kasenetz-Katz, the New York 'bubblegum' organisation that knocked out chart fodder with the same lack of artistic pretension as the jobbing songwriters who had once done the same in the Brill Building.

Just after the Archies left the US Top Forty for the last time with 'Who's Your Baby' in 1970, an edition of *Oz* was to have Richard Neville noting with sadness that 'Some of my best friends are going straight – cutting hair, wearing suits, seeking respectable employment. These are the same people who were freaking out at the first UFOs.'

Much of the hair was disappearing of its own accord in the case of singer-songwriter Graham Larkbey (who 'had the usual arguments over length with my parents, but as soon as I left home and could do what I liked, it started to fall out. Unfair or what?'). The same applied to Dewi Pws, life-and-soul of Y Tebot Piws ('The Purple Teapot'), former Cardiff University students, who chose to sing exclusively in Welsh, thus setting the ceiling of their ambition on EPs, more common (and economical) than singles, on local labels, to be plugged on BBC Wales's weekly pop showcase, *Disc A Dawn*.

'I started losing my hair at 20,' recalled Dewi, 'so went to the Cardiff trichology centre and was given a concoction of chemicals to rub into my scalp. I did this in the garage, to save embarrassment, but the smell was terrible. My mother asked what on earth the revolting aroma emanating from there (and myself) could be. I did this for a fortnight, was banned from the rugby club and no one would sit by me on the bus. Eventually, I gave the solution to my mother, who used it as a very successful rat poison. My advice? Bald is beautiful! Grow old gratefully!'

Raging against the dying of this particular light, however, had been Andy Warhol who made no effort to disguise the obviousness of his trademark silver hairpiece, and 'Svengali of Sound' Phil Spector, once famous for multi-tracking an apocalyptic *mélange* (everything except the proverbial kitchen sink) behind beehive-and-net-petticoat ciphers like the Crystals and the Ronettes who'd submitted to his master plan. He was now becoming notable for being seen in public in often outlandish wigs when not at the recording studio or, as he grew increasingly reclusive, in his Californian mansion.

Yet the unembellished pates of Bobby Elliott and Beach Boy Mike Love[117] were now in full view either in publicity photos or before audiences. Moreover, that Great Leveller alopecia was attacking the hairlines of Mike Cooper, Van Morrison, Morgan Fisher (once of Love Affair), Sandy Newman of the latter-day Marmalade, and – although the good looks of his pop star prime were still apparent – Wayne Fontana, as it had his brothers before him. The night would come when he'd lift his onstage cloth cap for a self-mocking *bon mot* about Mother Nature's unkindness.

Brian Pendleton, an insurance underwriter after he left The Pretty Things, was not exempt either. He was, nonetheless, still sufficiently recognisable to be accosted by French fans when seen thumbing through wares in a London record shop. While

---

117. Love was the only mainstay of The Beach Boys not to receive a composing credit for their 1968 single 'Friends' – which contained the line 'I talked your folks out of making you cut off your hair'.

he would never so renege on his past that he wouldn't cash long-awaited royalty cheques, Brian thought it wisest to stonewall his over-attentive admirers and hasten away. By contrast, however, on becoming estate agents after their respective tenures with the Dave Clark Five and Alice Cooper were over, Denis Payton and Neal Smith were pleased to regale interested clients with stories of their more glamorous previous lives.

Long gone from the Move, Ace Kefford in grey flannels, short-sleeved shirt and a severe pudding-basin was evangelising door to door on behalf of a non-orthodox Christian organisation that had persuaded the 'ex-pop-star-who'd-seen-the-error-of-his-ways' to rope in other people. Ace was to lose his new faith, nevertheless, as mysteriously as he'd found it. He'd volunteered to man a drugs helpline at the telephone in the church's vestry. It was given executive clearance with one proviso: Kefford was to make it plain to each caller that it was nothing to do with the church.

As well as professing 'to try to live as Jesus did', John Lennon, like Ace, had gone as far as a short haircut (as had the second Mrs Lennon) for purposes of disguise, despite a public promise that he wasn't going to do so until world peace had been achieved. Nonetheless, it looked unkempt when, in the wake of the echo-drenched 'Instant Karma' from February 1970, recorded and mastered with his Plastic Ono Band within a day of its composition, he took the trouble to perform this solo single 'live' vocal over a backing tape – on consecutive showings of *Top of the Pops* with that creepy Yoko next to him on a stool, either blindfolded (with a sanitary towel) and holding up her scrawled signs with *PEACE*, *SMILE*, *BREATHE* and other cryptadia on them, knitting a jumper, or mouthing silently into a microphone.[118]

On the edition previous to the first 'Instant Karma' plug, incidentally, Ian Anderson of Jethro Tull was striking for his vagrant attire, matted hair and antics with a flute. Moreover, as

---

118. The essence of 'Instant Karma' and, more so, its 'Power to the People' follow-up was slogan-ridden musical journalism. As such they had something in common with 'Tokoloshe Man', a UK hit by John Kongos, a South African – and *Wedding Album*-period Lennon lookalike – who freighted his songs with uncompromising lyrics born of the socio-political situation back home.

Pete Feenstra observed, 'there were also other individuals who took the hair concept literally to a great length such as Deep Purple's Ian Gillan and Uriah Heep's Ken Hensley, though both seemed to me to be part of a commercial hard rock tradition outside of the hippie vibe of the time'.

Via an interview around that time headlined 'Shut Up And Listen!: The Thoughts of Chairman John' in *Record Mirror*, I discovered how yawnsome Lennon, who'd now changed his middle name by deed poll from 'Winston' to 'Ono', was becoming, holding forth about his peace mission and an oscillating commitment to other worthy (or not) causes he was espousing at the rate of roughly one a month.

He'd donated his and Yoko's freshly shorn hair to be sold in boxed packages in aid of the kingdom's Black Power movement which he publicised on an ITV chat show a few months before he left his country of birth forever for the United States on 3 September 1971.

Black Power was aligned with Rastafarianism, a religious cult that to the-man-in-the-pub was embodied in rope-like, coiled and seemingly ungroomed dreadlocks, regarded as a male symbol of strength as outlined in the Old Testament tale of Samson.

'Rastas' had entered the life of Chris Blackwell who, related to Crosse and Blackwell, the soup people, had spent most of his first decades untroubled by trade turmoil in his parents' mansion in the poshest borough of Kingston, Jamaica. This was worlds removed from the Trench Town neighbourhood with its dirt-poor shanties and reeking squatters' camps rife with disease and swarming with undernourished children descended from black slaves. Yet it would be brash, confident 'Rude Boy' music from Trench Town and other ghettos, declaring in no uncertain terms that a change was gonna come, that would be the making of Blackwell who, while gallivanting with pals in a motorboat round the lonely Hellshire coastline near Spanish Town, found himself at the inadvertent mercy of dope-smoking Rastas, a sect he'd always understood to be 'killers, anti-white'.

The supposed imperilment began when the launch had struck

a reef and sank. The party swam to shore and Chris went for help. Hours later, the exhausted playboy approached a hut miles along the desolate beach. When six dreadlocked Rastas emerged, Blackwell almost fainted. However, instead of being tortured to death, he enjoyed frugal hospitality of seafood, Bible readings and back-to-Africa sermons. The encounter led Blackwell to sympathy in place of ingrained fear for the island's most shunned subculture.

Going further against the instincts of his upbringing, Blackwell started hanging around the clubs of downtown Kingston. Owned by various liquor distributors, these provided recreation for those too hard up to buy record players. From huge speakers at tinnitus-inducing volume poured discs from both US rhythm-and-blues and, soon, from Jamaica itself after one of the foremost spinners, Clement 'Sir Coxone' Dodd, turned to recording local musicians, thereby ensuring quality control and ready servings of 'sound system' fodder. Others followed suit and so evolved the island's record industry, welding North American – and, later, British – pop to West Indian *patois* and rhythms.

Access to this raw material in the UK was mainly via import shops in suburbs with a pronounced Caribbean immigrant population, and 'turntable hits' at exclusive discotheques in the bigger cities. This led to the infiltration of 'bluebeat' into the UK Top Fifty in 1964. An example of the real McCoy – 'King of Kings' by Ezz Reco and the Launchers – drifted into its lower regions that March, while soaring into the Top Ten came 'My Boy Lollipop' by Jamaica's own Millie, a Chris Blackwell discovery after he had founded his Island record label five years earlier. Also released was a revival of 'Mockin' Bird Hill' from the 1940s, which had been invested with a galumphing bluebeat-type lope by the Migil Five, who'd replaced the Dave Clark Five as resident act at Tottenham's Royal dance hall.

Bluebeat had been spooned from a cauldron of ska, mento, calypso and other Caribbean forms that were to amalgamate into reggae which Chris Blackwell in particular helped to popularise. Even though, by the close of the 1960s, it had a glut of white rock, his Island, probably more than any other British independent label, had always championed 'ethnic' sounds, especially after merging with Trinidad-based Trojan – which facilitated the channelling of remunerative reggae such as the *Club Ska '67* compilation, seen under the arm of many a Mod that was still around in spring 1967 – and creating its own Mango subsidiary specifically for reggae less universally accessible than that of Prince Buster, Desmond Dekker and similar practitioners whose isolated hits had engendered a snooty attitude towards the stuff by white so-called intelligentsia, even when pastiches were attempted – like 'Ob-la-di Ob-la-da' by The Beatles and Marmalade, Locomotive's 'Rudi's In Love' and 'To Rassman' by Island's own Blodwyn Pig.

Yet, through Bob Marley and the Wailers, Burning Spear, Ijahman, Sly and the Revolutionaries, Big Youth *et al*, reggae was soon to outflank even blues as the 'twisted voice of the underdog' and student disco accessory, and its stars' names were dropped in hip circles. Marley reminded George Harrison 'so much of Dylan – and as for his rhythm, it's so simple and yet so beautiful', and one of Eric Clapton's bestselling singles would be a version of Marley's 'I Shot the Sheriff'.

Paul Simon's solo career would be stabilised with 'Mother and Child Reunion', actually recorded in Jamaica while Cat Stevens, a 1960s pop star who'd re-emerge as a post-Woodstock singer-songwriter, penned Montego Bay ska exponent Jimmy Cliff's 1970 UK smash, 'Wild World'. Mentioned as long ago as 1966 by Spencer Davis in his *Midland Beat* column, Cliff (whose backing outfit were to assist Paul Simon) would star as a West Indian gunman in *The Harder They Come*, underwritten by Chris Blackwell and on at a cinema near you in 1972. That this violent film and its soundtrack album were liked by sixth formers and undergraduates demonstrated that reggae was no longer such an alien aspect of the general pop market.

Such was the distance reggae had travelled so rapidly since being despised as 'skinhead music' as the Sixties began to stop Swinging, *circa* 1968, and a moth-eaten 'hard' Mod, once the lord of creation, would be stepping aside for a taunting gang of youths with Prussian army haircuts. His spiritual descendants, they'd sprayed *SKINHEAD BOVVER* on a Stonehenge monolith – while a wall of St Paul's Cathedral was paint-splashed with *THE SHED*, the name of a terrace on the south side of the Stamford Bridge stadium, home ground of Chelsea, the First Division soccer club that vied with Arsenal and Millwall as the London team most favoured by skinheads who expressed their loud support so violently before and after each match that their steel-toed boots, ideal for stomping on fallen devotees of rival teams, were often confiscated by police stewards.

Footballers tended to be admired more than pop stars to the extent that Arsenal centre-forward – and former skinhead – Charlie George's betrayal of lank, straggly long hair was overlooked, and a 'get your hair cut, get your hair cut, get your hair cut, Charlie George' chant from opposing spectators, particularised outside the arena by team scarves (not always tied round the neck), would necessitate bloody retribution. Yet such factionalism counted less than the tribal identity forged outside school and workaday limits by youths with braces attached to jeans frequently discoloured with streaks of bleach, and hair shaved to uniform iron-filing length that triggered as much furore as that 'BEATLE YOUR ROLLING STONE HAIR!' business had half a decade earlier at some education establishments. 'I went from a fourteen-year-old longhair to a skinhead,' laughed Mancunian music biographer Mick Middles, 'and they threatened to expel me.'[119]

Like their Teddy Boy forebears, skinheads went around in packs – though the objectives of their belligerence tended to be more akin to those of American rednecks. For all their fondness for reggae, there were pronounced racist elements to the 'bovver' of many gangs, although this extended, as it did among Alf Garnett-like Britons in general, far less to West Indians than to Asians. This had been illustrated in the 1969 ITV sitcom Curry and Chips by Johnny Speight, writer of Till Death Us Do Part, which, under the weight of pressure from the Race Relations Board, was cancelled after six episodes. What lived in hostility towards a Pakistani immigrant

---

119. Unlike the Pilzkopf, there was hardly any room for variations beyond maybe a severe parting, though sideburns down to the jaw line and hints of moustache were permissible. In the early 1970s, 'suedeheads' came into being as more mannered and slightly longer-haired skinheads. Their very much more formal appearance embraced furled umbrellas with tips customised on grinder-wheels for use as stiletto blades.

with an Irish name that didn't apply to a West Indian on the same factory floor.

More widespread, however, was dislike of hippie males, seen, without supporting evidence, as 'queer', minimising a homoerotism perceivable, according to an autumn 1969 feature in *Disc and Music Echo*, in the skinhead preference for the company of 'mates' to that of female adherents debasingly called 'boilers'.

While there were attempts to appease the aggressors on disc with such as a reggaefied 'Give Peace A Chance' by Hot Chocolate, a multi-racial (four blacks, two white) outfit from south London, it didn't prevent a skinhead at a vegetable stall hurling a huge rotted potato at me and shouting 'you long-haired lump!' as I proceeded through Aldershot market.[120]

Andy Pegg reports starting at a college in Reading as an art student 'with hair down below my chin and a bushy beard, not unlike George Harrison at that time. I shared a flat above a jeweller's shop in the centre of town – which, in the late 1960s, was almost deserted at night. It was as late as that when I was walking back – and a bunch of skinheads spotted me and gave chase with bloodcurdling shouts. I was so scared that I could hardly run, but I got to the ground floor door just in time, opened it and slammed it shut. From my third floor window I could see them prowling the street below, still searching for me: a scary experience and a narrow escape.'

Also resident in the Berkshire county town, reckoned by makers of television documentaries to be the most 'average' in Britain, Clive Chandler, once bass guitarist in Turnpike – a folk-rock quintet that had dwelt seven miles south-east of where Traffic had 'got it together in the country' with more success – was reconciling himself to the fact that pop celebrity would not be his. Thus he obtained employment at a London university where, 'I expected there to be a dress code. Instead, I found a relaxed attitude and a group of colleagues who were ex-musos too, referring to delivering a lecture as "doing a gig".

'One morning at the bus stop at the start of my commute, an uncouth skinhead youth approached and said – literally – "Get

---

120. In turn, my coterie and I liked baiting lone skinheads during bus journeys to and from Farnborough Tech.

your hair cut!" Never short of a *bon mot* in such situations, I span round and told him to piss off. This oik looked me up and down and said, "You're an under-cover cop, ain't you? I can smell you lot a mile off." As I was mentally rehearsing my riposte – along the lines of "If I was, you'd already be nicked", the bus arrived, possibly saving me from physical as well as verbal assault.'

In the north-west, such attacks were inclined to be more targeted. 'There were so few people with long hair around, particularly in Formby,' John Townsend noted, 'that the town skinheads knew us and tried to hunt us down – and it wasn't always local. I remember once hiding out in a friend's house because we'd been told that skinhead nutters from the Marsh Lane gang from Bootle had arrived on the train with an axe and a hammer, and were roaming Formby looking for me.'

'John, who had a pretty dramatic head of curly hair, was really pushing the boundaries of tonsorial rebellion,' qualified Graham Humphreys, a Merseyside contemporary, 'and so did our friends Alan Barwise and Garry Jones, once the owner of hair that, if I remember correctly, was virtually waist-length. Somehow they managed to get away with it but perhaps the freedom of college life once they'd fled the restrictions of home and school did help.'[121]

A more generalised manifestation of skinhead contempt for hippies was their disruption of the free outdoor concerts that dotted the counter-culture's social calendar in post-flower-power Britain. Most such extravaganzas were triumphs because everyone wanted them to be – though the threat of 'bovver' caused some organisers to suggest the recruitment of vigilante squads.

While they didn't forget their British fans entirely, Led Zeppelin had no time for such events as they concentrated on North America. Furthermore, loud became louder and then loudest at 70,000 watts. Present at New York's capacious Madison Square Gardens for a

121. John Townsend and Garry Jones were to be bastions of El Seven, a group that ploughed an appealing post-punk furrow. Alan Barwise drummed for Clayson and the Argonauts during our 'imperial' period in the late 1970s, and when we reformed in 2005.

Zeppelin *blitzkrieg*, former Yardbird Chris Dreja remembered the volume from the PA system and flat-out amplifiers 'literally moving the concrete in front of 50,000 people. Having not been to many such events since the Yardbirds, it completely freaked me out'.

Maybe Robert Plant's ears had once been burning too when the nascent Slade, then the 'N Betweens, had been pondering the recruitment of a second lead vocalist. 'The others didn't know him, but I did,' recalled Noddy Holder. 'Personally, I didn't mind, although I knew I could front the band myself, and I preferred being in a four-piece.' Could it be that in another world, it is Plant with a guitar round his neck and his similar cement-mixer tenor rather than Holder who became the rabble-rouser-in-chief with Slade, co-writing their six-year UK chart run of mostly unremitting ravers with misspelt titles? Yet would Robert have conceded to removing his crinkly golden hair when Chas Chandler, now Slade's manager, recommended a corporate 'skinhead' cut?

'In this respect, Chas was a visionary,' thought Dave Hill, 'and he'd seen so many post-hippie bands, looking the same. So he told us to get our hair shaved off! We tussled with this suggestion, but decided to go with it. We also bought all the skinhead gear. I flippin' hated him then, and, as soon as glam-rock was starting in the early 1970s, we grew our hair back. Noddy kept his short on top. My 'Cleopatra' style developed through not having a full fringe.

'Yet Chas was right in that we certainly stuck out, and got a lot of press, but some places wouldn't book us because they thought there'd be "bovver". Also, the son of the *Top of the Pops* producer had been beaten up by skinheads – and Keith Altham, our publicist at that time, backed out because he didn't like the new image. I could understand his attitude – because if anyone wasn't a skinhead at heart, Slade wasn't either.'

In due course, *Top of the Pops* caved in, and Slade were granted a slot on 2 April 1970 to showcase their 'Shape Of Things To Come' 45 – which was at heavy rock odds with music associated with their putative followers. 'Some blokes got off on the hard image,' estimated Hill, 'but skinheads in general didn't particularly like Slade because we didn't play reggae, and Jim Lea, our bass player, doubled on violin. We were still playing gigs where hippies smoked

dope and sat cross-legged. It was hard to live with – because we
hated that look really.'[122]

On the following week's *Top of the Pops*, Roy Wood of the Move,
now streamlined to a trio, betrayed only hints of how he was to
look in 1972 as leader of Wizzard in which multi-coloured hair
would explode round a visage caked in patterns of paint. As such,
Roy was as far beyond Jethro Tull's Ian Anderson as Phil May had
been past Mick Jagger, even if hardship and bitter disappointment
were to induce The Pretty Things to take a brief sabbatical in
1971, allowing a legend to take shape until the 'wilderness years'
ended with a regrouping in 1978 when everything was different,
everything the same. Supported by Taylor's comment that, 'he has a
capacity to upset people that's unparalleled,' someone had insisted
that Viv Prince had fled Portugal because of a Mafia-like vendetta
against him, but Dick and Phil next saw Viv in Sidmouth where,
uninvited, they jammed with a pub's resident balalaika band until
the police were summoned.

Nonetheless, the tide was to turn, albeit with majestic slowness,
thanks largely to new manager and diehard fan, Mark St John, who
unravelled enough disregarded percentages and petty cash fiddles
to give the bank balances of individual Pretty Things welcome
boosts.

It hadn't been all smiles for the Stones either – though their type
of problems might have touched a raw nerve or two in queues at
UK labour exchanges in the early 1970s. With *Mick* Taylor, Brian
Jones's replacement, they'd embarked on a coast-to-coast assault on
North America which had sold out within hours. The comeback
had finished on an ugly note, however, via a buckshee bash on 6
December 1969 at Altamont, a speedway race track under more
usual circumstances, just an hour's drive from San Francisco. The
20-mile traffic jams in every direction and the shortage of portable
toilets were the least of it.

122. In 1972, Arthur Lee of Love, a Los Angeles group whose 1967 album
Forever Changes spawned decades of – often sheep-like – critical acclaim, was
pictured with his formerly long hair a stubble on the cover of *Vindicator*, his
first 33 rpm solo offering.

Altamont would be portrayed by US tabloids and broadsheets as a pop hybrid of the Siege of Cawnpore during the Indian Mutiny and the Hillsborough disaster, but for those who collate macabre allusions in pop, was it 'karma' for the previous August when half a million rain-soaked North Americans braved Woodstock, the outdoor rock festival that, from a distance of years, would be viewed as the climax of hippie culture?

Back home, the demands of the Inland Revenue had driven the Stones to tax havens on the Côte d'Azur where the ennui-shrouded making of their *Exile on Main Street* double-LP marked time artistically. Yet their rebel rocker aura glowed still, and a nosy world remained interested whenever an inkling of some aspect of their off-stage lives was leaked, even a minor instance of jack-in-office unpleasantness that occurred during British dates that preceded the exile to France.

Prior to a flight from Glasgow to London, a puppy dozing on the seat-belted lap of Anita Pallenberg, now Keith's 'constant companion', was to be placed in a bag and removed to the craft's chilly hold by a blue-jacketed airline official flanked by two Scottish policemen. Bringing himself into the altercation, Mick Jagger, still buzzing from the evening's performance at the city's Green's Playhouse, protested, 'all they have to do is search the luggage and it's 20 years in the Glasgow jail'. This provoked the words, 'I wouldn't give you the publicity, *chummy*,' from one of the cops who, nevertheless, might have been wondering whether to turn the incident into one on the scale of the one that had radiated from the urinations at the Romford garage in 1965.

The officer also would or would not learn of Jagger volunteering financial aid when the saga of the notorious 'Schoolkids' edition of *Oz* came home to roost in the summer of 1971. It became the subject of the longest trial under the 1959 Obscene Publications Act at the Old Bailey, a year after Richard Neville plus fellow proprietors Felix Dennis and Jim Anderson had surrendered the 28th edition to teenage contributors (of which I was one) just as a with-it curate might Evensong to the youth club. John Lennon weighed in too. As well as testifying on behalf of the journal, he and Yoko Ono were to write and produce 'God Save Us' by Bill

Elliot and the Elastic Oz Band, a 45 issued to help raise the defence costs.

The outlook was ominous from the beginning. In the British air that February had been an intended staging of Frank Zappa's *200 Motels* - to be stamped by the *New York Times* as 'a subjective *Hard Day's Night*' - at the Albert Hall with the Royal Philharmonic Orchestra. However, disapproval from enough of the musicians had forced its abandonment three days before by the Hall's tipped-off executive body because of what general manager, Frank Mundy, was to describe as 'filth for filth's sake'. The Albert Hall's specific objections were instanced, noted Zappa, by 'one of the pieces that was going to be performed at the concert that had the line in it, "What sort of girl wears a brassiere to a pop festival?"'

The *shock-horror!* of *200 Motels* was deemed worthy of mention in news bulletins with comments from both accosted orchestra members - like 'revolted' trumpeter John Wilbraham, one of two who walked out of a rehearsal - and Zappa when he was apologising to those among 5,000 ticket-holders queuing for their money back, and intimating that it was less a cancellation than a postponement. He'd ascertained already that there were grounds for making a litigational kerfuffle, but the civil action wasn't to be heard beneath the stained-glassed windows of the High Court in the Strand for four years.

The judge who presided then was elderly and out of his depth when it came to pop music, supposing it 'to do with rhythm, banging and an infectious atmosphere. I didn't know it was anything to do with sex'. Zappa's nod towards formality by the donning of a characterless brown-check suit, white shirt and tie was negated by the defence counsel showing all and sundry the *International Times* 'toilet' centre-spread, once purchasable as a poster.

It was inevitable that the Royal Albert Hall would be pledged leniency when found in breach of contract at the conclusion of a sitting in which there'd been no way either that the Crown was going to award the plaintiff damages or even recouping of costs.

Back at the Old Bailey in 1971, it had been decided that Anderson, Dennis and Neville were more than purely technically guilty - albeit not of the original offence of 'conspiracy to corrupt public morals' but of two lesser ones. An initial prison sentence would be quashed within a week, but not before the three had been 'tidied up' as instanced by Dennis's memory of, 'Richard's luxuriant mop lying on the floor around him'. The regulation haircuts caused as much of an outcry as anything else surrounding the trial and verdict.

During the month when 'my' Oz was on sale, I gave it some showbiz at college, albeit in a guarded fashion because there'd be hell to pay if my Mum and Dad heard about it. With mingled excitement and anxiety, however, in the heat of a particularly violent row one day, I'd alluded to it broadly and then clammed up at the barrage of questioning that only died away with Dad's conclusion that what I'd done – if, indeed, I *had* done it – was abhorrent but ultimately 'harmless'.

There was a wrong-headed attempt by Mum to form an alliance with Jane by asking her to withdraw her affections until I went to the barber's. Belying her non-committal nod at this request, Jane had given me a tie-dyed hippie shoulder-bag for my birthday, and, more seriously, still wanted me to have hair as long as Robert Plant's. The conflict was soon to embrace a cruel and stupid overt act on the day an inner devil spoke to my mother when, to blunt the edge off her day-in-day-out moaning, I trusted her to trim an – inappreciable few millimetres before the three-way mirror in her bedroom. What on earth possessed me to put myself in such a vulnerable position?

Probably the fault's all mine for not getting over it, but even now, I experience slight but definite trauma, and my hand wanders involuntarily to the nape of my neck, usually at 10.40 am – the approximate time she seized the entire overhanging hank at the back of my thick, wavy blond hair in her fist, and hacked it off almost to the crown.

This ultimate vengeance for me not mirroring her and Dad's lives and certainly not their expectations and mores had an immediate effect. My eyes went out on stalks, I screeched 'Oh fuck you!' – the first time I'd ever used the f-word in front of her – and my blood pressure was raised to the extent of claret spurting from my nostrils. Then, with my psyche on fire, I stumbled into the bathroom, bolted myself in and, raving loud enough to be heard in Aldershot, contemplated the horror of the most complete desecration of my self-image.

It crossed my mind to follow the footsteps of Christopher Holligan out of spiteful bravado. This wasn't made less likely by Richard, my younger brother, who was having the time of his life with pseudo-innocent chirrupings like 'Coo, his hair isn't half long!' on noticing an especially hirsute singer – it might have been Free's Paul Rodgers – on *Top of the Pops*.

My knuckles whitened, but I didn't punch Richard. Neither did I trash my bedroom as a jailbird might his cell. During the weeks when I uttered not a word that wasn't a domestic imperative, I didn't do anything you might have expected, not even totally stonewall the engineer of my disfigurement. Indeed, I toyed fleetingly with the idea of unnerving Mum by going the whole hog with a – very – short-back-and-sides; dressing in quiet good taste at all times; and attending every church service going, blasting out the psalms and hymns and every 'Amen!' at the top of my voice. Also, I thought about switching off the television whenever a long-haired bloke was on the screen, 'because we have to be sensitive to the fact that Mum is profoundly offended by it'. I couldn't, however, have brought myself to complete the lightning conversion from rebellious adolescent to godly young adult.

Ideally, Mum wanted me now to be a Church of England primary school teacher out of harm's way in some bucolic village. That became a more distinct possibility when, almost too late, I was summoned for interview at Berkshire College of Education. If uncomfortable about my peculiar hairstyle – still just bristles at the back, long everywhere else – what tipped the balance in my favour for the two open-necked lecturers grilling me was my slipping my *Oz* involvement into the conversation. One of them, an Australian of about 45, capped this with the information that he'd tutored Richard Neville at the University of New South Wales. Further reasons for me to feel hopeful were his Zapata moustache and him saying 'fuck' and 'man' a lot while trying finger-clickingly hard to make me suspect that he *smoked* LSD and planned to divorce his missus so they could *live together*.

My mother was furious at both this man's behaviour and my delight in relating it to her. Nevertheless, I was to start college in September, and would be destined to begin a concurrent University of Reading honours degree course in history, my main teaching certificate subject, thus prolonging my stay at Berkshire College of Education until June 1975.

EPILOGUE

'My hair is a statement and always will be, even when I no longer have any'

Standing among the common herd on the pitch, I caught The Rolling Stones at Wembley Stadium on Friday 25 June 1982. I was with Kevin Delaney. He was then a frozen-food executive, but any pretensions to respectability evaporated from him immediately. In seeing the Stones again, too, I'd come up for air and reaffirmed my most abiding self-image. When home by dawn, I saw in the bathroom mirror an 18-year-old boy, long-haired, as beautiful as a girl, and as daft as a brush, rather than a mortgaged 30-something with a wife soon to give birth.

I was next to see the Stones in person when they headlined at 2007's Isle of Wight Festival, brushing aside all those acts that had preceded them like so many matchsticks. Present too was Dick Taylor, who, despite obvious physical signs that his journey to his seventh decade hadn't been peaceful, was attractive in his candour. Rather than bitterness at missing the millions he might have earned had he gone the distance with Mick and Keith, he reflected that he might, alternatively, have gone the way of poor Brian Jones.

Yet, while drifting rather than breaking away from the Stones' orbit, there would always be occasional encounters as there was when Dick was conducted into the VIP enclosure at the Isle of Wight. Back in the 1990s when, during one of The Pretty Things' tours of Europe, he spent a night off at a Stones recital near Brussels, chatting to his two old mates as if the aeons that had passed since Dartford Grammar and Sidcup Art College had been but nothing. He was also central to a 2005 edition of the BBC2 series, *My Best*

Friend Is... , in which he discussed Jagger against a backdrop of their old haunts.[123]

Further news chronicled on Mark St John's regular page in *Ugly Things*, a heroic US periodical trading in 'Wild Sounds From Past Dimensions', has included a piece about his hand in gaining the group ownership of rights to all recorded output for releases spanning every avenue of its career. This guaranteed a clear run for output which, like that of the Stones, will continue to sustain interest for those faithful for whom every new Pretty Things release has always been a special event.

As the new century got underway too, it was revealed that the friendship between Mick Jagger and Princess Margaret had long been closer than the *Evening Standard* had had it way back when. On Mustique, a Caribbean colony for British multi-millionaires and blue bloods, he and she were near-neighbours, often thrown together at a composite of candlelit regimental dinner and Polynesian *tamara* ('great meal') with other materially successful local guests from all walks of life.

Over coffee, he may have indulged sometimes in orgies of reminiscence about the town of his childhood – of which he had become something of a patrician, presenting his old primary school with a computer and endorsing the naming of the Mick Jagger Performing Arts Centre on the site of Dartford Grammar. He had been standing by with his parents as the Duke of Kent snipped the ribbon at its opening on Thursday 30 March 2000.

Mick's altruism stretched beyond Dartford too when he donated a synthesiser to Instruments Amnesty, a children's music charity. Long before that, it had been reported that Jagger had put his hand in his pocket to sponsor Britain's gymnastic team for the Los Angeles Olympic Games to please his father – a retired lecturer in PE at a teachers' training college – as a 'backing Britain' gesture, and to help clear the way for his election in 1994 as honorary president of the LSE Students Union. Among runners-up was the beatified Mother Teresa of Calcutta.

---

123. The *Pointless* quiz show on BBC1 once included a question about the past and present personnel of The Rolling Stones. Everyone was mentioned apart from Dick Taylor, the first musician with the same surname to leave the group.

What was his game? If he had one, it was to attain its end in June 2002 when Prime Minister Tony Blair, former member of Ugly Rumours, advised the Queen to bestow a knighthood upon the showbusiness icon. This investiture was, Blair explained, for 'services to music' because, as well as being the most public face of The Rolling Stones, he'd been foremost among those who'd persuaded the arts ministry in 1991 to inaugurate an annual National Music Day filled with festivals, concerts and eisteddfods across the land – causing Mick to be much in evidence in laudatory newspaper articles, although he declined to be photographed with Screaming Lord Sutch at one open-air event.

Impending knighthood bred fine sensibilities that affected Jagger's partner-in-crime, who, to Dick Taylor, seemed to be even more changed. 'Mick always had affectations of speech – especially during his Cockney phase – but he was essentially a well-spoken grammar school boy. Keith had a rougher accent, but suddenly he was all la-di-da: "How fabulous! Lovely to see you!" – just like Alexis Korner rather than Keith, the barrow-boy I knew of old.'

Yet Keith was one of many for whom the notion of 'Sir Mick Jagger' was as absurd as that of Prime Minister Sutch. Nonetheless, the fellow was chauffeured at last to Buckingham Palace on 12 December 2003 to kneel and have his shoulders tapped with a ceremonial sword. Outside the great double-doors to the chandeliered royal drawing room, he grinned at Gerry of the Pacemakers and Procol Harum's Gary Brooker, there to receive lesser honours. Facing the press in the courtyard afterwards, cameras caught the flash of a diamond-studded front molar as he smiled again when commenting, 'I don't think the Establishment we knew exists any more.'

A police officer is more likely to request a Rolling Stone's autograph than arrest him these days. A few hours after Mick left the Palace, the noise of the subsequent celebration lacerated the night air outside the Temple, a club founded by the first Viscount Astor in the nineteenth century. Less than a mile away, a listed building that had once been Marlborough Street Magistrates' Court had opened as the five-star Courthouse Hotel in July 2004. The cell to which Mick Jagger had been taken to await a trial for drug possession two years after the legendary one, now catered for up to eight diners, who used what had been its toilet as a champagne bucket.

Having wed a Stuart, Phil May was in with the Royal Family too. 'Decades after I'd been one of the country's foremost social pariahs,' he smiled in 2014, 'I'd be invited to the Prince of Wales' wedding. My father-in-law had a grace-and-favour studio in the Palace. I'm probably eighty-fifth in line for the throne of Scotland.'

Hair loss had been visible for at least a decade before Phil's death, aged 75, in May 2020, just before the release of *Bare as Bone, Bright as Blood*, a final studio album by The Pretty Things. On it his voice was attractively rougher if more reposeful, as it had been the previous December when the group completed a sell-out farewell tour at the 2,400-capacity IndigO2 within London's O2 Arena, an event thought worthy of transmission in full on the Sky Arts television channel.

Phil seemed ecstatic that he and the Things were so rabidly remembered and, in a more objective fashion, his joy was shared by one who hadn't ended up cemented in place as a deputy headmaster in a Church of England primary school where nothing much was calculated to happen beyond the revolving of the seasons – though I'd been implored to succumb to Straightsville when, in spring 1972, on the very first day of my very first teaching practice, the headmaster relayed a memo to my tutor. He was worried about my long hair.

Then in his first year at Berkshire College of Education a certain John Battersby was sent to a junior school in Slough with a female student where, 'we were greeted by the head teacher who invited us into his office. He looked us up and down – me wearing a navy blue double breasted suit (borrowed from my dad), shirt, tie and polished black shoes, and my colleague in smart blouse and skirt. He smiled at her and showed her to her classroom, leaving me standing by his desk. On returning he said "How on earth do you expect to appear in front of children looking like that?" When I looked surprised and gestured at the great sartorial efforts I had made, he continued, "You know what I mean! I want *this* sorted by tomorrow," pointing at my hair and then showing me the door. I hitched back to campus, and was found a placement in a lovely school in Reading where I had a successful six weeks. Mind you, you could have done topiary on my head at the time.

'Even after college – when I went to Jersey on honeymoon – long hair wasn't allowed in any lounge bars or restaurants. Many had signs depicting "Hippies" on doors to smoke-filled public saloons where you *could* drink.'

Behind closed residential doors too, the haircut war had entered its *nth* year with my mother bellowing 'You're not to come home again until you've had a haircut!' just as I was leaving to catch the bus back to college after Easter 1972. Her attitude had softened, however, by the summer recess perhaps because Mark Ellen, undergraduate son of a Fleet preacher man,[124] had also become a Long-Haired Git. This became evident when he and I were employed for the duration at County Commercial Cars, manufacturers of agricultural transportation, mostly tractors, in its depots in Fleet, Hazeley Heath, Church Crookham – and Aldershot where I was dubbed 'Budgie' through a perceived resemblance to Adam Faith in the title role of a current ITV series. With Faith's hair then touching his shoulders, this was flattery of a kind, although the day after one middle-aged and crew cut charge hand – a Mr Bennett – spied me combing and stroking my own tousled blondness in the gents, the mirror was replaced by a square of opaque sheet metal to discourage Budgie and his sort from spending too long prettifying themselves. It's likely that Mr Bennett was at most a fitful reader of mail-order catalogues for men's clothing which nowadays pictured models with long hair and sideburns.

There was an increase too in oases of toleration at schools such as High Wycombe's Royal Grammar, *alma mater* of Fraser Massey, where, 'they were quite relaxed about it. I was there at the same time as 1980s hitmaker Howard Jones when he and I were fifteen in 1971. He had shoulder-length hair with a central parting and John Lennon granny specs'. Linked perhaps with Trunky Cotgreave's retirement and the fact that membership of the Combined Cadet

124. A University of Oxford crony of future Prime Minister Tony Blair, Mark was drawing towards a future as host of BBC2's *Old Grey Whistle Test*, *Live Aid* co-presenter and launch editor of *Q* and *Mojo*.

Force was no longer obligatory, Farnborough Grammar was OK about long hair too.

Yet, then and further into the decade, schoolboys still suffered as they'd done since the sunrise of rock 'n' roll. When Russell Newmark, a journalist whose passion for music often informed his output, began as an 11-year-old at Harrow County School for Boys where 'the school rules had a section associated with "sideboards" and a warning about the length of hair in conjunction with the nape of the neck', whilst Wokingham's Peter Rowe 'was suspended from Forest Grammar in 1975 where the regulation length was no longer than one inch over the collar, maximum. I was reinstated once I'd had it cut and measured: an indignity to say the least. My friend Nick Clark was punished likewise but having been to the barber's to have a trim, his father, a headmaster at another school, was not satisfied with the results and marched him back there. I vividly remember seeing Nick the next day wearing a bobble hat and being horrified at how little hair he had upon slowly raising the hat above his ears.'

Poacher-turned-gamekeeper Oliver Gray taught English and became popular among with-it older students over two decades in Winchester as 'an example of secondary education at its best'. Nevertheless, he became cognisant that, 'Even there, hair was of tremendous significance to those in power. Although there is no reason to believe that it is true, school executives think that an unconventional hairstyle is a sign of evil. That this is false is plain to see. For example, I myself am a fine upstanding citizen with no criminal or anti-social tendencies, but I have tended towards confrontational hairstyles ever since I have had a choice. Of youngsters I have known, those with the Mohicans and the green gel have turned into the most gentle and responsible family men while many of those with the most "appropriate" haircuts have turned into hardened criminals and wife-beaters.'

Nothing had changed on the other side of the planet either, as confirmed by Australian film director Baz Luhrmann: 'I grew up in a country town in New South Wales. It was like living on an island. When my father came out of the Vietnam War, I was forced to have short hair, and if you didn't have long hair in the mid-1970s, you were a dead person – so it was a big problem. Then my parents broke up, and I got estranged from my dad, and ended up in Sydney with the freedom to grow my hair.'

To do so in North Korea, however, remains unlawful. Aligning with Supreme Leader Kim Jong Il's short-sided bouffant, what translates as 'Let's Trim Our Hair In Accordance With The Socialist Lifestyles' was a programme in a series entitled *Common Sense*, broadcast on state-run television between 2004 and 2005. It recommended a once-a-fortnight trim, claiming that otherwise male intelligence could be compromised. Unstated, however, was that failure to do so – detectable by hidden cameras in public places – could also lead to arrest.

Whatever 'alternative' types in North Korea did, there remained untold millions in a freer world who still had – and have – an uncomplaining haircut roughly every month, and were and are OK about looking like their fathers and either not desiring or even knowing how to rebel. For Graham Humphreys, 'That I was on the job scene did mean that a degree of respectability was required. In addition, my first job at a farm animal feed factory required touring the mill, getting samples for analysis, and climbing onto grain lorries to do moisture checks. Also, a combination of malodorous and dusty ingredients, not to mention the sometimes acrid fumes in the lab, the dust produced by a powerful grinding machine and the smell of the medicinal or appetite-enhancing products we had to weigh out (no health-and-safety in those days when dealing with antibiotics, etc.) required a frequent bathing programme once home, and anything other than easily manageable hair would have been a nuisance.'

Upon retirement, Graham gave his workaday hair its head – and Warren Walters, who was to branch out as a freelance Personal Injury Claims Consultant, was also to 'go from a conservative haircut to a more rock 'n' roll look', but that was yet to come when, 'On 16 November 1970, I was due to attend my first Frank Sinatra concert, a midnight charity event at the Royal Festival Hall, introduced by both David Frost and Princess Grace. I thought it would be nice for my hair to look good so went to my hairdresser that morning. In the chair, I boasted about where I was going that evening; I was that excited. There was a man in the chair next to me having his hair cut. I didn't look at him, but when he got up I saw it was David Frost!'

Among Frost's less trumpeted activities later in the decade was promoting a tour of Australasia by The Beach Boys who'd be among many acts from the 1960s who'd seize upon pop's yesterdays as much as its present as a means of selling associated goods. Hence the Boys and other 1960s relics remained operational in what was no longer such a nostalgia netherworld, frequently drawing remarkably young crowds.

With repackaging factories in full production as the end of the century rolled around, it made sense for overripe artistes, supported by saturation television advertising, to plug recordings up to 30 years old as heavily as a latest release. This would be demonstrated by Slade, who'd almost packed it in before 1982 – a red-letter year that saw the group in Britain's Top Twenty in December with both the umpteenth reissue of their 1973 Number One, 'Merry Xmas Everybody', and their new 45, 'My Oh My'. The New Year would bring their biggest US chartbuster, 'Run Runaway', and even a modest clamber up its album list with *Keep Your Hands Off My Power Supply*.

Back in the early 1970s, they'd thrived as brand-leaders of glam-rock, conspicuous by its absence on most technical college and university jukeboxes, which instead were full of album-enhancing 45s of heavy business by Deep Purple, Humble Pie, Black Sabbath and further craftsmen who appealed largely to male consumers recently grown to man's estate.

Emanating from the bedsits of many young women in higher education were the 'beautiful' cheesecloth-and-stone-washed denim ho-hums of singing songwriters such as Neil Young, Elton John, James Taylor and – most precious of all – Melanie. Crosby-Stills-and-Nash – sometimes with, sometimes without Neil Young – and America, also peddled musical gentility and lyrics that made many embarrassed to be alive. Even a purring Mr Wonderful like Andy Williams enjoyed a period of being thought Truly Hip by association with what was called 'self-rock' if you liked it, and 'drip-rock', if, like *Melody Maker*'s Allan Jones in a scathing article, you didn't.

It had been gratifying for me to discover that quite a few girls at Berkshire College of Education genuinely preferred Shakin' Stevens and the Sunsets, the main attraction at the October 1971 Freshers' Ball, to Crosby, Stills and Nash. They applauded the swing back to the flash and cheap thrills of a more recent past as Slade, T Rex, David Bowie, Alice Cooper, Wizzard and the Sweet paved the way for the theatrical 'glam rock' excesses of other acts which contained people who had been relative non-starters in the Swinging Sixties – Gary Glitter, Bryan Ferry, Elton John and Rod Stewart, who fronted the Faces. Glam left its mark on other realms of entertainment too. Wrestler Adrian Street – to Jackie Pallo what David Bowie had been to Mick Jagger – whose first paying bout had been in 1957, developed an outrageously attired, effeminate public character.

Woodstock denim-and-cheesecloth was, therefore, chic no more. In the ascendant were sequins, lurex, mascara-ed gentlemen dressed like ladies and liberal nonconformities such as Ferry's performances in formal evening dress and layered blue-black hair that flopped flawlessly into place; Suzi Quatro in a leather jumpsuit and hair streaked silver on a blonde base; and Bowie with hair dyed red-hot and tailored like a distant and bolt-upright derivation of the style he'd adopted from one of Rave's 'Fashion and Beauty for Boys' Mod Styles' for the cover of his eponymous maiden LP in 1967. In the same way, Rod Stewart's more chopped-up version wasn't far removed from what he'd worn when he was in Long John Baldry's Hoochie Coochie Men. Moreover, following flop 45s as plain 'Gilbert', the tide turned for British singing pianist Gilbert O'Sullivan who, freakish in a pudding-basin haircut topped with a cloth cap like something out of Dickens, commenced a long run of self-penned hits in the domestic Top Forty – and his 'Alone Again (Naturally)' also topped the US Hot 100 in 1972.

All Elton John and Gary Glitter could do, however, was disguise hereditary pattern baldness by, respectively, expensive transplant and what one of Gary's fans excused as a 'rock 'n' roll busby'. The similarly afflicted Brian Eno of Roxy Music cultivated a severe fringe and let the rest grow as long as possible within its split-ended limits until he had it close-cropped after his career extended beyond Roxy

Music to a solo output, the foundation of Obscure Records (which pushed Gavin Bryars, Harold Budd, the Penguin Cafe Orchestra and others closer to a pop audience), the propagation of ambient music and collaborations with acts as diverse as the Portsmouth Sinfonia and David Bowie. In parenthesis, when famously bald US film actor, Telly Savalas, maximised exposure emanating from his titular role in the TV crime drama series *Kojak* by flirting with pop, he notched up international chart strikes, notably with 1975's spoken-word 'If'.

Important in more understated fashion than glam, pub-rock was a movement that narrowed the distance between a group and its audience – a V-sign at both the chirpy-chirpy-cheapness of *Top of the Pops* and, especially, the post-Woodstock megastar forever in North America, throwing a tantrum because of the promoter's misconstruing of a backstage amenities rider stipulating *Remy Martin*, not *De Kuyper* brandy. How much more gratifying it was to spend an evening in the jovial atmosphere of licensed premises where the musicians would finish their game of bar billiards to pile onstage – if there was a stage – and deliver a show that had less to do with self-aggrandisement than the satisfaction of a job well done.

As well as all manner of newcomers, there were places in pub-rock's nicotine-hazed sun for entities ranging from the Troggs to Johnny Kidd's surviving Pirates to the lowly Rockin' Vickers. 'Street-level' acclaim was also accorded to the Searchers, The Pretty Things, the Downliners Sect and other outfits who'd been famous – or not so famous – long ago. No more the has-beens they once imagined they had become, they juxtaposed their good-old-good-ones with new songs, the words of which were mouthed as accurately as the ancient smashes by those onlookers who didn't want their Swinging Sixties medicine neat.

Such material might have been added to the repertoire as a result of contracts waved before them by record company talent scouts investigating what might be a grassroots goldmine, judging by the clusters chattering excitedly as they spilled out onto the pavements at High Wycombe's Nag's Head, the Hope and Anchor in Islington, Hammersmith's Red Cow or as far afield as the Pheasant in Sheffield or the circuit of pubs in Bristol where the remarkable Duke Duke and the Dukes, led by an elderly bus conductor, held sway.

This otherwise unsung gentleman warranted a centre-spread in the *New Musical Express*, but fast comes the hour when fades the fairest flower, despite growing media coverage, the snowballing of specialist 'fanzines' and chart strikes by Ace, Eddie and the Hot Rods, Dr Feelgood, the Kursaal Flyers, Ian Dury and Rocky Sharpe and the Razors. For, while paving the way for the fiercer onslaught of punk, pub-rock was, arguably, to be marginalised by it.

It had been Johnny Rotten's habit to parade up and down the thoroughfares of Chelsea in a self-customised T-shirt bearing the legend 'I HATE PINK FLOYD'.[125] He had only fractionally more time for pub-rock then in the light of his contempt for its 'denim and plaid shirts, tatty jeans and long droopy hair'. Nevertheless, passing muster with him and his fellow Sex Pistols – guitarist Steve Jones, drummer Paul Cook and, on bass, Glen Matlock, arguably the group's creative pivot – were 30-something Ian Dury, disabled and pugnacious, spitting out in Oi! Oi! Cockney his perspectives on London low life, and Dr Feelgood with their blokeist haircuts and refusal to 'milk' the audience.

With a take-it-or-leave-it approach too, when four suede-headed louts first sauntered onto the boards at a metropolitan art college in 1975, onlookers wondered whether it was actually *meant* to be crap. Tellingly, some concluded that it was neither laughable nor 'so-bad-it's-good', but possessed an intangible something else. Others thought that these Sex Pistols weren't so much new as a culmination of strands of earlier pop that they'd either heard on disc or encountered directly. Further slipshod appearances were frequently accompanied by violence but drew gobbets of appreciative spit from a growing body of 'punks'. If nothing else, the Pistols maintained artistic consistency for, unfettered by slickness, they continued to

125. This was directed at what the group had become after the departure of Syd Barrett, the *ultima thule* of pop hermits, from Pink Floyd in 1968. Furthermore, to Glen Matlock, 'The Syd Barrett edition of Pink Floyd sounded to me like punk. Malcolm McLaren met Syd at the Hilton in Park Lane with a view to getting him to produce us – but Syd went off to the Gents and never came back.'

revel in frantic verve, and the thrilling impression that something was always about to go wrong.

Late 1970s pop was soon to be dated either pre- or post-Sex Pistols just as 1960s pop is pre- or post-Beatles, and, more relevantly, 1950s pop (in Britain anyway) is pre- or post-Lonnie Donegan because, like skiffle before it, anyone could try punk. As genre fanzine *Sniffin' Glue* proclaimed, all you needed was three chords.

It was a fierce time and no mistake. Among extramural activities Oliver Gray supervised at school, there was a 'rock club' which, during 1977, hosted 'a battle royal between punk rockers and the "progressive" music old guard, which the punks won'. During that year, not a week went by without changes being rung by another hot punk (or, if you prefer, New Wave or Blank Generation) combo, although much of their attendant expletive-filled obnoxiousness resulted from inverted snobbery by upper middle-class youths brutalising themselves.[126]

Somehow, nearly all of them looked and sounded just like The Sex Pistols: torn clothes, safety-pins, slim-jim ties and two-minute bursts of racket thrashed at speed to machine-gun drumming, those three chords and some johnny-one-note ranting at the old, the wealthy and the established. Then there was the hair – short, though frequently titivated with spikes and bright dyeing in unnatural colours. Mohawks of more extreme character than that of the newly retired Billy Two Rivers and even dreadlocks on white scalps emerged too.

As well as the Pistols, brand leaders were to include the Damned, Generation X, X-Ray Spex, the Clash, the Slits, Adam and the Ants, the Mekons and the Stranglers, all accumulating armies of devotees both in Britain and overseas. When in New York about 20 years ago, I watched a TV documentary about punk in North America. The very appearance among its talking heads of a pleasant young man with a Mohican haircut plus a groomed beard demonstrated that, perhaps, the Yanks hadn't quite got the idea. This was despite fearless attempts like those of New Jersey's

---

126. As did Joe Strummer of the Clash, who'd studied at a posh seat of education in Surrey at the behest of his father, a senior clerical officer in Her Majesty's Diplomatic Service.

Misfits, creators of the 'devilock' (not unlike an exaggerated jellyroll or elephant's trunk) and Darby Crash and his Germs. The latter's personnel included Belinda Carlisle, then calling herself 'Dottie Danger', on drums. In Los Angeles, they worked the clubs along Sunset Strip before the overreaching Darby fronted a poorly received new outfit after an exploratory visit to London from which he returned with a Mohawk and an Adam Ant white stripe across his nose.

Yet it had been in the States where punk precedents had been created up to seven years before catching on in Britain. They came courtesy of such acts as Iggy Pop's Stooges in Michigan and the New York Dolls, even though the latter had started in 1972 by modelling themselves on The Rolling Stones, both in appearance and personal excesses. In reciprocation, various Stones had hazarded excursions to investigate the British branch of what amounted to nascent punk. As the Pistols' quasi-fetishist wardrobe was bespoken by a shop called 'Sex' (formerly 'Let It Rock', specialising as much in Teddy Boy garments as associated discs) not far from the shabby flat where Jagger, Jones and Richards had once dwelt. The story goes that Mick once peered into this boutique – and pretending not to notice him, carriers of the punk bacillus exchanged titters. *We hate your guts, you long-haired, complacent, millionaire git.*

Improved with age, the incident also had Johnny Rotten banging the door in Jagger's face – a measured disrespect that belied a diligence in making private observations when, purportedly, Rotten and his odious friend, Sid Vicious, had attended a Stones extravaganza at Earl's Court the previous year. Indeed, the Pistols were to turn out to be more like the Stones than they'd ever imagined. Perhaps Led Zeppelin too, as illustrated years later when the calculatedly iconoclastic Rotten telephoned Robert Plant to ask for the lyrics of 'Kashmir' from their sixth album, as he was considering reviving it. During the ensuing conversation he might have mentioned Plant and Jimmy Page conducting themselves with observed good humour when they went to a punk haunt in London. There, Johnny and his chums had spoken in low voices as Robert and Jimmy settled at a table with their drinks.

Rotten's penchant for Led Zeppelin had to be hidden away from the type of folk who sprayed a punky *BREL EST MORT. HOURRA!* along a railway cutting between Liege and Brussels to mark Jacques Brel's passing in 1978 – or, the previous August, raised a gleeful cheer when Elvis Presley's fatal heart attack was announced in another dungeon-like hangout frequented by London punks.[127]

'It's just too bad it couldn't have been Mick Jagger,' had been Malcolm McLaren's charitable comment as his Sex Pistols continued to feed off the notoriety they had gained from cursing on one of Britain's early evening TV magazines and beer-induced vomiting in an airport's departure lounge. This was soon followed by a drunken invasion of a major record company's offices and the issue of their second single, 'God Save The Queen', a swipe at the royal family that almost topped the charts at the apogee of the sovereign's Silver Jubilee celebrations, sparking off widespread condemnation in the news; some roughnecks trying to re-sculpt Rotten's face with a razor; and an advisedly 'secret' UK tour by a group already prey to 11th hour nixing of scheduled concerts by municipal committees. Yet, as acknowledged by Keith Richards: 'I loved the media thing that was happening, but, hell, we'd done that. It was a replay of 1963, 1964...'

Certainly, there was to be an element of *déjà vu* between, say, the Stones' refusal to mount the revolving stage on *Sunday Night at the London Palladium* and the Pistols' pointed absence from the banqueting hall podium at New York's Waldorf-Astoria Hotel when inducted into the Rock 'n' roll Hall Of Fame in 2006. For good measure, when the late Sid Vicious, who replaced Glen Matlock just before the release of 'God Save The Queen', was arrested in New York for the murder of girlfriend Nancy Spungen,[128] a morning-

127. A month earlier, the front page *TEDS VERSUS PUNKS* headline in *Melody Maker*, focussed on a – possibly set-up – confrontation in Sloane Square, repeated on subsequent Saturday afternoons – for plain fact was that Teddy Boys had endured – whether as, say, a delegation welcoming Gene Vincent at the airport when, in 1969, he commenced his final UK tour or keen patronage of Sex when it was Let It Rock.

128. Who'd once invited The Pretty Things over for an open-minded afternoon by the swimming pool in her Philadelphia family home while her parents were out; their unexpected return triggering a hurried winding-up of

after comment from ex-New York Doll Johnny Thunders surfaced in *Rolling Stone*: 'Well, he beat Keith Richards[129] for the story of the year.' There were also mixed feelings both ways when the Stones offered financial aid to Vicious as he was awaiting trial.

Noted, too, was the thrilling margin of error that had put punkish teeth into music when the world was younger – as exemplified by the Stones' jagged and high-velocity 'She Said Yeah' or just one degree short of chaos, 1965's 'Honey, I Need' from The Pretty Things, which lived in a careering lurch of chords thrashed at speed behind Phil May's rant. Punk or what? Indeed, the Pistols were sufficiently free-wheeling to disassociate the extra-long hair visual trademark with what Rotten heard as the agreeably 'chaotic-sound' of the reformed Pretty Things when the Pistols had supported them in 1976.

Glen Matlock was to perform with the Things when the group was knocking 'em dead every Tuesday in the Bridge House tavern in Maida Vale. This was long after punk had been succeeded by a hyped fad for 'power pop' like the 'Thamesbeat' of the Pleasers, who had moptops, went 'ooo' and promptly blew it with a dud revival of The Who's 'The Kids Are Alright' in 1978. The logic behind this choice of make-or-break A-side was that it coincided with a so-called Mod Revival punier than the Swinging Sixties article.

The Jam, the guitar, bass and drums trio from Woking that made hay in the Revival's wake, had an associate from 1978 until 1981 in Peter Rowe, now gone from Wokingham's Forest Grammar. He'd be driven close to a self-administered end when, 'I started prematurely losing my hair. So, against the advice of my parents, my doctor and even the cosmetic surgery representative (who advised I wait several years), I went ahead with a hair transplant in March 1981, aged 20. This was a physically painful and traumatic procedure that resulted in a complete mental breakdown that lasted three months. I was too scared to sleep, eat, socialise or watch/read any media, and was prescribed antidepressants. I contemplated suicide on

---

(cont.) the party – and frank exchanges in the Spungen living room that evening.
129. Then on bail for 'possession of controlled drugs with intent to resell' for which, according to his designated lawyer, he could have been facing decades in jail.

several occasions[130] what with image and youth being of the utmost importance and good hair especially being an integral part of a cool Mod look.'

Another *après*-punk movement involved a resurgence of unadulterated psychedelia with the likes of Mood Six and Green Telescope showing the way – as Iron Maiden, Saxon, Diamond Head *et al* did the New Wave Of British Heavy Metal (NWOBHM). However, this growing habit of finding old-time 'opposite numbers' to contemporary groups reached an apotheosis with 'Britpop', although it would prove too black-and-white to categorise Blur and Oasis as the respective Beatles and Stones of the 1990s. Apart from anything else, here was a radically different economic, sociological and technological climate when being in a pop group was already an acceptable vocational option to former Mods, Rockers and hippies who, becoming parents themselves, bought MIDI equipment for 16th birthday presents. More insidiously, the notion of the 'two-guitars-bass-drums' line-up of a self-contained group had been instilled from the cradle in children for whom a bad attitude and adult fault-finding were not prerequisites for rock stardom now that academia had ceased distancing itself from music that has been recorded for the masses since before the death of Victoria.

This had started falling into place long before the disintegration of The Sex Pistols, following a tawdry last hurrah on 29 August 1978 at San Francisco's Candlestick Park, the same venue where The Beatles too had finished as a working band. Since then, Matlock, Jones, Cook and Rotten have re-emerged, both collectively and individually, on disc and in concert and via a lucrative revelling in junk culture as radio presenters, in ITV commercials, as 'talking heads' on 'list' programmes, contestants on editions of *Pointless* and as central figures in further televised 'celebrity' ordeals. Perhaps, as Andy Warhol said of Pop Art, 'There's nothing to explain or understand.'

---

130. In the early 1970s, I shared a flat with a bloke called Mike who was as vain about his appearance as I was – though he had the charm to admit both this and to being even more of a poseur than myself. I wasn't sure whether to disbelieve him, but I empathised when he told me he'd kill himself if he started going bald. He did, but he didn't.

Yet the sleeves of two 1980s solo albums by Steve Jones depicted the artist with hair nearly midway down his back like Robert Plant,[131] but that of an eponymous 1989 album by four-fifths of the original Jefferson Airplane had the men with their hair cut vaguely like the Pistols. Such images looked strange to both diehard punks and those like me who'd fought a long and ferocious campaign that had won punk rockers the right to keep their hair *short* – but maybe that was almost the point.

The war had dragged on way past the Swinging Sixties. Thirty-something Mark Stokes and his family went to a village pub near Farnham deep into the 1980s where, 'I was shocked to be told they would not serve people with long hair as it was quite a long time after all that nonsense.' It had reared up too when the then-all-female Slits arrived at the old Decca studio in West Hampstead in 1977 to record a session for John Peel's *Top Gear*, the principal outlet for their sort of pop on BBC Radio One. Guitarist Viv Albertine recalled, 'heaving the gear backwards and forwards past two grumpy old doormen who look like they've been there since the 1960s. One says to the other, "You can't tell if they're boys or girls." I bet that's exactly what they said when the Stones came through the door!'

Being judged by personal appearance became apparent to me during a low point in my career when I lost count of application forms completed for teaching posts. After a while, I was summoned to a Kent primary school where the pupils had been trained to stand and greet any adult entering the classroom with a polite and fixed-smiling chant. As I closed the door after the interview, a woman representing the board of governors snarped, 'I didn't like that hair!' So, in readiness for the following month's cross-examination at a place within a Devon surfing resort, I allowed someone to shear what had been defiantly long throughout punk, the very basis of so much trouble back in the 1960s and of the individuality I'd enjoyed at Farnborough Tech and Berkshire College of Education. Perhaps you can imagine how I felt driving home, having not been offered

131. Though Steve himself reckoned he looked more like Italian-American model and actor Fabio (who, like Johnny Rotten, appeared in a TV commercial for a brand of sandwich spread).

the job – though I suspect that, as it was elsewhere, it was because I emitted a sort of vibe that told the headmaster and his panel that I only wanted to work there because it was by the sea.

Frank Zappa had made such a compromise, too, when seen in public in a sober suit, shirt-and-tie and the short-back-and-sides that he grew out when a diagnosis of terminal cancer put paid to political ambitions.

These had been furthered after the Czech government appointed him its 'Special Ambassador to the West on Trade, Culture and Tourism', much to the displeasure of James Baker III, US Secretary of State, 'particularly when he was greeted so enthusiastically over there,' according to Zappa's wife, Gail. 'Thousands,' she said, 'showed up at the airport in Prague when he flew in.' On a visit there himself, Baker grumbled about this to President Václav Havel: 'You can do business with the United States or you can do business with Zappa.' Not wishing to cause further embarrassment to the Czechs, Zappa resigned immediately – and also gave up a long-considered notion of standing for supreme office in the USA. 'That had been his intention for as long as I knew him,' confirmed Gail. 'It wasn't to do with ambition. He was a visionary who saw problems and was prepared to do something about them.'

Four years after Frank departed for that bourne from which no traveller returns in 1993, the issue of hair re-erupted nationally after a school in Texas shuttered a boy in a windowless office each time he arrived with the ponytail he'd refused to have removed. In the next century, another such institution in the same state was compelled by a federal court to set a precedent by allowing a Native American of the same age to keep a braid trailing down his back because what the school regarded as an affectation was part of a tribal culture from time immemorial – although, as a concession, he wrapped it in a *chignon* during lessons.

As late as autumn 2023, fifteen-year-old Toby Quinn of Sunderland's St Aidan's Catholic Academy was separated from his classmates, kept in isolation for an entire day and then suspended from school for a 'mullet' hairstyle – popularised at various points over the past two centuries by such diverse individuals as US Seventh

Cavalry commander George Armstrong Custer and Jason Donovan, pop star and former star of Australian soap opera *Neighbours*[132] – that was deemed 'unacceptable'. Furthermore, two summers previously, a campaign in France against hair discrimination 'linked to texture, length, colour and style' drew public attention to the decade it took for an industrial tribunal to pass judgement concerning access to a flight not permitted to a black male flight attendant with braids tied in a bun just like those of female colleagues.

A year earlier, a similar crusade across the Channel cited the tribulations of Danson Njoka whose dreadlocks were described as 'wild' by others in the same corporate finance establishment, and who decided to quit the job 'after speaking to my grandmother about hair care practices in Kenya. It really got me thinking about why we were told we had to cut off our hair for it to be seen as professional'.

Where else are we in a year when a spoof article in *The Guardian* had Lee Anderson, Deputy Chairman of the Conservative Party, enquiring, 'Aren't you sick of not being able to tell if someone is a man or a woman? So all men should be made to have short hair, while women's hair should come down at least below their ears. Then we'll know?' What of Mick Pini's observation that, 'those who called us names have now grown their hair'? How about what were once rednecks portrayed with now acceptable Rolling Stone-length locks in the third series of the *Auf Wiedersehen, Pet* comedy-drama on BBC1? Why has the sight become common of elderly men with nothing much on top, with strands of hair twisted into a ponytail?

'Mine isn't a fashion statement,' protests Hans Alehag. 'I always had thin hair and, at my age, it's more of a necessity before it all falls off.' For Oliver Gray, 'The only thing possible was once a ponytail, but now it's a kind of spiky mod cut. This does mean often being derided for supposedly trying to be an ageing trendy, but my hair is a statement and always will be, even when I no longer have any – and it still demonstrates the required attitude of rebelling against convention. Daft really, in view of how deeply conventional I am.

---

132. Kurri Kurri in New South Wales hosts an annual 'Mulletfest'.

'My own children are divided. Annabel would dearly love me to look "like everyone else's dad" and, if I felt that I was causing her genuine embarrassment, I would cut it off. However, it seems that enough of her friends think I'm "cool" for her to be prepared to tolerate it. Lucy, on the other hand, specifically does not want me to look "like everyone else's dad". She looks tearful every time I suggest any sort of change. As for my wife Birgit, she doesn't show any sign of not wanting to be seen with me. We all enjoy knocking people's preconceptions and I know that many people have uttered the words, "He's actually quite nice really, despite the mess he looks." Mess! It's not easy to maintain an image, I can tell you!'

Neil Kinnock, former Parliamentary Leader of Her Majesty's Opposition, and ex-member of the South Wales skiffle combo, the Rebels, ceased bothering. As philosophical was Peter Miles: 'As I have pretty well no hair left now, it's someone else's problem!' It was the same for Martin Dimery, the bewigged 'John Lennon' character in the now-disbanded Sgt. Pepper's Only Dart Board Band, a tribute band of practised ease that could make the most serious-minded adult regress into teenage Beatlemania, abandoning his or her tip-up seat to dance in the aisles. Yet, when merchandising after a show, Martin, changed out of stage attire, was often unrecognised by customers as the person they'd been watching for the previous two hours, principally because 'my "hairstyle" is dictated by encroaching baldness and the desire to avoid the dreaded comb-over'.

Conversely, Ace Kefford's natural light blond hair remains unmarred by silver threads or recession around a boy's face with a lot of miles in the eyes. Also, while Ray Dorset's trademark thick sideburns have long gone, he too has clung onto suspicious jet-black hair as well as youthful looks and stick-insect physique. Indeed, sometimes the years fall away entirely, and a gesture or a look betrays a glimpse of a profile once defined by *Top of the Pops* arc lights during a plug for Mungo Jerry's chart-topping 'Baby Jump'.

'Why was hair such an important issue?' asks Mick Middles. 'It seems bonkers now, doesn't it?' In agreement, Tim Fagan 'regrets how much time and energy I spent on it when both rebelling against my mother and on being indoctrinated by Catholicism. I should have ignored them both and got on with my own life. There were many opportunities I missed by being enmeshed in the struggle'.

Me too, Tim – and so I will close with mention of another incident in the life of the all-important personage of Alan Clayson, among whose family are two grandsons, both under eleven, with Phil May-length hair, just as mine was around 1974 when, unshaven and radiating rock 'n' roll depravity, I was messing about on a cheap electric organ in Fleet's Woolworth's. Sensing someone behind me, I turned and met the glance of a promenading Mrs Diver, the orchestrator of oppression and depression when I was at junior school. For a split second, the old dread peeped out, but I carried on vamping the noisy keys. Her mouth twitched, but she changed her mind, shot me a look of purest hatred and strode on.

AUTHOR'S NOTE

Although much of this account is drawn from my own direct experiences and deeply absorbed memories of printed and electric media, much new and rediscovered information was brought to light as I waded through oceans of press and other archives, notably within the British Library's Newspaper Archive, whose staff proved helpful and courteous, often beyond the call of duty.

I am indebted also to Inese Pommers for helping me to hold real life at arm's length; Jack Clayson for being of immediate assistance for computer maintenance and technical advice; and Peter Doggett for lending various ears.

For their cooperation, trust and candour, let's have a big hand too for Hans Alehag, Penny Baldwin, Alan Barwise, Dave Berry, Eddy Bonte, Rob Boughton, Clive Chandler, Mike Cooper, Kevin Delaney, Rod Demick, Martin Dimery, Ray Dorset, Tim Fagan, Oliver Gray, John Farley, Alan Franks, Gary Gold, Brian Harrington, Paul Hearne, John Arthur Hewson, Graham Humphreys, Jack Irving, Robb Johnson, Graham Larkbey, Jonathan Meades, Fraser Massey, Peter Miles, Stephen Mills, Russell Newmark, Ray Nichol, Malcolm Noble, Philip Norman, Andy Pegg, Dewi Pws, Mark St John, Peter Rowe, Charles Salt, Peter Scott, Jim Simpson, Mark Stokes, Dick Taylor, John Townsend, Lennart Wrigholm, Warren Walters, Rick West and John Whittaker.

I have also drawn from conversations with Frank Allen, the late Ian 'Tich' Amey, Cliff Bennett, the late Jimmy Carl Black, Bruce Brand, Chris Britton, Eric Burdon, Trevor Burton, Clem Cattini, Dave Clark, the late Don Craine, the late Tony Dangerfield, Dave Davies, Ray Davies, the late Trevor 'Dozy' Ward-Davies, the late

Dave Dee, the late Denis D'Ell, the late Lonnie Donegan, Chris Dreja, Bobby Elliott, the late Wayne Fontana, Steve Gibbons, 'Wreckless' Eric Goulden, Keith Grant, the late Wee Willie Harris, Tony Hicks, Dave Hill, the late Alun Huws, the late Garry Jones, Mick Jones, Chris 'Ace' Kefford, the late Denny Laine, the late Cynthia Lennon, Glen Matlock, the late Phil May, Jim McCarty, Tom McGuinness, Ralph McTell, Mick Middles, Sandy Newman, the late Harry Nilsson, Brian Poole, the late Reg Presley, Vodak Pryliński, the late Twinkle Rogers, Paul Samwell-Smith, the late Vivian Stanshall, Mike Stax, the late Lord David Sutch, Paul Tucker, the late Hilton Valentine, the late Art Wood, Bill Wyman, Ted Woodings and the late Gail Zappa.

How about a round of applause too for Phil Allen, Steve Allen, Arthur Brown, Ron Cooper, the late Rick Hardy, Rob Johnstone, Stephen MacDonald, Sean McGhee, the late Chris Phipps, Anne Taylor, John Tobler, Michael Towers and Gina Way?

Very special appreciation is in order as well for Ellie Lavender, Ion Mills, Steven Mair, Jane Heaton and the rest of the team at Oldcastle for their faith in the intrinsic merit of this project, encouragement as I worked at this book, and for seeing it through to publication.

Whether they were aware of providing assistance or not, thanks are also due in varying degrees to Sue Allen, Pete Auton, the late Roger Barnes, Robert Bartel, Graham Bartholomew, the late Geoff Belcher, David Bonser, the late Stuart Booth, Carol Boyer, Mike Byrne, Donna Cichocki, the late Terry Clarke, Frank Clayson, Harry Clayson, Henry Clayson, Stanley Clayson, Ron Cooper, Tony Cousins, Pete Cox, Paul Critchfield, Magret Damaschke, Ian Drummond, the late Mary Emmott, the late Veronica Filbee, Pete Frame, Roddy Gilliard, Sue Glover, Andrew Greenaway, Ross Hannan, John Harries, the late Vashti Emma Hayes, Michael Heatley, the late Susan Hill, Brian Hinton, Kevin Howlett, Dave Humphreys, Allan Jones, Tim Jones, Andy Lavery, Brian Leafe, the late Jon Lewin, Martin Lewis, Jean Lindsay, the late Kenny Lynch, Stephen MacDonald, Dave Maggs, Steve Maggs, Buddy McAlpin, Joel McIver, Denny Mills, Stefan Mlynek, Clinton Morgan, Adrian Moulton, Alistair 'The Curator' Murphy, Mike Ober, Amy Rigby,

John Roberts, Alan Robinson, the late Mike Robinson, the late Pete Sargeant, David Scott, Liz Swain, Mick Taylor, Derrik Timms, Vic Thomas, Trish Thomas, the late Judy Totton, Marthy van Lopik, Pamela Wiggin and Fran Wood. Let those who come after see that their names are not forgotten!

It may be obvious to the reader that I have received help from sources that prefer not to be mentioned. Nevertheless, I wish to express my appreciation of what they did.

BIBLIOGRAPHY

The following books are recommended for further reading:

A CONSUMER GUIDE TO THE PLASTIC PEOPLE OF THE UNIVERSE by Joe Yanosik (Joe Yanosik, 2021);

A DYSFUNCTIONAL SUCCESS: THE WRECKLESS ERIC MANUAL by Eric Goulden (Do-Not Press, 2003);

THE BEATLES: ALL THESE YEARS: VOLUME ONE – TUNE IN by Mark Lewisohn (Little, Brown, 2013);

AWOPBOPALOOBOPALOPBAMBOOM: POP FROM THE BEGINNING by Nik Cohn (Vintage Classics, 2015);

BEAT MERCHANTS: THE ORIGINS, HISTORY, IMPACT AND ROCK LEGACY OF THE 1960S BRITISH POP GROUPS by Alan Clayson (Blandford, 1995);

BENT COPPERS by Norman Pilcher (Clink Street, 2020);

BRIAN JONES by Alan Clayson (Sanctuary, 2003);

COSH BOY by Bruce Walker (Ace Books, 1959);

DON'T BRING ME DOWN... UNDER: THE PRETTY THINGS IN NEW ZEALAND, 1965 by Mike Stax, Andy Neil and John Baker (Ugly Things, 2006);

FAMILY IN THE SIXTIES by Alison Hurst (A & C Black, 1987);

GROWING UP: SEX IN THE SIXTIES by Peter Doggett (Bodley Head, 2021);

HELLFIRE: THE JERRY LEE LEWIS STORY by Nick Tosches (Plexus, 1982);

HAMBURG: THE CRADLE OF BRITISH ROCK by Alan Clayson (Sanctuary, 1997);

KEITH RICHARDS by Alan Clayson (Sanctuary, 2004);

KINK: AN AUTOBIOGRAPHY by Dave Davies (Hyperion, 1997);

LONDON BABYLON: THE BEATLES AND THE STONES IN THE SWINGING SIXTIES by Steve Overbury (Steve Overbury, 2009);

LONDON CALLING: A COUNTER-CULTURAL HISTORY OF LONDON SINCE 1945 by Barry Miles (Atlantic, 2010)

OVERPAID, OVERSEXED AND OVER THERE: HOW A FEW SKINNY BRITS WITH BAD TEETH ROCKED AMERICA by David Hepworth (Bantam, 2020);

MICK JAGGER by Alan Clayson (Sanctuary, 2005);

POET MCGONAGALLL THE BIOGRAPHY OF WILLIAM MCGONAGALL by Norman Watson (Birlinn, 2010);

RIOT ON SUNSET STRIP: ROCK 'N' ROLL 'S LAST STAND IN HOLLYWOOD by Domenic Priore (Jawbone, 2015);

ROCKIN' ROUND BRITAIN: ROCK 'N' ROLL LANDMARKS OF THE UK AND IRELAND by Pete Frame (Omnibus, 1999);

ROOTS, RADICALS AND ROCKERS: HOW SKIFFLE CHANGED THE WORLD by Billy Bragg (Faber & Faber, 2017);

SCOUTING FOR BOYS: A HANDBOOK FOR INSTRUCTION IN GOOD CITIZENSHIP (original 1908 edition) by Lord Baden-Powell of Gilwell (Oxford University Press, 2001);

STARMAKERS AND SVENGALIS: THE HISTORY OF BRITISH POP MANAGEMENT by Johnny Rogan (Macdonald & Co.,1989);

TALKBACK: AN EASY GUIDE TO BRITISH SLANG by Brian Poole (Avon, 1995);

TEDDY BOYS: POST-WAR BRITAIN AND THE FIRST YOUTH REVOLUTION by Max Décharné (Profile, 2024)

THE BEATLES AND SOME OTHER GUYS: ROCK FAMILY TREES OF THE EARLY SIXTIES by Pete Frame (Omnibus, 1997);

THE BRITISH INVASION: HOW THE BEATLES AND OTHER UK BANDS CONQUERED AMERICA by Bill Harry (Chrome Dreams, 2004);

THE MAN WHO WAS SCREAMING LORD SUTCH by Graham Sharpe (Aurum, 2005);

THE REBEL by Alan Holmes (Mayfair, 1961);

THE RESTLESS GENERATION: HOW ROCK MUSIC CHANGED

THE FACE OF 1950s BRITAIN by Pete Frame (Rogan House, 2007);

THE ROLLING STONES: THE ORIGIN OF THE SPECIES by Alan Clayson (Chrome Dreams, 2007)

THE SOUND OF THE CITY by Charlie Gillett (Book Club Associates, 1970);

THE STONES by Philip Norman (Elm Tree, 1984);

THE TRUE STORY OF THE BEATLES by Billy Shepherd (Beat Publications, 1964);

TILL DEATH US DO PART: SCRIPTS by Johnny Speight (Routledge, 1973);

TURN UP THE RADIO!: ROCK, POP AND ROLL IN LOS ANGELES 1956-1972 by Harvey Kubernik (Santa Monica, 2014);

'TWIXT TWELVE AND TWENTY by Pat Boone (Prentice Hall, 1958);

WE DANCED ON OUR DESKS by Philip Norman, (Mensch Publishing, 2022);

WILLIAM THE FOURTH by Richmal Crompton (George Newnes Limited,1924);

X-RAY: THE UNAUTHORIZED AUTOBIOGRAPHY by Ray Davies (Viking, 1994),

YOU DON'T HAVE TO SAY YOU LOVE ME by Simon Napier Bell (New English Library 1983).

INDEX

Bikini Beach (film) (see also: Avalon, Frankie), 173
Bilk, Acker and his Paramount Jazz Band, 69, 80
Birkin, Jane, 208
Black Sabbath, 120, 293
Black, Cilla, 24, 74, 100
Black, Jimmy Carl (see also: Mothers of Invention), 52, 168, 210, 307
Blackboard Jungle (film), 29, 31, 39, 41
Blackwell, Chris, 273-5
Blackwells, 163
Blair, Tony, 87, 288, 290
Blousons noirs, 32, 59
Bōsōzoku, 32
Bodgies, 32
Bolan, Marc (see also: T Rex), 219
Bonnie and Clyde (film), 234
Bonzo Dog Doo-Dah Band, The, 28, 44
Boone, Pat, 54, 70
Bowie, David (see also: Manish Boys), 13, 127, 137-8, 150, 294-5
Brando, Marlon, 29, 41, 259
Branson, Richard, 109, 266
Brel, Jacques, 34, 262, 299
Brubeck, Dave, 35, 44, 268
Bruce, Lenny, 49, 211
Brylcreem, 10, 25, 77, 106, 255
Brynner, Yul, 36, 109, 123, 149
'Bubbles' (painting), 141
Budgie (TV series) (see also: Faith, Adam), 290
Burdon, Eric (see also: Animals, The), 69, 235, 245, 266, 307
Burning Spear, 275
Bygraves, Max, 36, 123, 215
Byrds, The, 16, 175, 181, 210, 218
Byrnes, Edd 'Kookie', 79

Cadillac, Flash and the Continental Kids, 261
Caesar, Sid, 36
Caligula, 20
Candid Lads, The, 182
Capaldi, Jim (Traffic), 219, 239

Capone, Al, 233-4
Carnaby Street, 144, 213
Castro, Fidel, 42, 265
Cattini, Clem (see also: Tornados), 307
Cavan, Crazy and the Rhythm Rockers, 261
Chandler, Chas (see also: Animals, The; Hendrix, Jimi), 235, 279
Chants R&B, 183
Clapton, Eric (see also: Yardbirds), 111, 275
Cocker, Joe, 268
Cogan, Alma, 81, 195
Cohen, Leonard, 262
Cohn-Bendit, Daniel ('Danny the Red'), 265-6
Coleman, Ray, 132-3, 250
Collins, Ray (see also: Mothers of Invention), 210
Commodus, 20
Como, Perry, 30, 80
Cook, Peter, 215, 218
Coon, Caroline, 217, 230
Cooper, Mike, 236, 271, 307
Corbett, Harry H, 233
Coronation Street (TV series), 39, 90, 111, 123, 173, 209
Cosh Boy (novel and film), 29
Cowsills, 246
Crazy World of Arthur Brown, The, 86, 220
Cream, 256
Creation, The, 44
Crewcuts, The, 33
Cribbins, Bernard, 13
Crisp, Quentin, 17, 39
Crompton, Richmal, 23
Crosby, David (see also: Crosby, Stills and Nash), 253
Crosby, Stills and Nash, 253, 294
Curry and Chips (TV series), 276
Curtis, Chris (see also: Searchers), 64
Curtis, Tony, 33-4

Damned, The, 86, 93, 297

Revere, Paul and the Raiders, 41, 176
Richard, Cliff, 65-7, 92, 147, 268
Richards, Keith (see also: Rolling
    Stones, The), 24, 48, 72, 113-4,
    117, 124, 133, 136, 138, 170-1,
    200, 215, 218, 227-8, 266, 299
Roger, Bunny, 17
Rolling Stone, 113, 133, 169, 172, 182,
    222-3, 226, 228, 230, 255, 288,
    300, 304
Rolling Stones, The, 9-10, 13, 24, 40,
    44, 51, 83, 85, 90, 94, 104, 113,
    115, 117-8, 122-3, 127, 131-3, 135,
    138, 169-70, 174, 179, 182-3, 185-6,
    199-200, 204, 210-2, 216, 218, 239-
    40, 247, 252-3, 286-8, 298
Rossi, Brian, 149
Rotten, Johnny (see also: Sex Pistols,
    The), 71, 226, 296, 298-302
Rowe, Dick, 96, 115, 149, 291, 300,
    307
Roxy Music, 150, 294
Royal Variety Show, 100
Rustiks, 107

Saigon Saucers, 266
Samson, 21, 273
Samwell-Smith, Paul (see also:
    Yardbirds, The), 109, 175, 308
Sapphires, 120
Savalas, Telly, 295
Savile, Jimmy, 28, 205
Scooter Boys, 80, 111
Scouting for Boys (book), 26
Scowcroft, Wallace, 131
Searchers, The, 64, 96, 105-6, 115,
    175, 295
Sellers, Peter, 86
Sex Pistols, The, 103, 129, 136-7, 185,
    226, 296-7, 299, 301
Shadows, 65, 70, 103, 115, 169, 175,
    188
Shaw, Sandie, 183-4
Sheeley, Sharon, 180
Sheridan, Tony, 162
Sherwood, Jim 'Motorhead', 158-9,
    165

Simon and Garfunkel, 262
Simpson, Jim, 14, 263, 307
Sinatra, Frank, 34, 37, 60, 80, 172,
    210, 292
Sinclair, John, 258-9
Sir Douglas Quintet, 165, 179
Six-Five Special (TV series), 66, 90
skinheads, 270, 275-9
Slade, 195, 279, 293-4
Small Faces, The, 194, 212, 216, 218
Social Deviants, 257
Sonny and Cher, 207, 211
Soper, Dr Donald, 50, 66, 148
Spartans, 18-9
Spector, Phil, 271
Speight, Johnny, 276
Spencer Davis Group, The, 147, 208,
    235
Spinning Wheels, The, 183
St John, Mark (see also: Pretty
    Things, The), 280, 287, 307
Standells, 168-9, 182
Stanshall, Viv (see also: Bonzo Dog
    Doo-Dah Band), 28, 214, 308
Stardust (film), 79
Starr, Freddie, 30
Starr, Ringo (see also: Beatles, The),
    97-8, 102, 123, 161, 178, 233
Stevens, Cat, 275
Stevens, Shakin' and the Sunsets,
    261, 294
Stewart, Ian (see also: Rolling Stones,
    The), 115, 126, 136
Stewart, Rod, 195, 294
Stooges, 298
Street, Adrian, 294
Stuart, Charles Edward ('Bonnie
    Prince Charlie'), 20
Student (magazine), 266
Sunday Night at the London Palladium
    (TV series), 50, 112, 123, 199, 211,
    215, 299
Sutch, David 'Screaming Lord', 13,
    83-93, 95-7, 126, 136, 214, 248,
    261, 288, 308
Sutcliffe, Stuart (see also: Beatles,
    The), 77